EXPERIENCE

Also by NORBERT ENGELS and JOHN ENGELS

WRITING TECHNIQUES
with illustrative readings

For ELEANORE *and* GAIL

EXPERIENCE
and
IMAGINATION

An Anthology for Freshman English

By

NORBERT ENGELS
and
JOHN ENGELS

DAVID McKAY COMPANY, INC.

New York

Experience and Imagination
AN ANTHOLOGY FOR FRESHMAN ENGLISH

LIBRARY OF CONGRESS CATALOG CARD NUMBER: 65–12288

MANUFACTURED IN THE UNITED STATES OF AMERICA

VAN REES PRESS   •   NEW YORK

TABLE OF CONTENTS

Contents vii

INTRODUCTION

I. Creative Thinking

A MAN'S EDUCATION might be said to be successful to the degree that it has taught him an awareness of the world and that he exists in a certain vital relationship to it. The educated man can be said, in fact, to be the curious and observant man, who recognizes the particularity of things, who sees each object in the world as having its own form and being distinguishable from every other thing. A reality of great liveliness and variety opens for him, in the face of which he will not find it possible to go through life like "a patient etherized upon a table," [1] but will instead live always observantly and creatively. The educated man also possesses the synthesizing mind; as Cardinal Newman says, he "enlarges" his intellect. He is not merely an accumulator of facts, but learns to put things together inductively to seek new knowledge and insights. The educated man is one who comes to see not only the particularity of things but the patterns of essential unity in the endless diversities of man, of nature, of all things and all ideas.

Education is the process, then, of helping a man to see and understand the world around him, and what his relationship to that world is. William Van O'Connor has noted that it is "hardly an exaggeration to say that we do not know what kind of world we live in until we have experienced it through the coherent and meaningful configurations of our most original and perceptive artists." [2] The artist, the philosopher, the scientist—all are concerned with the clear perception of the world and its unities, and with the expression of that perception. To paraphrase Mr. O'Connor, it is hardly an exaggeration to say that we do not know the world we live in until such minds have taught us how and what to see. They teach us loves, values, and choices; techniques of observation and organization; to abhor surfaces, façades, masks, and the easy solution; to recognize the complexities of existence, thus teaching us respect for the world and our own identities; and, finally, that there is no such thing as truly

[1] T. S. Eliot, "The Love Song of J. Alfred Prufrock," *The Complete Poems and Plays* (New York: Harcourt, Brace & Co., 1952), 11, 2–3, p. 3.
[2] William Van O'Connor, "The Novel in Our Time," *Forms of Modern Fiction*, ed. by William Van O'Connor (Bloomington: Indiana University Press, 1961), p. 3.

ix

independent observation, once it is understood that every action we take and every thought we think is based upon, and therefore part of, a tradition of disciplined investigation and thought. Robert Browning says in "Fra Lippo Lippi":

> God uses us to help each other so,
> Lending our minds out.

The important thing to remember is that while we cannot ignore and must acknowledge our debt to the intellectual tradition which gives life to our minds, we must not at the same time allow ourselves to be trapped by it. T. S. Eliot observes in his essay, "Tradition and the Individual Talent":

> ...if the only form of tradition, of handing down, consisted in following the ways of the immediate generation before us in a blind or timid adherence to its successes, "tradition" should positively be discouraged.[3]

A man is "judged," says Eliot, "not amputated" by the standards of the past.[4] He means, of course, that a tradition is of its nature a growing thing, an instrument for freedom which provides us with a structure of thought and a language to express what we think. It is a point of intellectual organization. It carries nourishment from the past to our whole intellectual body; whatever we do, invent, discover, or create, we do in terms of this tradition. Dr. J. Bronowski has this notion in mind when he writes that *Othello* is "genuinely a creation":

> ...not because *Othello* came out of a clear sky; it did not. There were Elizabethan dramatists before Shakespeare, and without them he could not have written as he did...within their tradition *Othello* remains profoundly personal; and though every element in the play has been a theme of other poets, we know that the amalgam of these elements is Shakespeare's; we feel the presence of his single mind. The Elizabethan drama would have gone on without Shakespeare, but no one else would have written *Othello*.[5]

In brief, a man learns from the past and from other minds, is given the power to think and speak by tradition, and yet, when he speaks, retains his particular voice. *He is articulate in an individual manner in terms of tradition.*

3 T. S. Eliot, *The Sacred Wood* (New York: Barnes & Noble, 1960), pp. 47–48.
4 *Ibid.*, p. 50.
5 J. Bronowski, "The Creative Process," *Scientific American*, 199:46 (September, 1958), 58.

Now this is the ideal we have in mind for our student. We want to help him rise above the usual intellectual plain, develop curiosity, an excitement for ideas, a taste for exploration and independence, all directed toward the gradual formation of a free and creative imagination that will enable him to think independently. We want to encourage him to try to do some things that may be far beyond his present abilities, whatever the results. (John Stuart Mill says, "... the best way of improving one's faculties is to be continually trying what is above one's present strength.") We want him to feel deeply but to learn to control this capacity so that he will avoid any variety of sentimentalism. We do not want him to be easily satisfied, or to accept the past as something exclusive, permanent, and whole. We want him to develop a critical mind, and to further this end, we hope to introduce our student to a method of thinking, reading, and writing which will turn the processes of his mind away from the merely receptive to the more active. We would like to help him start a fire of his own from time to time, instead of always warming his bones by another's—but still to understand that there is warmth to be found at firesides other than his own.

II. Creative Reading

One means toward development of the critical and constructive mind is reading, not merely routine but close, critical, and creative reading which enables the student to judge not only the truth of what he has read, but also to determine its validity in the light of established logical and literary values, including matters of form as well as content. Specifically, we would ask the student to challenge the statement or main thesis of practically everything he reads; to question, not merely to be contentious, but as a means of testing prime principles and premises; to reject whatever he finds to be artificial, incomplete, or false; to ask if there are alternate solutions to the problem other than that which the author proposes; to discuss important books and articles with others; and finally to try to relate ideas, motivations, and significant patterns of action he has discovered in the course of his reading to his own experience, whenever possible.

This process is time consuming, but so are all things which are worth doing. Life itself is not simple, and why, therefore, should we expect that the products of artistic or philosophical processes should be simple, and susceptible of immediate apprehension? We should not be guilty of hasty reading, and above all we should avoid making immediate revelation of meaning a standard for judging human works. It is up to us to discover what demands various kinds of reading material make upon us. Scanning, for example, is useful during preliminary reading for a research project, but is not appropriate for more than merely gathering information. Certain other kinds of reading may require time, not speed. The original meaning of the word "school," which is derived from the same root as the word "scholar," is "leisure." To the ancient Greeks, masters of orderly thinking, keen observation, and creative imagination, *leisure* was the time one could devote to intellectual discussion, to the development of mind, after one's material and professional duties had been taken care of. It was a time for the joy of discovery and realization, not a rat race against the traps of time. The creative mind is not necessarily a fast mind, although sometimes it may intuit truth and beauty in a "white blinding flash."

III. Writing Creatively

To read well, that is, comprehensively and creatively, is in itself a rewarding and invaluable experience. It has a multiple value in that it not only allows the reader to participate in the skilled writer's ideas, but also provides models of good organization, development, diction, and imagery; and it gives evidence of the relationship which exists between writer, materials, and technique. The reader is given an opportunity of meeting interesting, individual personalities and of observing their particular ways of thinking.

But being a good reader does not automatically make one a good writer. Good reading is certainly an aid to good writing if only because it shows the student some ways of developing his own ideas more clearly, logically, and completely, and, consequently, how to express them more effectively. The student must learn to read as a *writer,* not only as a reader. He will be bountifully rewarded in all his courses (and his life) for the time he spends in learning to read well. But it is in the Freshman English course that he must master the fundamentals of good writing if he is ever to master them at all, for his other teachers will reasonably assume that he is capable of clear and effective, not merely correct, writing when he enters their classes. He should be able to conceive an idea of his own drawn from his reading or observation, develop it fully, provide sharply profiled definitions, and illustrate with concrete examples, logical and imaginative comparisons, and vivid details, all presented in a coherent and unified manner.

Very often the freshman's composition suffers from what might be called a formal and intellectual neutrality, there's nothing right about it, and yet there's nothing really wrong, either, except what is perhaps the worst fault of all: it has nothing to say and no way of saying it. It is often dull, commonplace, and hackneyed, a matter of putting the same old ideas in the same old ways. This book is concerned not only with providing materials to stimulate the student's thinking, and with exercises to improve his ability to read critically and well, but also with relating both of these skills to the ultimate goal of effective writing.

It should be pointed out here that our purpose in this book is not to teach "creative writing" as the term popularly applies to courses which provide instruction in the writing of novels, short stories, drama, and poetry, although we have included readings from each of these genres, as well as numerous examples of the essay. By writing creatively we mean simply writing out of a functioning imagination and with a good sense of organization.

One help in learning how to write well is to imitate what good writers have already accomplished. It is commonly and falsely assumed that a writer, unlike a dancer or a pianist, needs no practice, that if he is any good at all he writes spontaneously, that he is, somehow, as Plato believed, a writing-pen of the Gods. Actually, the regular exercise of the writer, beginner or professional, is absolutely necessary for the development and maintenance of his skill. Exercises such as we suggest in this book, including the occasional suggestions for imitation, are designed to achieve nothing more or less than the development of an ease and clarity of style, plus a broadening of experience, imagination, and point of view. Imitation, it must be emphasized, is a means and not an end in itself. Nothing is accomplished if the apprentice writer does not eventually develop his own mind and voice. He must always take note of what has gone before, and what underlies his work; but he must work freely within the tradition.

It should further be emphasized that imitation is not creation nor, as E. E. Cummings noted, is contrivance. But the imitative exercise, while it is not guaranteed to develop a creative facility in the student, is a great help toward that end. It teaches the ear the basic cadences of good written English and tends to instill in the student a sense of standards to be maintained, equalled, excelled—in any case, absorbed. And most importantly, it provides him with a point of reference from which he can venture, and upon which he can build with confidence.

IV. Plan of the Book

The materials in this book are grouped together in eight related categories, so arranged as to start with the easiest and most
appealing to the college student, and then to progress to the
more intellectual and challenging. A considerable variety of
readings are found in each category: some deep, some light;
some short, some long; some formal, others informal, and so on.
Teachers will note that some selections could as well be placed
in one category as another and, in fact, may prefer to rearrange
the material to suit a completely different plan of their own.

Each of the readings has, we believe, a complete and separate
interest of its own for the reader. Most of them are whole essays,
chapters, stories, or poems, but even the shortest excerpts have
a beginning, middle, and end.

Most of the selected pieces, but not all, are followed by analytical questions and related exercises. A few in each category are
left for the student to work out in his own way, for we do not
believe it is either necessary or good for the student to "tenderly
be led by the nose," the entire length of every path he must
follow. Nor is our treatment exactly the same for each selection,
for we fear that too rigid a formula might fix instead of flex the
student's approach. This freer range of treatment allows us to
help the reader inquire into the most important features that
the various pieces separately present: but the whole range will
include questions and exercises relating to diction, sentence structure, paragraphing, précis, ideas, organization, idioms, comparative readings, rhetorical development—in other words, a three-
dimensional view of the subject of reading, thinking, and writing.

The questions and suggestions also range from the simple to
the sophisticated. We do not expect that even the brightest
freshman will be able to answer some of the questions without
considerable study and thought, or even that every student will
be able to work out all the exercises, but we are trying to appeal
to as many different interests and talents among the students as
possible. Students who may have a special interest in science, or
in art, for example, may well be the principal contributors to
classroom discussion in those fields. Some of the suggestions may
require help from the teacher, or, in turn, even provide him
with ideas for an occasional lecture hour.

Numerous topics for student writing are to be found at the
end of many of the related exercises. Others are clearly implied
and, of course, many more may be supplied by the teachers and
students themselves.

As for the readings, we regret that we could not include many more. Yet we have tried to provide a cross-sectional view, a sampler, of at least a few of the ideas that every student who considers himself reasonably intelligent and well read should absorb and integrate sooner or later.

No attempt has been made to include representative pieces of every phase of modern life. After all, we are caught in the vortex of one of the most exciting periods of all time. We are knee-deep in our own history, but there are so many good books, magazine articles, and newspaper stories in which the student may read about the nuclear age, its science, politics, and philosophy, that we feel it is better to have at least one book which skirts around the edge of this excitement and concentrates on more timeless values. History, like a vast mural, is better seen from a little distance.

Finally, we have provided a cross-reference index of titles arranged according to rhetorical devices and literary types, as an aid to both students and teachers who may wish to emphasize or combine prescriptive forms of writing and fundamental instruction in literature.

We trust, all in all, that this book may help the college freshman gradually realize more of his critical and creative capabilities, as it makes keener his awareness of the basic values and purposes of man in the world of things and ideas. We hope and believe that he will, as a result of following diligently and intelligently the course of study we have laid out, discover his own challenges and be better able to plan ways to meet them.

—Norbert Engels and John Engels

CLASSIFICATION OF TITLES
ACCORDING TO RHETORICAL
AND LITERARY TYPES

As an extra aid to those who use this book, the reading selections have been rearranged to serve as examples of writing techniques for topical development and also of basic literary types. It is not our purpose to provide a comprehensive textbook of rhetoric or anthology of literature, however.

Most of these titles could be listed under several classifications, but, instead of attempting the almost endless task of criss-crossing them on the basis of every detail, we have tried to place each piece, except for the few repeated and the few omitted, in a category to which it seems reasonably, if not exclusively, to belong.

EXAMPLES

"A Defense of Nonsense," by G. K. Chesterton
"Party of One," by Eric F. Goldman
"Concerning Liberality and Meanness," by Nicolò Machiavelli
"Conclusion of *The Origin of Species,*" by Charles Darwin
"The Two Cultures," by C. P. Snow
"Touch and Sight," by Bertrand Russell

COMPARISON AND CONTRAST

"Science in the Liberal Arts," by Dael Wolfle
"English in 2061: A Forecast," by Mario Pei
"Greek and Hebrew Story-Tellers," by Mary Ellen Chase
"The Cave," by Plato

DEFINITION

"Liberal Knowledge its Own End," by Cardinal Newman
"The Educational Issue," by The Ford Foundation
"On Scientific Truth," by Albert Einstein
"The Case For and Against Psychology," by Gordon W. Allport

CAUSE AND EFFECT

"How They Killed the Buffalo," by Wayne Gard
"Notre Dame of Chartres," by Henry Adams
"Declaration of Independence"
"Fury of D-Day," by Omar N. Bradley

INDUCTION AND DEDUCTION

"Party of One," by Eric F. Goldman
"English in 2061: A Forecast," by Mario Pei
"Conclusion of *The Origin of Species*," by Charles Darwin

CLASSIFICATION AND DIVISION

"Of Studies," by Francis Bacon
"Chronological Cycles and Eras," by Colin Simkin

EXPOSITION

"Woodpeckers, Sparrows, and Starlings," by H. T. Pfitzenmeyer
    and Dirck Benson
"Man the Tool-Maker," by Kenneth P. Oakley
"The Indian in His Environment," by William A. Ritchie
"Pony Show in Connemara," by William Sansom
"Culture," by Matthew Arnold
"Fury of D-Day," by Omar N. Bradley
"Cylinder Seals," by Mary Chubb
"Of the Origin of Our Ideas," by David Hume

NARRATION

"Good, Clean Fun," by Red Smith
"Poor Man's Marlin," by Isaac Nae Walton
"Weekend with Henry," by Peg Boland
"The Hiding of Black Bill," by O. Henry
"The Battle of the Ants," by Henry D. Thoreau
"Reveries," by William Butler Yeats
"Susanna," Old Testament
"Odysseus and Penelope," by Homer
"Rigoletto," by Carlo Gatti
"Traveling Man," by Peter Matthiessen

"Whan that Aprille, etcetera," by Ernest Sandeen
"Montoya's Bestiary," by Suzanne Gross
"Landscapes with Set-screws," by X. J. Kennedy
"When I Heard the Learn'd Astronomer," by Walt Whitman
"Fra Lippo Lippi," by Robert Browning
"A Scene from *Othello*," by William Shakespeare
"The Perfect State," by William Shakespeare
"This England," by William Shakespeare
"Gold, the King-Killer," by William Shakespeare
"Stanzas from *In Memoriam*," by Alfred Lord Tennyson

Part One

LAUGHTER FOR A MONTH

Or

Wit, Wisdom, and Humor

A DEFENSE OF NONSENSE *

By G. K. Chesterton

There are two equal and eternal ways of looking at this twilight world of ours: we may see it as the twilight of evening or the twilight of morning; we may think of anything, down to a fallen acorn, as a descendant or as an ancestor. There are times when we are almost crushed, not so much with the load of the evil as with the load of the goodness of humanity, when we feel that we are nothing but the inheritors of a humiliating splendor. But there are other times when everything seems primitive, when the ancient stars are only sparks blown from a boy's bonfire, when the whole earth seems so young and experimental that even the white hair of the aged, in the fine biblical phrase, is like almond-trees that blossom, like the white hawthorn grown in May. That it is good for a man to realize that he is "the heir of all the ages" is pretty commonly admitted; it is a less popular but equally important point that it is good for him sometimes to realize that he is not only an ancestor, but an ancestor of primal antiquity; it is good for him to wonder whether he is not a hero, and to experience ennobling doubts as to whether he is not a solar myth.

The matters which most thoroughly evoke this sense of the abiding childhood of the world are those which are really fresh, abrupt, and inventive in any age; and if we were asked what was the best proof of this adventurous youth in the nineteenth century we should say, with all respect to its portentous sciences and philosophies, that it was to be found in the rhymes of Mr. Edward Lear and in the literature of nonsense. *The Dong with the Luminous Nose*, at least, is original, as the first ship and the first plow were original.

It is true in a certain sense that some of the greatest writers the world has seen—Aristophanes, Rabelais, and Sterne—have written nonsense; but unless we are mistaken, it is in a widely different sense. The nonsense of these men was satiric—that is to say, symbolic; it was a kind of exuberant capering round a discovered truth. There is all the difference in the world between the instinct of satire, which, seeing in the Kaiser's moustaches something typical of him, draws them continually larger and

* From *The Defendant,* by G. K. Chesterton (London: J. M. Dent & Sons Ltd., 1901), pp. 63–70. Reprinted by permission of Miss D. E. Collins and J. M. Dent & Sons Ltd., Canada.

larger; and the instinct of nonsense which, for no reason whatever, imagines what those moustaches would look like on the
present Archbishop of Canterbury if he grew them in a fit of
absence of mind. We incline to think that no age except our own
could have understood that the Quangle-Wangle meant absolutely nothing, and the Lands of the Jumblies were absolutely
nowhere. We fancy that if the account of the knave's trial in
Alice in Wonderland had been published in the seventeenth century it would have been bracketed with Bunyan's *Trial of Faithful* as a parody on the state prosecutions of the time. We fancy
that if *The Dong with the Luminous Nose* had appeared in the
same period every one would have called it a dull satire on
Oliver Cromwell.

It is altogether advisedly that we quote chiefly from Mr. Lear's
Nonsense Rhymes. To our mind he is both chronologically and
essentially the father of nonsense; we think him superior to Lewis
Carroll. In one sense, indeed, Lewis Carroll has a great advantage.
We know what Lewis Carroll was in daily life: he was a singularly
serious and conventional don, universally respected, but very
much of a pedant and something of a Philistine. Thus his strange
double life in earth and in dreamland emphasises the idea that
lies at the back of nonsense—the idea of *escape*, of escape into a
world where things are not fixed horribly in an eternal appro-
priateness, where apples grow on pear-trees, and any odd man you
meet may have three legs. Lewis Carroll, living one life in which
he would have thundered morally against any one who walked
on the wrong plot of grass, and another life in which he would
cheerfully call the sun green and the moon blue, was, by his very
divided nature, his one foot on both worlds, a perfect type of the
position of modern nonsense. His Wonderland is a country pop-
ulated by insane mathematicians. We feel the whole is an escape
into a world of masquerade; we feel that if we could pierce their
disguises, we might discover that Humpty Dumpty and the March
Hare were Professors and Doctors of Divinity enjoying a mental
holiday. This sense of escape is certainly less emphatic in Edward
Lear, because of the completeness of his citizenship in the world
of unreason. We do not know his prosaic biography as we know
Lewis Carroll's. We accept him as a purely fabulous figure, on
his own description of himself:

> "His body is perfectly spherical,
> He weareth a runcible hat."

While Lewis Carroll's Wonderland is purely intellectual, Lear
introduces quite another element—the element of the poetical

and even emotional. Carroll works by the pure reason, but this is not so strong a contrast; for, after all, mankind in the main has always regarded reason as a bit of a joke. Lear introduces his unmeaning words and his amorphous creatures not with the pomp of reason, but with the romantic prelude of rich hues and haunting rhythms.

"Far and few, far and few,
Are the lands where the Jumblies live,"

is an entirely different type of poetry to that exhibited in *Jabberwocky*. Carroll, with a sense of mathematical neatness, makes his whole poem a mosaic of new and mysterious words. But Edward Lear, with more subtle and placid effrontery, is always introducing scraps of his own elvish dialect into the middle of simple and rational statements, until we are almost stunned into admitting that we know what they mean. There is a genial ring of common sense about such lines as,

"For his aunt Jobiska said 'Every one knows
That a Pobble is better without his toes,' "

which is beyond the reach of Carroll. The poet seems so easy on the matter that we are almost driven to pretend that we see his meaning, that we know the peculiar difficulties of a Pobble, that we are as old travelers in the "Gromboolian Plain" as he is.

Our claim that nonsense is a new literature (we might almost say a new sense) would be quite indefensible if nonsense were nothing more than a mere aesthetic fancy. Nothing sublimely artistic has ever arisen out of mere art, any more than anything essentially reasonable has ever arisen out of the pure reason. There must always be a rich moral soil for any great aesthetic growth. The principle of *art for art's sake* is a very good principle if it means that there is a vital distinction between the earth and the tree that has its roots in the earth; but it is a very bad principle if it means that the tree could grow just as well with its roots in the air. Every great literature has always been allegorical—allegorical of some view of the whole universe. The *Iliad* is only great because all life is a battle, the *Odyssey* because all life is a journey, the Book of Job because all life is a riddle. There is one attitude in which we think that all existence is summed up in the word "ghosts"; another, and somewhat better one, in which we think it is summed up in the words *A Midsummer Night's Dream*. Even the vulgarest melodrama or detective story can be good if it expresses something of the delight in sinister possibilities—the healthy lust for darkness and terror which may come on us any night in walking down a dark lane. If, therefore, nonsense is really to be the literature of the future, it must have its own version of the Cosmos to offer; the world must not only be the tragic, romantic, and religious, it must be nonsensical also. And here we fancy that nonsense will, in a very unexpected way, come to the aid of the spiritual view of things. Religion has for centuries been trying to make men exult in the "wonders" of creation, but it has forgotten that a thing cannot be completely wonderful so long as it remains sensible. So long as we regard a tree as an obvious thing, naturally and reasonably created for a giraffe to eat, we cannot properly wonder at it. It is when we consider it as a prodigious wave of the living soil sprawling up to the skies for no reason in particular that we take off our hats, to the astonishment of the park-keeper. Everything has in fact another side to it, like the moon, the patroness of nonsense. Viewed from that other side, a bird is a blossom broken loose from its chain of stalk, a man a quadruped begging on its hind legs, a house a gigantesque hat to cover a man from the sun, a chair an apparatus of four wooden legs for a cripple with only two.

This is the side of things which tends most truly to spiritual wonder. It is significant that in the greatest religious poem existent, the Book of Job, the argument which convinces the infidel is not (as has been represented by the merely rational religionism of the eighteenth century) a picture of the ordered beneficence of the Creation; but, on the contrary, a picture of the huge and undecipherable unreason of it. "Hast Thou sent the rain upon the desert where no man is?" This simple sense of wonder at the shapes of things, and at their exuberant independence of our intellectual standards and our trivial definitions, is the basis of spirituality as it is the basis of nonsense. Nonsense and faith (strange as the conjunction may seem) are the two supreme symbolic assertions of the truth that to draw out the soul of things with a syllogism is as impossible as to draw out Leviathan with a hook. The well-meaning person who, by merely studying the logical side of things, has decided that "faith is nonsense," does not know how truly he speaks; later it may come back to him in the form that nonsense is faith.

Notebook Assignment for Class Discussion

1. Look up the meaning and etymology of the following words:

primitive	chronology	aesthetic
bonfire	don	allegory
solar	pedant	journey
evoke	Philistine	sinister
portentous	biography	quadruped
satire	amorphous	infidel
exuberant	mosaic	beneficence
parody	peculiar	syllogism

2. Note the crisp, direct opening of the essay—it is not a long-winded "warm-up" filled with vague generalizations and clichés. Instead, Chesterton begins: "There are two equal and eternal ways of looking at this twilight world..." What do the two ways have to do with the author's defense of nonsense?

3. Chesterton saw practically everything in the world in a pattern of paradoxes—the whole of life as a sort of unified dichotomy. What is a dichotomy? What is a paradox? List all the examples of paradox you can find in this essay.

4. Note the contrasts in balanced form in the first sentences: "twilight of evening" or "twilight of morning"; "a descendant" or "an ancestor." What contrast is found in the next sentence? What contrast between the second and third sentences? In various places throughout the essay? In the character of Lewis Carroll?

5. How does Chesterton exemplify the difference between the "instinct of satire" and the "instinct of nonsense"? Do these closely juxtaposed examples make the difference immediately clear? Try to provide a few examples of your own.

6. What does the author say is behind the idea of nonsense? Again provide a few of your own examples to augment Mr. Chesterton's apples on pear trees and a man with three legs.

7. How does the author distinguish between the nonsense of Lewis Carroll and that of Edward Lear? Write these essential differences in a brief statement.

8. Compare the dictionary definition of "nonsense" with Chesterton's literary explanation, paying special attention to his sense of depth and breadth.

Related Exercises

1. Read *Alice in Wonderland,* by Lewis Carroll, *A Book of Nonsense,* by Edward Lear, and *Winnie the Pooh,* by A. A. Milne; then write down several questions and topics on each book for possible class discussion. Which recent writers would you classify as nonsense authors?

2. Is it true that mankind "has always regarded reason as a bit of a joke"? Try to think of some important historical occasions during which "reason" was denied or ridiculed. Does the average student "bull session" prove that Chesterton was probably right or wrong about this point?

3. Mr. Chesterton is dissatisfied with the trichotomy: "tragic, romantic, and religious." He would add "nonsensical." Summarize his argument that if a thing is *sensible* it cannot be *wonderful,* i.e., capable of evoking wonder. What does *wonder* mean? Chesterton validates and equates nonsense with the serious side of life. How does he find nonsense a serious matter, too, and thus the basis of a sublime paradox? Explain.

4. The wife of a poet once said that women are less struck by the wonder of things than men are. Did she mean all men, or only men who are poets? Is it part of the poet's nature to see things that others pass by?

5. Develop a paragraph on any part of Chesterton's tri-formed sentence concerning the *Iliad, Odyssey,* and the Book of Job by explaining the book in broad terms supported by a few carefully selected and compressed details.

6. Write a short essay or a poem full of nonsense.

JABBERWOCKY *

By LEWIS CARROLL

'Twas brillig, and the slithy toves
Did gyre and gimble in the wabe;
All mimsy were the borogoves,
And the mome raths outgrabe.

"Beware the Jabberwock, my son!
The jaws that bite, the claws that catch!
Beware the Jubjub bird, and shun
The frumious Bandersnatch!"

He took his vorpal sword in hand;
Long time the manxome foe he sought—
So rested he by the Tumtum tree,
And stood awhile in thought.

And, as in uffish thought he stood,
The Jabberwock, with eyes of flame,
Came whiffling through the tulgey wood,
And burbled as it came!

One, two! One, two! And through and through
The vorpal blade went snicker-snack!
He left it dead, and with its head
He went galumphing back.

"And hast thou slain the Jabberwock?
Come to my arms, my beamish boy!
O frabjous day! Callooh! Callay!"
He chortled in his joy.

'Twas brillig, and the slithy toves
Did gyre and gimble in the wabe;
All mimsy were the borogoves,
And the mome raths outgrabe.

* From *Through the Looking Glass,* by Lewis Carroll (Charles Lutwidge Dodgson).

SELF-PORTRAIT OF
THE LAUREATE OF NONSENSE *

By EDWARD LEAR

How pleasant to know Mr. Lear!
Who has written such volumes of stuff!
Some think him ill-tempered and queer,
But a few think him pleasant enough.

His mind is concrete and fastidious,
His nose is remarkably big;
His visage is more or less hideous,
His beard it resembles a wig.

He has ears, and two eyes, and ten fingers,
Leastways if you reckon two thumbs;
Long ago he was one of the singers,
But now he is one of the dumbs.

He sits in a beautiful parlour,
With hundreds of books on the wall;
He drinks a great deal of Marsala,
But never gets tipsy at all.

He has many friends, laymen and clerical;
Old Foss is the name of his cat;
His body is perfectly spherical,
He weareth a runcible hat.

When he walks in a waterproof white,
The children run after him so!
Calling out, "He's come out in his night-
Gown, that crazy old Englishman, oh!"

He weeps by the side of the ocean,
He weeps on the top of the hill;
He purchases pancakes and lotion,
And chocolate shrimps from the mill.

He reads but he cannot speak Spanish,
He cannot abide ginger-beer:
Ere the days of his pilgrimage vanish,
How pleasant to know Mr. Lear!

* From *The Complete Nonsense of Edward Lear.*

GOOD, CLEAN FUN *

By Red Smith

The Lady of the Bath glanced up without curiosity when four gents tottered out of the steam room of the sauna all naked as jaybirds and broiled like proper sirloins, charred on the outside, medium rare in the middle. The Lady of the Bath, an old doll wearing spectacles and a long rubber apron, was busy soaping and scrubbing the tract of masculine meat on her pine board table, and the newcomers represented more work on an already crowded day.

The sauna (pronounced "sow-na") is a Finnish bath, and a great deal more. It is a sacred rite, a form of human sacrifice in which the victim is boiled like a missionary in the cannibal islands, then baked to a turn, then beaten with sticks until he flees into the icy sea, then lathered and honed and kneaded and pummeled by the high priestess of this purgatorial pit.

Nothing relaxes a Finn like this ritual of fire-worship, water-worship, and soap-worship. It is an ancient folk custom dating from forgotten times, and it explains why Finland produces so many great marathon runners. Anybody who can survive a sauna can run twenty-six miles barefoot over broken beer bottles.

The most gracious gesture of hospitality a Finn can make is to bathe with his guest. From an American host, a suggestion that everybody go get washed might imply that the guest was getting a trifle gamey, but Americans don't know everything. Lots of them haven't been bathed by a doll since they were six.

"A foreigner," says a pamphlet on the subject, "who leaves Finland without the intimate acquaintance of a sauna cannot boast of having got into grips with the Finnish mentality. Through it the creature of civilization is enabled to get in touch with the primal forces of nature—earth, fire, and water."

Curious about primal forces, three Americans and Kai Koskimies, their Finnish keeper, had taxied out to Washington on the outskirts of Helsinki, where a birch forest meets the blue waters of the Gulf of Finland. There they stripped to the buff, bowed cordially to the Lady of the Bath, and entered the steam room.

* From the New York *Herald Tribune,* July 30, 1952. Reprinted in Red Smith, *Views of Sport* (New York: Alfred A. Knopf, 1954), 131–4.

In a murky, low-ceilinged cubicle recognizable to anybody who ever read Dante, several other lost souls attired in sweat sat on benches with faces buried in their hands. The room was heated— an understatement, as ever was—by a sort of Dutch oven in which cobblestones cooked over a fire of birch logs. A thermometer registered only 130 degrees Fahrenheit and Kai, making a snort of disapproval, scooped water onto the hot rocks to get up a head of steam.

The visitors were destined to discover the differences between dry heat and the steamy coziness of this inferno. The steam room is the simple, ancient type of sauna which is part of the humblest Finnish home. There are 400,000 of them in Finland, one for every ten people. "The air gives off a slight but exhilarating aroma of smoke," says the pamphlet. "The effect of the open fireplace feels strong to sensitive people."

Four sensitive people stood it as long as any hickory-smoked ham could have done. Then they oozed out of the cell like melted tallow, and Kai led the way to another room providing dry heat. There the thermometer outraged him. It registered only 176 degrees, not even warm enough to boil an egg. The sauna proprietor agreed that this was ridiculous.

"This is no sauna!" He did something with the fireplace. "In one, two, three minutes, it will be warm." In one, two, three minutes the thermometer raced up to 219 degrees. Missionaries are fricasseed at 212.

Bundles of leafy birch branches were provided as knouts so the bathers could beat themselves. Kai splashed water around to cool the wooden floor and benches but it evaporated instantly. Even with the insulation of a folded Turkish towel, the seats were like stovelids.

Relaxing Finnish style, everybody sat rocking from cheek to cheek to avoid being fried outright. At the same time, all laid about with the birch, flogging themselves like flagellants. After that came a refreshing dip in the sea.

The Gulf of Finland is colder than an Eskimo spinster. However, all feeling had been left behind in the stew pot. The instant a guy hit the water he turned numb; he suffered no more than a corpse.

Cleanliness was next on the schedule, and the Lady of the Bath was the babe to provide it. She starts with a shampoo, then works on the subject in sections—just as one eats a lobster, cleaning up one claw, laying it aside and picking up another.

Her powerful fingers probe deep, finding muscles the doctors never have charted. She is skillful, efficient, and thorough. She scrapes the hull with a rough wet towel. The combination massage-and-scouring process is genuinely relaxing, easing muscles, untying knotted nerves.

That's all there is to a sauna, except for one technicality. The technicality is that as soon as you're finished you do it all over: the heat, the swim, and the shower. In the winter, when the sea drops two degrees in temperature and freezes over, you can't swim. You go outdoors and roll in the snow instead.

On the second time around, the temperature in the dry oven had got satisfactorily cozy. It was slightly over 269 degrees. This created some excitement around the sauna. They said it was a world record.

When it's all over you get a diploma testifying that you are alive and clean. This is partly true.

Notebook Assignment for Class Discussion

1. Locate several of Red Smith's witty "gimmicks," such as exaggeration, understatement, allusion, slang, alliteration, and comparisons and contrasts.

2. Try substituting comparisons in three or four of Smith's similes. Where he says, "they oozed out of the cell like melted tallow," you might write, for example, "they slid off the hot rack like smoked herring." Or, in place of "The Gulf of Finland is colder than an Eskimo spinster," you could try, "The Gulf of Finland is colder than the inside of an icicle." Don't be discouraged if you fail to improve Red Smith's writing; the chances are, even Red himself couldn't, for he is known as a perfectionist who "bleeds out" every word.

3. Where the student would write, "covered with sweat," Red writes, "attired in sweat"; instead of "a bit smelly," Red says, "a trifle gamey." Pick out ten or twelve other examples of striking and amusing phrases in this essay, then suggest what words you probably would have used in their place if you had been the original writer.

4. The several allusions to "the Lady of the Bath," as well as the language of paragraph 2 and the beginning of paragraph 3, are examples of the mock-heroic style. What does that mean? Is it an effective device for humorous writing? Wherein does the incongruity appear? Why is incongruity often funny? When is it not?

5. Note how Red Smith includes the term, "primal forces," in a quotation at the end of one paragraph and then uses it again

at the beginning of the next as a close connecting link. Between what other paragraphs does he employ similar connectors, or transitions?

Related Exercises

1. The reference to Dante suggests an interesting association of words and ideas: the steam of the sauna suggests heat and fire; heat and fire suggest Hell; Hell suggests the Inferno; the Inferno suggests Dante; and Dante the lost souls. But Smith jumps over the intermediate steps and writes, "In a murky, low-ceilinged cubicle recognizable to anybody who ever read Dante . . ." In the next paragraph, however, he uses the intermediate "Inferno," too.

2. The association of the Inferno with Dante should be obvious to all. But what ideas or patterns are associated with:

Hercules	John Henry
Prometheus	Davey Jones
Mars	Geronimo
Damocles	Nosey Parker
doubting Thomas	Rube Goldberg?

3. What are the origins and associations of such allusions as:

Alibi Ike	clowder of cats	pretty kettle of fish
apple-pie order	donnybrook	Madison Avenue
April Fool	get down to brass	Maggie's drawers
bring home the	tacks	red dog
bacon	hit the panic	red tape
blue-chip stocks	button	schlock shop
cheesecake	hoist by his own	three sheets in the
cockles of the	petard	wind
heart	Hollywood ham	tinhorn gambler
cock-and-bull	pull the wool over	wild and wooly
stories	his eyes	West?

4. Wide reading exercise and a good sense of allusion can enrich your writing, whether it be witty or serious. But don't overuse it. For handy reference to popular allusions, see *Dictionary of Word and Phrase Origins,* by William and Mary Morris (New York: Harper & Row, 1962). Also, *Unusual Words and How They Came About,* by Edwin Radford. (New York: The Philosophical Library, Inc., 1946).

POOR MAN'S MARLIN *

By Isaac Nae Walton

Northern pike are the poor man's marlin. They come in all sizes, I am sad to say, because the ones I catch are usually the pygmies of the family *Esox*, while the other guys, even the scarce-bearded beginners, are hauling in the lunkers.

Just the other day I was reading about a novice named Lee Perry who caught a 27-pound northern pike while he was fishing walleyes with a night crawler. As he later told a reporter, it was "just dumb luck. The big fish rose straight up to the surface, so I merely grabbed my net and grunted him right into the boat. It was that simple.

"He didn't even know he was caught until he hit the bottom of the boat. Then he came alive. Man! I learned one thing: don't ever leave your tackle box lying open in the bottom of the boat. What a mess!

"Once in the boat, he ripped my net to shreds, but I didn't care. I tried to stab him in the head with my pocket knife, missed, and broke the blade. It's still sticking in the bottom of the boat. I nearly cut a finger off, too."

Perry's final observation: "Any darn fool can catch a big fish— if he's lucky!"

Only three months before that my son, John, hooked into a 22-pound northern on a small, marsh-rimmed lake at the end of an old lumber-jack road in Wisconsin. He is not exactly a beginner at this game except when it comes to tackle-busting pike. He has always preferred the fast-stream and dry-fly combo for trout, but this time, probably influenced by his old man's lazy way of doing things, he was drowsing in the aluminum canoe sans landing net or gaff hook. His 4-ounce fly rod was dangling over the side, soaking a minnow along the edge of the pickerel weed beds where they suddenly go way-down-deep-inside. Once in a while he would come to just long enough to relight his corncob and take a disinterested look at his bobber.

At one of these intervals of twilight consciousness he suddenly realized that the bobber was gone. Then he spotted it swimming three or four inches below the surface. When John struck, this

* From *The South Bend Tribune Magazine*, February 19, 1961, pp. 8–9.

brute struck right back at him. Forty-five minutes later the lad
jabbed his fingers into the eye sockets of grand-daddy-o and
hauled him over the tipping side. When he got back to the cot-
tage, bug-eyed with excitement, the monster was still gasping, the
bottom of the canoe was strewn with tackle, one paddle and the
minnow bucket were missing, and the night crawlers he had taken
along "just in case" looked like last week's hamburger.

When we showed up at the resort to weigh the prize, three
weekenders from Milwaukee gaped, hastily gulped their remaining restoratives, fervently chorused "Wow-EE" and tore out of
the vitamin palace in the general direction of the small, marsh-
rimmed lake none of them ever had considered worth bothering
about.

A few years ago I was perch fishing off one of the Coast Guard
piers that jut out into Lake Michigan. But the perch weren't
having any that day and I finally gave up and had walked back
almost to shore when I met a friend, a chemical engineer, who
was up there for a week's vacation. While we chatted about this
and that, I picked up a stiff, dry minnow from the concrete causeway, hooked it on just for fun, threw it overboard, canal-side,
and stood with one foot on the cane pole. All of a sudden the
bamboo began to jerk, and next thing we knew there was a 4½-
pound northern flopping around on the end of the perch hook,
scraping his scales against the rough cement. To this day it remains my biggest fish.

"Egads!" said my friend. "How I'd like to get hold of something like that on my trout rod. What luck!"

Luck is right. Half an hour earlier I would gladly have settled
for a few eight-inch perch. Maybe the best way to go fishing is
never to concentrate on it. Just spend your time soaking a dead
minnow and chatting about world affairs, or lighting your perique, or going somnolent. No pressing. Just taking it easy-like,
not even thinking about fish.

Another lucky fellow once caught a big pike with a full bottle
of beer in his stomach. Which of the two catches he considered
the better is not for me to say, but I do know he ate the fish and
washed it down with the same bottle of brew. He had been fishing all day without a single strike when that big fellow started
banging on his front door. Apparently some earlier fisherman had
been cooling the bottle on a string hung from his boat, and the
pike had nuzzled and guzzled without even bothering to pop off
the cap. Imagine yourself, if you can, going out pike fishing with
a six-pack for bait! What chance would you have without the
combination of beginner's luck and an alcoholic pike?

If you aren't yet convinced, how about the fellow who had never even pricked his finger on a fish hook? He had bought a few chances on a punch board just for kicks and won a complete fishing outfit: rod, reel, lines, and lures. His pal, an old, wise hand at the game, insisted they try it out the next weekend. They showed up at Gilas Lake about dawn, and while the friend went up to the farmer's house to rent a boat, the rank but lucky tyro made a practice cast from the shore. When the pal returned with the oars he found his friend lying flat on the grass, an 18-pound northern flopping feebly beside him. "I made only that one cast," he gasped, "and this crazy fish grabbed ahold of it and I horsed him in. You can have my whole outfit. I've had it. I'm all through!"

This lad had made the perfect score. One trip, one cast, one big fish. Batting average: 1000! He never went back.

There is also the story of the duck hunter sitting in his blind on one of those days when nothing is flying around except rumors. He finally put away his gun and took up his casting rod, which he had taken along out of habit—and hooked into a 19-pounder. Would you call that skill, chance, or ingenious foresight? Nobody had caught anything but runt panfish in that lake for years.

To wind it all up, there are the usual stories of the city slickers who go up to the north woods all dressed up like store-window mannikins, knowing nothing at all about fishing except that some restaurant in Rockford or Aurora serves a wonderful plate of shrimp or lobster tails and they'd like to catch some in a nearby lake and cook them up themselves. One of these fellows actually snagged into a big pike not long ago while he was fishing for tuna steaks on the reservoir at High Falls. When the lunker came up to the boat the fellow took one look at the mammoth head, threw his tackle into the water and headed for shore and home. That's how scared he was!

Another carried a revolver and hunting knife in his belt. When his big fish came rolling up, this fellow took out his gun (the fastest draw in East St. Louis) and shot the hook right out of the fish's jaws. This time it was the pike that had all the luck. All it had to do was sulk down there in the soft, clean mud and let the bullet hole heal instead of waiting for the hook to rust itself out.

My brother Jimmy, who is anything but a drug-store fisherman, once tied into a regular log of a pike on Otter Lake, up there in the northwoods country. Jimmy had no net, either, but hauled in his "beeg" one head over tail and wrestled with him in the boat until it seemed the floor boards would give way. He actually lay on this fish and paddled not with oars but his bare hands over the side of the craft until he was safely on shore, soggy, and full of scales and slime. Jimmy would say his luck was not so much in hooking and boating this Loch Otter monster but in bringing it in for his skeptical (and envious) brothers to see and wonder at.

There are lots of different kinds of fisherman's luck, you see. And if some of you do not believe these stories, just stop in at the Golden West sometime, or Van Beek's on County W, or almost any other traveler's haven around there, and ask about it. They can always furnish a few tales of their own while you eat a bowl of hot, home-made pea soup and get the car gassed up for the tall trip back home.

Notebook Assignment for Class Discussion

1. The title of this essay is taken from the opening sentence. Why would this title be likely to attract the attention of the reader, especially one who loves outdoor life and its sports? Find several other "catchy" titles in the essay or supply a few of your own.
2. The writer obviously uses a pen name, but why does he choose "Isaac Walton"? Who was Isaac Walton?
3. How would you describe the style of the first paragraph? Does the same style continue throughout the essay?
4. "...family *Esox*" refers to the family of fishes known popularly as *pike* because of their long, pointed snout which resembles a spear, or *pike*, a word deriving from Old French *piquer*, to pierce. The term, "scarce-bearded beginners" is a reference to line 21 of the opening scene of Shakespeare's *Antony and Cleopatra*, and it obviously means "very young." Select and explain several other allusions in this essay, such as "lighting your perique," and "Loch Otter monster."
5. Select and explain several of the more colorful words and phrases, such as "(I) *grunted* him right into the boat," "the big fellow started *banging on his front door*," and "the *tall* trip back home."
6. What is a *lunker, dry fly, gaff hook, night crawler, causeway, tyro, panfish?*
7. What is a euphemism? Locate two examples of euphemism in the paragraph beginning, "When we showed up . . ." How do these euphemisms contribute to the sense of fun?
8. What basic details contribute to the sense of realism underlying and supporting the fun? Do you believe the several inci-

dents which make up the body of this essay really happened? (They did!) Is an essay or story of this kind more enjoyable when, despite the "gimmicks," its essential experience is credible? Explain.

THE MAGIC TOOT *

By Newton F. Tolman

Watching the televised Boston Symphony one day last winter, I was startled when the camera swung toward the musician trilling out an intricate cadenza for first flute. The close-up showed a very pretty woman. When I was young and still spending two hours a day attempting to conquer the hemidemisemiquavers, a female wind-instrument player was rarer than a female plumber. Ladies took up strings or piano.

Though I am no virtuoso, there was a day when I had a youthful dream of earning a living with my flute. Looking back, I am glad that this was at the time that the saxophone craze, aided by the Six Brown Brothers, was sweeping the country. Wherever I went, there was always a blaring sax to drown me out. But I was just stubborn enough to cling to the flute as a hobby. And all through life it has proved a handy way of getting rid of unwanted callers. It also provides an emotional outlet, and one never knows when an emotional outlet may be needed in my house.

A century ago, musical instruments began to increase everywhere, led by the eternal duo of violin and piano. But for a long time the flute lost ground; it seemed to be following its cousins, the flageolet and chalumeau, into gradual extinction. Only in very recent years, with the uprising of all minorities—and the aid of microphones—have flute players begun to be heard again.

While there has never been much love lost between violinists and flautists, my own reaction to fiddles was aggravated by years of unavoidable exposure to square-dance musicians. Firmly lodged in my memory is the comment of one of the early Bachs in a letter I came across while poking around for flute lore in Vienna. It was written when woodwinds, particularly flutes, were still

* From *Our Loons Are Always Laughing*, by Newton F. Tolman (New York: Ives Washburn, Inc., 1964), pp. 88–96.

supreme. Here is a loose translation: "Violinists, besides obtaining the clear, true tone of which they are reasonably capable, are constantly given to vibrato, tremolo, swelling, diminuendo, quavering, shaking, quivering, sobbing, wailing, plucking, clucking, plinking, twanging, groaning, moaning, and squeaking, whilst flautists follow the score in a dignified manner, blowing either loud or soft as called upon, and leaving further intricacy of tone to its proper province, that of the vocalists."

Unfortunately, as time went on the balance of power shifted. It got so bad that most composers would toss off only a few trifling notes here and there for the gaunt and hungry flute players. Some composers came right out and showed their true colors. "The only thing worse than a flute is two flutes," said Cherubini.

This trend accounted for the endless lines of rests that I sat through in my orchestra days—page after page of the degrading little things, while everybody else was blowing and scraping and pounding away like mad. It is noteworthy that this kind of music is always written by second-raters. Great composers always give the flute its due, as witness Bach and Mozart, Stravinsky and Bartok.

It was in Beethoven's day that large orchestras, ancestors of today's symphonies, first began to assemble. The strings got in on the ground floor somehow, in spite of Sidney Lanier's prediction that flutes would gain in popularity until they would outnumber strings in all orchestras. Soon flutes were snowed under, twenty to one, by violins alone. Ever afterward, the poor flute player was always crouched somewhere in the background, nursing his small piece of plumbing and his neurosis. He could play or not; nobody ever knew the difference.

Without the mike, the soft and fluid lowest octave of a flute is no match for louder instruments, even in a quartet or quintet. The middle octave can hold out against a slightly larger group, but this takes an aggressive nature and the lungs of a pearl diver. Orchestrations traditionally confine the flute player pretty much to his highest octave, where he is about as happy as a pianist with the lower two thirds of the keyboard out of action.

He is further bedeviled by eyestrain, trying to read up to "six lines above," and cramps from the hopeless fingering combinations of the top scale. This upper-register fingering, eliminated on other woodwinds by merely pressing an octave key, breaks the hearts of most serious flute students early in the game. They turn to clarinet, sax, or horns; almost anything seems easier.

As a youngster of nine, I began an all-out attack on *Wind Amongst the Trees*. This ornate melody was obscured by triple tonguing, runs, octave jumps, and arpeggios, finally ending with an anguished shriek on high C. After seven or eight years, I had the first movement somewhat whipped. Then I quit and turned to an easier masterpiece, the piccolo obbligato in *The Stars and Stripes Forever*.

This repertoire did not take me as far as a Petrillo man. But it led to some insight into the general character of flute players. As Frederick the Great remarked severely when a careless courtier said, "Out of twenty-nine flute players here in town, only twenty-eight are eccentric enough to be noticeable": *"Ich bin ein Flöte-spieler!"*

Flute players are perhaps not more peculiar than their instruments. Tones do not come out of the end, as with any respectable woodwind or horn, but right from the lips. And the flautist's ears are only five inches from his mouth, where the sound emanates. It may be that the internal reverberation affects the mind. Anyway, once he has got well into habitual playing, the flautist begins a gradual retreat into his mysterious, solitary world. After a few years, he seldom emerges entirely. He does not even care much when nobody is listening to him. But if deprived of his instrument for long, his sinuses fairly scream for their accustomed doses of vibration.

Mention the instrument casually, and someone is likely to pipe up, "How about George Washington—didn't he play the flute?" True. He didn't indulge very deeply, but it shows that, like all great men, he had at least one psychotic habit. Even my own modest research proves that flute playing is apt to denote genius. Watching the ranks of politicians, we find that ukuleles and pianos mean little. What we need is another President who plays the flute.

The pipes of Pan were nothing but a simple double-barreled flute. Pan had goat legs, and horns on his human head. So we may assume that, like all flautists, he was considered somewhat odd, even among his mythological confreres. But the effect of his music was scientifically logical. The low notes of a flute are as soothing and enticing as the high notes are blood-curdling. And the precisely engineered silver tubes that we play today are perfectly capable of producing the same results attributed to Pan's instrument.

In younger days, I tried an experiment along these lines, after some research on Pan's mode of operation—moonlit nights, black he-goats, nymphs, and so on. It worked. One night I caught an enormous contralto. I managed to get away from her, but I gave up pastoral fluting on moonlit nights. It is too risky.

The recorder craze gives rise to a popular misconception. It is

time to set the record straight: it is *not* an early, simplified form
of our present-day flute. These gurgling, cooing wooden spouts
are rather ancestors of clarinets and oboes. Take a recorder out
on a moonlit night, and if you attract anything, it will be an
elderly spinster with a passion for morris dancing.

It is true that, before 1700, the recorder was often included in
the general family of *flûte-à-bec, Blockflöte,* fipple flute, and
heaven knows how many kinds of flute. However, when the trans-
verse flute, our present type, was adapted to modern pitch with
chromatics, the recorder was as good as dead. Dead, that is, until
recent tone-deaf dilettantes began exhuming every old contrap-
tion they could find, from virginals to serpents. Dickens was probably thinking of the recorder when he had Dick Swiveller call
flute playing a "good, sound, dismal occupation."

Around 1915, prima donna Galli-Curci drew attention to the
flute with her famous soprano and flute duet. Unfortunately, it
did little for the musical standing of flautists. Every music-loving
home had the recording; it was the talk of the day. The celebrated coloratura's warblings were said to be such a perfect imitation of the accompanying flute you couldn't tell one from the
other. It never seemed to occur to anyone that the flute player
was imitating Galli-Curci—a feat no less impressive because she
often sang a little flat.

Many of us remember the diva as clearly as if she had sung
only last week. But who remembers the name of the remarkable
flautist who could duplicate her voice? This is the kind of thing
flautists have always been up against, and it is why we are so
moody.

Some reason can be found to explain why the orchestra flute
player was treated for so long like Wayne Morse in the Senate.
A flautist can also play a piccolo, just as a violinist can double
on viola. And the piccolo is a real menace. A fountain-pen-sized
flute, it has all the volume its big brother lacks. Turn a couple of
piccolos loose in a symphony orchestra, and the whole string section might as well pack up and go home.

Aware of this, composers and conductors have long toadied to
the string-dominated majority, telling the public some guff or
other about tonal groupings—a mere smoke screen hiding the
flautist's basic urge to be heard. How did so many wailing violins,
cellos, and bass fiddles get into the symphonies in the first place?
And why is first violin always chosen concertmaster? Pure jealousy is the answer.

There may be those who hesitate to accept the unsupported
word of a humble flute player; luckily, there is at hand the *Music*

Lovers' Encyclopedia (Rupert Hughes and Deems Taylor, Double-day). This work includes a "Dictionary of Musicians," seven to eight thousand names—violinists, singers, pianists in droves. Every fiddler who ever drew bow, except perhaps Jack Benny. But I can't find a single one of several top-rank contemporary flute men. Important violin makers have all been listed, back to Amati, Stradivarius, and Guarnerius. And there is Sax, inventor of you know what. But Boehm, the originator of the modern flute, is dismissed with a couple of lines. The authors do better by a forgotten character who, around 1690, devised an instrument called a rackettenfagott. Just wait until the recorder tootlers discover the rackettenfagott!

So much for research, having proved our point: the flute player always gets the short end of the fagot.

So-called brass bands have also flouted the flautist. Bandsmen love noise, and they can never be sure when a flute player will take to his piccolo. One tiny piccolo can shrill out above a hundred-piece band. This infuriates the rest, chuffing and puffing into such heavy equipment as trombones and tubas. So, ignoring an audience which always loves to hear it, the piccolo is allowed only a few mean little trills and peeps, with an obbligato only when all hands are blasting away fortissimo. In the flute chair, you know what it is really like to feel alone.

Flute prestige hit bottom early in the twentieth century. Professional flautists, found only in the largest orchestras, were thin, furtive-looking chaps who went around with their instrument cases held under their coats like concealed weapons. Defensively cynical, to a man, they all played with repressed technique, shunning all tonal diversity—a technique we still hear too often.

This was known as the classical approach: thin, clear tone without color or expression. My teacher was fanatical about it. He was no less abnormal than most flautists. He spent his last twenty-five years whistling away like an old B & M locomotive, all to himself, locked in his bedroom.

For years I accepted the classical style without question. Then, some twenty years ago, I heard a flute featured in Cab Calloway's band. The performer thawed all the ice with which his instrument had been encrusted in the hands of symphony flautists. He played like a Heifetz, though the vehicle was jazz. And I declared a personal war on the traditions of flute playing.

I am still some way from Carnegie Hall, but now when I romp into Mozart's Concerto in G Major, people do not start climbing out the windows. And far greater flautists, here and there, are starting to swell their lungs with free air and deliver. There is

Hubert Barwahser, with the Vienna Symphony; listen to his recordings if you wish to hear a flute really sing.

But perhaps no flautist can ever gain the following of a Menuhin or a Rubinstein or a Casals. We who whistle are a strange lot, as I have intimated. But strange or not, when I sit down with my flute all the small children in the neighborhood gather around. They are my public. Television forgotten, they give me an attention that more skilled performers, with any other instrument, could never hold. The Pied Piper may be a legend, but it did not come out of thin air.

Notebook Assignment for Class Discussion

1. The title of this essay is a take-off on that of an opera by a famous German composer. Identify him and the title of his opera (in both English and German) through the *Encyclopedia of the Opera,* by David Ewen (New York: A. A. Wyn, Inc., 1955), pp. 282 ff., *The World of Music, An Illustrated Encyclopedia* (New York: Abradale Press, 1963), pp. 788 ff., or some other dictionary of music and musicians. Is the take-off of the original title appropriate and catching? Why?

2. Look up "semiquaver" in your dictionary and from its definition construct the author's meaning of "hemidemisemiquaver" in paragraph 1. How does the sentence containing "hemidemisemiquaver" quickly establish the tone or mood of the whole essay?

3. Make a list of unusual words in this essay, such as *virtuoso, flautist, arpeggio, obbligato, chromatic, virginals, coloratura,* and *prima donna,* and discover what they mean in a musical context. Explain why so many technical terms of music are derived from Italian.

4. Analyze the sentence structure to discover differences in length as well as structural variety. How does the sentence style fit the mood of the writer? Select a few sentences that strike you as being particularly witty and well timed. What is the importance of timing in wit and humor? In sports, such as tennis, golf, baseball, or football?

5. Try to rewrite the first sentence of the penultimate paragraph in a completely serious way, then explain why the original is funny and yours is not.

6. Does the author's humorous approach to his subject indicate a lack of respect for it? Does he write out of personal experience? How do you know? If he is as truly devoted to the flute

and to music as he asserts, should he not have dealt with them more seriously? Is it possible that humor may be directed toward a serious end?

Related Exercises

1. Generally speaking, have women equalled men as music composers, instrumentalists, singers? What is their record in painting, ballet, theater, literature?
2. Is the saxophone truly a "blaring" instrument? How does it compare in tone quality with the other reed instruments? Have you ever heard a sweet, mellow "sax" tone, or a musical classic played on a saxophone? If so, what was your impression of it? Should it be rated as a first-class instrument?
3. Where does the word *saxophone* come from? The word *sousaphone, cornet, oboe, trombone, tuba, tympani?* What is the etymological relationship between *trumpet* and *triumph, clarinet* and *clarion?*
4. Do you agree with what Cherubini said about flutes? Who was Cherubini? Would you be willing to say the same about a flügelhorn, sackbut, cymbal, or sistrum?
5. Do you think a flute has a place in a modern dance orchestra? Explain.
6. Listen to some good flute recordings of Bach sonatas, and concertos by Vivaldi, Mozart, Gluck, Pergolesi, and Boccerini. Then try to pick out the flute and other single instruments and follow their parts through some symphonic recordings. Train your ear to identify all the separate instruments of the band or orchestra and to follow the rhythmic or contrapuntal patterns they play. Also, note how sometimes a choir of brass instruments will "speak" and a choir of reeds will answer, as in Tchaikovsky's *Romeo and Juliet Overture.*
7. Students of music sometimes practice the fundamentals of composition by first learning to imitate. Here is the opening theme of "Swing Low, Sweet Chariot," for example, with two imitative melodies based on the same rhythmic pattern. Ask someone to play them for you. Then try the same method to imitate sentence patterns in prose. Try to describe, for instance, a saxophonist in a sentence which imitates the structure and style of the quoted sentence in the second half of paragraph 4, "Violinists, besides obtaining ..." Or describe some other instrumentalist, or group.

Original melody

Imitation 1

Imitation 2

8. Develop some striking statement in this essay, such as ". . . it has proved a handy way of getting rid of unwanted callers," or "What we need is another President who plays the flute." Feel free to adapt the selected line to your own art or hobby, substituting terms as needed. Shift your mind and mood into the "fun" gear. Let yourself go. But remember that your revisions must be as careful and critical as though you were writing a serious paper.

9. If you are a musician, write an amusing analysis of the limitations or lack of appreciation of your own instrument. Or, similarly treat any talent, hobby, or subject in which you take particular delight.

10. Do you think the typical college band when playing between halves of a football game "sounds right" as a musical organization? Is it primarily a marching unit, a musical one, or a bunch of horn blowers who ran into a hornets' nest? Write an argumentative paper expressing your views, or organize a classroom debate on this question.

THE CRITIC ART *

By A. C. Greene

A few years ago I was appointed a sort of catchall critic on a small-town newspaper. I was worried, at the start, because my reviews seemed to lack the professional aesthetic tone achieved by my big-city and periodical critic compatriots.

* From *The Atlantic Monthly,* Vol. 207, No. 6 (June, 1961), 87–88.

As so often happens in life, I discovered the solution to the problem too late to help my own cause, as I stopped being a critic. However, in case others face the need to write (or read) contemporary criticism, let me say that the solution is fairly simple: review one medium in terms of another.

For example, you are doing a criticism of a symphony orchestra concert. Then write in terms of a painting exhibit: "Maestro Pogany worked from a muted palette, applying first an under-layer of brown tones with a somber display of *Tuonela,* then adding pastels with a brace of French modernists."

The technique is even more adaptable to soloists:

"Using lighter strokes as he sketched in the fugue, Violinist Hraknurv flew across the central figures, splashing primary colors as he went, doodling for a moment in contemplation of the coda. . . ."

It is a shame that you cannot simply reverse the process and apply musical terms to painting, but it isn't done. Musical terms have been appropriated by the architectural commentators. (There aren't very many of them, so you might be able to get away with thieving the semantics, if there is no question of your conscience.)

On the other hand, Blatburg often described Shambles House, the now famous etude in tonality which he achieved shortly before the "Dancing Mud" motif began dominating his composition, as "staccato in conception but legato in execution."

If colored photos accompany the piece, particularly blobby night shots, then another type of architectural-musical vocabulary is used, which, for purposes of identity, I privately call "lifetime" style:

"High above the growling bass of the traffic at its feet, the golden soprano of the Knifegrinders Trust and Mercantile Bank soars into lilting, spatial lyrics of almost Wagnerian power."

Poetry nomenclature is also employed in architectural criticism, but I, for one, think this can be disregarded. Poetry nomenclature is used in just about all forms of criticism. Frankly, I predict that, if it is not already old hat, poetry nomenclature in criticism soon will be old hat—even for small-town newspapers.

Having mentioned painting, I'd best get it out of the way. Working painters usually wear old clothes and go sockless, and I have found that any of the arts which are practiced in this way are usually handled in either psychiatric or philosophical jargon:

"But why this instinctive groping toward womb acceptance in the work of Von Shmier? One must look for total disappearance of entity into the symmetry of his bold withdrawal in rejecting the whole society of his predecessors to achieve the fluid empathy his canvases cry out for with their huge areas of nothingness and inchoate movement."

Now and then, in the thinner magazines, is a tougher, more personal kind of philosophy-art criticism encountered:

"Then this critic said to Normuh Sklizk, 'No, damn it, no. He can't confuse life with living. He absolutely has not the authority to tell me I am a man.' Which, of course, is exactly what *Composition #9 by Northwest* tries to do."

Most critics who write in the first person are pretty tough, philosophically speaking, regardless of the field:

"As music, it schizzed—and I failed to derive inwardness from it. . . ."

"Sometimes I ask myself, 'Can he have read Kierkegaard? Can he? Can he? And then go on such a metaphysical binge as the spiritual spewings of his quasi-novel, *Spluster's End'*?"

Ballet criticism has preserved a certain purity, but in some instances use can be made (I'm quite serious) of sports writing:

"The corps de ballet, having kept the spectators in the tense mood created when the principals left the field, itself retired, and there was an unbearable moment before Undaluva came leaping onstage in a wild burst of footwork, whirling across the arena until we, whose memories go back that far, were holding our breaths, half believing, half fearing that another Nijinsky was about to score."

Actually, ballet criticism is based on two simple points which, if kept in mind, reduce it to routine: never say anything was bad, except in French, and always mention Nijinsky.

Book reviewing is a troublesome, nonprofit sort of work at best, and for my part, I suggest not dabbling in it. However, on a now-and-then basis it seems best handled, currently, from a tauromachian frame of reference.

"Having disposed, in his first two chapters, of the picadors (rather crudely draped under the Freudian cloak of a double seduction, this reviewer thought), O'Malville then blows a tremendous deguello in chapter three, ushering in his beautiful afternoon of *sangre y arena,* leading, predictably, to the moment of truth in which his protagonist sees his own soul, and Dorothy's, passing irretrievably through life, as it were, in a series of poorly executed veronicas."

You may ask, where, then, does the critic use literary terms? Serious students of LP records can answer that instantly—modern jazz reviews:

"Butterball Baker negates the stream of consciousness theory, never deviating from the chapter and verse of Bubba Benson's arrangements. 'I try to choose our literature from the classics in a nonclassic manner. To me, jazz is definitive of mind or it denies its *raison d'être*. The genius virtue of the combo as opus is its keen attention to the penned manuscript.' "

The weakest spot in my theory of modern criticism is that of the theater. I can't seem to put my finger squarely on its source. The closest I can manage is to say that much theater criticism sounds like someone apologizing for a domestic wine:

"Certainly this playgoer would not recommend *She Can't Can-Can* as the kind of stage for steady consumption—heady as a few draughts may be. Nor will critic ask connoisseur to forget his vintage O'Neill or even good Miller '49 for it. But does one want the bouquet, the richness of the great years, week in, week out? Is it, one asks, after swishing a thoughtful mouthful, theater?"

You must be careful, I will say in closing, not to get into the predicament one of our sports writers found himself in when, for a lark, he wrote up a wedding as though he were covering a track meet. He wound up in a journalistic morass of double-entendre and libelous description which was hilariously successful but which cost him his job.

Of course, I must add that sports writers (and critics) do not make a great deal of money on small-town newspapers, so the loss was easily survived.

Notebook Assignment for Class Discussion

1. Look up the meaning of:

critic	spatial	tauromachian
aesthetic	nomenclature	*raison d'etre*
pastel	jargon	opus
semantics	entity	morass
etude	empathy	double-entendre
staccato	inchoate	libelous
legato	quasi	veronica

2. Why is this essay included in the section on wit and humor instead of language, literature, and criticism? Is it essentially critical? What are the elements of true criticism?
3. Do you think that in this essay A. C. Greene intends to be ironic, sarcastic, or satiric? What is the difference between these terms?

4. Is his mood serious, playful, cynical, whimsical, or what? Explain.
5. The author uses "lifetime" as the label of the particular style he exemplifies in "High above the growling bass . . ." Why "lifetime"? Can you think of a more accurate descriptive term?

Related Exercises

1. Read some of the music reviews, or criticisms, in *Time* and other popular periodicals to test Greene's theory that you simply "review one medium in terms of another." Locate several other examples in which so-called critics review one medium (any) in terms of another (any).
2. Greene says you cannot reverse the process and apply musical terms to painting. Do you agree? Write one or two sentences in which you try to apply musical terms to a particular painting, e.g., "The bold staccato brush strokes at first tongue muffled sounds of gray, then rise swiftly in leaping arpeggios to etch a profile of modulations, and finally fade into the dim, wavering uncertainty of a French horn *sustenato diminuendo*." Above all, remember that you are doing this for practice and for fun, not for developing a lifelong style.
3. Mr. Greene tells how hilarious the account of the wedding was, told in terms of a track meet, but he fails to give the reader even the slightest taste of the fun. Try to supply the fun by writing such an account in a single paragraph.

WEEKEND WITH HENRY *

By Peg Boland

Henry took over the ramshackle rabbit cage in our back yard with the flourish of a marine C.O. on a new post. He strutted back and forth and preened endlessly. Then he *cluk, cluked* furiously, and drawing himself majestically to full banty height, crowed in the high melodious voice of the chanticleer.

* From *Don't Panic, Mother,* by Peg Boland (Milwaukee: Bruce Publishing Co., 1964), pp. 3–9.

Was it notice to all that some mighty good things come in small packages? Or fair warning that he was not to be reckoned with lightly?

If the slightest misgiving rose in my bosom as I tucked Henry into his new home that summer afternoon, I laid it to the fourth doughnut I'd had at lunch.

Cocker spaniels bury their old bones in the neighbors' tulip beds; rabbits send up their own peculiar scent to the four winds. But Henry was such a *little* thing. How could he possibly be any trouble?

Certainly the new tenant was the most elegant of our long array of pets. Not his the meekness of Dagwood the tricolor guinea pig, nor the stoic silence of Midnight the black rabbit. Nor was he covered with confusion like Murgatroyd the rat-like hamster. Henry was all brilliant plumage and importance.

Henry drank in the oh's and ah's of the neighborhood who came on the double to inspect our newest piece of livestock. His banty heart must have swelled to king-size at their admiration for the gold and russet of his wings and the sweep of his black tail feathers, gleaming iridescent in the summer sunshine. Mr. John or Sally Victor would have seen Henry through different eyes. What a time *they* would have had dreaming up bonnets to tempt Milady with Henry's magnificent coq feather tail!

Most fascinating to all was the way Henry arched his neck and sent forth his *cock-a-doodle-doo*. An effort definitely on the soprano side, compared with the more raucous endeavors of the commonplace brethren in his species. Furthermore, from the moment of his arrival Henry continued to sound off with the relentless fire and cadence of a platoon command drilling green-as-grass G-I's.

At bedtime it took force to tear the children from their watch over the new pet. And that night it seemed I had just closed my eyes when Henry's shrill call dragged me from sleep. The clock in the early light said 4 A.M. I could have wrung Henry's neck, russet feathers and all.

He crowed again, loud, clear, compelling. My muscles tensed and I shuddered, waiting for the next crow. It came, and another. Unable to help myself I began timing their regularity. How many minutes between crows? Four? Five? And how many of my sleep-loving neighbors were already awake and cursing Henry? Henry crowed and I fretted for three hours. By seven o'clock I was ready to toss Henry in a soup pot. Just plain murder was too good for him.

I wondered bitterly why nostalgia for one's youth so often betrays one. I remembered the day the youngsters asked, "Mother, what did *you* do when you were a little girl"

"Well," I had told them, "I had two of the cutest little banties you ever saw ... they even let me put them to sleep in my doll bed." There was more, much more. The booby traps we lay for ourselves!

Just one crack-of-dawn session like this and it was evident that Henry had to quiet down or we would all be in the doghouse along with our assorted livestock.

That night I covered every inch of Henry's cage with ragged patchwork quilts and old pieces of slip-cover. A wild looking roost it was, but it would fool Henry. Henry would think it was still night time, and he would sleep.

That was *my* idea, not Henry's. Henry slept. Until 5 A.M. One hour later, to be sure, when he shrilly welcomed the new day, but definitely not the hour our neighbors were accustomed to greeting it.

All that day I was so vexed with Henry I didn't once go out to admire him, and turned a deaf ear to the children's raptures over his antics. My affair with Henry was over right then, but neither of us knew it.

When I tucked him in that night I was determined that Henry would settle down, or else! When I covered his roost I made some mention of this fact to him, along with a few dire threats. The banty blinked solemnly and closed both eyes.

Long before the first robin chirped Henry let go again. *Cock-a-doodle-doo!* Loud, clear, piercing. Either Henry was the victim of insomnia or he expected the world to begin the day at his shrill command. I burrowed down under the bed clothes but there was no shutting him out. Covered cage or not, Henry was still in good voice.

My disposition that day resembled the Shrew—untamed. And in the mail, to add to my dismay, came an anonymous letter.

"Remember the Golden Rule," it said. "How would you like it if *all* the neighbors kept chickens?"

Silly question. Obviously our family would like it. The kids would not be the least impressed by vague threats. I could hear their Bronx cheer. And for my money, it wasn't the number one griper in our neighborhood that bothered me. It was no sleep.

Henry's stock skidded to a new low, and it didn't climb even a notch when my husband, blissfully unaware of the letter, went to bat for the pest. "Henry's as good as a watch dog," he said cheerfully. Hadn't he chased away a bullying mongrel dog that annoyed everybody around the place? The stray had appeared practically at Henry's first note, to inspect the upstart. Henry had cocked one eye at the intruder, clucked furiously and let go in his most frightening voice. The dog took off like a streak, tail between his legs. This feat delighted the family no end, but failed to stir me.

At this stage of the game Henry needed kind words, but the only others in his favor came from a gentle lady on the next street. She liked his musical crow. It reminded her of her childhood on a Dakota farm. By now I wished fervently that my own early years had been less vivid, and I less of a soft touch for animals.

Our visiting list increased by the hour. They were amazed. Why, he was only a pint-size rooster! How could such a *little* piece make such a ruckus? There was surprise, disappointment, too, in their faces. I found out why when several so-called friends, after frankly admiring Henry's plumage, took leave admitting he was "hardly a mouthful," but wondering if he "would be any good in a stew." Their interest, strictly of the gastronomical variety, and their innuendos, did not improve the painful situation, nor my disposition, ragged at the edges from lack of sleep.

I was fed up. Particularly was I fed up with Henry. By now even I could see that chickens don't belong in the city. With Henry wound up like an eight-day clock, the neighbors would demand a general housecleaning of all livestock on our place.

The family were unimpressed. They accused me of being stuffy, and warned if I got rid of Henry, I could expect no help from them. But my hackles were up.

After a little quiet investigating I had lined up just the spot for the rooster—Healy's farm in the country. *There* was banty paradise if I ever saw one.

Came Sunday, D-day for Henry, and with it the rain and the wind. The skies opened and water came down in sheets.

But so bent on getting rid of the rooster was I by now that the elements only fired me with more determination. The heck with the deluge. I put on a raincoat and made for the yard.

Things got off to a bad start. The little hellion was unco-operative when I tried to get him from his cage into a small cardboard box. My early schooling was peculiarly lacking—it included no tactical course on snagging chickens.

Clumsily I was grasping Henry by his squirming middle and Henry didn't like it. Sputtering and scolding fiercely, the saucy character gave an angry jerk and exploded out of the box like a pheasant heading for cover.

In my wrath I stripped the raincoat from my Sunday best and

took after the chicken, using my coat like the toreador as he makes feints at the bull. My raincoat went one way, Henry the other.

The chase grew wilder and hotter, over bushes, into the hedge, behind the wisteria vines. Already I was soaked to the skin and mud to the ankles. Every move I made, Henry outwitted, diving into the underbrush or taking off over a fence.

In the heat of the chase I refused to consider the spectacle I presented. Low comedy was not my dish, and my frustration at being outsmarted by this twisting, diving mite was outweighed only by my overwhelming desire to lay my hands on him. Abbott and Costello could have sold out the house for the performance ... but I had no comedy aspirations. Creeping on all fours in the dripping bushes, I suddenly encountered Henry where he had squeezed in beside a fence. I grabbed him quickly, and stuffed his sopping, clucking carcass into the box. Gasping, spent from the exertion, I drew a deep breath and relaxed my hold on the lid. Henry was off again.

Field hockey in baggy bloomers at a girls' school was no training for cross-country in the mud. Frustrated, panting, I hurled my weight into one desperate lunge at Henry, and sprawled flat in the soggy earth. I picked myself up from my final ignominy, grateful that my family had deserted me. Worst of all, I had only myself to thank for this debacle.

Disgusted, I made a half-hearted attempt to pull myself together and peered into the murky downpour. I could just make out Henry taking off over the trees.

Then I remembered an awful thing: the day the farmer gave Henry to me we had to coax him down from his roost in an apple tree. Henry always slept in a tree. He didn't *like* being cooped up. Maybe I'd never catch him and he would go to bed in Morgan's cherry tree and sound off under their bedroom window at four o'clock next morning. I felt like blowing my brains out; then on second thought wondered, *what* brains?

For an hour more I sloshed and slopped through the mud in the gloom of the lot, poking in every thicket and hedge. Finally, fed up, soaked, my hair in wet scraggles against my face, I was ready to call the whole thing off—let the chips fall where they may.

Disgustedly I looked down at my eight double A's, wrecked beyond repair, and from the corner of my eye detected something move. Henry was eyeing me balefully from one small dry spot under a forsythia bush. Maybe Henry was at low ebb, too, for he offered me no back talk when I grabbed him by his saturated feathers and plumped him into the box.

Unfortunately my mission was far from accomplished, for a good ten miles lay ahead of me to Healy's farm on the river.

It took half the trip to get my blood pressure down to normal, and I was still talking to myself when I made the turn that would bring me around a hill and into view of the house. There I found the road torn up and a sign, "Road under construction. Travel at your own risk."

But nothing was going to keep me from getting rid of that rooster. So, blood pressure soaring again, I stepped hard on the gas. And there I was, mired to the hub cap . . . a long trek from home.

My thoughts at that moment would have singed asbestos. I climbed out of the car in mud to my knees and sloshed a mile up the hill to the nearest farm.

The farmer owned a jeep, which he obligingly, and for a fee, used to tow my struggling car out of the mud. When I attempted to take off under my own steam, I hit another bog and in again I sank. The farmer was agreeable. This time he pulled me two miles, also for a fee.

Which character, Henry or I, was more bedraggled is hard to say. When we appeared in the Healy barnyard my friend took me in from stem to stern. Then, with a glint in her eye, she asked, "You just get off the Ark? Or maybe you've taken to lying in gutters."

"Look, friendship is a beautiful thing, but lay off the funny stuff." I pushed Henry into her hands.

With all the dignity I could muster, I brushed a dripping lock out of one eye, blew a stray banty feather from its perch on my wet bosom, and made for the car.

I looked back only once, to see Henry settle himself manfully down in the henyard. He surveyed his new kingdom, and preened himself, then drawing up with a lordly air he sounded off with a full-throated, "*Cock-a-doodle-doo!*"

But the females in the chicken yard held no lasting allure for Henry. Before I was out of sight, the explosive mite lifted his wings and sailed over the fence.

Henry spends what he considers his nights in princely splendor high in the mulberry tree below the Healy's bedroom window.

There undoubtedly he mingles his high melodious tones with the call of the loon, the chirp of the crickets, and the quack of the ducks feeding on the river. No one has ever complained. After all, it's quiet in the country.

Notebook Assignment for Class Discussion

1. What use does Peg Boland make of allusion in paragraph 1?
2. Do you find the author's mood and point of view infectious? Do you get a real sense of fun out of her dramatic account of a family experience, or not?
3. Do the occasional fragmentary sentences add to or detract from the mood the author is attempting to create? Are there times when the strict rules of grammar may be violated to produce an effect, in this case the humanization of the rooster and excitement of the whole experience?
4. Which concrete words and details contribute most to the establishment of Henry's personality?
5. Which details best reveal the author's own personality? How would you describe her?

Related Exercises

1. Does a rooster actually make a sound like *cock-a-doodle-doo?* Is *cock-a-doodle-doo* imitative or descriptive language? Since the sounds of nature are basically the same in all parts of the world, ask some of the foreign students in your classes to pronounce and write their vernacular term for the crow of a rooster, and other onomatopoeic, or *sound,* words, e.g., their equivalents of *splash, sizzle, drone, hum, crackle, meow, gurgle,* and so on.
2. What is it about naming pets that brings out the worst, or silliest, in people? Elliot Paul says that "the bourgeois French (in the 1920's) called their parrots 'Coco,' cats 'Minou,' small dogs 'Frou-frou,' and police dogs 'Hanibal.' " [1] What are some favorite American names for pets?
3. The essay of self-disparagement, based on the author's minor complaints and confusions, has long been a favorite form of humorous writing. James Thurber, E. B. White, Robert Benchley, Cornelia Otis Skinner, and many others have occasionally had great fun themselves and provided many laughs for others by relating in whimsical fashion their *faux pas,* humiliations, hopeless entanglements, and the like. There is a touch of it in Red Smith's "sauna" experience, too. Try to

---

[1] From *The Last Time I Saw Paris,* by Elliot Paul (New York: Random House, 1942), p. 6.

recall some similar experience of your own and write a humorous sketch of 400 words, imitating the style of Peg Boland, or some other writer whose sense of fun you admire.

THE HIDING OF BLACK BILL *

By O. Henry

A lank, strong, red-faced man with a Wellington beak and small, fiery eyes tempered by flaxen lashes, sat on the station platform at Los Pinos swinging his legs to and fro. At his side sat another man, fat, melancholy, and seedy, who seemed to be his friend. They had the appearance of men to whom life had appeared as a reversible coat—seamy on both sides.

"Ain't seen you in about four years, Ham," said the seedy man. "Which way you been traveling?"

"Texas," said the red-faced man. "It was too cold in Alaska for me. And I found it warm in Texas. I'll tell you about one hot spell I went through there.

"One morning I steps off the International at a water-tank and lets it go on without me. 'Twas a ranch country, and fuller of spite-houses than New York City. Only out there they build 'em twenty miles away so you can't smell what they've got for dinner, instead of running 'em up two inches from their neighbors' windows.

"There wasn't any roads in sight, so I footed it 'cross country. The grass was shoe-top deep, and the mesquite timber looked just like a peach orchard. It was so much like a gentleman's estate that every minute you expected a kennelful of bulldogs to run out and bite you. But I must have walked twenty miles before I came in sight of a ranchhouse. It was a little one, about as big as an elevated-railroad station.

"There was a little man in a white shirt and brown overalls and a pink handkerchief around his neck rolling cigarettes under a tree in front of the door.

"'Greetings,' says I. 'Any refreshment, welcome, emoluments, or even work, for a comparative stranger?'

* From *Options*, by O. Henry (O. Henry Authorized Editions; Garden City: Doubleday, Page and Co., 1920), pp. 38–55.

" 'Oh, come in,' says he, in a refined tone. 'Sit down on that stool, please. I didn't hear your horse coming.'

" 'He isn't near enough yet,' says I. 'I walked. I don't want to be a burden, but I wonder if you have three or four gallons of water handy.'

" 'You do look pretty dusty,' says he; 'but our bathing arrangements—'

" 'It's a drink I want,' says I. 'Never mind the dust that's on the outside.'

"He gets me a dipper of water out of a red jar hanging up, and then goes on:

" 'Do you want work?'

" 'For a time,' says I. 'This is a rather quiet section of the country, isn't it?'

" 'It is,' says he. 'Sometimes—so I have been told—one sees no human being pass for weeks at a time. I've been here only a month. I bought the ranch from an old settler who wanted to move farther west.'

" 'It suits me,' says I. 'Quiet and retirement are good for a man sometimes. And I need a job. I can tend bar, salt mines, lecture, float stock, do a little middle-weight slugging, and play the piano.'

" 'Can you herd sheep?' asks the little ranchman.

" 'Do you mean *have* I heard sheep?' says I.

" 'Can you herd 'em—take charge of a flock of 'em?' says he.

" 'Oh,' says I, 'now I understand. You mean chase 'em around and bark at 'em like collie dogs. Well, I might,' says I. 'I've never exactly done any sheep-herding, but I've often seen 'em from car windows masticating daisies, and they don't look dangerous.'

" 'I'm short a herder,' says the ranchman. 'You never can depend on the Mexicans. I've only got two flocks. You may take out my bunch of muttons—there are only eight hundred of 'em —in the morning, if you like. The pay is twelve dollars a month and your rations furnished. You camp in a tent on the prairie with your sheep. You do your own cooking, but wood and water are brought to your camp. It's an easy job.'

" 'I'm on,' says I. 'I'll take the job even if I have to garland my brow and hold on to a crook and wear a loose-effect and play on a pipe like the shepherds do in pictures.'

"So the next morning the little ranchman helps me drive the flock of muttons from the corral to about two miles out and let 'em graze on a little hillside on the prairie. He gives me a lot of instructions about not letting bunches of them stray off from the herd, and driving 'em down to a water-hole to drink at noon.

" 'I'll bring out your tent and camping outfit and rations in the buckboard before night,' says he.

" 'Fine,' says I. 'And don't forget the rations. Nor the camping outfit. And be sure to bring the tent. Your name's Zollicoffer, ain't it?'

" 'My name,' says he, 'is Henry Ogden.'

" 'All right, Mr. Ogden,' says I. 'Mine is Mr. Percival Saint Clair.'

"I herded sheep for five days on the Rancho Chiquito; and then the wool entered my soul. That getting next to Nature certainly got next to me. I was lonesomer than Crusoe's goat. I've seen a lot of persons more entertaining as companions than those sheep were. I'd drive 'em to the corral and pen 'em every evening, and then cook my corn-bread and mutton and coffee, and lie down in a tent the size of a table-cloth, and listen to the coyotes and whippoorwills singing around the camp.

"The fifth evening, after I had corralled my costly but uncongenial muttons, I walked over to the ranch-house and stepped in the door.

" 'Mr. Ogden,' says I, 'you and me have got to get sociable. Sheep are all very well to dot the landscape and furnish eight-dollar cotton suitings for man, but for table-talk and fireside companions they rank along with five-o'clock teazers. If you've got a deck of cards, or a parcheesi outfit, or a game of authors, get 'em out, and let's get on a mental basis. I've got to do something in an intellectual line, if it's only to knock somebody's brains out.'

"This Henry Ogden was a peculiar kind of ranchman. He wore finger-rings and a big gold watch and careful neckties. And his face was calm, and his nose-spectacles was kept very shiny. I saw once, in Muscogee, an outlaw hung for murdering six men, who was a dead ringer for him. But I knew a preacher in Arkansas that you would have taken to be his brother. I didn't care much for him either way; what I wanted was some fellowship and communion with holy saints or lost sinners—anything sheepless would do.

" 'Well, Saint Clair,' says he, laying down the book he was reading, 'I guess it must be pretty lonesome for you at first. And I don't deny that it's monotonous for me. Are you sure you corralled your sheep so they won't stray out?'

" 'They're shut up as tight as the jury of a millionaire murderer,' says I. 'And I'll be back with them long before they'll need their trained nurse.'

"So Ogden digs up a deck of cards, and we play casino. After

five days and nights of my sheep-camp it was like a toot on
Broadway. When I caught big casino I felt as excited as if I had
made a million in Trinity. And when H. O. loosened up a little
and told the story about the lady in the Pullman car I laughed
for five minutes.

"That showed what a comparative thing life is. A man may see
so much that he'd be bored to turn his head to look at a $3,000,-
000 fire or Joe Weber or the Adriatic Sea. But let him herd sheep
for a spell, and you'll see him splitting his ribs laughing at 'Cur-
few Shall Not Ring Tonight,' or really enjoying himself playing
cards with ladies.

"By-and-by Ogden gets out a decanter of Bourbon, and then
there is a total eclipse of sheep.

" 'Do you remember reading in the papers, about a month
ago,' says he, 'about a train hold-up on the M. K. & T.? The
express agent was shot through the shoulder, and about $15,000
in currency taken. And it's said that only one man did the job.'

" 'Seems to me I do,' says I. 'But such things happen so often
they don't linger long in the human Texas mind. Did they over-
take, overhaul, seize, or lay hands upon the despoiler?'

" 'He escaped,' says Ogden. 'And I was just reading in a paper
to-day that the officers have tracked him down into this part of
the country. It seems the bills the robber got were all the first
issue of currency to the Second National Bank of Espinosa City.
And so they've followed the trail where they've been spent, and
it leads this way.'

"Ogden pours out some more Bourbon, and shoves me the
bottle.

" 'I imagine,' says I, after ingurgitating another modicum of
the royal booze, 'that it wouldn't be at all a disingenuous idea for
a train-robber to run down into this part of the country to hide
for a spell. A sheep-ranch, now,' says I, 'would be the finest kind
of a place. Who'd ever expect to find such a desperate character
among these song-birds and muttons and wild flowers? And, by
the way,' says I, kind of looking H. Ogden over, 'was there any
description mentioned of this single-handed terror? Was his lineaments or height and thickness or teeth fillings or style of habili-
ments set forth in print?'

" 'Why, no,' says Ogden; 'they say nobody got a good sight of
him because he wore a mask. But they know it was a train-robber
called Black Bill, because he always works alone and because he
dropped a handkerchief in the express-car that had his name
on it.'

" 'All right,' says I. 'I approve of Black Bill's retreat to the sheep-ranges. I guess they won't find him.'

" 'There's one thousand dollars' reward for his capture,' says Ogden.

" 'I don't need that kind of money,' says I, looking Mr. Sheepman straight in the eye. 'The twelve dollars a month you pay me is enough. I need a rest, and I can save up until I get enough to pay my fare to Texarkana, where my widowed mother lives. If Black Bill,' I goes on, looking significantly at Ogden, 'was to have come down this way—say, a month ago—and bought a little sheep-ranch and—'

" 'Stop,' says Ogden, getting out of his chair and looking pretty vicious. 'Do you mean to insinuate—'

" 'Nothing,' says I; 'no insinuations. I'm stating a hypodermical case. I say, if Black Bill had come down here and bought a sheepranch and hired me to Little-Boy-Blue 'em and treated me square and friendly, as you've done, he'd never have anything to fear from me. A man is a man, regardless of any complications he may have with sheep or railroad trains. Now you know where I stand.'

"Ogden looks black as camp-coffee for nine seconds, and then he laughs, amused.

" 'You'll do, Saint Clair,' says he. 'If I *was* Black Bill I wouldn't be afraid to trust you. Let's have a game or two of seven-up to-night; that is, if you don't mind playing with a train-robber.'

" 'I've told you,' says I, 'my oral sentiments, and there's no strings to 'em.'

"While I was shuffling after the first hand, I asks Ogden, as if the idea was a kind of a casualty, where he was from.

" 'Oh,' says he, 'from the Mississippi Valley.'

" 'That's a nice little place,' says I. 'I've often stopped over there. But didn't you find the sheets a little damp and the food poor? Now, I hail,' says I, 'from the Pacific Slope. Ever put up there?'

" 'Too draughty,' says Ogden. 'But if you're ever in the Middle West just mention my name, and you'll get foot-warmers and dripped coffee.'

" 'Well,' says I, 'I wasn't exactly fishing for your private telephone number and the middle name of your aunt that carried off the Cumberland Presbyterian minister. It don't matter. I just want you to know you are safe in the hands of your shepherd. Now, don't play hearts on spades, and don't get nervous.'

" 'Still harping,' says Ogden, laughing again. 'Don't you suppose that if I was Black Bill and thought you suspected me, I'd

put a Winchester bullet into you and stop my nervousness, if
I had any?'

" 'Not any,' says I. 'A man who's got the nerve to hold up a
train single-handed wouldn't do a trick like that. I've knocked
about enough to know that them are the kind of men who put
a value on a friend. Not that I can claim being a friend of yours,
Mr. Ogden,' says I, 'being only your sheep-herder; but under
more expeditious circumstances we might have been.'

" 'Forget the sheep temporarily, I beg,' says Ogden, 'and cut
for deal.'

"About four days afterward, while my muttons was nooning
on the water-hole and I deep in the interstices of making a pot of
coffee, up rides softly on the grass a mysterious person in the
garb of the being he wished to represent. He was dressed somewhere between a Kansas City detective, Buffalo Bill, and the town
dog-catcher of Baton Rouge. His chin and eye wasn't molded on
fighting lines, so I knew he was only a scout.

" 'Herdin' sheep?' he asks me.

" 'Well,' says I, 'to a man of your evident gumptional endowments, I wouldn't have the nerve to state that I am engaged in
decorating old bronzes or oiling bicycle sprockets.'

" 'You don't talk or look like a sheep-herder to me,' says he.

" 'But you talk like what you look like to me,' says I.

"And then he asks me who I was working for, and I shows him
Rancho Chiquito, two miles away, in the shadow of a low hill,
and he tells me he's a deputy sheriff.

" 'There's a train-robber called Black Bill supposed to be
somewhere in these parts,' says the scout. 'He's been traced as
far as San Antonio, and maybe farther. Have you seen or heard
of any strangers around here during the past month?'

" 'I have not,' says I, 'except a record of one over at the
Mexican quarters of Loomis' ranch, on the Frio.'

" 'What do you know about him?' asks the deputy.

" 'He's three days old,' says I.

" 'What kind of a looking man is the man you work for?' he
asks. 'Does old George Ramey own this place yet? He's run sheep
here for the last ten years, but never had no success.'

" 'The old man has sold out and gone West,' I tells him. 'Another sheep fancier bought him out about a month ago.'

" 'What kind of a looking man is he?' asks the deputy again.

"Oh,' says I, 'a big, fat kind of a Dutchman with long whiskers
and blue specs. I don't think he knows a sheep from a ground-
squirrel. I guess old George soaked him pretty well on the deal,'
says I.

"After indulging himself in a lot more non-communicative information and two-thirds of my dinner, the deputy rides away.

"That night I mentions the matter to Ogden.

" 'They're drawing the tendrils of the octopus around Black Bill,' says I. And then I told him about the deputy sheriff, and how I'd described him to the deputy, and what the deputy said about the matter.

" 'Oh, well,' says Ogden, 'let's don't borrow any of Black Bill's troubles. We've a few of our own. Get the Bourbon out of the cupboard and we'll drink to his health—unless,' says he, with his little crackling laugh, 'you're prejudiced against train-robbers.'

" 'I'll drink,' says I, 'to any man who's a friend to a friend. And I believe that Black Bill,' I goes on, 'would be that. So here's to Black Bill, and may he have good luck.'

"And both of us drank.

"About two weeks later comes shearing-time. The sheep had to be driven up to the ranch, and a lot of frowzy-headed Mexicans would snip the fur off of them with back-action scissors. So the afternoon before the barbers were to come I hustled my under-done muttons over the hill, across the dell, down by the winding brook, and up to the ranch-house, where I penned 'em in a corral and bade 'em my nightly adieus.

"I went from there to the ranch-house. I find H. Ogden, Esquire, lying asleep on his little cot bed. I guess he had been overcome by anti-insomnia or diswakefulness or some of the diseases peculiar to the sheep business. His mouth and vest were open, and he breathed like a second-hand bicycle pump. I looked at him and gave vent to just a few musings. 'Imperial Caesar,' says I, 'asleep in such a way, might shut his mouth and keep the wind away.'

"A man asleep is certainly a sight to make angels weep. What good is all his brain, muscle, backing, nerve, influence, and family connections? He's at the mercy of his enemies, and more so of his friends. And he's about as beautiful as a cab-horse leaning against the Metropolitan Opera House at 12:30 A.M. dreaming of the plains of Arabia. Now, a woman asleep you regard as different. No matter how she looks, you know it's better for all hands for her to be that way.

"Well, I took a drink of Bourbon and one for Ogden, and started in to be comfortable while he was taking his nap. He had some books on his table on indigenous subjects, such as Japan and drainage and physical culture—and some tobacco, which seemed more to the point.

"After I'd smoked a few, and listened to the sartorial breathing of H. O., I happened to look out the window toward the shearing-

pens, where there was a kind of a road coming up from a kind
of a road across a kind of a creek farther away.

"I saw five men riding up to the house. All of 'em carried guns
across their saddles, and among 'em was the deputy that had
talked to me at my camp.

"They rode up careful, in open formation, with their guns
ready. I set apart with my eye the one I opinionated to be the
boss muckraker of this law-and-order cavalry.

" 'Good-evening, gents,' says I. 'Won't you 'light, and tie your
horses?'

"The boss rides up close, and swings his gun over till the opening in it seems to cover my whole front elevation.

" 'Don't you move your hands none,' says he, 'till you and me
indulge in a adequate amount of necessary conversation.'

" 'I will not,' says I. 'I am no deaf mute, and therefore will not
have to disobey your injunctions in replying.'

" 'We are on the lookout,' says he, 'for Black Bill, the man
that held up the Katy for $15,000 in May. We are searching the
ranches and everybody on 'em. What is your name, and what do
you do on this ranch?'

" 'Captain,' says I, 'Percival Saint Clair is my occupation, and
my name is sheep-herder. I've got my flock of veals—no, muttons—
penned here to-night. The shearers are coming to-morrow to give
them a hair-cut—with baa-a-rum, I suppose.'

" 'Where's the boss of this ranch?' the captain of the gang
asks me.

" 'Wait just a minute, cap'n,' says I. 'Wasn't there a kind of
reward offered for the capture of this desperate character you
have referred to in your preamble?'

" 'There's a thousand dollars' reward offered,' says the captain,
'but it's for his capture and conviction. There don't seem to be
no provision made for an informer.'

" 'It looks like it might rain in a day or so,' says I, in a tired
way, looking up at the cerulean blue sky.

" 'If you know anything about the locality, disposition, or
secretiveness of this here Black Bill,' says he, in a severe dialect,
'you are amiable to the law in not reporting it.'

" 'I heard a fence-rider say,' says I, in a desultory kind of voice,
'that a Mexican told a cowboy named Jake over at Pidgin's store
on the Nueces that he heard that Black Bill had been seen in
Matamoras by a sheepman's cousin two weeks ago.'

" 'Tell you what I'll do, Tight Mouth,' says the captain, after
looking me over for bargains. 'If you put us on so we can scoop
Black Bill, I'll pay you a hundred dollars out of my own—out

of our own—pockets. That's liberal,' says he. 'You ain't entitled to anything. Now, what do you say?'

" 'Cash down now?' I asks.

"The captain has a sort of discussion with his help-mates, and they all produce the contents of their pockets for analysis. Out of the general results they figured up $102.30 in cash and $31 worth of plug tobacco.

" 'Come nearer, capitan meeo,' says I, 'and listen.' He so did.

" 'I am mighty poor and low down in the world,' says I. 'I am working for twelve dollars a month trying to keep a lot of animals together whose only thought seems to be to get asunder. Although,' says I, 'I regard myself as some better than the State of South Dakota, it's a come-down to a man who has heretofore regarded sheep only in the form of chops. I'm pretty far reduced in the world on account of foiled ambitions and rum and a kind of cocktail they make along the P.R.R. all the way from Scranton to Cincinnati—dry gin, French vermouth, one squeeze of a lime, and a good dash of orange bitters. If you're ever up that way, don't fail to let one try you. And, again,' says I, 'I have never yet went back on a friend. I've stayed by 'em when they had plenty, and when adversity's overtaken me I've never forsook 'em.

" 'But,' I goes on, 'this is not exactly the case of a friend. Twelve dollars a month is only bowing-acquaintance money. And I do not consider brown beans and corn-bread the food of friendship. I am a poor man,' says I, 'and I have a widowed mother in Texarkana. You will find Black Bill,' says I, 'lying asleep in this house on a cot in the room to your right. He's the man you want, as I know from his words and conversation. He was in a way a friend,' I explains, 'and if I was the man I once was the entire product of the mines of Gondola would not have tempted me to betray him. But,' says I, 'every week half of the beans was wormy, and not nigh enough wood in camp.

" 'Better go in careful, gentlemen,' says I. 'He seems impatient at times, and when you think of his late professional pursuits one would look for abrupt actions if he was come upon sudden.'

"So the whole posse unmounts and ties their horses, and unlimbers their ammunition and equipments, and tiptoes into the house. And I follows, like Delilah when she set the Philip Steins on to Samson.

"The leader of the posse shakes Ogden and wakes him up. And then he jumps up, and two more of the reward-hunters grab him. Ogden was mighty tough with all his slimness, and he gives 'em as neat a single-footed tussle against odds as I ever see.

" 'What does this mean?' he says, after they had him down.

" 'You're scooped in, Mr. Black Bill,' says the captain. 'That's all.'

" 'It's an outrage!' says H. Ogden, madder yet.

" 'It was,' says the peace-and-good-will man. 'The Katy wasn't bothering you, and there's a law against monkeying with express packages.'

"And he sits on H. Ogden's stomach and goes through his pockets symptomatically and careful.

" 'I'll make you perspire for this,' says Ogden, perspiring some himself. 'I can prove who I am.'

" 'So can I,' says the captain, as he draws from H. Ogden's inside coat-pocket a handful of new bills of the Second National Bank of Espinosa City; 'Your regular engraved Tuesdays-and-Fridays visiting-card wouldn't have a louder voice in proclaiming your indemnity than this here currency. You can get up now and prepare to go with us and expatriate your sins.'

"H. Ogden gets up and fixes his necktie. He says no more after they have taken the money off of him.

" 'A well-greased idea,' says the sheriff captain, admiring, 'to slip off down here and buy a little sheep-ranch where the hand of man is seldom heard. It was the slickest hide-out I ever see,' says the captain.

"So one of the men goes to the shearing-pen and hunts up the other herder, a Mexican they call John Sallies, and he saddles Ogden's horse, and the sheriffs all ride up close around him with their guns in hand, ready to take their prisoner to town.

"Before starting, Ogden puts the ranch in John Sallies' hands and gives him orders about the shearing and where to graze the sheep, just as if he intended to be back in a few days. And a couple of hours afterward one Percival Saint Clair, an ex-sheep-herder of the Rancho Chiquito, might have been seen, with a hundred and nine dollars—wages and blood money—in his pocket, riding south on another horse belonging to said ranch."

The red-faced man paused and listened. The whistle of a coming freight-train sounded far away among the low hills.

The fat, seedy man at his side sniffed, and shook his frowzy head slowly and disparagingly.

"What is it, Snipy?" asked the other. "Got the blues again?"

"No, I ain't," said the seedy one, sniffing again. "But I don't like your talk. You and me have been friends, off and on, for fifteen year, and I never yet knew or heard of you giving anybody up to the law—not no one. And here was a man whose saleratus you had et and at whose table you had played games of cards—

if casino can be so called. And yet you inform him to the law and take money for it. It never was like you, I say."

"This H. Ogden," resumed the red-faced man, "through a lawyer, proved himself free by alibis and other legal terminalities, as I so heard afterward. He never suffered no harm. He did me favors, and I hated to hand him over."

"How about the bills they found in his pocket?" asked the seedy man.

"I put 'em there," said the red-faced man, "while he was asleep, when I saw the posse riding up. I was Black Bill. Look out, Snipy, here she comes! We'll board her on the bumpers when she takes water at the tank."

Part Two

A MIRROR HELD TO NATURE

Or

The World Outside the World of Man

ZOOLOGICAL NOTES *

By Mona Gardner

Monster crickets from the Kalahari regions have begun a slow but persistent invasion of the vast western desert above Cape Town, where flourishing karakul and merino flocks are being raised these days. Called "barbers" because their favorite diet is human hair and they nibble a sleeping man bald in a couple of hours, these glossy black giants have a leg spread which covers a tennis ball, yet they do not hop, but only crawl at the slow-motion pace of a foot a minute. Because their present excursion south is through sparsely settled regions which provide scant human hair, the creeping barbers are making do with karakul and merino hair. Herdsmen are swapping data on an all-out search for natural enemies that will exterminate the fleecers, but so far have only established the dismal fact that birds refuse to eat them.

Bull elephants have a fondness for the sap of the *lala* palm, which provides native villages with a seasonal liquor supply. Toward the end of the rainless months these palms are trimmed down to stumps, a circular groove is cut below the top, and a leaf is inserted to act as a spout, which drains into a hanging calabash. Shortly after, a sweetish, tangy fluid begins to flow, which makes an invigorating drink when fresh, but when fermented is said to have the kick of a giraffe. During this season old bulls regularly make the rounds of native villages, toss off the contents of all available calabashes, and then go crashing through the bush squealing and trumpeting boisterously. Native calendars appropriately call this the "ho-ho month."

Rains are sometimes eighteen to twenty-two months apart in the Western Cape, but settlers there claim they have an infallible weather forecast provided by the trek of insect armies from the dry pans which fill with water during one of these infrequent downpours. Hours before the first drop, millions of scorpions, beetles, and tarantulas, who inhabit the baked and cracked mud of these saucerlike depressions, start moving out toward high ground.

The red-billed weaver of the finch family is a very formidable invader. Flying in solid clouds three miles long and one mile

* From *The Atlantic Monthly*, Vol. 207, No. 3 (March, 1961), 96–97.

wide, these devastating millions eat their way through wheat
fields and leave them as barren as an ant army on the march
would. Only two ways have been found to interrupt this grim
migration—dynamiting the trees where they roost at night, and
nocturnal sorties by aircraft spraying poison on these roosting
spots.

Hottentot legend is that baboons *can* talk but don't because
the white man would make them work. These brown-haired, dog-
faced Chacma baboons are the most cunning and daring crop
robbers that veld farmers have to contend with. They will maneuver and deploy in troops for hours to confuse pursuers. Baboons
can readily count to six, farmers maintain, and they say that if
five armed men disappear into a corn patch and four come out,
leaving one behind to kill marauders, the baboons know and
won't enter that patch. It is the same if six go in and five come
out. But raise the number to seven, and evidently it does something to baboon computation, for they will charge in as soon as
six men leave.

Baboon tribes still flourish on the peninsula below Cape Town,
which is now a nature reserve. One colony of over a thousand
has been cut off from other colonies for more than a century by
a motor road and railway line. They are bold, playful, and intelligently adaptable, often throw rocks at passing motorcars, and
have learned to scoop fish out of rock pools and to bait lobsters.
Curiously enough, they are afraid of men but not of women. Let
a man in woman's dress come toward them, and they will scatter.
But if a woman appears in slacks, even though she is carrying a
gun, they will charge her ferociously.

Baboons suffering from gastric ulcer, rheumatism, influenza,
and malnutrition have taught medical men several effective remedies. During the 1918 flu epidemic, sick baboons were seen totter-
ing from their mountain caves to burrow for wild garlic and
gorge on it. When stricken farm families ate the same raw bulbs,
they found both fever and congestion were relieved. The sight
of rheumatic baboons stuffing themselves with willow leaves led
Cape householders to brew a strong infusion of willow leaves,
which they drink to alleviate rheumatic pains. These same willow
leaves are the basis of one of today's world-famous specifics for
rheumatism.

During hot, dry weather, farmers hunting stores of wild honey
go into the bush and wait for an unerring honey diviner to lead
them to a well-stocked hive. This small brown-gray bird does a

series of anxious fluttering passages to and from the man in one direction, meanwhile keeping up a loud insistent chatter. The note changes exultantly when the man reaches the hive and cuts through the hard sugary shell, which the bird's beak cannot penetrate. Hottentots always leave a share for the honey guide, because they say it has a vindictive nature and if cheated would probably lead them next time to a leopard or to the deadliest of snakes, the black mamba.

Notebook Assignment for Class Discussion

1. What is the basis of Miss Gardner's organization in this selection?
2. What has each section of "Zoological Notes" in common with the others? Are they stylistically similar? Thematically similar?
3. Has the author a central idea? Does she make it clear?
4. Both introduction and conclusion are lacking here. Is it harmful to the clarity and tone of the whole?
5. What kind of unity has "Zoological Notes"? What kind of coherence?
6. For what effect is the author working in these "notes"? Is the form she chooses more likely to achieve this effect than another? In what other ways might she have achieved the same effects?
7. There is little impressionistic description in these "notes"; but in what sense might this selection be called "impressionistic"?
8. Notes usually serve as the raw materials from which a finished essay is constructed. Does this collection of anecdotes, news items, and short expository paragraphs seem to you finished, and if so, in what sense?

Related Exercises

1. Write an essay in which you discuss possible points of comparison between "Zoological Notes" and Thoreau's "The Battle of the Ants."
2. Neither Thoreau nor Gardner makes an explicit judgment about the behavior of either animals or men, though it is clear that Thoreau is drawing a parallel. Does he also contrast human and animal behavior?

3. Is it Miss Gardner's intention to draw a parallel, or is her first concern to point out contrasts?
4. What are the important implications which derive from her notes on animal behavior?
5. Taken singly, are they particularly relevant? Or are they significant only when read in the context of each other?
6. Thoreau's *Walden* is organized, to a degree, episodically, and proceeds, at times, anecdotally. Are there instances in *Walden* which are greatly similar in technique to "Zoological Notes," where Thoreau merely presents the natural object or circumstance with no attempt at explanation or the drawing of an analogy?
7. What are the advantages of Thoreau's direct analogical technique, and what are its disadvantages? What are the advantages and disadvantages of Miss Gardner's indirectly analogical technique?
8. Do you consider Thoreau as less precise and objective in his description of nature and animal behavior than Miss Gardner? Does his meaning seem to be of a higher order than Miss Gardner's? How do you account for this?

INSECT WEATHER PROPHETS *

By J. Henri Fabre

During the whole winter, the Pine Caterpillars are active only at night. In the daytime, when the weather is fine, they readily repair to the dome of the nest and there remain motionless, gathered into heaps. It is the hour of the open-air siesta, under the pale December and January sun. As yet none leaves the home. It is quite late in the evening, towards nine o'clock, when they set out, marching in an irregular procession, to browse on the leaves of the branches hard by. Their grazing is a protracted affair. The flock returns late, some time after midnight, when the temperature falls too low.

Secondly, it is in the heart of winter, during the roughest

* Reprinted by permission of Dodd, Mead & Company from *The Insect World of J. Henri Fabre,* edited by Edwin Way Teale. Copyright, 1916, by Dodd, Mead & Company. Copyright, 1949, by Edwin Way Teale.

months, that the Processionary displays his full activity. Indefatigably at this time of year he spins, adding each night a new web to his silken tent; at this time, whenever the weather permits, he ventures abroad on the neighboring boughs to feed, to grow and to renew his skein of silk.

By a very remarkable exception, the harsh season marked by inactivity and lethargic repose in other insects is for him the season of bustle and labor, on condition, of course, that the inclemencies of the weather do not exceed certain limits. If the north wind blow too violently, so that it is like to sweep the flock away; if the cold be too piercing, so that there is a risk of freezing to death; if it snow, or rain, or if the mist thicken into an icy drizzle, the caterpillars prudently stay at home, sheltering under their weatherproof tent.

It would be convenient to some extent to foresee these inclemencies. The caterpillar dreads them. A drop of rain sets him in a flutter; a snowflake exasperates him. To start for the grazing-grounds at dark of night, in uncertain weather, would be dangerous, for the procession goes some distance and travels slowly. The flock would fare ill before regaining shelter did any sudden atmospheric trouble supervene, an event of some frequency in the bad season of the year. So that he may be informed in this particular during his nocturnal winter rambles, can the Pine Caterpillar be endowed with some sort of meteorological aptitudes? Let me describe how the suspicion occurred to me.

Divulged I know not how, my rearing of caterpillars under glass acquired a certain renown. It was talked about in the village. The forest-ranger, a sworn enemy to destructive insects, wanted to see the grazing of the famous caterpillars, of whom he had retained a too poignant memory ever since the day when he gathered and destroyed their nests in a pinewood under his charge. It was arranged that he should call the same evening.

He arrives at the appointed hour, accompanied by a friend. For a moment we sit and chat in front of the fire; then, when the clock strikes nine, the lantern is lit and we all three enter the greenhouse. The visitors are eager for the spectacle of which they have heard such wonderful things, while I am certain of satisfying their curiosity.

But, but...what is this? Not a caterpillar on the nests, not one on the fresh ration of branches! Last night and on the previous nights they came out in the countless numbers; tonight not one reveals himself. Can it be that they are merely late in going to dinner? Can their habitual punctuality be at fault because appetite has not yet arrived? We must be patient...Ten o'clock.

Nothing. Eleven. Still nothing. Midnight was at hand when we abandoned our watch, convinced that it would be vain to prolong the sitting. You can imagine what an abject fool I looked at having thus to send my guests away.

Next day I thought that I dimly perceived the explanation of this disappointment. It rained in the night and again in the morning. Snow, not the earliest of the year, but so far the most abundant, whitened the brow of the Ventoux. Had the caterpillars, more sensitive than any of us to atmospheric changes, refused to venture forth because they anticipated what was about to happen? Had they foreseen the rain and the snow, which nothing seemed to announce, at all events to us? After all, why not? Let us continue to observe them and we shall see whether the coincidence is fortuitous or not.

On this memorable day, therefore, the 13th of December, 1895, I institute the caterpillars' meteorological laboratory. I have at my disposal absolutely none of the apparatus dear to science, not even a modest thermometer, for my unlucky star continues in the ascendant, proving as unkind today as when I learned chemistry with pipe-bowls for crucibles and bottles that once contained sweets for retorts. I confine myself to visiting nightly the Processionaries in the greenhouse and those in the garden. It is a hard task, especially as I have to go to the far end of the enclosure, often in weather when one would not turn a dog out of doors. I set down the acts of the caterpillars, whether they come out or stay at home; I note the state of the sky during the day and at the moment of my evening examination.

To this list I add the meteorological chart of Europe which the *Temps* publishes daily. If I want more precise data, I request the Normal School at Avignon to send me, on occasions of violent disturbances, the barometrical records of its observatory. These are the only documents at my disposal.

Before we come to the results obtained, let me once more repeat that my caterpillars' meteorological institute has two stations: one in the greenhouse and one in the open air, on the pines in the enclosure. The first, protected against the wind and rain, is that which I prefer: it provides more regular and more continuous information. In fact, the open-air caterpillars often enough refuse to come out, even though the general conditions be favorable. It is enough to keep them at home if there be too strong a wind shaking the boughs, or even a little moisture dripping on the web of the nests. Saved from these two perils, the greenhouse caterpillars have only to consider atmospheric incidents of a higher order. The small variations escape them; the great alone make an impression on them: a most useful point for the observer and going a long way towards solving the problem for him. The colonies under glass, therefore, provide most of the material for my notes; the colonies in the open air add their testimony, which is not always quite clear.

Now what did they tell me, those greenhouse caterpillars who, on the 13th of December, refused to show themselves to my guest, the forest-ranger? The rain that was to fall that night could hardly have alarmed them: they were so well sheltered. The snow about to whiten Mont Ventoux was nothing to them: it was so far away. Moreover, it was neither snowing yet nor raining. Some extraordinary atmospheric event, profound and of vast extent, must have been occurring. The charts in the *Temps* and the bulletin of the Normal School told me as much.

A cyclonic disturbance, coming from the British Isles, was passing over our district; an atmospheric depression the like of which the season had not as yet known, had spread in our direction, reaching us on the 13th and persisting, in a more or less accentuated form, until the 22nd. At Avignon the barometer suddenly fell half an inch, to 29.1 in., on the 13th and lower still, to 29 in., on the 19th.

During this period of ten days, the garden caterpillars made no sortie on the pine-trees. True, the weather was changeable. There were a few showers of fine rain and some violent gusts of the mistral; but more frequently there were days and nights when the sky was superb and the temperature moderate. The prudent anchorites would not allow themselves to be caught. The low pressure persisted, menacing them; and so they stayed at home.

In the greenhouse things happen rather differently. Sorties take place, but the staying-in days are still more numerous. It looks as though the caterpillars, alarmed at first by the unexpected things happening overhead, had reassured themselves and resumed work, feeling nothing, in their shelter, of what they would have suffered outdoors—rain, snow and furious mistral blasts— and had then suspended their work again when the threats of bad weather increased.

There is, indeed, a fairly accurate agreement between the oscillations of the barometer and the decisions of the herd. When the column of mercury rises a little, they come out; when it falls they remain at home. Thus on the 19th, the night of the lowest pressure, 29 in., not a caterpillar appears.

As the wind and rain can have no effect on my colonies under glass, one is led to suppose that atmospheric pressure, with its physiological results, so difficult to define, is here the principal

factor. As for the temperature, within moderate limits, there is
no need to discuss it. The Processionaries have a robust constitution, as behooves spinners who work in the open air in midwin-
ter. However piercing the cold, so long as it does not freeze, when
the hour comes for working or feeding they spin on the surface
of the nest or browse on the neighboring branches.

Another example. According to the meteorological chart in the
Temps, a depression whose center is near the Iles Sanguinaires,
at the entrance of the Gulf of Ajaccio, reaches my neighborhood
with a minimum of 29.2 in., on the 9th of January. A tempestuous
wind gets up. For the first time this year there is a respectable
frost. The ice on the large pond in the garden is two or three
inches thick. This wild weather lasts for five days. Of course, the
garden caterpillars do not sally forth on the pine-trees while
these are battered by such a gale.

The remarkable part of the business is that the greenhouse
caterpillars do not venture out of their nests either. And yet for
them there are no boughs dangerously shaken, no cold piercing
beyond endurance, for it is not freezing under the glass. What
keeps them in can only be the passage of that wave of depression.
On the 15th the storm ceases; and the barometer remains between
29.6 and 30 in. for the rest of the month and a good part of
February. During this long period there are magnificent sorties
every evening, especially in the greenhouse.

On the 23rd and 24th of February, suddenly the Processionaries stay at home again, for no apparent reason. Of the six nests
under cover, only two have a few rare caterpillars out on the
pine-branches, while previously, in the case of all six, I used every
night to see the leaves bending under the weight of an innumerable multitude. Warned by this forecast, I enter in my notes:

"Some deep depression is about to reach us."

And I have guessed right. Two days later, sure enough, the
meteorological record of the *Temps* gives me the following information: a minimum of 29.2 in., coming from the Bay of Biscay
on the 22nd, reaches Algeria on the 23rd and spreads over the
Provence coast on the 24th. There is a heavy snowfall at Marseilles on the 25th.

"The ships," I read in my paper, "present a curious spectacle,
with their yards and rigging white. That is how the people of
Marseilles, little used to such sights, picture Spitzbergen and the
North Pole."

Here certainly is the gale which my caterpillars foresaw when
they refused to go out last night and the night before; here is the
center of the disturbance which revealed itself at Serignan by a

violent and icy north wind on the 25th and the following days. Again I perceive that the greenhouse caterpillars are alarmed only at the approach of the wave of atmospheric disturbance. Once the first uneasiness caused by the depression had abated, they came out again, on the 25th and the following days, in the midst of the gale, as though nothing extraordinary were happening.

From the sum of my observations it appears that the Pine Processionary is eminently sensitive to atmospheric vicissitudes, an excellent quality, having regard to his way of life in the sharp winter nights. He foresees the storm which would imperil his excursions.

His capacity for seeing bad weather very soon won the confidence of the household. When we had to go into Orange to renew our provisions, it became the rule to consult him the night before; and according to his verdict, we went or stayed at home. His oracle never deceived us.

Notebook Assignment for Class Discussion

1. Analyze the logical development of this essay. At what point does the introduction conclude and the body of the essay begin? At what point does the conclusion begin? Are there very definite lines of demarcation between the major parts of the essay?
2. What kind of coherence does this essay have? Does it proceed primarily inductively? Deductively? Or both? Or neither?
3. Does the prose have an archaic ring? In what ways do the diction and figurative language seem old-fashioned? Do any other elements of style or organization contribute to this quality of tone? Analyze and discuss.
4. What purpose do you see in the author's constant switching from past to present tense, as in paragraph 6? How many times does he do this? Is it always done in the same circumstances?
5. Abstract from the essay and state in your own words what seems to you to be the central proposition. Make a topic sentence outline of the essay. Outline the logical argument of the essay. What, in each instance, is the *essential* difference between your abstraction and the whole essay?

Related Exercises

1. Is the tone of this essay what you might ordinarily think of as being "scientific"? What elements of the tone and point of view seem to you to be decidedly unscientific? Stipulate a definition of both "scientific" and "unscientific" tone and point of view.
2. Does it seem to you that Fabre proceeds very scientifically? What are the deficiencies of his scientific method? Does he seem to recognize them and take account of them in the course of his exposition? Do you think that he proves his proposition?
3. What are the criteria for a valid experiment? Does Fabre fulfill these? Is a valid experiment necessarily successful? Is a succesful experiment necessarily valid?
4. Go to the library and find materials which might corroborate or deny M. Fabre's conclusions.
5. These experiments were performed a long time ago with inadequate materials under rather loosely controlled conditions. Might not these constitute sufficiently extraordinary circumstances for you to properly anticipate your findings in the library? What do you think they will be? How, in fact, do they correspond to your anticipations? Examine your conscience, and try to state the presumptions which were the basis of your first critical response to this essay.

HOW THEY KILLED THE BUFFALO *

By Wayne Gard

Stories of the vast size of the buffalo herds that once roamed the Great Plains of the West sound like the imaginings of a Paul Bunyan. They would hardly be credited today except that they were attested by many reliable travelers and by early settlers.

Often the herds of shaggy beasts darkened the whole horizon. In 1832, after skirting the north fork of the Platte River, Captain Benjamin Bonneville climbed a high bluff that gave him a wide view of the surrounding plains. "As far as the eye could see," he

* From *American Heritage*, Vol. VII, No. 5 (August, 1956), 34–39.

reported, "the country seemed absolutely blackened by innumerable herds." John K. Townsend, while crossing the Platte Valley, stopped on the rise of a hill to view a similar scene. The whole region, he wrote, "was covered by one enormous mass of buffaloes. Our vision, at the least computation, would certainly extend ten miles; and in the whole of this vast space, including about eight miles in width from the bluffs to the river bank, there apparently was no vista in the .incalculable multitude."

These accounts were matched by others that came from the high plains of northwest Texas. One pioneer there described a herd which he said covered fifty square miles. Another reported that he saw between two and three million buffaloes at one time. A third told of herds that he estimated held four million head. Many frontiersmen, like the Indians, thought there were enough buffaloes to last forever.

Sometimes the herds were so solid that they impeded travel. On the upper Missouri River in the summer of 1867, the steamer *Stockdale,* in charge of Captain Grant Marsh, was held up while a herd of snorting and bellowing shaggies crossed the stream. The buffaloes became so thick that the boat could not move, and the captain had to stop its engines. Many of the animals became entangled with the wheel, while others beat against the sides and stern, blowing and pawing. It was hours before the whole herd had crossed and the boat could continue its voyage.

Two years later, buffaloes were so thick in Western Kansas that an immense herd held up a Kansas Pacific train for nine hours while it crossed the track. As late as the early 1870's, Texas drovers taking longhorn cattle up the Chisholm Trail had to stop in the Indian Territory to let buffalo herds cross their path. The cowmen feared that the buffaloes would cause the cattle to stampede and that some of the longhorns would join the shaggies.

Many of those who saw the enormous buffalo herds in the West and assumed that they always would be there lived to see the plains cleared of them. Except for a remnant in the north, the whole slaughter was completed in little more than a decade. The near extermination of the buffalo came because his hide was worth a dollar or so to hardy hunters willing to take chances on being scalped by Indians.

For as long as they could remember, the Indians had been hunting buffaloes. The tribes living on the Great Plains were especially dependent on them for their meat, for robes for winter warmth, and for hides used in making tepees. When the early Spanish explorers first saw the buffaloes on the plains, they called them Indian cattle.

Yet the Indians, although sometimes they hunted for pleasure, as a rule killed the buffaloes only when they needed meat or hides. Until the Spaniards brought horses from Europe, the Indians hunted afoot with bows and arrows or with lances, sometimes disguising themselves under wolf skins. After they began to steal horses from the Spaniards and to capture and tame those that had gone wild, they became expert riders and used their mounts in hunting.

"The Indian is a great epicure," said Colonel Richard Irving Dodge. "He knows the choicest tidbits of every animal and how to cook them to his taste. The great fall hunt yields him the fullest enjoyment of his appetite." Most of the red men, though, were less patient. The warrior who killed a buffalo likely would cut it open and eat at once the raw liver and some of the other meat.

Some of the early travelers in the West hunted buffaloes for sport as well as for meat. One such was Washington Irving, who, with several companions, went on a buffalo hunt in the Indian Territory in October, 1832. Irving, after several misses, downed an enormous bull with his pistol. He took the tongue on his saddle and carried it back to camp.

A number of European visitors traveled to the West to try their marksmanship on the shaggies. Among them was Sir William Drummond Stewart, who came from Scotland in 1843 to shoot buffaloes. In the Platte Valley he and his party found all they could want—a herd estimated at a million head. On some days when they finished shooting the prairie was strewn for miles with dead animals.

The most publicized hunt of this type was that of the Grand Duke Alexis, a son of Czar Alexander II of Russia. Early in 1872 the Grand Duke went by rail to the Kansas frontier town of Hays, where General Philip Sheridan arranged a hunting party. Chief Spotted Tail of the Sioux staged a war dance for the entertainment of the royal visitor, and William F. Cody, better known as Buffalo Bill, coached him on shooting. As soon as Alexis had downed a buffalo and the other hunters had drunk his health in champagne, he was ready to return to his private car.

At the time of the Grand Duke's hunt, the decade of the slaughter of the buffaloes for their hides was about to begin. In that span the vast herds—estimated to have held 75,000,000 head before the Indians acquired horses—were reduced to a fragmentary herd in the north and a few stragglers elsewhere. Already the mounted Indians had begun to trim the size of the herds, especially after they could sell choice robes to white fur traders and mountain trappers.

In the 1840's the American Fur Company sent large cargoes of robes down the Missouri River to St. Louis. The count included 76,000 robes in 1840, and 110,000 robes and 25,000 tongues in 1848. The skins of the cows only were used for robes, since those of the bulls were too heavy. Meanwhile, butchering by the whites was increasing. Pioneer farmers in Kansas and Nebraska killed thousands of buffaloes for their meat. On January 9, 1873, the Wichita *Eagle* reported, "Choice humps and rounds of buffalo are selling at three cents a pound on our streets." As early as 1844, Josiah Gregg had viewed with alarm the excessive killing of the buffaloes, and other warnings followed. Yet to most eyes the herds seemed as large as ever.

The start of the great buffalo hunt is linked with the name of J. Wright Mooar, who became the mightiest of the hide men. Mooar, of Scotch ancestry, was born in Vermont in 1851. He traveled west in 1869 and, after working as a horsecar conductor in Chicago and as a carpenter at Rochelle, Illinois, went on to Hays, Kansas, in the fall of 1870. There he chopped cordwood for a government contractor on Walnut Creek, thirty miles south of the fort.

As this was buffalo country, Mooar soon joined in the more lucrative occupation of hunting. With five associates he equipped a small outfit, with two horse teams and one ox team. At that time the market for hides was limited largely to their use in making lap robes. Mooar and his fellows killed for meat. Mooar shipped the hind quarters to Quincy, Illinois, and to Kansas City, leaving the rest of the carcass, including the hide, to rot on the prairie.

In the winter of 1871–72, Mooar learned from another hunter, Charlie Rath, that the Leavenworth firm of W. C. Lobenstein had an order for 500 buffalo hides. A firm in England wanted them for experimental use in making leather. After Mooar had provided a quota of this order, he had 57 hides left. He shipped the surplus hides to his brother, John Wesley Mooar, who was a clerk in a jewelry store in New York, asking him to see if he could interest tanners in them.

The tanners were so interested that Wright Mooar soon had orders for all the hides he could deliver, and his New York brother went to Kansas to handle the business end of the enterprise. As more tanners discovered that buffalo hides made leather good for many uses, the demand became so great that a whole army of hunters surged into the buffalo ranges.

With Dodge City as the principal outfitting and shipping point, most of the hunters worked in small groups, going out with wagons for hauling back the hides. They used heavy rifles, some of them Sharps made especially for killing buffaloes. In some cases, two hunters worked together, sharing both the shooting and the skinning. In a bigger outfit, two or three expert marksmen might hire a larger number of less skilled men for the more menial work of skinning and drying.

The buffaloes, although suspicious of strange smells, had poor eyesight and were less alert than most game animals. If the hunter approached against the wind, usually he could come close to the herd without being noticed. Often he could kill many of the animals before the others sought safety in flight. Some hunters fired from the saddle, but more preferred to work afoot and thus have steadier aim and take more hides with less ammunition. The hunter tried to shoot the buffalo just behind the shoulder blade and to penetrate the heart. A wounded bull could be dangerous, but usually the rifleman could dodge long enough to place the mortal shot.

One of the Kansas hunters, who hired fifteen skinners, claimed to have killed 1,500 buffaloes in a week, 250 of them in a single day. Billy Tilghman took 3,300 hides in one season. With a long-range Sharps rifle, even an ordinary marksman could average fifty hides a day. At one place on the prairie a surveying party found 6,500 carcasses from which the hides had been stripped. The untouched meat had been left to rot or to be devoured by wolves. A Santa Fe railway conductor, J. H. Helton, said he could have walked for a hundred miles along the right of way without stepping off the carcasses. So great was the slaughter that in 1872 and 1873 the railroads hauled 1,250,000 hides out of Kansas and nearby territory.

This hide hunting, plus the killing of an estimated 350,000 head by Indians in that period, thinned the Kansas herds enough to make further shooting less profitable there. In search of new herds, J. Wright Mooar and John Webb saddled their horses and took a trip through the Texas Panhandle. For five days they rode through a sea of grazing buffaloes.

Their report excited the other hunters, but there was some hesitation because the Medicine Lodge Treaty of 1867 had reserved for the Indians all the hunting grounds south of the Arkansas River. On the other hand, Texas, which owned the land now in question, had not been a party to the treaty. Mooar asked advice from the commander of the Third Infantry at Fort Dodge, Richard Irving Dodge.

"Boys," replied the officer, "If I were hunting buffalo, I would go where the buffalo are."

That was enough for the hunters. Willing to risk the danger of Indian scalpers, they quickly formed parties and set out to the south. They were followed in the spring of 1874 by dealers in hunting supplies and hides. The first of these, Charlie Myers, drove south with about forty hunters and teamsters, taking eight wagons and six-yoke teams of oxen. On the Canadian River in the Texas Panhandle he cut cottonwood logs and built a branch of his Dodge City store. This site was a mile and a half east of the ruins of the Adobe Walls trading post that a party sent out by William Bent had established about 1843. Around the Myers store the men built a corral and a stockade.

Soon afterward another Dodge merchant, Charlie Rath, also arrived to set up a Texas branch. He opened for business in a sod house near the Myers cabin. Next, James Hanrahan, also from Dodge City, came in with a supply of whisky and built a sod-house saloon between the two stores and near the Myers stockade. Then Tom O'Keefe set up a picket house for a black-smith shop between the saloon and the Rath store. All were ready for business by the first of May, and the newcomers called their village Adobe Walls.

Business flourished with the success of the hide hunters, but danger from Indians was never far away. Hostile warriors, who had killed and scalped several of the hunters in isolated camps, made a concentrated attack on Adobe Walls at dawn on the morning of June 27, 1874. The 700 attackers were mainly from the Cheyenne, Comanche, and Kiowa tribes and were led by Quanah Parker and Lone Wolf. Mooar and others had gone north with hides, but the outpost had 28 men and one woman. The defenders successfully fought off the Indians, but lost four men.

Other temporary headquarters of the Texas buffalo hunters in the next few years included Tepee City, on Tepee Creek, and Rath City, near the Double Mountain Fork of the Brazos River. The latter outpost, established by Charlie Rath in January, 1877, lasted until May of the following year. In addition to offering supplies and a market for hides, it had a wagon yard, a Chinese laundry, and a combination saloon and dance hall.

In the middle and late 1870's the principal Texas headquarters for the hunters was Fort Griffin, on the Clear Fork of the Brazos. From this outpost long wagon trains hauled the hides to Dallas and Denison. One of the trains might include as many as forty wagons, each drawn by six or eight mules. As the hides made light freight, they were piled high, and were held in place with poles and ropes. After Fort Worth obtained its first railroad, on July 4, 1876, it became the chief Texas shipping point for hides.

In the winter of 1876–77 an estimated 1,500 hunters were shooting buffaloes on the Texas plains, and by early spring Fort Griffin had about four acres filled with piles of hides waiting for the wagon trains to haul them to Fort Worth. In the latter town, one morning in May, 1877, a reporter noted a caravan of ten wagons coming in. "In front were eleven yoke of oxen driven by one man and dragging after them four large wagons, heavily laden. Two other teams, with seven yoke each, drawing three wagons, followed. There probably were 2,500 to 3,000 hides in the train."

In the same spring another Fort Worth observer was impressed with one lot of 60,000 hides piled high on a platform near the Texas and Pacific Railroad. During the season, Fort Griffin sent in about 200,000 hides, which brought the hunters about a dollar each. But the peak of the slaughter had passed, and the end was in sight. The hunters had broken up the great southern herd, leaving only scattered remnants.

In the winter of 1877–78 the skinners took more than 100,000 hides in Texas. This virtually wiped out the southern herd. The only noteworthy commercial hunting left was that in the northern plains in the early 1880's. Like so many of his fellows, J. Wright Mooar put away his buffalo guns and turned to cattle ranching in Texas. His careful aim had downed 20,000 of the shaggies in eight years.

The widespread and wasteful slaughter had aroused shocked opposition, especially in the East. Several western states passed laws to curb the killing, but these measures came too late and were not strictly enforced. Realists in the West knew that the buffaloes would have to go before the hostile Indians of the Great Plains could be subdued and the ranges opened for cattle ranching.

Representative James A. Garfield expressed this view in 1874 when, in a debate in Congress, he reported that the secretary of the interior would rejoice, as far as the Indian question was concerned, when the last buffalo was killed. Early in the following year General Phil Sheridan put it even more clearly when he addressed a joint session of the Texas legislature, which was considering a bill to protect buffaloes.

The hunters, said the General, "... will do more in the next year, to settle the vexed Indian question than the entire regular army has done in the last thirty years. They are destroying the Indians' commissary ... Send them powder and lead ... let them kill, skin and sell until the buffaloes are exterminated. Then your prairies can be covered with speckled cattle and the festive cowboy, who follows the hunter as a second forerunner of an advanced civilization."

When the hunters had completed their slaughter, only the white bones remained strewn over the plains. Many a pioneer farmer and ranchman eked out his meager income in a drought year by gathering these bones and hauling them in his wagon to the nearest railroad town, where they were shipped off to be made into carbon or fertilizer.

In isolated valleys enough buffaloes were left to let the breed survive and to supply circuses and zoos and those ranchmen who liked to keep a few for sentimental reasons. Today the federal game preserves are so well supplied that every year or two the government has to sell a few hundred head to keep the ranges from being overgrazed. Yet the vast herds have vanished; they roam only in song and story and in the minds of a few old men with long memories.

Notebook Assignment for Class Discussion

1. This essay is an attempt to deal with the history of the plains buffalo for a period of about thirty-five years. What seem to you to be the special difficulties of such a project? What are some of the more important elements to be considered by the author in planning his essay?
2. How does the author manage to be economical without at the same time diminishing the scope of his subject matter, or having his essay seem thin and insubstantial?
3. How are his tone and point of view affected by his attempt at so panoramic a view?
4. This essay begins with a number of general assertions which are then given substance through illustration and example. For instance, one section begins: "Sometimes the herds were so solid that they impeded travel." This sentence is followed by two paragraphs of examples. Is this the general pattern of the author's discourse? Is it appropriate to the special demands of his subject matter?
5. Is the author present in his essay, or is he so objective in his treatment of the subject matter as to make it impossible for us to discern his attitudes toward it?
6. Make a list of words or phrases which might provide some evidence of a personality or point of view present in the work.

7. Is it necessary for the author to provide a judgment about the question of the morality of such a slaughter? If so, might we consider his cool objectivity a flaw in the work? Or is it enough to simply present the situation, as he has done, to make the moral issue clear?

8. The author makes no attempt to invest any of the people he mentions with a personality. Does it matter to the reader that he knows nothing of the particular character of, say, J. Wright Mooar? Why is it neither necessary nor fitting that the author attempt to dramatize issues or personalities in this essay?

Related Exercises

1. In the library, search out additional examples to substantiate each of the general assertions which Mr. Gard makes at the beginning of each division of his essay.

2. Write an essay in which—through quoting from primary source materials—you provide examples of the various moral attitudes toward the slaughter of the buffalo that you can find. Provide a bibliography of the works in which the primary sources you use are found.

3. Read about the extinction of the greater auk, the dodo, the Carolina parakeet, and the passenger pigeon; and the near extinction of the fur seal, the white rhinoceros, and the Tasmanian devil. Write an essay in which you compare and contrast the fate of the American buffalo in its various causes with that of one of these other animals.

4. Debate the issue raised by General Sheridan: which is of greater importance—to save the buffalo, or to eliminate the Indians and make the West safe for settlers? What is the moral position of the white settler who settles on Indian lands? Can it be said that there is a moral imperative which gives force to such a wave of progress as that which overwhelmed the Indian during the last century? Can questions such as these be debated generally, in the abstract? Or must the conditions for argument be carefully determined through—among other things—research?

5. Using the library, provide an anthology of attitudes toward the Indian as an obstruction in the way of progress, using, again, primary sources wherever possible. Provide an anthology of contrary attitudes.

6. How do you think the contemporary notion of progress differs

from that held by General Sheridan? Try to define the notion of progress as it was entertained by the men of the American frontier, using primary sources wherever possible.

WOODPECKERS, SPARROWS, AND STARLINGS *

I. WOODPECKERS VS. SCIENTISTS

By H. T. Pfitzenmeyer

A familiar topic among utility companies throughout the United States concerns the subject of woodpeckers and their damaging attacks upon wooden utility poles. Why the woodpeckers damage poles and how this damage can be prevented—that is still in the realm of conjecture and theory. The pileated woodpecker (*Dryocopus pileatus*), possessed of extreme cunning, agility, and determination, holds the secret to this perplexing problem in the Northeast. So proficient has this particular bird been in eluding all practical devices designed by the utility companies to keep them off these poles that scientists at the Pennsylvania State University have been called upon to test their ingenuity against that of the woodpecker.

In order to have a complete and unbiased view of the pileated woodpecker's role in today's problem, a look at earlier accounts of the bird reveals some interesting facts.

The pileated woodpecker naturally is at home when among mature forest trees and exhibits considerable reaction upon the slightest intrusion. Even before the White settlers arrived on this continent there was an apparent awareness among the North American Indians of the pileated woodpecker. The Indians showed a great deal of respect for this bird: frequently its magnificent head was included in part of their ceremonial worship and its crest was often found decorating their peace pipes.

When the early pioneers began to exploit new territories and

* From *The New York State Conservationist*, Vol. 10, No. 4 (February–March, 1956), pp. 6–8, and 28–29. Reprinted by permission of the New York Conservation Department.

clear the virgin forests for farm land, they of course encountered some resistance from the woodpeckers. Peter Kalm in 1748, writing of his experiences in North America in obtaining new seed material for Sweden, tells of the pileated woodpecker being seen frequently in the forests of Pennsylvania, and destroying much of the settlers' corn crop. But as civilization became more firmly established, the pileated woodpeckers gradually succumbed to its advance. It was not uncommon to see bunches of these birds on sale for food in the market places of the cities. Man with his musket, axe, and plow apparently had again won this battle for existence, and it seemed that the pileateds were about to join other non-conforming species in the ranks of the extinct. Furthermore, the extensive lumbering typical of our early history destroyed the original habitat of the bird, and that, along with other harassments of civilization, forced it to become adapted to civilized conditions or become an extinct species.

The population of woodpeckers diminished throughout the nineteenth century to the extent that in sections of the country where they were once abundant they became absent. Outdoors authors and bird-lovers wrote of the pileated woodpecker but admitted they had never seen one. Naturalists and egg collectors invaded what seemed to be the last few remaining localities where the bird had taken refuge against civilization with the hopes of adding the rare specimens to their collections.

Although the extreme rarity of this species is shown by a study of ornithological notes of the early 1900's, it was evident by this time that the birds were at least holding their own in some localities. And some observers reported seeing them once again in areas where they hadn't been seen for many years. So, without any help from man, this beneficial bird chose to adapt its mode of living to civilization and accept the terms of the conqueror.

In the woodpecker's desperate attempt to become accustomed to the revised environment it acquired certain habits which proved disagreeable to man. In place of forest trees the woodpeckers found other wooden structures and apparently the birds derived a great deal of satisfaction from drumming upon or damaging houses and barns. Another favorite subject of attack were high church spires.

The damage to wooden power poles commenced just after the turn of the century when the rapidly expanding utility companies laid thousands of miles of electric and communication lines throughout the country. This rapid installation of tempting timbers was too much for the ever-curious woodpeckers to resist, especially over deforested areas.

The Southern States were the first to report damage to utility poles. Apparently the climatic conditions and swampy areas of the Deep South are the most suitable habitat for the pileated woodpecker, and it is here one finds the heaviest concentration. The late Dr. Hoyt of Cornell University reported that in open forested areas in Louisiana during the years 1938 to 1940 there was an average of a nesting pair of pileateds to the acre.

In 1906 the State of Louisiana reported that 41 per cent of the poles on one line had been damaged. On a line in Indiana, damage occurred on 59 per cent of the poles. Damage to the utility lines in our Northeastern States was not so serious at this time. This is attributed to the fact that practically all of the woodpeckers' natural habitat had been destroyed by large-scale lumbering operations. Consequently, drastic reduction of the woodpecker population took place to the extent of near extinction, especially in the case of the large pileated woodpecker. Time was needed for the second growth timber to become large enough to support a woodpecker population able to inflict serious damage.

It was a common expression of the line crews in Louisiana that the woodpeckers "got fat off of creosote." Early preventive methods taken on these lines were: hanging the birds by placing a noose of horse hair around the entrance to their holes; filling their holes with pebbles, and shooting the birds off the poles. However, no practical method of eliminating the damage was found.

Pole damage in the Northeast is not just a recent problem but one that has been gradually increasing in direct proportion to the increasing woodpecker population. In the past the utility companies were able to contend with the woodpeckers and withstand the cost of replacing an occasional pole, but when damage took place to the extent that a pole had to be replaced within six months after being installed the problem became one of critical importance, especially when the average life expectancy of the treated pole is considered to be 30 to 40 years. The areas where they frequently must be replaced are nearly always very inaccessible, and the cost of getting man-power and equipment into these remote areas amounts to more than twice the cost of the pole. Also, frequently the line which has serious damage is the only source of power for distant communities. Therefore it is necessary to give maximum service and replace the poles—with uninterrupted electric power. So, besides amounting to many thousands of dollars per year, the woodpecker problem is also very perturbing to the utility companies.

Over a period of years these companies have tested various

methods to make the poles as undesirable to the woodpeckers as possible. But these expedients did not appear to discourage the birds in the least, and some even seemed to concentrate their activity. A few methods attempted were: (1) leaving the ruined old pole in place beside the new one; (2) lashing sections of the old pole, which contains woodpecker holes, to the replacement; (3) attaching metal flashers that would revolve in the wind; (4) hanging strips of red cloth from the cross-arm and pole; (5) wrapping the pole in wire hardware cloth; (6) enclosing the pole with tarpaper; (7) placing sections of garden hose around the pole to represent snakes; and (8) filling the holes with a sticky tar-like substance.

In March, 1955, the Pennsylvania State University in co-operation with the Pennsylvania Power and Light Company, New Jersey Power and Light Company, Northern Pennsylvania Power Company, and West Penn Power Company, began a study of woodpecker damage to wooden utility poles. The initial phase of this project has been a life history and behavior study of the pileated woodpecker in relation to utility line poles and, secondly, development of a practical method of preventing the woodpecker from causing damage to wooden poles.

Sections of four separate power lines have been designated as the study areas and periodic observations of these areas have been continued since the start of the study. The woodpecker damage to these poles is seasonal. The period of activity begins approximately the first of October and lasts throughout the Winter months until about March. This season of pole damage corresponds to the season of increased woodpecker activity among the forest trees. It is at this time of year the pileated must secure its principal food supply from the hearts of the trees infested with carpenter ants and wood borers. Consequently it is during the winter months one finds new wood exposed and extensive tree excavation—an indication of a pileated woodpecker in the vicinity.

This would lead one to believe that the reason for damage to the poles was relatively simple: to secure food. However, when a pole which has been creosoted under pressure and erected on the line exactly three weeks, is then extensively damaged by woodpeckers, one becomes somewhat skeptical about the food theory.

There has been some proof that the pileated woodpeckers use the holes they make in the poles as shelter or roosting cavities. But this cannot reasonably account for numerous poles which have received damage four or five feet from the ground line, or the ones which have holes not in the slightest resembling the characteristics of a roosting or shelter cavity.

It was once thought that the vibrations or humming caused by the wind against the wires was responsible for misleading the woodpeckers into thinking that insects were moving within the pole. But: whenever a new utility line is being constructed all the poles are first set in the ground; after this is completed the wires are then attached to the poles; and it so happened that on one line under study some of the poles had to be replaced because of woodpecker damage even before the wires were attached.

With these facts before them, members of the School of Forestry and the wildlife management experts at the Pennsylvania State University have undertaken this disturbing problem.

To test the pileated woodpeckers' reaction to colors, a color repellent experiment was established on a section of 24 poles which had the most recent damage. Four poles, or two adjacent structures, were each painted with four ten-foot bands of red, white, green, and yellow paint. One adjoining structure (two poles) was then left unpainted to serve as control for the sake of comparison. On the next two structures proceeding along the line, the colors were rotated; i.e., white, green, yellow, and red as compared with the first color sequence. Again the next single structure was left as a control. This method was continued until each color had appeared in four possible positions on the pole. In this way, if the damage occurred only in one color or two or three colors, the assumption could be made that a color or colors would repel the woodpeckers.

Since the establishment of this experiment in March, 1955, approximately 42 per cent of the poles in the test area have received light damage in all four colors—as well as the unpainted control poles. Therefore, the colors used in the experiment do not appear to repel the pileated woodpecker, although they may prove discouraging enough so that the bird will leave before doing damage.

Experiments on several commercial repellents as well as other chemicals are now in progress, using a pileated woodpecker which has been in captivity since May, 1955. This bird has become surprisingly well adapted to the limited natural habitat within the confines of its aviary. Its behavior and capability of damaging poles or trees is nearly the same as that of a wild bird.

Repellents are placed on wooden sections in which there is known to be food—so the bird has every reason to attack them. Those which are being tested are believed to be most practical for use on an actual utility line; thus for observations under practical conditions, repellents found effective in connection with the captive woodpecker can be applied to poles of a section of line which is receiving damage.

An ideal solution to the problem would be a chemical repellent which would treat the wood against woodpeckers when mixed at the same time with a wood preservative necessary to prevent decay. Thereby, one operation would serve a dual purpose. However, the battle is but joined and the victor is not ready for crowning. Woodpecker or scientist, that is the question!

II. Two of Our Exotics

By Dirck Benson

Among exotics from the plant world are such things as the nightshade or European bittersweet, a pest at times but a fine Winter food for the pheasant; the wild carrot or Queen Anne's lace, a nuisance in hayfields but in its improved form a welcome addition to the dinner table; or the hawkweeds and thistles which certainly beautify the landscape when in flower but are otherwise undesirable members of pasture lot society. And then, of course, practically nobody has a good word for the water chestnut.

Among our exotic animals some are quite generally condemned, including the Japanese beetle, cockroach, house mouse, and the Norway rat. Others in the animal world, as with the plants, receive mingled blessings and curses. For example, the carp is welcomed by some as a culinary delicacy but widely condemned by hosts of sport fishermen. Likewise, the ringnecked pheasant is sought after by many a gunner, yet cursed by gardeners.

The European house sparrow (the English sparrow to most of us—but improperly so) and the starling fall into the in-between category. There are some who sing their praises but far more who sincerely wish neither species were here.

The house sparrow was first introduced to America in 1850 to help control the cankerworm. Eight pairs were released in Brooklyn that year, and more were released there in 1852. In later years others were liberated in various New England communities. This species took hold rapidly and by 1900 had spread from the Atlantic to the Pacific. Many factors favored the almost lightning-like spread of this weaverbird. As a nonmigratory group the birds are here in the early spring to start nesting, allowing time for up to three broods each season. An aggressive bird, they take and keep the best nesting sites and feeding territories, assuring a relatively high rate of nesting and rearing success. As a race that tolerates no weaklings, competition for mates is vigorous, with few delicate social refinements. When the parents are ready to start a new brood, the fledglings are left to shift for themselves. This feature contributes greatly to their spread, for the young form into flocks which keep pushing on into new territories. The house sparrow is fairly tolerant of crowding and if food is abundant will be content with a small territory and practically colonial nesting.

Man and his stage of civilization and mechanical progress aided this species in its spread. The house sparrow made good use of the horse and buggy era, thrived best in the cities and villages but also followed the post road to new communities. Undigested grain and spilled oats were their main fare, but were amply supplemented with crumbs from workers' lunch pails, uncontrolled garbage dumps, grain about the chicken yards, and even some weed seeds and insects.

Times have changed now. There is little food for the sparrow in exhaust fumes or on the macadam around a gas pump. Their populations in the cities have declined and their diet changed but year around they are still our most abundant avian urban dweller. Large flocks, however, now are most frequently seen in the country around the barns and chicken yards or in the grain fields about harvest time. The house sparrow is a most adaptable soul, feeding cheerily on weed seeds or switching to a nearly pure diet of grasshoppers, cutworms, or cankerworms when these reach peaks of abundance.

Though commonly called a sparrow, this bird really belongs to the weaverbird or Old World sparrow family. They differ in part from the New World sparrows and finches in their adeptness at weaving quite complicated nests. Furthermore, there are few that can compete in song with our native sparrows. The house sparrow is an exception, though there is something cheery in their happy but unmusical chatter. True to their family background, the house sparrow is still capable of weaving a fancy, bulky, wind-resistant nest, but as many an immigrant before, most of our American residents have put aside the customs of their native land and made the best of available resources. Open gutter pipes, fancy cornices, holes under the eaves or hollows in trees are frequently used as nesting sites. Any site offering shelter and a firm base will do but, true to their heritage, almost invariably the nests will be lined with feathers.

Considering their dietary habits, one can neither completely condone nor condemn the house sparrow. Assuredly their feeding on grasshoppers, cutworms, and cankerworms is commendable and one can rejoice at the quantity of weed seeds they eat. The cherry grower, on the contrary, is justifiably rankled at the damage to his fruit. In the field the house sparrow is quite adept at harvesting wheat and has no compunctions about cleaning up a freshly seeded lawn, pulling seedlings, or stealing chicken feed.

Other activities of the house sparrow also tend to put them on the black list. In their aggressiveness they steal the nest sites and drive away some of our more welcome native species, such as the bluebird. In their gregariousness, especially in winter flocks, they become noisy, smelly, and a minor hazard to pedestrians. Naturally they are not on the protected list but there is little chance of that having much effect on their numbers.

The introduction and establishment of the starling in North America parallels that of the house sparrow in many ways. In 1890 some 60 birds were set free in Central Park in New York and an additional release of 40 birds was made the following year. For the first ten years the starling did not get beyond New York City but in the next ten years radiated out for 200 miles. Within fifty years the starlings had spread north to the Gulf of St. Lawrence, south to Florida, and west to the edge of the Great Plains, and by 1950 a few individuals had been seen in the Pacific Coast states.

Some claim the releases were made to control the house sparrow, others for insect control. Perhaps it was a little of both and perhaps there was an element of yearning for a species from the homeland. In any case the starling, like the house sparrow, seems to be here to stay.

The starling is an early nester, often starting the first week of April, and may produce three broods by August. The nest may be built in holes in trees or in houses, barns, or churches where the birds can find a sheltered entry. Frequently the starling will dispossess the flicker or other hole-nesting species. The starling, again like the house sparrow, seems to prefer solitary nesting sites but will readily adapt to tenement conditions when nesting sites are at a premium.

The song of the starling is not very accomplished or harmonious but they make up for this with their versatility in imitating other birds. They are particularly adept in mimicking the bobwhite, the chickadee, and the peewee; do well in copying the woodthrush, whitethroat, crow, and clucking chickens; and get out moderate imitations of other species.

The starling is a strong flier and quite gregarious outside of the mating season. As soon as the young are on the wing they form into flocks which range the agricultural areas in search of both grain and insects. As the season advances, late hatching broods and adults that have completed their domestic duties join the flocks so that by wheat harvest time groups of over 1,000 birds are not unusual. In these flocks the more numerous young of the year stand out with their much lighter and browner plumage. In late summer and through the fall the starlings usually seek out conifer plantations for night roosts and often mingle with redwings, grackles, cowbirds, and even crows so that the common roost may have many thousands of birds.

The starling is not a highly migratory species but as winter draws nigh many thousands push south into less rigorous climes. Like other tourists they find Washington, D.C., a very pleasant stopping point. Many more thousands hold no brief with long trips and have a simpler solution. They just move into the nearest city, roosting for the night in church towers and old buildings which offer shelter from the wind, or next to factory chimneys and advertising signs where they can cuddle up to a convenient heat supply. During the day some will range the city and trash dumps for food but others will fly ten or more miles to the country to feed. Being a size larger than the house sparrow the starling does things in just a little bit bigger way—the sparrow is noisy but the starling is noisier; in winter roosts the sparrow is smelly but the starling is smellier. And if the sparrow makes walking under a roost somewhat of a gamble, the starling makes it a real hazard.

Most ground-feeding songbirds hop, but the starling walks, leaving practically no stone unturned in his search for insects and worms. The insect diet of the starling, including cutworm, wire, inch and tomato worms, and the click, May, potato, bean and Japanese beetles, puts these birds in a beneficial class. On the other hand, their penchant for cultivated fruits and grains tends to put them on the other side of the ledger. On the whole it seems as if the starling is more beneficial than harmful but since their winter flocks often become quite obnoxious, no one would mind if this species were a little less numerous.

Various methods have been tried to disperse large winter roosts —shooting, scarecrows, intermittent noises, and even the playing back of the call of a scared starling—but so far none has proved very successful. Similarly, attempts have been made to control both starling and sparrow populations by trapping and nest destruction. In a local area this may be temporarily effective but it isn't long before other members of the species move into the void.

Another aspect of the economic importance of both the sparrow and starling is their part in the transmission of disease. Both species have been demonstrated to be potential agents in the transmission of diseases which may be important in domestic poultry and game birds, though at the present time there is no indication that they create a serious problem in this respect.

At any rate, for better or for worse, both the starling and the house sparrow are with us to stay. And since they appear perfectly willing to overlook our "seamier" characteristics, it seems only fair to extend them the same courtesy.

THE BATTLE OF THE ANTS *

By Henry D. Thoreau

One day when I went out to my wood-pile, or rather my pile of stumps, I observed two large ants, the one red, the other much larger, nearly half an inch long, and black, fiercely contending with one another. Having once got hold they never let go, but struggled and wrestled and rolled on the chips incessantly. Looking farther, I was surprised to find that the chips were covered with such combatants, that it was not a *duellum,* but a *bellum,* a war between two races of ants, the red always pitted against the black, and frequently two red ones to one black. The legions of these Myrmidons covered all the hills and vales in my wood-yard, and the ground was already strewn with the dead and dying, both red and black. It was the only battle which I have ever witnessed, the only battle-field I ever trod while the battle was raging; internecine war; the red republicans on the one hand, and the black imperialists on the other. On every side they were engaged in deadly combat, yet without any noise that I could hear, and human soldiers never fought so resolutely. I watched a couple

* From *Walden,* Chapter 12, "Brute Neighbors."

that were fast locked in each other's embraces, in a little sunny valley amid the chips, now at noon-day prepared to fight till the sun went down, or life went out. The smaller red champion had fastened himself like a vise to his adversary's front, and through all the tumblings on that field never for an instant ceased to gnaw at one of his feelers near the root, having already caused the other to go by the board; while the stronger black one dashed him from side to side, and, as I saw on looking nearer, had already divested him of several of his members. They fought with more pertinacity than bulldogs. Neither manifested the least disposition to retreat. It was evident that their battle-cry was Conquer or Die. In the meanwhile there came along a single red ant on the hillside of this valley, evidently full of excitement, who either had despatched his foe, or had not yet taken part in the battle; probably the latter, for he had lost none of his limbs; whose mother had charged him to return with his shield or upon it. Or perchance he was some Achilles, who had nourished his wrath apart, and had now come to avenge or rescue his Patroclus. He saw this unequal combat from afar,—for the blacks were nearly twice the size of the red,—he drew near with rapid pace till he stood on his guard within half an inch of the combatants; then, watching his opportunity, he sprang upon the black warrior, and commenced his operations near the root of his right foreleg, leaving the foe to select among his own members; and so there were three united for life, as if a new kind of attraction had been invented which put all other locks and cements to shame. I should not have wondered by this time to find that they had their respective musical bands stationed on some eminent chip, and playing their national airs the while, to excite the slow and cheer the dying combatants. I was myself excited somewhat even as if they had been men. The more you think of it, the less the difference. And certainly there is not the fight recorded in Concord history, at least, if in the history of America, that will bear a moment's comparison with this, whether for the numbers engaged in it, or for the patriotism and heroism displayed. For numbers and for carnage it was an Austerlitz or Dresden. Concord Fight! Two killed on the patriots' side, and Luther Blanchard wounded! Why, here every ant was a Buttrick,—"Fire! for God's sake fire!"—and thousands shared the fate of Davis and Hosmer. There was not one hireling there. I have no doubt that it was a principle they fought for, as much as our ancestors, and not to avoid a three-penny tax on their tea; and the results of this battle will be as important and memorable to those whom it concerns as those of the battle of Bunker Hill, at least.

I took up the chip on which the three I have particularly described were struggling, carried it into my house, and placed it under a tumbler on my window-sill, in order to see the issue. Holding a microscope to the first-mentioned red ant, I saw that, though he was assiduously gnawing at the near foreleg of his enemy, having severed his remaining feeler, his own breast was all torn away, exposing what vitals he had there to the jaws of the black warrior, whose breastplate was apparently too thick for him to pierce; and the dark carbuncles of the sufferer's eyes shone with ferocity such as war only could excite. They struggled half an hour longer under the tumbler, and when I looked again the black soldier had severed the heads of his foes from their bodies, and the still living heads were hanging on either side of him like ghastly trophies at his saddle-bow, still apparently as firmly fastened as ever, and he was endeavoring with feeble struggles, being without feelers and with only the remnant of a leg, and I know not how many other wounds, to divest himself of them; which at length, after half an hour more, he accomplished. I raised the glass, and he went off over the window-sill in that crippled state. Whether he finally survived that combat, and spent the remainder of his days in some Hotel des Invalides, I do not know; but I thought that his industry would not be worth much thereafter. I never learned which party was victorious, nor the cause of the war; but I felt for the rest of that day as if I had my feelings excited and harrowed by witnessing the struggle, the ferocity and carnage, of a human battle before my door.

Kirby and Spence tell us that the battles of ants have long been celebrated and the date of them recorded, though they say that Huber is the only modern author who appears to have witnessed them. "Aeneas Sylvius," say they, "after giving a very circumstantial account of one contested with great obstinacy by a great and small species on the trunk of a pear tree," adds that " 'This action was fought in the pontificate of Eugenius the Fourth, in the presence of Nicholas Pistoriensis, an eminent lawyer, who related the whole history of the battle with the greatest fidelity.' A similar engagement between great and small ants is recorded by Olaus Magnus, in which the small ones, being victorious, are said to have buried the bodies of their own soldiers, but left those of their giant enemies a prey to the birds. This event happened previous to the expulsion of the tyrant Christiern the Second from Sweden." The battle which I witnessed took place in the Presidency of Polk, five years before the passage of Webster's Fugitive-Slave Bill.

Notebook Assignment for Class Discussion

1. Describe the technique most commonly used in this selection to draw a parallel between the actions of ants, or brute creation, and of men.
2. Cite some descriptive passages, figures of speech, and use of detail which lend to Thoreau's account of the battle an air of the mock-heroic.
3. Does Thoreau's use of the mock-heroic in any way detract from the essential seriousness of the passage?
4. By what rhetorical device does Thoreau prevent his narrative from becoming merely farcical?
5. Analyze the general effect of Thoreau's consistent use of long, highly compounded and modified, and periodic sentences; or sequences of sentences separated not by periods, but by semicolons. How, for example, does the *cadence* of Thoreau's prose underline his essential thesis? Will your response to this question be of any help in your attempt to answer item 3?
6. Describe and analyze the important instance in which Thoreau discerns a higher law or *universal* principle of action at work in the *particular* drama of the ant-war.
7. Does Thoreau abandon, at any point, his close focus on the literal microcosm in favor of abstract speculation? Is his meaning perfectly clear to you?
8. Is he in any way cramped by his careful consideration of the particular and immediate world of his experience? Can you describe the major techniques by which he maintains this simultaneous view of the particular and universal worlds as distinct, yet intermingled?

Related Exercises

1. Thoreau's allusions are, as usual, legion. How would you go about discovering the identities of the names with which you are not familiar?
2. Go to the library and produce a list of short biographies identifying—by those qualities, circumstances, or characteristics which make them relevant to Thoreau's main purpose —the individuals alluded to in this essay.
3. Does Thoreau emphasize the brutishness or the intelligence of the ants? To what ends?
4. Does he justify, so that it does not seem inappropriate, his

comment to the effect that he "felt for the rest of that day as if (he) had (his) feelings excited and harrowed by witnessing the struggle, the ferocity and carnage, of a human battle before (his) door."? Why doesn't the essay end with this sentence? What do the few sentences which follow add? Are they necessary to Thoreau's purpose?

5. What is his reason for ending the narrative by parodying the ancient accounts of ant-wars? Does he achieve the same effect here as he does earlier by his reference to the battle of Austerlitz or Dresden? Define that effect.

6. Read all of Chapter 12 of *Walden*. Is the meaning of the battle of the ants clearer in the context of the whole chapter? Is its general effect in any way altered? Write an essay in which you judge this excerpt in its important relationships to the other elements of Chapter 12, "Brute Neighbors."

WHAN THAT APRILLE, ETCETERA *

By ERNEST SANDEEN

Here is the sun, nothing but explosion,
Exuding light to hide in, soft as shadow,
And sweetly warming the tongues of the wind's erosion
To lick away the trivial April snow.

Walking in nudes of dreams where nothing but news
In sheerest algebras occurred all night,
We quickly dress to meet the springtime views
Spread thick like old prints along the public street.

Our nighteyes blinking to watch the shrubs unfold
Their walls along the sidewalks in ordered curves
Can see nothing but seething suns. The old
Indolent leafing is triggered now on nerves

Of sleep stretched to the torment of all we know.
Houses in their rows poise like gases
On abstract lawns. Under the failing snow
Fuses wait in a billion violent grasses.

* From *Children and Older Strangers* (Notre Dame, Ind.: University of Notre Dame Press, 1961), p. 62.

Before noon strikes, nothing is left but spring
And as we cross the street archaic-legged,
Bare concrete particles set our feet to tingling.
We cringe across on shells immensely egged,

And yet the future fossiling at our bone
Has not erupted. It's strange how strange it seems
That streets of twigs budding with wings have gone
Right on sleeping through our real dreams.

Notebook Assignment for Class Discussion

1. Characterize the poet's language in this poem, by comparing
   and contrasting it with Mr. Kennedy's and Miss Gross's in
   the other two poems in this section, "Landscapes with Set-
   Screws," and "Montoya's Bestiary."
2. What is the subject matter of this poem?
3. Has this poem an obvious thesis?
4. Point out what seem to you to be the most striking metaphors
   and images in this poem, and explain how they contribute to
   the whole feeling, or tone, of the poem.
5. Upon what common experience is this poem based?
6. Has this poem a logical progression?
7. Has this poem an associational coherence?
8. Are the images in this poem capable of being categorized?
   If so, what idea seems to be their "common denominator"?
9. In what way does the rhyme contribute to the movement of
   the poem?
10. Does the poet seem to be "moving easy in harness," as Robert
    Frost would phrase it? Are there any lines, for example, which
    seem to have been dictated by the need for a rhyme? Does
    the poet seem to be in control of his idea?
11. The clarity, or intelligibility, of poetry differs from that of
    expository prose. In *what* does the essential clarity of this
    poem consist: The logical development of an argument? The
    scientific exposition of a human feeling?

Related Exercises

1. The title makes reference to the opening lines of the General
   Prologue to Chaucer's *Canterbury Tales*. In the Prologue,

Chaucer describes the coming of spring as a time of joyous
rebirth and a time when "longen folk to goon on pilgrimages."
Read and compare the first 19 lines of the Prologue with
"Whan that Aprille, etcetera."

2. In what respects do the tones of the two poems differ?
3. In what respects do the imageries of the two poems differ?
4. For what purpose does Mr. Sandeen allude, by so entitling
   his poem, to the Prologue to *The Canterbury Tales?*
5. Why does the title conclude with "etcetera"? Does Mr. Sandeen use this phrase merely as a convenience, so he doesn't
   have to reproduce the first 19 lines of the Prologue, or does
   he have another idea in mind?
6. What idea does the poet introduce with the exceptional
   phrase "And yet..." in the final stanza of the poem? Is it
   anticipated earlier in the poem, either directly or indirectly?
7. What has the poet proposed in the first five stanzas of the
   poem to which he must take exception, or which he must at
   least qualify, in the sixth stanza? In order to answer this
   question, note the images which receive special emphasis, the
   organization of details, the occasional assertions. What do
   all of these things *taken together* suggest as a special experience of Spring and human life?
8. Attempt a logical paraphrase of the poem. Is it possible? What
   difficulties do you encounter? Is a poem diminished because
   it cannot be paraphrased exactly, and exalted because it can
   be? What is the use of paraphrase?

MONTOYA'S BESTIARY *

By SUZANNE GROSS

La mariposa
    has four wings
to mock the seraphim.
It will be found a choke of brightness
shattered, caught in the radiator of a car,
and a smear of gold powder pressed
in the asphalt on Candelaria Road.

* From *Sand Verbena* (Notre Dame, Ind.: University of Notre Dame Press,
1962), pp. 92–94.

El gorrión
    never migrates, never sings.
In small brotherhoods it spins all seasons
from curb to curb on ash-blank wings,
not always avoiding the smash of wheels.
On Lead and Iron, at Fourth and Gold,
it is busy in the gutters, rattling
empty peanut sacks to find no crumb forgotten,
stepping into fragrant popcorn bags
to find a greasy emptiness.
It pierces cigarette butts with its bill
and eats the stale tobacco.
It chirps. The sounds it makes
for pleasure and for pain
are indistinguishable.

La paloma
    lives on the flat roofs
of the Albuquerque National Bank,
the Federal Courthouse and the Sunshine Building.
Dragging his wings in the dust the male struts
and swells his sleek, soft, feathered sex;
the black and purple female squats on debris
of eggs fallen from a nest
hidden in the red clay rooftiles.
Songs say the dove
speaks love *y canta cu cu.*
But these are the sweet songs
of another country.

La trucha
    is a fish from whose rose flash
and glittering repose the heights
of the Sangre de Cristo take their name.
Agents of the Interior Department plant them,
in thousands, in the old trout streams,
from which they are fished out, in thousands,
by Rocky Mountain Fresh Fish of Los Angeles,
and sportsmen from West Texas and Dakota
whose glass rods bend like whips.
It is served skinned-out and fire-dried
in the Liberty Cafe, with cole slaw
and brown slices of a shrivelled lemon.

El venado
    of all antlered cattle,
men agree is prettiest,
with his delicate nose, proud mouth and graceful neck,
his soft pelt the color of fifteen-cent tokay.
Multiplied, his luminous, dark-sorrowing glass eyes
look down from the walls of Charlie's Bar,
La Casablanca and the Golden West.

El buey
    is eunuch to his kind,
helplessly false friend to the brave bulls.
His strength deprived of its heat
he is yoked to servitude.
His horns are mounted in his hide
to hang in offices and clubrooms
in Minnesota, Carolina and the Hilton Hotel.
Men say, in Còrdova,
in Trampas, Truchas, Péna Blanca,
that when San Ysidro knelt in the furrow to pray,
an angel came to him from heaven,
and ploughed the land with his oxen.
But these are old men
who have never left the mountains
called Sangre de Cristo.

Notebook Assignment for Class Discussion

1. What unifies the parts of this poem so that it is one poem
   and not five?
2. What formal devices for coherence are evident here?
3. Characterize the language, imagery, formal organization, and
   movement of this poem.
4. What is the tone of this poem? From what qualities of language, imagery, organization, and movement does it derive?
5. How does the employment of particular place names and
   Spanish names and phrases "work" in this poem? How does
   it add to the poem's effect?
6. Does Miss Gross's great insistence upon particular detail seem
   to you to clarify or obscure the broader implications of the
   poem?

Related Exercises

1. What is a bestiary? Look up the subject in the library.
2. To what extent does Miss Gross utilize the traditional allegorical technique of the bestiary?
3. Is her poem fabulous in character?
4. Is her poem moralistic in character?
5. Is this poem an attempt at scientifically objective description? How do you think a scientific approach to *el gorrión* might differ from Miss Gross's in *intention* and in *technique?*
6. Do you see any basis for comparison between "Montoya's Bestiary" and "Whan that Aprille, etcetera" in general theme? With Part II of "Landscapes with Set-Screws"?
7. Do we rend the world, do we ignore it, do we fail of purpose? What relevance have these questions in the light of "Montoya's Bestiary"?

LANDSCAPES WITH SET-SCREWS *

By X. J. KENNEDY

I. *The Autumn in Norfolk Shipyard*

Is a secret one infers
From camouflage. Scrap steel
Betrays no color of season,
Corrosion works year-round.
But in sandblasted stubble
Lurks change: parched thistle burr,
Blown milkweed hull—dried potholes
After tides reassume their foam.

Destroyers mast to mast,
Mechanical conifers,
Bear pointed lights. Moored tankers
Redden slow as leaves.

Under the power crane
Dropped girders lie like twigs,
In drydock ripened tugs
Burst pod-wide—ringbolts bobble
To quiet upon steel-plate
Mud. A flake of paint falls,

Green seas spill last year's needles.

II. *Airport in the Grass*

Grasshopper copters whir,
Blue blurs
Traverse dry air,
Cicadas beam a whine
On which to zero in flights
Of turbojet termites,

A red ant carts
From the fuselage of the wren that crashed
Usable parts

And edging the landingstrip,
Heavier than air the river
The river
The rustbucket river
Revs up her motors forever.

Notebook Assignment for Class Discussion

1. Part I of this poem centers around a paradox. What is it?
2. How is the paradox embodied in the imagery of Part I?
3. What are the contrasting sets of images in Part I, and how are they made to work with one another?
4. Part II of this poem centers around a contrast. What is it?
5. How would you answer the criticism that these poems are "merely descriptive"?
6. How would you answer the criticism that they sketch merely fanciful pictures in which objects are arbitrarily assigned equivalents, e.g., destroyers = evergreens, paint-flakes = falling leaves, grasshoppers = helicopters, etc?

7. In both parts of this poem the meter is unobtrusive and irregular; the lines in Part I do not rhyme; the language is certainly not "literary" or "poetic," but, on the contrary, the kind of language we might use in everyday speech. It seems, in short, a rather relaxed kind of poetry—it seems, perhaps, even a little unpoetic. How would you respond to these remarks?
8. Why not set up Part I in a block, like prose? Would doing that make it prose?
9. Why are Part I and Part II tied together with a general title? In other words, what relationship do they have to one another? Does the title give us a hint?
10. How do you explain "with set-screws" in the general title?

Related Exercises

1. This poem, by X. J. Kennedy, deals, in Part I, with a vision of life embodied in images of the inanimate. Does this give rise to a very evident ironic tone?
2. Part I presents us with a picture of pseudo-life and season in the midst of which the pitiful remnants of real life are overwhelmed and go unnoticed. Is it, therefore, a pessimistic poem, in the sense that the selections in Part Eight of this book from Tennyson and Arnold are pessimistic poems?
3. Part II presents us with a picture of furious, but incidental, activity, contrasted with the eternal, great dull force of the river. Does this contrast give rise to an ironic tone? Why should one expect that it would?
4. How would you characterize the tone of Part II, as it is comparable to or contrastable with "Montoya's Bestiary," which also treats the subject of animals?

A FACE ON WHICH TIME MAKES
BUT LITTLE IMPRESSION *

By Thomas Hardy

A Saturday afternoon in November was approaching the time of twilight, and the vast tract of unenclosed wild known as Egdon Heath embrowned itself moment by moment. Overhead the hollow stretch of whitish cloud shutting out the sky was as a tent which had the whole heath for its floor.

The heaven being spread with this pallid screen and the earth with the darkest vegetation, their meeting-line at the horizon was clearly marked. In such contrast the heath wore the appearance of an instalment of night which had taken up its place before its astronomical hour was come: darkness had to a great extent arrived hereon, while day stood distinct in the sky. Looking upwards, a furze-cutter would have been inclined to continue work; looking down, he would have decided to finish his faggot and go home. The distant rims of the world and of the firmament seemed to be a division in time no less than a division in matter. The face of the heath by its mere complexion added half an hour to evening; it could in like manner retard the dawn, sadden noon, anticipate the frowning of storms scarcely generated, and intensify the opacity of a moonless midnight to a cause of shaking and dread.

In fact, precisely at this transitional point of its nightly roll into darkness the great and particular glory of the Egdon waste began, and nobody could be said to understand the heath who had not been there at such a time. It could best be felt when it could not clearly be seen, its complete effect and explanation lying in this and the succeeding hours before the next dawn: then, and only then, did it tell its true tale. The spot was, indeed, a near relation of night, and when night showed itself an apparent tendency to gravitate together could be perceived in its shades and the scene. The somber stretch of rounds and hollows seemed to rise and meet the evening gloom in pure sympathy, the heath exhaling darkness as rapidly as the heavens precipitated it. And so the obscurity in the air and the obscurity in the land closed

* From *The Return of the Native*, Book One, Chapter 1.

together in a black fraternization towards which each advanced half-way.

The place became full of a watchful intentness now; for when other things sank brooding to sleep the heath appeared slowly to awake and listen. Every night its Titanic form seemed to await something; but it had waited thus, unmoved, during so many centuries, through the crises of so many things, that it could only be imagined to await one last crisis—the final overthrow.

It was a spot which returned upon the memory of those who loved it with an aspect of peculiar and kindly congruity. Smiling champaigns of flowers and fruit hardly do this, for they are permanently harmonious only with an existence of better reputation as to its issues than the present. Twilight combined with the scenery of Egdon Heath to evolve a thing majestic without severity, impressive without showiness, emphatic in its admonitions, grand in its simplicity. The qualifications which frequently invest the facade of a prison with far more dignity than is found in the facade of a palace double its size lent to this heath a sublimity in which spots renowned for beauty of the accepted kind are utterly wanting. Fair prospects wed happily with fair times; but alas, if times be not fair! Men have oftener suffered from the mockery of a place too smiling for their reason than from the oppression of surroundings oversadly tinged. Haggard Egdon appealed to a subtler and scarcer instinct, to a more recently learnt emotion, than that which responds to the sort of beauty called charming and fair.

Indeed, it is a question if the exclusive reign of this orthodox beauty is not approaching its last quarter. The new Vale of Tempe may be a gaunt waste in Thule: human souls may find themselves in closer and closer harmony with external things wearing a somberness distasteful to our race when it was young. The time seems near, if it has not actually arrived, when the chastened sublimity of a moor, a sea, or a mountain will be all of nature that is absolutely in keeping with the moods of the more thinking among mankind. And ultimately, to the commonest tourist, spots like Iceland may become what the vineyards and myrtle-gardens of South Europe are to him now; and Heidelberg and Baden be passed unheeded as he hastens from the Alps to the sand-dunes of Scheveningen.

The most thorough-going ascetic could feel that he had a natural right to wander on Egdon: he was keeping within the line of legitimate indulgence when he laid himself open to influences such as these. Colours and beauties so far subdued were, at least, the birthright of all. Only in summer days of highest feather did its mood touch the level of gaiety. Intensity was more usually reached by way of the solemn than by way of the brilliant, and such a sort of intensity was often arrived at during winter darkness, tempests, and mists. Then Egdon was aroused to reciprocity; for the storm was its lover, and the wind its friend. Then it became the home of strange phantoms; and it was found to be the hitherto unrecognized original of those wild regions of obscurity which are vaguely felt to be compassing us about in midnight dreams of flight and disaster, and are never thought of after the dream till revived by scenes like this.

It was at present a place perfectly accordant with man's nature —neither ghastly, hateful, nor ugly: neither commonplace, unmeaning, nor tame; but, like man, slighted and enduring; and withal singularly colossal and mysterious in its swarthy monotony. As with some persons who have long lived apart, solitude seemed to look out of its countenance. It had a lonely face, suggesting tragical possibilities.

This obscure, obsolete, superseded country figures in Domesday. Its condition is recorded therein as that of heathy, furzy, briary wilderness—"Bruaria!" Then follows the length and breadth in leagues; and, though some uncertainty exists as to the exact extent of this ancient lineal measure, it appears from the figures that the area of Egdon down to the present day has but little diminished. "Turbaria Bruaria"—the right of cutting heath-turf—occurs in charters relating to the district. "Overgrown with heth and mosse," says Leland of the same dark sweep of country.

Here at least were intelligible facts regarding landscape—far-reaching proofs productive of genuine satisfaction. The untameable, Ishmaelitish thing that Egdon now was it always had been. Civilization was its enemy; and ever since the beginning of vegetation its soil had worn the same antique brown dress, the natural and invariable garment of the particular formation. In its venerable one coat lay a certain vein of satire on human vanity in clothes. A person on a heath in raiment of modern cut and colors has more or less an anomalous look. We seem to want the oldest and simplest human clothing where the clothing of the earth is so primitive.

To recline on a stump of thorn in the central valley of Egdon, between afternoon and night, as now, where the eye could reach nothing of the world outside the summits and shoulders of heathland which filled the whole circumference of its glance, and to know that everything around and underneath had been from prehistoric times as unaltered as the stars overhead, gave ballast to the mind adrift on change, and harassed by the irrepressible

New. The great inviolate place had an ancient permanence which the sea cannot claim. Who can say of a particular sea that it is old? Distilled by the sun, kneaded by the moon, it is renewed in a year, in a day, or in an hour. The sea changed, the fields changed, the rivers, the villages, and the people changed, yet Egdon remained. Those surfaces were neither so steep as to be destructible by weather, nor so flat as to be the victims of floods and deposits. With the exception of an aged highway, and a still more aged barrow presently to be referred to—themselves almost crystallized to natural products by long continuance—even the trifling irregularities were not caused by pickaxe, plough, or spade, but remained as the very finger-touches of the last geological change.

The above-mentioned highway traversed the lower levels of the heath, from one horizon to another. In many portions of its course it overlaid an old vicinal way, which branched from the great Western road of the Romans, the Via Iceniana, or Ikenild Street, hard by. On the evening under consideration it would have been noticed that, though the gloom had increased sufficiently to confuse the minor features of the heath, the white surface of the road remained almost as clear as ever.

Notebook Assignment for Class Discussion

1. What is the tone of this descriptive passage? Is it in any sense ambiguous? Is its ambiguity a fault, or a strength?
2. Try to state Hardy's theme in one or two sentences. Can it be done? Would you say that paraphrasability is a criterion of all good literature? Does the difficulty of paraphrasing this passage indicate, necessarily, a lack of clarity?
3. How would you define *clarity* as the word that might be applied to works of the following kind:
   a. imaginative literature (fiction, poetry, drama)
   b. structural analysis (exposition)
   c. logical argumentation
   d. objective natural description
   e. subjective natural description
4. Can you discern an argumentative thread running through this passage? Try to state Hardy's main thesis. Is it consistent with the tone of this passage?
5. How does Hardy employ argumentation here? How does it reenforce or detract from the general effect for which he is working?

6. Does the prose seem awkward at times? Are there some awkward passages which seem *purposeful,* while others appear merely *accidental?* Cite the evidence upon which you base your answer.

7. Note the passages which seem to you to be particularly badly written, and rewrite them to your own satisfaction. Then reread the corrected piece. How have you altered it, *considering the work as a whole?*

8. Does Hardy seem unnecessarily discursive at times? Are there points where he seems lacking in rhetorical subtlety?

9. How would you describe what seems to you to be his most characteristic rhetorical fault? What do you consider to be his greatest rhetorical virtue?

10. Explain Hardy's tonal effects through an examination and analysis of the following:
    a. sentence structure, rhythms, and cadences
    b. the selection and arrangement of detail
    c. the type and use of allusion
    d. the diction
    e. the discursive and "philosophical" passages

Related Exercises

1. Compare and contrast the themes of "The Battle of the Ants" and "A Face on Which . . ." What are the obvious similarities and differences? Are these authors of *opposite* temperaments, bents, and attitudes?

2. How does Hardy's work differ in tone and rhetorical technique from Thoreau's?

3. How does the vision of Nature held by each of these authors agree with and illustrate his vision of life?

4. By what devices do both Thoreau and Hardy extend the scope of their themes beyond the immediate particularities of the battling ants and Egdon Heath? In other words, how might their work be said to have achieved "universality"? How are the subjects transcended?

5. Why does Hardy call the Heath "Ishmaelitish"? For the same, or different, reasons that he cites the old literature pertaining to the Heath, and mentions the Roman roads?

6. In the context of the whole passage, what function does the description of the present road serve? Why is this descriptive paragraph a fitting conclusion to the chapter?

7. Why, in Hardy's view, is man likely to turn from the beauties of a lusher and more benevolent nature to the ascetic grandeurs of cold and wild places?

8. Does Hardy, like Thoreau, finally perceive an order in what appears to be the wild and disordered tangle of brute nature? What is it?

9. In what final and contrasting relationship does Hardy see humankind and the Heath? What, finally, does the Heath symbolize?

Part Three

THE PROPER STUDY

Or

A Sampler of Views on Education

IN ONE ERA AND OUT
THE OTHER *

By Phyllis McGinley

Children can be academic failures as early as kindergarten. For prosperous middle-class America has suddenly discovered the prestige of Education and is bowing down before it as before a Golden Calf. I am not, naturally, against education. To enlarge and elevate the mind, particularly the child-mind, is the noblest of all human activities. What I deplore is the new race toward measured achievement, the frantic struggle of all the Smith parents to set their children competing against their peers for grades, marks, triumphs in aptitude tests, not for the love of knowledge but because only triumph will get them into future colleges.

That the struggle has innocent motives, that the snobbery of a high I.Q. proceeds from a good cause, does not reduce tensions for the children involved. There used to be room in childhood's world for every kind of mentality. If schools offered less challenge in my day than in this, at least they gave to us, who sat in unassorted classrooms, a kind of anonymous safety. We were not branded by the Test. Now the specter of the Intelligence Test, the examinations of aptitude, achievement, special skills, hangs over our schools like a nightmare, haunting our young from the time they enter first grade until they walk on stage for a diploma. Tests sort them, classify them, winnow them out as if they were gradable peas from a commercial garden. Into one compartment go the jumbo-sized I.Q.'s; into another the medium, into a third the inferior. And the fact that such tests measure neither leadership nor talent nor emotional adjustment, not even promise, stops no educator from doing the classifying—nor the sortee from feeling its effect. Again, success or failure comes too soon.

"Jane isn't a student," Jane's mother used to say with a lenient smile. She knew perfectly well Jane could straggle on somehow toward graduation, no doubt marry young, and let fall her lines in pleasant places. Jane was able to wear her academic inability gaily, as if it were a corsage.

Or, "Howard's impossible at math," Howard's father was in-

* Reprinted with permission of the Macmillan Company from *Sixpence in Her Shoe* by Phyllis McGinley, pp. 236–8. Copyright © 1964 by Phyllis McGinley.

clined to boast. "Just like his old man. But you ought to see the way he'll hit that scrimmage line when he gets to Princeton."

Now Howard Sr. is having his eight-year-old son tutored in arithmetic, burdening him with summer-school lessons, making him feel guilty of some juvenile sin for not achieving the same marks as the Jones lad. He is aware, and makes the boy aware, that there will be no Princeton in his future—perhaps not even a Siwash University—unless things improve. Jane's mother, eager for the prestige a good college bestows now on a girl (socially important as a debut) is nagging her daughter into hysterics or moving her from school to school, hoping somehow to redesign her charming if unscholarly mind. No wonder the neuroses of childhood increase and unsuccessful victims of the System turn delinquent at 12.

I know a young woman with several small children who lives in a delightful suburb. But she is deserting it for Larkspur Manor. In Larkspur Manor she has no friends, her house will not be so attractive as the one she owns.

"But Larkspur has this awfully good school," she says candidly. "The principal gets practically the entire senior class into college. I have to think ahead."

Already, you see, she is waging that battle for status. Higher education is not a dim vision on a faraway horizon but a prize for which the battle begins in the perambulator. And the prize is a pragmatic one—a social rather than an intellectual reward. Her brood will be trained for winning scholastic merit as they will be groomed for appearance and poise. First-rate schooling has to her the identical value of orthodontics, summer camps, riding lessons and a talking doll for the baby.

FROM HARD TIMES *

By Charles Dickens

THE ONE THING NEEDFUL

"Now, what I want is Facts. Teach these boys and girls nothing but Facts. Facts alone are wanted in life. Plant nothing else, and root out everything else. You can only form the minds of reason-

* From Book the First, Chapter 1.

ing animals upon Facts: nothing else will ever be of any service to them. This is the principle on which I bring up my own children, and this is the principle on which I bring up these children. Stick to Facts, sir!"

The scene was a plain, bare, monotonous vault of a schoolroom, and the speaker's square forefinger emphasized his observations by underscoring every sentence with a line on the schoolmaster's sleeve. The emphasis was helped by the speaker's square wall of a forehead, which had his eyebrows for its base, while his eyes found commodious cellarage in two dark caves, overshadowed by the wall. The emphasis was helped by the speaker's mouth, which was wide, thin, and hard set. The emphasis was helped by the speaker's voice, which was inflexible, dry, and dictatorial. The emphasis was helped by the speaker's hair, which bristled on the skirts of his bald head, a plantation of firs to keep the wind from its shining surface, all covered with knobs, like the crust of a plum pie, as if the head had scarcely warehouse-room for the hard facts stored inside. The speaker's obstinate carriage, square coat, square legs, square shoulders—nay, his very neckcloth, trained to take him by the throat with an unaccommodating grasp, like a stubborn fact, as it was—all helped the emphasis.

"In this life, we want nothing but Facts, sir; nothing but Facts!"

The speaker, and the schoolmaster, and the third grown person present, all backed a little, and swept with their eyes the inclined plane of little vessels then and there arranged in order, ready to have imperial gallons of facts poured into them until they were full to the brim.

MURDERING THE INNOCENTS

Thomas Gradgrind, sir. A man of realities. A man of facts and calculations. A man who proceeds upon the principle that two and two are four, and nothing over, and who is not to be talked into allowing for anything over. Thomas Gradgrind, sir—peremptorily Thomas—Thomas Gradgrind. With a rule and a pair of scales, and the multiplication table always in his pocket, sir, ready to weigh and measure any parcel of human nature, and tell you exactly what it comes to. It is a mere question of figures, a case of simple arithmetic. You might hope to get some other nonsensical belief into the head of George Gradgrind, or Augustus Gradgrind, or John Gradgrind, or Joseph Gradgrind (all suppositious, non-existent persons), but into the head of Thomas Gradgrind—no, sir!

In such terms Mr. Gradgrind always mentally introduced himself, whether to his private circle of acquaintance, or to the public in general. In such terms, no doubt, substituting the words "boys and girls" for "sir," Thomas Gradgrind now presented Thomas Gradgrind to the little pitchers before him, who were to be filled so full of facts.

Indeed, as he eagerly sparkled at them from the cellarage before mentioned, he seemed a kind of cannon loaded to the muzzle with facts, and prepared to blow them clean out of the regions of childhood at one discharge. He seemed a galvanizing apparatus, too, charged with a grim mechanical substitute for the tender young imaginations that were to be stormed away.

"Girl number twenty," said Mr. Gradgrind, squarely pointing with his square forefinger, "I don't know that girl. Who is that girl?"

"Sissy Jupe, sir," explained number twenty, blushing, standing up, and curtseying.

"Sissy is not a name," said Mr. Gradgrind. "Don't call yourself Sissy. Call yourself Cecilia."

"It's father as calls me Sissy, sir," returned the young girl in a trembling voice, and with another curtsey.

"Then he has no business to do it," said Mr. Gradgrind. "Tell him he mustn't. Cecilia Jupe. Let me see. What is your father?"

"He belongs to the horse-riding, if you please, sir."

Mr. Gradgrind frowned, and waved off the objectionable calling with his hand.

"We don't want to know anything about that, here. You mustn't tell us about that, here. Your father breaks horses, don't he?"

"If you please, sir, when they can get any to break, they do break horses in the ring, sir."

"You mustn't tell us about the ring, here. Very well, then. Describe your father as a horsebreaker. He doctors sick horses, I dare say?"

"Oh yes, sir."

"Very well, then. He is a veterinary surgeon, a farrier, and horsebreaker. Give me your definition of a horse."

(Sissy Jupe was thrown into the greatest alarm by this demand.)

"Girl number twenty unable to define a horse!" said Mr. Gradgrind, for the general behoof of all the little pitchers. "Girl number twenty possessed of no facts, in reference to one of the commonest of animals! Some boy's definition of a horse. Bitzer, yours."

The square finger, moving here and there, lighted suddenly on Bitzer, perhaps because he chanced to sit in the same ray of sunlight which, darting in at one of the bare windows of the intensely whitewashed room, irradiated Sissy. For the boys and girls sat on the face of the inclined plane in two compact bodies, divided up the center by a narrow interval; and Sissy, being at the corner of a row on the sunny side, came in for the beginning of a sunbeam, of which Bitzer, being in the corner of a row on the other side, a few rows in advance, caught the end. But whereas the girl was so dark-eyed and dark-haired that she seemed to receive a deeper and more lustrous color from the sun when it shone upon her, the boy was so light-eyed and light-haired that the selfsame rays appeared to draw out of him what little color he ever possessed. His cold eyes would hardly have been eyes but for the short ends of lashes which, by bringing them into immediate contrast with something paler than themselves, expressed their form. His short-cropped hair might have been a mere continuation of the sandy freckles on his forehead and face. His skin was so unwholesomely deficient in the natural tinge, that he looked as though, if he were cut, he would bleed white.

"Bitzer," said Thomas Gradgrind. "Your definition of a horse."

"Quadruped. Graminivorous. Forty teeth, namely, twenty-four grinders, four eye-teeth, and twelve incisive. Sheds coat in the spring; in marshy countries, sheds hoofs, too. Hoofs hard, but requiring to be shod with iron. Age known by marks in mouth." Thus (and much more) Bitzer.

"Now girl number twenty," said Mr. Gradgrind. "You know what a horse is."

She curtseyed again, and would have blushed deeper if she could have blushed deeper than she had blushed all the time. Bitzer, after rapidly blinking at Thomas Gradgrind with both eyes at once, and so catching the light upon his quivering ends of lashes that they looked like the antennae of busy insects, put his knuckles to his freckled forehead and sat down again.

The third gentleman now stepped forth. A mighty man at cutting and drying he was; a government officer; in his way (and in most other people's too), a professed pugilist; always in training, always with a system to force down the general throat like a bolus; always to be heard of at the bar of his little public-office, ready to fight all England. To continue in fistic phraseology, he had a genius for coming up to the scratch, wherever and whatever it was, and proving himself an ugly customer. He would go in and damage any subject whatever with his right, follow up with his left, stop, exchange, counter, bore his opponent (he always fought All England) to the ropes, and fall upon him neatly. He was certain to knock the wind out of common sense, and render that unlucky adversary deaf to the call of time. And he

had it in charge from high authority to bring about the great
public-office Millennium, when Commissioners should reign upon
earth.

"Very well," said this gentleman, briskly smiling, and folding
his arms. "That's a horse. Now, let me ask you girls and boys:
Would you paper a room with representations of horses?"

After a pause, one half of the children cried in chorus, "Yes,
sir!" Upon which the other half, seeing in the gentleman's face
that Yes was wrong, cried out in chorus, "No, sir!"—as the custom
is in these examinations.

"Of course, No. Why wouldn't you?"

A pause. One corpulent slow boy, with a wheezy manner of
breathing, ventured the answer, Because he wouldn't paper a
room at all, but would paint it.

"You *must* paper it," said the gentleman, rather warmly.

"You must paper it," said Thomas Gradgrind, "whether you
like it or not. Don't tell *us* you wouldn't paper it. What do you
mean, boy?"

"I'll explain to you, then," said the gentleman, after another
and a dismal pause, "why you wouldn't paper a room with representations of horses. Do you ever see horses walking up and
down the sides of rooms in reality—in fact? Do you?"

"Yes, sir!" from one half. "No, sir!" from the other.

"Of course, No," said the gentleman, with an indignant look
at the wrong half. "Why, then, you are not to see anywhere what
you don't see in fact; you are not to have anywhere what you
don't have in fact. What is called Taste is only another name for
Fact."

Thomas Gradgrind nodded his approbation.

"This is a new principle, a discovery, a great discovery," said
the gentleman. "Now, I'll try you again. Suppose you were going
to carpet a room. Would you use a carpet having a representation
of flowers upon it?"

There being a general conviction by this time that "No, sir!"
was always the right answer to this gentleman, the chorus of No
was very strong. Only a few feeble stragglers said Yes: among
them Sissy Jupe.

"Girl number twenty," said the gentleman, smiling in the
calm strength of knowledge.

Sissy blushed, and stood up.

"So you would carpet your room—or your husband's room, if
you were a grown woman, and had a husband—with representations of flowers, would you?" said the gentleman. "Why would
you?"

"If you please, sir, I am very fond of flowers," returned the girl.

"And that is why you would put tables and chairs upon them and have people walking over them with heavy boots?"

"It wouldn't hurt them, sir. They wouldn't crush and wither, if you please, sir. They would be the pictures of what was very pretty and pleasant, and I would fancy—"

"Aye, aye, aye! But you mustn't fancy," cried the gentleman, quite elated by coming so happily to his point. "That's it! You are never to fancy."

"You are not, Cecilia Jupe," Thomas Gradgrind solemnly repeated, "to do anything of that kind."

"Fact, fact, fact!" said the gentleman. And "Fact, fact, fact!" repeated Thomas Gradgrind.

"You are to be in all things regulated and governed," said the gentleman, "by fact. We hope to have, before long, a board of fact, composed of commissioners of fact, who will force the people to be a people of fact, and of nothing but fact. You must discard the word Fancy altogether. You must have nothing to do with it. You are not to have, in any object of use or ornament, what would be a contradiction in fact. You don't walk upon flowers in fact; you cannot be allowed to walk upon flowers in carpets. You don't find that foreign birds and butterflies come and perch upon your crockery; you cannot be permitted to paint foreign birds and butterflies upon your crockery. You never meet with quadrupeds going up and down walls; you must not have quadrupeds represented upon walls. You must see," said the gentleman, "for all these purposes, combinations and modifications (in primary colors) of mathematical figures which are susceptible of proof and demonstration. This is the new discovery. This is fact. This is taste."

The girl curtseyed, and sat down. She was very young, and she looked as if she were frightened by the matter-of-fact prospect the world afforded.

"Now, if Mr. McChoakumchild," said the gentleman, "will proceed to give his first lesson here, Mr. Gradgrind, I shall be happy, at your request, to observe his mode of procedure."

Mr. Gradgrind was much obliged. "Mr. McChoakumchild, we only wait for you."

So Mr. McChoakumchild began in his best manner. He and some one hundred and forty other schoolmasters had been lately turned at the same time, in the same factory, on the same principles, like so many pianoforte legs. He had been put through an immense variety of paces, and had answered volumes of head-breaking questions. Orthography, etymology, syntax, and prosody, biography, astronomy, geography, and general cosmography, the sciences of compound proportion, algebra, land-surveying and leveling, vocal music, and drawing from models were all at the ends of his ten chilled fingers. He had worked his stony way into Her Majesty's most Honorable Privy Council's Schedule B, and had taken the bloom off the higher branches of mathematics and physical science, French, German, Latin and Greek. He knew all about the watersheds of all the world (whatever they are), and all the histories of all the peoples, and all the names of all the rivers and mountains, and all the productions, manners, and customs of all the countries, and all their boundaries and bearings on the two-and-thirty points of the compass. Ah, rather overdone, McChoakumchild. If he had only learnt a little less, how infinitely better he might have taught much more!

He went to work in this preparatory lesson, not unlike Morgiana in the Forty Thieves: looking into all the vessels ranged before him, one after another, to see what they contained. Say, good McChoakumchild: When from thy boiling store, thou shalt fill each jar brimful by-and-by, dost thou think that thou wilt always kill outright the robber Fancy lurking within—or sometimes only maim him and distort him?

AN APOLOGY FOR IDLERS *

By Robert Louis Stevenson

Boswell: We grow weary when idle.

Johnson: That is, sir, because others being busy, we want company; but if we were idle, there would be no growing weary: we should all entertain one another.

Just now, when everyone is bound, under pain of a decree in absence convicting them of lèse-respectability, to enter on some lucrative profession, and labor therein with something not far short of enthusiasm, a cry from the opposite party who are content when they have enough, and like to look on and enjoy in the meanwhile, savors a little of bravado and gasconade. And yet this should not be. Idleness so called, which does not consist in

* From Cornhill Magazine, Vol. XXXVI (July, 1877), 80–86.

doing nothing, but in doing a great deal not recognized in the dogmatic formularies of the ruling class, has as good a right to state its position as industry itself. It is admitted that the presence of people who refuse to enter in the great handicap race for sixpenny pieces, is at once an insult and a disenchantment for those who do. A fine fellow (as we see so many) takes his determination, votes for sixpences, and in the emphatic Americanism, "goes for" them. And while such an one is ploughing distressfully up the road, it is not hard to understand his resentment, when he perceives cool persons in the meadows by the wayside, lying with a handkerchief over their ears and a glass at their elbow. Alexander is touched in a very delicate place by the disregard of Diogenes. Where was the glory of having taken Rome for those tumultuous barbarians, who poured into the Senate-house, and found the Fathers sitting silent and unmoved by their success? It is a sore thing to have labored along and scaled the arduous hilltops, and when all is done find humanity indifferent to your achievement. Hence physicists condemn the unphysical; financiers have only a superficial toleration for those who know little of stocks; literary persons despise the unlettered; and people of all pursuits combine to disparage those who have none.

But though this is one difficulty of the subject, it is not the greatest. You could not be put in prison for speaking against industry, but you can be sent to Coventry for speaking like a fool. The greatest difficulty with most subjects is to do them well; therefore, please to remember this is an apology. It is certain that much may be judiciously argued in favor of diligence; only there is something to be said against it, and that is what, on the present occasion, I have to say. To state one argument is not necessarily to be deaf to all others, and that a man has written a book of travels in Montenegro, is no reason why he should never have been to Richmond.

It is surely beyond a doubt that people should be a good deal idle in youth. For though here and there a Lord Macaulay may escape from school honors with all his wits about him, most boys pay so dear for their medals that they never afterwards have a shot in their locker, and begin the world bankrupt. And the same holds true during all the time a lad is educating himself, or suffering others to educate him. It must have been a very foolish old gentleman who addressed Johnson at Oxford in these words: "Young man, ply your book diligently now, and acquire a stock of knowledge; for when years come upon you, you will find that poring upon books will be but an irksome task." The old gentleman seems to have been unaware that many other things besides reading grow irksome, and not a few become impossible, by the time a man has to use spectacles and cannot walk without a stick. Books are good enough in their own way, but they are a mighty bloodless substitute for life. It seems a pity to sit like the Lady of Shalott, peering into a mirror, with your back turned on all the bustle and glamour of reality. And if a man reads very hard, as the old anecdote reminds us, he will have little time for thought.

If you look back on your own education, I am sure it will not be the full, vivid, instructive hours of truantry that you regret; you would rather cancel some lack-luster periods between sleep and waking in the class. For my own part, I have attended a good many lectures in my time. I still remember that the spinning of a top is a case of Kinetic stability. I still remember that Emphyteusis is not a disease, nor Stillicide a crime. But though I would not willingly part with such scraps of science, I do not set the same store by them as by certain other odds and ends that I came by in the open street while I was playing truant. This is not the moment to dilate on that mighty place of education, which was the favorite school of Dickens and of Balzac, and turns out yearly many inglorious masters in the Science of the Aspects of Life. Suffice it to say this: if a lad does not learn in the streets, it is because he has no faculty of learning. Nor is the truant always in the streets, for if he prefers, he may go out by the gardened suburbs into the country. He may pitch on some tuft of lilacs over a burn, and smoke innumerable pipes to the tune of the water on the stones. A bird will sing in the thicket. And there he may fall into a vein of kindly thought, and see things in a new perspective. Why, if this be not education, what is? We may conceive Mr. Worldly Wiseman accosting such an one, and the conversation that should thereupon ensue:

"How now, young fellow, what dost thou here?"

"Truly sir, I take mine ease."

"Is not this the hour of the class? and should'st thou not be plying thy Book with diligence, to the end thou mayest obtain knowledge?"

"Nay, but thus also I follow after Learning, by your leave."

"Learning, quotha! After what fashion, I pray thee? Is it mathematics?"

"No, to be sure."

"Is it metaphysics?"

"Nor that."

"Is it some language?"

"Nay, it is no language."

"Is it a trade?"

STEVENSON: *An Apology for Idlers* 109

"Nor a trade neither."

"Why then, what is't?"

"Indeed, sir, as time may soon come for me to go upon Pilgrimage, I am desirous to note what is commonly done by persons in my case, and where are the ugliest Sloughs and Thickets on the Road; as also, what manner of staff is of the best service. Moreover, I lie here, by this water, to learn by root-of-heart a lesson which my master teaches me to call Peace, or Contentment."

Hereupon Mr. Worldly Wiseman was much commoved with passion, and shaking his cane with a very threatful countenance, broke forth upon this wise: "Learning, quotha!" said he; "I would have all such rogues scourged by the Hangman!"

And so he would go his way, ruffling out his cravat with a crackle of starch, like a turkey when it spreads its feathers.

Now this, of Mr. Wiseman's, is the common opinion. A fact is not called a fact, but a piece of gossip, if it does not fall into one of your scholastic categories. An inquiry must be in some acknowledged direction, with a name to go by; or else you are not inquiring at all, only lounging; and the workhouse is too good for you. It is supposed that all knowledge is at the bottom of a well, or the far end of a telescope. Sainte-Beuve, as he grew older, came to regard all experience as a single great book, in which to study for a few years ere we go hence; and it seemed all one to him whether you should read in Chapter XX, which is the differential calculus, or in Chapter XXXIX, which is hearing the band play in the gardens. As a matter of fact, an intelligent person, looking out of his eyes and hearkening in his ears, with a smile on his face all the time, will get more true education than many another in a life of heroic vigils. There is certainly some chill and arid knowledge to be found upon the summits of formal and laborious science; but it is all round about you, and for the trouble of looking, that you will acquire the warm and palpitating facts of life. While others are filling their memory with a lumber of words, one-half of which they will forget before the week be out, your truant may learn some really useful art: to play the fiddle, to know a good cigar, or to speak with ease and opportunity to all varieties of men. Many who have "plied their book diligently," and know all about some one branch or another of accepted lore, come out of the study with an ancient and owl-like demeanor, and prove dry, stockish, and dyspeptic in all the better and brighter parts of life. Many make a large fortune, who remain underbred and pathetically stupid to the last. And meanwhile there goes the idler, who began life along with them—by your leave, a different picture. He has had time to take care of his health and his spirits; he has been a great deal in the open air, which is the most salutary of all things for both body and mind; and if he has never read the great Book in very recondite places, he has dipped into it and skimmed it over to excellent purpose. Might not the student afford some Hebrew roots, and the business man some of his half-crowns, for a share of the idler's knowledge of life at large, and Art of Living? Nay, and the idler has another and more important quality than these. I mean his wisdom. He who has much looked on at the childish satisfaction of other people in their hobbies, will regard his own with only a very ironical indulgence. He will not be heard among the dogmatists. He will have a great and cool allowance for all sorts of people and opinions. If he finds no out-of-the-way truths, he will identify himself with no very burning falsehood. His way takes him along a by-road, not much frequented, but very even and pleasant, which is called Commonplace Lane, and leads to the Belvedere of Common-sense. Thence he shall command an agreeable, if no very noble prospect; and while others behold the East and West, the Devil and the Sunrise, he will be contentedly aware of a sort of morning hour upon all sublunary things, with an army of shadows running speedily and in many different directions into the great daylight of Eternity. The shadows and the generations, the shrill doctors and the plangent wars, go by into ultimate silence and emptiness; but underneath all this, a man may see, out of the Belvedere windows, much green and peaceful landscape; many fire-lit parlors; good people laughing, drinking, and making love as they did before the Flood or the French Revolution; and the old shepherd telling his tale under the hawthorn.

Extreme *busyness*, whether at school or college, kirk or market, is a symptom of deficient vitality; and a faculty for idleness implies a catholic appetite and a strong sense of personal identity. There is a sort of dead-alive, hackneyed people, about, who are scarcely conscious of living except in the exercise of some conventional occupation. Bring these fellows into the country or set them aboard ship, and you will see how they pine for their desk or their study. They have no curiosity; they cannot give themselves over to random provocations; they do not take pleasure in the exercise of their faculties for its own sake; and unless Necessity lays about them with a stick, they will even stand still. It is no good speaking to such folk: they *cannot* be idle, their nature is not generous enough; and they pass those hours in a sort of coma which are not dedicated to furious moiling in the gold-mill. When they do not require to go to office, when they are not hungry and have no mind to drink, the whole breathing world is a blank to them. If they have to wait an hour or so for a train, they fall into a stupid trance with their eyes open. To see them, you would suppose there was nothing to look at and no one to speak with; you would imagine they were paralyzed or alienated; and yet very possibly they are hard workers in their own way, and have good eyesight for a flaw in a deed or a turn of the market. They have been to school and college, but all the time they had their eye on the medal; they have gone about in the world and mixed with clever people; but all the time they were thinking of their own affairs. As if a man's soul were not too small to begin with, they have dwarfed and narrowed theirs by a life of all work and no play; until here they are at forty, with a listless attention, a mind vacant of all material of amusement, and not one thought to rub against another, while they wait for the train. Before he was breeched, he might have clambered on the boxes; when he was twenty, he would have stared at the girls; but now the pipe is smoked out, the snuff-box empty, and my gentleman sits bolt upright upon a bench, with lamentable eyes. This does not appeal to me as being Success in Life.

But it is not only the person himself who suffers from his busy habits, but his wife and children, his friends and relations, and down to the very people he sits with in a railway-carriage or an omnibus. Perpetual devotion to what a man calls his business, is only to be sustained by perpetual neglect of many other things. And it is not by any means certain that a man's business is the most important thing he has to do. To an impartial estimate it will seem clear that many of the wisest, most virtuous, and most beneficent parts that are to be played upon the Theatre of Life are filled by gratuitous performers, and pass, among the world at large, as phases of idleness. For in that Theatre, not only the walk-ing gentlemen, singing chambermaids, and diligent fiddlers in the orchestra, but those who look on and clap their hands from the benches, do really play a part and fulfil important offices towards the general result. You are no doubt very dependent on the care of your lawyer and stockbroker, or the guards and signalmen who convey you rapidly from place to place, and the policemen who walk the streets for your protection; but is there not a thought of gratitude in your heart for certain other benefactors who set you smiling when they fall in your way, or season your dinner with good company? Colonel Newcome helped to lose his friend's money; Fred Bayham had an ugly trick of borrowing shirts; and yet they were better people to fall among than Mr. Barnes. And though Falstaff was neither sober nor very honest, I think I could name one or two long-faced Barabbases whom the world could have better done without. Hazlitt mentions that he was more sensible of obligation to Northcote, who had never done him anything he could call a service, than to his whole circle of ostentatious friends; for he thought a good companion emphatically the greatest benefactor. I know there are people in the world who cannot feel grateful unless the favor has been done them at the cost of pain and difficulty. But this is a churlish disposition. A man may send you six sheets of letter-paper covered with the most entertaining gossip, or you may pass half-an-hour pleasantly, perhaps profitably, over an article of his; do you think the service would be greater if he had made the manuscript in his heart's blood, like a compact with the devil? Do you really fancy you should be more beholden to your correspondent, if he had been damning you all the while for your importunity? Pleasures are more beneficial than duties because, like the quality of mercy, they are not strained, and they are twice blest. There must always be two to a kiss, and there may be a score in a jest; but wherever there is an element of sacrifice, the favor is conferred with pain, and, among generous people, received with confusion. There is no duty we so much underrate as the duty of being happy. By being happy we sow anonymous benefits upon the world, which remain unknown even to ourselves, or when they are disclosed, surprise nobody so much as the benefactor. The other day, a ragged barefoot boy ran down the street after a marble, with so jolly an air that he set everyone he passed into a good humor; one of these persons, who had been delivered from more than usually black thoughts, stopped the little fellow and gave him some money with this remark: "You see what sometimes comes of looking pleased." If he had looked pleased before, he had now to look both pleased and mystified. For my part, I justify this encouragement of smiling rather than tearful children; I do not wish to pay for tears anywhere but upon the stage; but I am prepared to deal largely in the opposite commodity. A happy man or woman is a better thing to find than a five-pound note. He or she is a radiating focus of goodwill; and their entrance into a room is as though another candle had been lighted. We need not care whether they could prove the forty-seven propositions; they do a better thing than that, they practically demonstrate the great Theorem of the Liveableness of Life. Consequently, if a person cannot be happy without remaining idle, idle he should remain. It is a revolutionary precept; but thanks to hunger and the workhouse, one not easily to be abused; and within practical limits, it is one of the most incontestable truths in the whole Body of Morality. Look at one of your industrious fellows for a moment, I beseech you. He sows hurry and reaps indigestion; he puts a vast deal of activity out to interest, and receives a large measure of nervous derangement in return. Either he absents himself entirely from all fellowship, and lives a recluse in a garret, with carpet slippers and a leaden inkpot; or he comes among people swiftly and bitterly, in a contraction of his whole nervous system, to discharge some temper before he returns to work. I do not care how much or how well he works, this fellow is an evil feature in other people's lives. They would be happier if he were dead. They could easier do without his services in the Circumlocution Office than they can tolerate his fractious spirits. He poisons life at the well-head. It is better to be beggared out of hand by a scapegrace nephew, than daily hag-ridden by a peevish uncle.

And what, in God's name, is all this pother about? For what cause do they embitter their own and other people's lives? That a man should publish three or thirty articles a year, that he should finish or not finish his great allegorical picture, are questions of little interest to the world. The ranks of life are full; and although a thousand fall, there are always some to go into the breach. When they told Joan of Arc she should be at home minding women's work, she answered there were plenty to spin and wash. And so, even with your own rare gifts! When nature is "so careless of the single life," why should we coddle ourselves into the fancy that our own is of exceptional importance? Suppose Shakespeare had been knocked on the head some dark night in Sir Thomas Lucy's preserves, the world would have wagged on better or worse, the pitcher gone to the well, the scythe to the corn, and the student to his book; and no one been any the wiser of the loss. There are not many works extant, if you look the alternative all over, which are worth the price of a pound of tobacco to a man of limited means. This is a sobering reflection for the proudest of our earthly vanities. Even a tobacconist may, upon consideration, find no great cause for personal vainglory in the phrase; for although tobacco is an admirable sedative, the qualities necessary for retailing it are neither rare nor precious in themselves. Alas and alas! you may take it how you will, but the services of no single individual are indispensable. Atlas was just a gentleman with a protracted nightmare! And yet you see merchants who go and labor themselves into a great fortune and thence into the bankruptcy court; scribblers who keep scribbling at little articles until their temper is a cross to all who come about them, as though Pharaoh should set the Israelites to make a pin instead of a pyramid; and fine young men who work themselves into a decline, and are driven off in a hearse with white plumes upon it. Would you not suppose these persons had been whispered, by the Master of the Ceremonies, the promise of some momentous destiny? and that this lukewarm bullet on which they play their farces was the bull's-eye and center-point of all the universe? And yet it is not so. The end for which they gave away their priceless youth, for all they know, may be chimerical or hurtful; the glory and riches they expect may never come, or may find them indifferent; and they and the world they inhabit are so inconsiderable that the mind freezes at the thought.

Notebook Assignment for Class Discussion

1. State in one sentence Stevenson's main thesis. State several of his subordinated theses. Is this essay digressive? How do the minor theses work to complement the main one?
2. In what sense does he use the word "apology"? "Idler"? Is Stevenson's idler merely a procrastinator? Is he useless, aimless, a squanderer?
3. Select several statements which Stevenson makes in this essay with which you entirely agree or disagree. Choose only those about which you feel strongly, and be prepared to explain and defend your point of view.
4. Analyze the essay to discover how Stevenson uses contrast, paradox, epigram, and anecdote. How do these devices help to express the author's main point? Is Stevenson writing with tongue in check, or do you think that he *literally* means everything he says?
5. Does the author make his main purpose clear? How often does he return to the statement of his thesis? Does he restate it according to a pattern?
6. What use does Stevenson make of historical and literary allusion? How does the use of allusion differ from the citing of authority?
7. The persuasion appears largely in a series of contrasting examples in which overdiligence is ridiculed and the proper kind of idleness is praised. Point out several of these contrasts, and explain their particular effectiveness.

Related Exercises

1. Does industry seem to you to be one of the great human virtues? Why is it not one of the theological virtues? Do most Americans consider it *morally* good to be industrious? Look up Benjamin Franklin's "spiritual exercises" in the *Autobiography;* how does he regard industry? Write an evaluation of this section of the *Autobiography,* [1] adopting what you think would be R. L. Stevenson's point of view and tone.

2. Can you imagine an industriousness which is detrimental to man and, therefore, to society? Does Stevenson cite any examples or propose any hypothetical cases of injurious industry?

3. Why will Stevenson's idler not be a dogmatist? What is wrong with being a dogmatist? In what sense does Stevenson use the word? What does he imply as the contrary of dogmatism? Why should he think it good that the idler "regard his [hobbies] with only a very ironical indulgence"? What is *irony?* In what sense does it differ from *cynicism?* From the *sardonic?* Would Stevenson think cynicism a desirable trait in a man?

4. Would not the idler's approach to learning, as Stevenson describes it, result in shallowness of intellect? Is some grubbing necessary in the process of being educated? Explain the author's paradoxical remark that "extreme *busyness,* whether at school or college, kirk or market, is a symptom of deficient vitality."

5. Does the allusion to Montenegro and Richmond mean that because one is customarily diligent he can never be idle? Or, because he has one point of view, he may never sample others?

6. Write a paper contrasting formal and "natural" education, alluding to actual or fictional persons who illustrate the contrast, e.g., Prospero and Caliban in Shakespeare's *The Tempest.*

7. Show in an analytical paper how Stevenson shapes the connotations of such words as "idler" and "industrious," and in the process destroys the conventional connotations.

8. Write an argumentative paper, using for your topic one of Stevenson's more provocative statements, such as "Books are good enough in their own way, but they are a mighty bloodless substitute for life." Try to employ some of the major rhetorical devices this author has used, including allusion, paradox, and epigram.

[1] *The Autobiography of Benjamin Franklin* (New York: Random House, 1944), pp. 87–104.

9. Write an essay on any phase or experience of nature that you know very well, and about which you can become excited. Try to infect the reader with your enthusiasm, avoiding merely impersonal exposition. *Show* the reader how you feel about your subject.

WHEN I HEARD
THE LEARN'D ASTRONOMER

By WALT WHITMAN

When I heard the learn'd astronomer,
When the proofs, the figures, were ranged in columns before me,
When I was shown the charts and diagrams, to add, divide, and measure them,
When I sitting heard the astronomer where he lectured with much applause in the lecture-room,
How soon unaccountable I became tired and sick,
Till rising and gliding out I wander'd off by myself,
In the mystical moist night-air, and from time to time,
Look'd up in perfect silence at the stars.

Notebook Assignment for Class Discussion

1. What makes the poet feel alone, apart from the other listeners in the lecture-room, as well as from the "learn'd astronomer"?
2. Which details in the poem stress the difference between the poet, the audience, and the lecturer?
3. With what particular mood of Stevenson's essay does the poem agree?
4. Do you think Stevenson's sense of humor makes his essay a more effective weapon against formal order than Whitman's poem?
5. Why does the poet say "How soon unaccountable . . . "? Why does he say "rising and gliding" instead of "(I) rose and glided"? How does "wander'd" help develop the contrast between the lecturer and the poet? What strong impact is provided by the word "silence" in the last line of the poem?

6. Might not the scientist's approach to astronomy be merely one valid way toward truth, and the poet's another? Is intuition a mode of knowledge? Is feeling? Does a scientist never make use of intuition? Do you think that Whitman's poem and Stevenson's essay make their attacks too general, too inclusive?
7. The poem is short; is it also *complete?* Exactly where is it divisible into the beginning, middle, and end?
8. This poem is organized around a contrast which the poet draws between two modes of knowledge. In what *concrete* terms is the contrast dramatized for us?
9. What contrary is implied for the term "mystical" as the poet uses it?
10. What contrasts can be made between the quality of the diction and the rhythmical movement of each of the major divisions in the poem?

Related Exercises

1. Look up the following poems, for the purpose of comparing and contrasting them with "When I Heard the Learn'd Astronomer" in theme, thesis, tone, imagery, figurative language, scope, formal techniques, etc.:
   a. William Blake, "Mock on, Mock on, Voltaire, Rousseau . . ."
   b. Edgar A. Poe, "Sonnet to Science"
   c. William Wordsworth, "Expostulation and Reply" and "The Tables Turned"
   d. Ezra Pound, "Canto XXXVI"
   e. Robert Frost, "The Egg and the Machine"
2. How do you regard the poet's response to the astronomer's lecture? What response would you make to the charge that the scientist in some way leaches mystery from the universe, and thereby diminishes the beauty of life?
3. In what sense might the following remark serve as a beginning for an argument in response to the second part of question 2: ". . . science deals with but a partial aspect of reality, and . . . there is no faintest reason for supposing that everything science ignores is less real than what it accepts." [1]

---

[1] J. W. N. Sullivan, *The Limitations of Science* (New York: Mentor, 1933), p. 147. Copyright, Viking Press.

LIBERAL KNOWLEDGE
ITS OWN END *

By Cardinal Newman

I consider, then, that I am chargeable with no paradox, when I speak of a Knowledge which is its own end, when I call it liberal knowledge, or a gentleman's knowledge, when I educate for it, and make it the scope of a University. And still less am I incurring such a charge, when I make this acquisition consist, not in Knowledge in a vague and ordinary sense, but in that Knowledge which I have especially called Philosophy or, in an extended sense of the word, Science; for whatever claims Knowledge has to be considered as a good, these it has in a higher degree when it is viewed not vaguely, not popularly, but precisely and transcendently as Philosophy. Knowledge, I say, is then especially liberal, or sufficient for itself, apart from every external and ulterior object, when and so far as it is philosophical, and this I proceed to show.

Now bear with me, gentlemen, if what I am about to say, has at first sight a fanciful appearance. Philosophy, then, or Science, is related to Knowledge in this way:—Knowledge is called by the name of Science or Philosophy, when it is acted upon, informed, or if I may use a strong figure, impregnated by Reason. Reason is the principle of that intrinsic fecundity of Knowledge, which, to those who possess it, is its especial value, and which dispenses with the necessity of their looking abroad for any end to rest upon external to itself. Knowledge, indeed, when thus exalted into a scientific form, is also power; not only is it excellent in itself, but whatever such excellence may be, it is something more, it has a result beyond itself. Doubtless; but that is a further consideration, with which I am not concerned. I only say that, prior to its being a power, it is a good; that it is, not only an instrument, but an end. I know well it may resolve itself into an art, and terminate in a mechanical process, and in tangible fruit; but it also may fall back upon Reason, and resolve itself into Philosophy. In one case it is called Useful Knowledge, in

* From *On the Scope and Nature of University Education,* by John Henry Cardinal Newman, Discourse IV.

the other Liberal. The same person may cultivate it in both ways at once; but this again is a matter foreign to my subject; here I do but say that there are two ways of using Knowledge, and in matter of fact those who use it in one way are not likely to use it in the other, or at least in a very limited measure. You see, then, gentlemen, here are two methods of Education; the one aspires to be philosophical, the other to be mechanical; the one rises towards ideas, the other is exhausted upon what is particular and external. Let me not be thought to deny the necessity, or to decry the benefit, of such attention to what is particular and practical, the useful or mechanical arts; life could not go on without them; we owe our daily welfare to them; their exercise is the duty of the many, and we owe to the many a debt of gratitude for fulfilling it. I only say that Knowledge, in proportion as it tends more and more to be particular, ceases to be Knowledge. It is a question whether Knowledge can in any proper sense be predicated of the brute creation; without pretending to metaphysical exactness of phraseology, which would be unsuitable to an occasion like this, I say, it seems to me improper to call that passive sensation, or perception of things, which brutes seem to possess, by the name of Knowledge. When I speak of Knowledge, I mean something intellectual, something which grasps what it perceives through the senses; something which takes a view of things; which sees more than the senses convey; which reasons upon what it sees, and, while it sees; which invests it with an idea. It expresses itself, not in a mere enunciation, but by an enthymeme: it is of the nature of science from the first, and in this consists its dignity. The principle of real dignity in Knowledge, its worth, its desirableness, considered irrespectively of its results, is this germ within it of a scientific or a philosophical process. This is how it comes to be an end in itself; this is why it admits of being called Liberal. Not to know the relative disposition of things is the state of slaves or children; to have mapped out the Universe is the boast of Philosophy.

Moreover, such knowledge is not a mere extrinsic or accidental advantage, which is ours to-day and another's to-morrow, which may be got up from a book, and easily forgotten again, which we can command or communicate at our pleasure, which we can borrow for the occasion, carry about in our hand, and take into the market; it is an acquired illumination; it is a habit, a personal possession, and an inward endowment. And this is the reason, why it is more correct, as well as more usual, to speak of a University as a place of education, than of instruction, though, when knowledge is concerned, instruction would at first sight have seemed the more appropriate word. We are instructed, for instance, in manual exercises, in the fine and useful arts, in trades, and in ways of business; for these are methods, which have little or no effect upon the mind itself, are contained in rules committed to memory, to tradition, or to use, and bear upon an end external to themselves. But education is a higher word; it implies an action upon our mental nature, and the formation of a character; it is something individual and permanent, and is commonly spoken of in connection with religion and virtue. When, then, we speak of the communication of Knowledge as being Education, we thereby really imply that that Knowledge is a state or condition of mind; and since cultivation of mind is surely worth seeking for its own sake, we are thus brought once more to the conclusion, which the word "Liberal" and the word "Philosophy" have already suggested, that there is a Knowledge, which is desirable, though nothing come of it, as being of itself a treasure, and a sufficient remuneration of years of labor.

SCIENCE IN THE
LIBERAL ARTS *

By Dael Wolfle

It is not uncommon to hear someone say with smugness and even a touch of pride, "I don't know a thing about science." Even among faculty members one sometimes encounters a complacent ignorance of most things scientific. Dr. James R. Killian tells the story of a faculty meeting that was deciding the fate of those students who were failing in one or more of their courses. When it was announced that a student named Cicero was failing in Latin, everyone laughed. A little later, when it was announced that a student named Gauss was failing in mathematics, only the scientists laughed.

Stories are also told about the fact that scientists, too, are sometimes ignorant in fields outside their own areas of specialization. I owe my favorite to William E. Dick, editor of the British maga-

* Reprinted from *The American Scholar*, Vol. 28, No. 2 (Spring, 1959). Copyright © 1959 by the United Chapters of Phi Beta Kappa. By permission of the publishers.

zine *Discovery*. He quotes a delightful anecdote from Lord Moulton, a brilliantly versatile patent lawyer who encountered a solitary German scientist on top of a mountain. As Lord Moulton tells the story:

I found he was a chemist, and I began to talk upon a chemical subject. He told me he was only an organic chemist. He had not exhausted my resources, and I began to talk of coal-tar and pharmaceutical products. Then he told me he was a coal-tar by-product chemist. That did not beat me, because I had just been fighting a case of canary yellow. I thought I would get some subject that was common to us, and I slipped into the subject of canary yellow. Still the same ominous silence for a time, and then he said, "I am only a coal-tar chemist dealing with blues." But I had not finished. With an Englishman's pertinacity, not believing I was beaten, I racked my brains for a coal-tar blue—I had had to advise on some case—and I gradually, without a too obvious change of subject, slipped into that. Then he finally defeated me, because he said in equally solemn tones, but equally proud of the fact, "I deal only with methyl blues."

I would not present this specialist on methyl blues as a typical scientist. Yet the fact that the story has enough reality to be told is indicative of the fact that scientists sometimes retreat into narrowness of specialization. Note, however, that it is other areas of science about which this chemist was ignorant. He may or may not have had a fair knowledge of music, the arts and other subjects. Quite possibly he did have, for many scientists do, if for no other reason than that most of them have had a substantial amount of work in the liberal arts during their college years. Remember that the scientists as well as the humanists laughed when it was reported that Mr. Cicero was failing in Latin.

There is, of course, better evidence than these anecdotes of the fact that there are some very real differences between the sciences and the liberal arts as those subjects are generally taught. We have, I am convinced, suffered a very substantial loss in allowing education in science to grow away from education in the liberal arts. When experimental science was young it was part of the liberal arts. But as science grew, as it became of greater practical importance, as it became necessary to train a substantial number of professional scientists, a widening gulf developed between what is usually thought of as a scientific education and what is usually thought of as a liberal education.

The difference has, I believe, been more largely the result of a major difference in attitude on the part of teachers of science and teachers of the humanities than the result of differences in the subject matters involved. Of course I am oversimplifying, but let me point out a fairly widespread difference between the two groups of teachers. The teacher of science knows that his subject matter is of very great importance to the welfare of the world and that it is the foundation of the whole vast field of applied science, in agriculture, in medicine, in engineering and in other fields of application. He knows, too, that a considerable number of his students will follow careers in science or applied science.

The teacher of the humanities also knows that his field is important; but there is, nevertheless, a contrasting attitude toward students. The teachers of music, of history, of English or of art expect only a few of their students to follow professional careers in these fields. Their teaching, in consequence, is not as vocationally oriented as is that of the science teacher. Their aim is to produce educated men and women rather than to produce professional musicians, historians, English scholars and artists.

This difference in attitude leads to different kinds of courses and different methods of instruction. The teacher of a humanistic subject attempts to develop those intellectual virtues that we traditionally associate with the liberal arts. First is the notion of breadth. As distinct from training that is primarily concerned with relatively narrow specialization, liberal education is broad in scope. It may include chemistry or history or any other discipline, but it goes beyond the borders of a single field or even a closely related group of fields. Second, liberal education involves the idea of depth. A course of instruction does not merit the label of liberal education unless it goes beyond the superficial to give a depth of understanding that includes the why, as well as the what and the how, of whatever is being studied. In the third place, liberal education gives the student exercise in reasoning and thinking for himself; it teaches him to ask questions, to criticize, to examine his own thinking, and to form conclusions that he can discuss and defend, but that he can also change.

The teaching of science may also exhibit these characteristics, but frequently it does not. The more immediately useful a field is thought to be, the greater is the temptation to teach practical information; and when this fare seems dull, the temptation is to compound the fault by making the teaching even more down to earth and practical. So college catalogues are crowded with such courses as household physics, chemistry for nurses, psychology for salesmen and mathematics for consumers. Rarely—perhaps never— in such courses does the student gain much in breadth or depth, nor through skillfully handled discussion is he led to an understanding of how and why he reached a conclusion.

To the extent that teachers of science are preparing their students for scientific work, they frequently get so obsessed with the importance, the complexity and the vastness of science that they dislike to see a student graduate with any gaps in his knowledge. So the textbooks get thicker and thicker, the print gets smaller and smaller, and the courses fuller and fuller. The teacher is so busy giving information that he has no time to explain and evaluate and criticize, and the student is so busy learning facts that he has no time to question and digest and think critically. This is a serious shortcoming of much teaching of science, for it represents an objective that is impossible of attainment. The ever growing body of scientific knowledge makes it increasingly impossible to teach all of it to any student, and the attempt to do so is a self-defeating effort.

These are serious shortcomings of much teaching of science, but they are not necessary shortcomings. For the truth is that the characteristics of liberal education are also characteristics of science—not of all the people who call themselves scientists and not of all courses in science, but of science itself, of what we call scientific method, and of the thinking of the great scientists. Important scientific advances exhibit the penetrating depth, the critical, inquiring attitude, and the logical reaching of conclusions that we hope to achieve as products of a liberal education: and frequently, too, they exhibit the scope and sweep of imagination that we attribute to liberal education at its best. The teaching of science can be broad. It can provide depth in selected areas. And it offers almost unequalled opportunities in the development of reasoning.

If we are to achieve these characteristics, however, many of our science courses must be changed, and so must the thinking of many of our science teachers. To start with, let us accept the fact that most students who enroll in elementary biology, physics or chemistry, or in freshman mathematics courses, are not going to become scientists; they are sampling a subject in which they think they may be interested, or they are fulfilling a college requirement that says they must have a certain number of hours in science. In a liberal arts college, the students who are never going to become scientists constitute the large majority. What is it that will contribute most to their education? Although I cannot answer this question in detail here, let me suggest the lines along which I think it should be answered. In the liberal arts kind of science course, we must select a limited number of areas of science to be included; there is no need to try to cover everything. Selected topics can be used to teach what science is and how the scientist works, to teach something of the history and philosophy of science, to give an understanding of the nature of science and of its beauty and elegance. There are several models in existence. Conant's "On Understanding Science" and the related general course in science at Harvard is one model. Another is provided by the excellent and up-to-date course in physics being developed by the Physical Science Study Committee at the Massachusetts Institute of Technology.

These courses are not easy to develop or to teach. They require the combined efforts of several scientists, usually representing different fields of science. They require the ruthless omission of some of the things that we want future scientists to learn. But in compensation we can have courses that make a greater contribution to the liberal education of our students and that provide a kind of intellectual fare that will remain with the student long after he would have forgotten a collection of facts and principles. If we want a student to appreciate the main streams of intellectual thought, we must certainly include science in his education. But if we want him to appreciate and understand science, we must avoid overwhelming him with a collection of facts, and we must give him time to understand science in its broad perspective and to incorporate into his own intellectual life some of the traditions, the philosophy, and the manner of thought of science.

So far I have been justifying the inclusion of science in the liberal arts curriculum on the grounds that the education of the individual student would be enriched thereby. This is perhaps justification enough for the effort that is required to develop the type of science course I have briefly sketched. But there is another reason to develop such courses, and one of great urgency.

The scientist's search for fuller understanding of the forces of nature has been so richly rewarded in recent decades and his fuller understanding of those forces has resulted in so many practical applications that there is a grave and growing danger to society in not understanding science. When science was less important than it is now, it was all very well to leave science to the scientist. It was perhaps stupid to say smugly, "I don't know a thing about science," but it was not dangerous, for all that one was relegating to the limbo of his own ignorance was a fascinating but not very practical branch of learning. But now it is dangerous as well as stupid to take such an attitude, for what one is doing is to turn his back on the forces responsible for the control of disease, the extension of life and the explosive increase in the world's population. Such a person is shutting himself off from the fields of knowledge that are responsible for the synthetic fibers in which he is clothed, the gadgets that make his life easier, the processes and devices that speed industrial production, multiply agricultural output, and bring the world of amusement and current events into his living room. He is dissociating himself from the basic sciences that have brought us to the threshold of exploration beyond the borders of earth and air that have confined man's wanderings for the whole of previous history, and that have produced weapons of such destructive power that a single trigger-happy pilot or missile-man could wipe out his city in one blazing flash. He is saying that he knows nothing and cares nothing about the methods of thought that are responsible, more than any other, for changing the world in which he lives and that show, as well as any other, the genius of the human intellect at its best.

Science has become the chief instrument of power in the world, power that can be used constructively or destructively. Decisions about the proper use of that power cannot and should not be made by scientists alone; in a democratic society such decisions are the proper responsibility of educated men and women of all walks of life. The decisions cannot be made wisely unless the men and women who make them understand something about the forces with which they are dealing.

Every man cannot be a scientist any more than everyone can be a historian, a linguist, an artist or an economist. Yet every educated man and woman knows something of history, something of economics, something of the traditions and cultures of other people. He knows these things because they are part of his intellectual heritage, part of his general education, part of his equipment for discharging his responsibilities as an informed and educated citizen. Science has become an instrument of such power in the world that it is essential that the educated citizen also know something of science—not the specialized knowledge of the professional scientist, but the general understanding of principles, of trends, of major developments that in other fields we think of as being proper parts of a liberal education.

Science has now become of necessity what it once was by virtue of interest, an essential part of the liberal arts curriculum.

Notebook Assignment for Class Discussion

1. How does the author's use of anecdote provide interest as well as information for the reader? Try to provide other anecdotes that might effectively illustrate some of the topics in this essay.

2. At precisely what points, and how, does the author make deliberate efforts to avoid antagonizing various elements among his readers?

3. After establishing a basic contrast between teachers of science and teachers of humanities, how does Wolfle project or develop that contrast in detail?

4. Explain how the basic contrast, which he calls an oversimplification of the matter, is related to the other contrasts here, as cause is related to effects.

5. Comment on Wolfle's style, paying particular attention to his choice of words, his techniques of developing a paragraph in relation to the whole theme, his sentence structure, clarity, and general appeal to the reader.

Related Exercises

1. Dael Wolfle argues for the inclusion of science as an important and necessary part of the liberal arts curriculum. Try to provide a functional definition of the liberal arts as he conceives them.

2. What is there about a democracy which might incline its citizens to prefer an "objective" or "practical" education to one less immediately useful? Does Wolfle feel that the study of science in America suffers from this tendency?

3. What distinction does the author make between "depth" as an aim of liberal studies and "specialization" as the term applies to the professional study of science?

4. Ortega y Gasset, the Spanish philosopher, in an essay entitled "The Barbarism of Specialization," calls the specialist "a learned ignoramus," saying that he is not really learned, being "formally ignorant of all that does not enter into his specialty; but neither is he ignorant, because he is 'a scientist' and 'knows' very well his own tiny portion of the universe ... he is a person who is ignorant ... with all the petulance of one who is learned in his own special line." [1] Try to anticipate Wolfle's reaction to this charge.

5. Wolfle himself indicates that it is not possible for one man either to teach or absorb all that there is to know about science in general, or even one field. Perhaps there is no alternative to the "barbarism" of specialization. Use this proposition as the basis of an essay. As a beginning, examine Wolfle's

[1] From *Great Essays in Science,* ed. by Martin Gardner (New York: Pocket Books, Inc., 1957), p. 123.

article for any indication that he sees a solution for the professional scientist.

6. Jacques Barzun, in arguing for the inclusion of the sciences among the humanities, says, "what makes a subject fit for the higher curriculum is ... that it shall enlighten all the corners of the mind and teach its own uses. The humble three R's begin in strict utility and end up in poetry, science, and the search for the Infinite. They can and should therefore be taught indefinitely. Men have known for three thousand years that other matters of knowledge naturally divide themselves into special and general, that both are needful, but that whereas the special *add* to one's powers, the general *enhance the quality* of all of them." [2] Write an essay emphasizing the importance of the distinction Professor Barzun makes at the end of this quotation. What is the particular relevance of this passage in the light of the essay by Dael Wolfle?

7. Both Professor Barzun and Dael Wolfle indicate that the borderlines of science, philosophy, theology, and poetry are sometimes overlapped. The scientist is not merely a dull categorizer obsessed with facts, but is often, on the contrary, possessed of a genuinely imaginative sweep of mind. Try to involve yourself in an investigation into the life of one of the following scientists, so that you may judge for yourself the truth of what Barzun and Wolfle say:

a. Sigmund Freud
b. Carl G. Jung
c. Albert Einstein
d. Louis Pasteur

e. Sir Isaac Newton
f. Johannes Kepler
g. Charles Darwin
h. Teilhard de Chardin

8. Do you agree with Wolfle's proposition that modern man has a moral responsibility to know about science? Why should we not merely take advantage of its benefits, and brave its dangers, since it is clear that few of us can ever know enough about science to alter the course of events through our own efforts? Respond to this question from your own point of view in an essay of whatever length seems appropriate.

9. After reading the complete essay referred to in question 4, write 500 words in answer to Ortega y Gasset using as your major proposition a line from Montaigne: "Men call that barbarism which is not common to them." [3]

2 Jacques Barzun, *Teacher in America* (Anchor A25; New York: Doubleday, 1954), p. 83.
3 Montaigne, *The Essays*, I:30, translated by John Florio.

10. After listening carefully to the various ideas brought out in the class discussion of items 5, 6, and 8 of these exercises, write a thoughtful essay *in imitation of Wolfle's style* on any one of them.
11. Write a biographical sketch of any one of the scientists listed in item 7, in order to emphasize the topic: "He had a genuinely imaginative sweep of mind."
12. Select any statement from Wolfle's essay that you find especially interesting and challenging, then write a well-reasoned defense or denial of it.

THE EDUCATIONAL ISSUE *

1. THE AMERICAN UNIVERSITY TRADITION

The American university has a public purpose, whether in domestic or world affairs, founded upon the traditions of American society and the heritage of other great universities in history. The purpose is the advancement of human welfare through the enlargement and communication of knowledge in a spirit of free inquiry. At its best, the university frees individual minds as it develops competence for the higher pursuits of life. It widens the horizons of the nation's judgment while supplying skills essential to the nation's tasks. As part of a larger community of scholarship, it also co-operates in an effort to enlarge man's understanding of the world and thereby to promote the welfare of mankind.

In pursuit of these ends the university in the United States over the generations has become a distinctively American institution, closely identified with growth and change in American society. Some of its counterparts in Europe embody Cardinal Newman's idea of a university as a "place of teaching universal knowledge." In many countries the university as a center of learning combines the functions of teaching and scholarship for the advancement of knowledge. The American university characteristically adds a third form of service to the society that nurtures it—activities such as professional training, consultation, extension work, and continuing education, serving directly the broader society beyond the campus.

* From *The University and World Affairs* (New York: The Ford Foundation, 1960), pp. 9–14.

These additional activities are particularly characteristic of the philosophy of the land-grant and state colleges and universities. But leading private universities also helped to pioneer the contributions of modern education to industry, agriculture, and government. Some of their departments in these fields are older than similar departments in the land-grant institutions. Their alumni and faculty helped staff the faculties of the younger state universities. They developed their own strong traditions of outside consultation by faculty members.

This amalgam of teaching, scholarship and other forms of service to society, in both public and private universities, has given the American university an outreach, a vitality and a practical concern that have contributed greatly to the agricultural, industrial and scientific revolutions of the past century, in the context of a free society.

Traditionally, American universities have been preoccupied with educational tasks centering on the development of American civilization on this continent. In an era when "the American experiment" was being carried out within a national compass, our educational system was shaped accordingly. The universities were mindful of their Western heritage, of the international scope of science and letters, and of the universal implications of the principles of a free society, but most were nevertheless predominantly domestic in their scope and character. Such was the condition of the past. Today, no university can afford to maintain so obsolescent a posture.

2. THE NEW DIMENSIONS

The profound transformations that are overtaking the world as we have known it demand a far broader conception of the university's role. Problems which an earlier generation conceived as local cannot be managed today except by an approach which takes into account their world scale. An adequate perspective must include the old cultures and new nations outside the familiar landscape of North America and Western Europe. In the words of President Cornelius de Kiewiet of the University of Rochester, "America's consciousness of its world must undergo the same transformation that occurred in Western Europe in the sixteenth and seventeenth centuries as a result of the great voyages of discovery ... To a degree we do not yet recognize, with an unparalleled speed, we are discovering a new world ... Our educational habits and practices have of necessity been deeply influenced by

Western Europe . . . Yet there simply must be room in general education . . . for the opportunity to bring into focus the new world . . ."

In the years since the Second World War, many universities in the United States have responded to changed conditions and to new demands. They have continued to display their traditional resourcefulness and capacity for effective growth. More than ever before, their scholars went abroad and they received scholars from other countries. They welcomed to their campuses in substantial numbers students from all continents. They introduced large numbers of new educational programs on foreign areas and languages and international relations. Some of them also undertook unprecedented programs of service overseas intended to assist educational and public institutions in other countries.

Much, but not all, of this expanded activity in world affairs has been undertaken by universities in cooperation with the United States Government and the larger private foundations. For them, too, particularly for the government, this activity was for the most part a new and pioneering effort. The government has increasingly recognized the essential contribution of universities in programs to aid foreign countries, to promote international understanding and to develop American competence needed for the nation's tasks.

In this new setting, the greater concern of American universities with world affairs is but an appropriate educational response to matters of paramount concern to the individual American, to the nation in its new role, and to men everywhere. To a greater degree than ever before, world affairs are American affairs, and American affairs are those of the world. These are matters not alone for the specialists. They are a dimension or whole new set of dimensions of the problems with which all American students and all American universities and colleges are or should be vitally concerned. In these new dimensions lie not only public responsibilities and duties but exciting opportunities for the individual to be enriched as an educated man and citizen.

3. ALTERNATIVE CHOICES

American universities are once again in an historic situation where they are challenged to show their capacity for growth and innovation. They cannot educate for tomorrow with yesterday's means. Lord Lindsay, a noted English educator, has said that universities "can be their beautiful selves only if they are something else as well, and remember that just as they are served by, so must they serve the community. They have to serve the community in their own characteristic way. They are not to do everything the community may ask them to do if that would destroy their higher powers of giving the community what no other institution can give it; but supply its high needs they must . . . It would be expected therefore that as society changes, and as its needs change, the universities will change also. That is indeed what has happened . . ."

The modern American university is a large and diversified institution. Given the richness and depth found in its faculties, it is small wonder that our society may fail to consider, in the varied demands it makes upon the university, that the university's resources are not inexhaustible. Faced with new tasks of formidable scope and magnitude in world as in domestic affairs, challenged by the educational opportunities and the stakes in human welfare, American universities are forced to make historic choices.

It is not surprising that conflicting views have been pressed upon the universities. On the one hand are those who, feeling keenly a grave sense of national urgency, would have the government tell the universities how they must serve the new and pressing needs of the nation in world affairs. On the other hand are those who, cherishing the university's ancient tradition and spirit of scholarship, contend that the university's main contributions to world affairs should come mainly as a byproduct of its scholarship.

If pressed to an extreme, these two points of view are incompatible and untenable. Each gives color to the fears expressed by those holding the other. Too much stress on the university's responsibility to meet pressing national needs, and to answer policy questions put to it by government, would risk overwhelming its distinctive tasks of scholarship and teaching with demands for topical research and emergency projects of service abroad. The university might well lose its autonomy. On the other hand, too much stress on the freedom of scholars to pursue their own interests would leave serious gaps in American competence of the kinds that only the universities can supply. To fulfill their public purpose, universities should take responsibility for contributing to these kinds of competence, and for defining and exploring the intellectual and educational issues that confront society.

What is needed is a relationship of mutual confidence and accommodation. Universities would participate in the process of government, through contributing to the determination and implementation of educational policies and programs in world affairs. Government would participate in the process of education, through contributing to the strength of the educational institutions upon which our own society and other societies depend for their growth and freedom.

Government would provide the means to do the educational tasks, at home and abroad, that the universities cannot undertake unaided. The universities would rise to the educational responsibilities which world affairs place on them and on their sister institutions in other nations.

4. Horizons of a Free Society

In the conditions of modern life the university is under a duty arising, as Whitehead has said, from our potential control over the course of events. "Where attainable knowledge could have changed the issue, ignorance has the guilt of vice." The judgments of the nation, from which its actions proceed, are shaped by the scholar's knowledge as by the statesman's decision. In a time of relative tranquility education in a free society can be a handmaiden to tradition. In a time of turbulent change, the universities in free societies must press their scholarship responsibly into new fields of knowledge and fresh perspectives of policy, if they are to enlarge the horizons of judgment and anticipate the needs of a changing world.

If the thrust and direction of a free society's purpose are hammered out by the political process of government, the process of education helps to shape its horizons and consensus. Emerson said, "It is the eye which makes the horizon." In free societies, the university is like the eye. With its help, nations' understanding of one another can be enlarged, thereby widening the horizons of a free international society.

Our age has been characterized as being the first in history to recognize the practical possibility of having all peoples throughout the world share in the fruits of civilization. At such a time, education, including international education, has been catapulted into the position of a major determinant in the dynamics of social change. Human welfare everywhere depends upon the conjunction of technological power and democratic freedoms. Without the first, men are slaves to nature; without the second, slaves to one another. Neither is possible without education. Neither can be advanced without the organized scholarship that is characteristic of great universities.

In those societies that approach the totalitarian model, the dependence of the nation upon education has led the government to conclude that it must tightly control the institutions of education. University and school are made the agents of the state, learning the servant of politics. Where everything is service to the state, one is taught so that he may serve the state better.

In those societies that deliberately cultivate freedom, the dependence of the nation upon education has led to the conclusion that the government must protect and strengthen the independence of the university so that it may perform its unique role. Knowledge is power and is good in itself, but even more important to the well-being of society is the freedom to seek and communicate knowledge. The public purpose thereby served is to secure the happiness and security of the nation through what Justice Black has described as "its ability to explore, to change, to grow, and ceaselessly to adapt itself to new knowledge born of inquiry free from any kind of governmental control over the mind and spirit of man."

Notebook Assignment for Class Discussion

1. The first paragraph of this essay attempts a definition. Of what? Restate the definition in your own words.
2. The second paragraph is organized around a comparison. Explain the comparison, and show how it begins the effective development of the body of the essay.
3. The last two paragraphs in section 1 are related causally. Explain.
4. Select other paragraphs from the essay to illustrate how a variety of methods of topical development may produce a unified impression.
5. In section 2, what functions and purposes of a university are embodied in the objectives of different schools in Europe and America?
6. In section 3, two points of view are suggested as being pressed upon the universities. Explain how they are incompatible and untenable "if pressed to an extreme." Be sure to take cognizance of the qualification of "extreme" in your consideration.
7. Why should the American university traditionally extend its services to the "society which nurtures it"?
8. What is one great difference between an American university of the present, and one of the past?

9. Does this paper present an effective argument from authority? What constitutes a proper authority upon which one may safely base an argument?

10. Is argument from authority particularly effective under *most* circumstances? What are its obvious limitations? What are its strengths?

11. Could a paper such as this one have been successful had it avoided any recourse to authority?

Related Exercises

1. In what particular ways, and in response to what particular pressures, have many American universities responded to changed conditions in and new demands of the "outside" world? Can you think of other ways in which their response might or should be extended?

2. In section 3 there is an epigram: "[American universities] cannot educate for tomorrow with yesterday's means." See if you can locate several other epigrammatic phrases in this essay. Select one of them, and write an essay of about 500 words using it as your topic and supporting it with examples, comparisons, and so on.

3. De Kiewiet refers to certain voyages of discovery in the sixteenth and seventeenth centuries that affected Western Europe greatly. Look into the bibliography of Renaissance exploration and write a report on one or two of the primary sources you found most interesting.

THE HUMANITIES *

By Douglas Bush

No one would ever speak of "the plight of the natural sciences," of "the plight of the social sciences," but it is always proper to speak of "the plight of the humanities," and in the hushed, melancholy tone of one present at a perpetual death bed. For some-

* From *The Educational Record*, Vol. XXXVI (January 6, 1955), 64–69. Originally written as an address to the annual meeting of the American Council on Education, October 14, 1954.

thing like twenty-five hundred years the humanities have been in more or less of a plight, not because they are themselves weak, but because their war is not merely with ignorance but with original sin; and as civilization has advanced, the means of stultifying the head and heart have multiplied in variety and power. As a sample of cultural leadership, or of a common attitude, I should like to read a declaration of faith delivered some years ago by the chairman of the department of humanities in a well-known technological institution. We will call him Professor X. This is most of the report, from the *New York Times,* of his speech to a convention of engineers:

> Professor X . . . asserted last night that it would be "morally wrong" for him to advise the reading of the literary classics in this fast-moving age of television, radio and movies. . . .
> One should read for the purpose of doing something with what one reads, he asserted: not of polishing one's mind like a jewel, but of improving the world around.
> Take up a book because it will tell you something of the world . . . ; read what you want to read, not what you think you should read. "This is the frame of mind that makes reading worthwhile and often deeply rewarding.
> "For example, it would be morally wrong of me to urge you to take up a classic like 'David Copperfield' and to settle yourselves in easy chairs for winter evenings' reading. If you tried 'David Copperfield' you would grow restive; you would think of all the other things you might be doing more consistent with your daily environment—looking at television, listening to the radio, going to the movies.
> "Moreover, you would wonder why you should spend so much time laboriously reading 'David Copperfield' when you could see the book as a film, should it return some time to the neighborhood movie.". . .
> "The single prescription for adult reading," he added, "should be to read something different, something that will change your mind. Herein lies compensation for the loss of the purely reflective life."

Engineers are not, to be sure, in common repute the most cultivated branch of mankind, but did even they deserve such counsel, and from such a source? The humanities, as I said, have always had to contend with the crude urges of the natural man, with his resistance to higher values than his own, but the speech I just quoted from reminds us of the many new ways there are of escaping from active thought and feeling into a state of lazy collapse, of passive surrender to unthinking action or external sensation. Many people would endorse our oracle's view that one should not read to polish one's mind like a jewel but for the sake of improving the world around. The humanistic tradition has always stood for improvement of the world, but it has always insisted that a man must make himself worthy of such an enterprise; one of our perennial troubles is that improvement of the world is undertaken by so many unpolished minds. Then our touching faith in machinery is illustrated by the quaint assumption that a movie is the same thing as a great book. And that *Ersatz* doctrine extends down through television to the comics, which have now joined the march of mind by reducing literary classics to capsule form. That sort of thing, by the way, was done, and done much better, a dozen centuries ago, and has been commonly labeled a symptom of the Dark Ages. But this is only a reminder; there is no need of enlarging upon such powerful elements in our popular civilization. The opposition to such elements comes from the humanities.

Negative terms, however, are not enough. The "humanities," in the original meaning of this and kindred words, embraced chiefly history, philosophy, and literature. These were the studies worthy of a free man, that ministered to *homo sapiens,* man the intellectual and moral being, and not to *homo faber,* the professional and technical expert. And these, with divinity, completed the central circle of human knowledge and understanding. Divinity went overboard long ago; history, which once was literature, is now a social science; and philosophy, though still grouped with the humanities, has become a branch of mathematics. Thus in common usage the humanities mean literature and the fine arts. That is an unfortunate narrowing but we may take things as we find them and concentrate on literature, which is central and representative.

One plain fact nowadays is that the study of literature, which in itself is comprehensive and complex, has had to take over the responsibilities that used to be discharged by philosophy and divinity. Most young people now get their only or their chief understanding of man's moral and religious quest through literature. Anyone who has been teaching literature for twenty-five or thirty years, as I have, can testify to the marked change there has been in the spiritual climate during that time. (A rigorously scientific colleague of mine, in psychology, will not permit the use of the word "spiritual," but I use it anyhow.) I am speaking mainly of the higher order of college students, but it would be hard to imagine even the better students of twenty-five or thirty years ago reading Dante and George Herbert and Milton and Hopkins and Eliot with the real sympathy that many now show. For the more intelligent and sensitive young people of today, and there are very many of that kind, are a serious and a conservative lot. They not only live in our unlovely world, they have no personal experience of any other. They are aware of hollowness and confusion all around them, and, what is still more real, of hollowness and confusion in themselves. They feel adrift in a cockboat on an uncharted sea, and they want a sense of direction, of order and integration. And in literature they find, as countless people have found before them, that their problems are not new, that earlier generations have been lost also. Most of the young people I see find in literature, literature of the remote past as well as of the present, what they cannot find in textbooks of psychology and sociology, the vision of human experience achieved by a great spirit and bodied forth by a great artist.

I apologize for elaborating what may be called clichés, but those familiar lists of courses in catalogues make one forget that the frigid label "English 10" or "French 20" may represent an illumination and a rebirth for John or Betty Doe. Not that courses are the only or even the main road to enriched experience and sensitivity, but they are one road; and a teacher can help as a guide or catalyst. Josiah Royce is said to have complained that a philosopher was expected to spiritualize the community. The modern philosopher is expected only to semanticize the community; the other function, as I said, falls upon the teacher of literature. I do not of course mean inspirational gush. I mean that teachers, conducting a critical discussion of a piece of great literature, necessarily deal not only with the artistic use of words and materials but with the moral and spiritual experience that are its subject matter. That is why, as President Pusey has said, the humanities must be the cornerstone of a liberal education. Naturally teachers will have their methods under constant scrutiny, but their material, the world's great literature, can hardly be improved; all it needs is a chance to work upon responsive minds and characters.

While I cannot guess the temper of this gathering, and while all the administrators present may, for all I know, regard the humanities as a pearl of great price, that is not their general reputation. Administrators are commonly said to prize the solid and tangible virtues of the natural and social sciences and to look upon the humanities as a nice luxury for the carriage trade. How far that general reputation is true or false I wouldn't know, but, just in casc it has a modicum of truth, I have been insisting that the humanities are not a luxury; they are the most practical of necessities if men and women are to become fully human. The humanities commonly suffer in esteem because they do not lend themselves to statistical reports of achievement. You cannot demonstrate with graphs and charts that John or Betty Doe, through reacting to a piece of literature, became a person of richer moral and imaginative insight, of finer wisdom and discrimination and stability. For the experience of literature is an individual experience, and nothing that is really important can be measured.

When we look at the American educational scene, the diversity of standards is so great that generalizations about this or that part of it may be violently contradictory. At any rate educational history of the past fifty years seems to furnish a pretty good forecast of the bad effects of the deluge to be expected in the next fifteen. In school, college, and university, the results of the huge increase in the student body suggest that the principle of education for all, however fine in theory, in practice leads ultimately to education for none. An editorial in the *New York Times* of September 13, 1954, takes the usual line of defense. The principle of education for all, it says, forces us "to accept the principle, also, that the function of education is primarily social and political rather than purely intellectual." "It cannot be denied," the *Times* proceeds, "that this means a down-grading of the learning process. We are adjusting to an 'average' that must be spread so widely that it comes down automatically. Education is no longer the intellectual privilege of the gifted few. It is held to be the democratic right of all." The *Times* does go a little beyond this orthodox assent to express uneasiness over the sacrifice, in elementary and secondary schools, of quality to quantity.

To mention one of many results, there has been an appalling growth of illiteracy at all levels, even in the graduate school. (Somehow stenographers are still literate, even if their college-bred employers are not.) At every orgy of Commencements one wonders how many of the hordes of new bachelors of arts can speak and write their own language with elementary decency, or read it with understanding. After all, the polished mind is suspect, whether in a student, a professor, or a Presidential candidate. And illiteracy, and contentment with illiteracy, are only symptoms of general shoddiness.

Obviously one main cause of this state of things has been the sheer pressure of numbers, along with a deplorable shrinkage in the number of qualified teachers. But the situation would not be so bad as it has been if the downward pressure of numbers had not been powerfully strengthened by misguided doctrine and practice. The training of teachers and the control of school curricula have been in the hands of colleges of education and their products, and these have operated on principles extracted from John Dewey's philosophy of barbarism. (If that phrase seems unduly harsh, I may say that I have in mind Dewey's hostility to what he regarded as leisure-class studies; his anti-historical attitude, his desire—intensified in his followers—to immerse students in the contemporary and immediate; and his denial of a hierarchy of studies, his doctrine that all kinds of experience are equally or uniquely valuable; and it would not be irrelevant to add his notoriously inept writing.) The lowest common denominator has been, not an evil, but an ideal. The substantial disciplines have been so denuded of content that multitudes of students, often taught by uneducated teachers, have been illiterate, uninformed, and thoroughly immature. There is no use in priding ourselves on the operation of the democratic principle if education loses much of its meaning in the process. When we think, for instance, of education for citizenship, which has been the cry of modern pedagogy, we may think also of the volume and violence of popular support given to the anti-intellectual demagoguery of the last few years. Mass education tends to reflect mass civilization, instead of opposing it. Even if education were everywhere working on the highest level, it would still face tremendous odds.

The great problem has been, and will be, first, the preservation of minority culture against the many and insidious pressures of mass civilization, and, secondly, the extension of that minority culture through wider and wider areas. The rising flood of students is very much like the barbarian invasions of the early Middle Ages, and then the process of education took a thousand years. We hope for something less overwhelming, and for a less protracted cure, but the principle is the same; Graeco-Roman-Christian culture not only survived but triumphed, and with enrichment. If we think of our problem in the light of that one, we shall not be disheartened but recognize both as phases of man's perennial growing pains.

Throughout history it has been a more or less small minority that has created and preserved what culture and enlightenment we have, and, if adverse forces are always growing, that minority is always growing too. In spite of the low standards that have commonly prevailed in public education during the last fifty years, I think the top layer of college students now are proportionately more numerous than they were thirty years ago and are more generally serious and critical. There is a growing nucleus of fine minds, and teachers are concerned with the enlargement of that all-important group. At the same time, without retreating from that position, one wonders what it is in our educational process or in our culture at large that often causes a liberal education to end on Commencement Day.

I have no novel and dramatic remedy for the evils that have shown themselves so clearly already and will become more formidable still. But I might mention a few things of varying importance which do not seem utopian. Of course I represent no one but myself, and I cannot even say, like a member of the House of Lords, that I enjoy the full confidence of my constituents.

In the first place, I see no reason why the flood of students should be allowed to pour into college, why automatic graduation from school should qualify anyone for admission. We ought to recognize, and make people in general recognize, that a desire for economic or social advantage, or for merely four years of idle diversion, is not enough. Under such pressure as is coming, surely the state universities have the strength to set up bars and select their student body, instead of admitting all who choose to walk in the front door and then, with much trouble and expense, trying to get rid of some through the back door. Doubtless such procedure would require a campaign of enlightenment and persuasion, but legislators always have an alert ear for the cry of economy, and the public must be convinced that higher education, or what passes for that, is neither a birthright nor a badge of respectability, and that useful and happy lives can be led without a college degree. As things are, we have an army of misfits, who lower educational standards and increase expense, and no branch of a university staff has grown more rapidly of late years than the psychiatric squad.

Secondly, many people have grounds for the belief that the multiplying junior colleges can and will drain off a large number of the young who for various reasons are unfitted for a really strenuous four-year course. Junior colleges, however, should not be recreational centers for the subnormal.

Thirdly, I think the need for formal education beyond high school would be much lessened, and the quality of both secondary and higher education obviously improved, if the colleges and universities, getting the public behind them, made a concerted and effectual demand that the schools do their proper work and do it better than a great many schools have been doing it. Quite commonly, a distressing proportion of a college course now consists of high school work. For example, we have grown so accustomed to a battalion of instructors teaching elementary composition to freshmen that we take it as a normal part of college education, whereas it is a monstrosity. Imagine a European university teaching the rudiments of expression! If high school graduates are illiterate, they have no business in college. For a long time and for a variety of reasons we have had slackness all along the line; somehow, some time, strictness and discipline have got to begin.

Increased enrollments have almost inevitably led to increased reliance upon large lecture courses. There are administrators who assume that there is no limit to the effectiveness of a lecture course except the size of the auditorium, and there are also teachers who see positive virtues in lectures and can themselves display them. Perhaps because I never remember anything I hear in a lecture, I do not share that faith. I favor classes small enough to allow discussion, and that is expensive. But there are possible economies that would be highly desirable in themselves. We do not need to maintain the naive doctrine that there has to be a course in anything in which anyone ever has been or might be interested. Many catalogues list courses that can only be called fantastic, and I don't think I am guilty of partisan prejudice if I say that these are rarely found among the humanities. If we had fewer and less specialized courses, and if we did not have our armies of composition teachers, a considerable number of man-hours would be released for smaller classes.

One thing that has suffered grievously and conspicuously in this last generation has been the study of foreign languages. The usual reason given is again the pressure of numbers, the numbers who are not going beyond high school, but again a positive reason has been open or quiet hostility. Languages have been pretty well crowded out of the school curriculum, and of course there has been a corresponding decline in college study. Nothing has been commoner in recent decades than the applicant for admission to a graduate school who has had little or no acquaintance with any foreign language except possibly a year or two of Spanish. Serious study of a foreign language means work, and a first principle of modern pedagogy has been the elimination of work. Thus, during the years in which we have all become conscious of one small world, and in which this country has become the leader of that world, educational theory and practice have retreated into cultural parochialism. There is no need to argue how necessary for the ordinary citizen is some knowledge of a foreign language and a foreign people. In the last few years a good many parents have been aroused, and the Modern Language Association has been putting on a vigorous campaign, so that progress has been made;

but there is a long way to go. It is encouraging that in some cities successful experiments have been made in the teaching of languages in elementary schools, where, for good psychological reasons, they ought to begin. I wish there were something encouraging to be said about the ancient languages, but we are concerned with actualities.

Finally, since I touched on the large number of young people who are in college and shouldn't be, I might mention those who are not and should be, and who may be lost in the oncoming flood. Educators and others are more conscious than they once were of our failure to recognize and foster promising students who cannot afford college, and increasing efforts are being made in that direction, but we are still very far behind England, where bright students are picked out at the age of 10 or 11 and brought along on scholarships. If we spent on exceptional students a fraction of the time and money we have spent on nursing lame ducks, there would be a considerable change in the quality of education.

One last word on a different matter. Like everything else, the Ph.D. has been cheapened by quantitative pressure, and it might be earnestly wished that it were not a union card for the teaching profession. There are plenty of young men and women who would be good teachers without such a degree, and the degree itself ought to mean something more than it does. Along with that may go another earnest wish, that both administrators and members of departments would abandon the principle of "publish or perish." Socrates would never have had a chance at an assistant professorship.

Notebook Assignment for Class Discussion

1. Point out the important divisions in this essay, and attempt to locate as precisely as possible the logical and formal lines of demarcation. Does the essay seem to you to be organized according to the classical rhetorical divisions of introduction, body, and conclusion? Or does Profesor Bush range rather freely back and forth, blurring his boundaries?
2. What use does he make of allusion in this essay? Does he base his argument primarily on reference to authority? If not, then what *is* the most general basis of his argument, i.e., what argumentative form does he employ?
3. Look up a biographical reference to Professor Bush. Does it seem to you that he might function adequately as his *own* au-

thority or are there no circumstances under which one's own authority need not be corroborated?

4. This is an essay in support of a general and abstract assertion, and yet it is formally neither general nor abstract. How does Professor Bush manage to accomplish so particular and concrete an argument? What are some of the devices he employs? List a number of the figures of speech he uses, and note in what context they appear.

5. Is his tone formal or informal? Loosely conversational? Folksy? Characterize his tone, and support your conclusion by reference to the quality of his diction. In what manner does the language of this essay differ from what you might expect of Professor Bush if you were to discuss this question with him while riding on a bus? Locate some particular constructions which would be inappropriate to a casual conversation.

6. Does Professor Bush *appear* in his essay? By this we mean to ask if he allows his personality to come into evidence. Are you able to characterize the author on the basis of his essay? What approach might be useful in pursuing such a character analysis? Is Professor Bush a man of wit? Is he stuffy and pedantic? Dogmatic? Passionate in his conviction? Does he feel superior to his audience? Supply evidence from the essay itself in an attempt to answer these questions.

Related Exercises

1. Comment on Professor Bush's quotation of President Pusey's remark that the humanities must be the cornerstone of a liberal education.

2. How does the author explain the loss of "divinity" which was once part of the humanities?

3. Why does Professor Bush feel that literature must now encompass all the other studies once considered to constitute the humanities?

4. Do you think that Bush's point about the small minority upholding culture against its enemies is true? Write an argumentative essay in which you take issue with the notion that culture is upheld by the many. Make use of Professor Bush's own point that the *more* people who are educated, the *less* any one of them is educated.

5. Write an essay in which you discuss the meanings of the following terms: "cultured," "culture," and "cultivated." Does Professor Bush use the term "culture" as synonymous

with national tradition or national characteristics, or does he loosely associate it with intellectualism?

6. Is Professor Bush being a snob, or undemocratic, when he favors the drastic raising of academic standards, thus eliminating the possibility of a great many young men and women entering college? What are the conditions to which he refers both directly and indirectly, which seem to provide that there is no alternative to his proposal?

7. Alexis de Tocqueville remarks that "Equality begets in man the desire of judging of everything for himself: it gives him, in all things, a taste for the tangible and the real, a contempt for tradition and for forms." [1] In an essay, evaluate this comment on the basis of your own experience and observation.

8. Write an essay in which you show the above remark by de Tocqueville to be relevant to and in agreement with one of Professor Bush's main points.

9. De Tocqueville also concludes that "Aristocratic nations are naturally too apt to narrow the scope of human perfectibility; democratic nations, to expand it beyond reason." [2] Upon examining this statement out of its proper context, does it seem to you to be in contradiction of the first quotation given in item 7? Write an essay in which you attempt to evaluate the first quotation in the light of the second.

10. Should reading be primarily for utilitarian purposes? How does Professor Bush feel about Professor X's comments on this question? How do *you* feel about them? How has your opinion been formulated?

11. How do you expect that Professor Bush would react to Bacon's conclusions about the values to be derived from reading and studies?

12. Using materials from Professor Bush's essay, formulate (in an essay of about 1000 words) an argument against the judgment that "Aristocratic nations are naturally too apt to narrow the scope . . ."

[1] Alexis de Tocqueville, *Democracy in America*, ed. by R. D. Heffner (New York: Mentor, 1956), p. 163.
[2] *Ibid.*, p. 158.

REVERIES *

By William Butler Yeats

Because I had found it hard to attend to anything less interesting than my thoughts, I was difficult to teach. Several of my uncles and aunts had tried to teach me to read, and because they could not, and because I was much older than children who read easily, had come to think, as I have learnt since, that I had not all my faculties. But for an accident they might have thought it for a long time. My father was staying in the house and never went to church, and that gave me the courage to refuse to set out one Sunday morning. I was often devout, my eyes filling with tears at the thought of God and for my own sins, but I hated church. My grandmother tried to teach me to put my toes first to the ground because I suppose I stumped on my heels and that took my pleasure out of the way there. Later on when I had learnt to read I took pleasure in the words of the hymn, but never understood why the choir took three times as long as I did in getting to the end; and the part of the service I liked, the sermon and passages of the Apocalypse and Ecclesiastes, were no compensation for all the repetitions and for the fatigue of so much standing. My father said if I would not go to church he would teach me to read. I think now that he wanted to make me go for my grandmother's sake and could think of no other way. He was an angry and impatient teacher and flung the reading-book at my head, and next Sunday I decided to go to church. My father had, however, got interested in teaching me, and only shifted the lesson to a weekday till he had conquered my wandering mind. My first clear image of him was fixed on my imagination, I believe, but a few days before the first lesson. He had just arrived from London and was walking up and down the nursery floor. He had a very black beard and hair, and one cheek bulged out with a fig that was there to draw the pain out of a bad tooth. One of the nurses (a nurse had come from London with my brothers and sisters) said to the other that a live frog, she had heard, was best of all. Then I was sent to a dame school kept by an old woman who stood us in rows and had a long stick like

* Reprinted with permission of the publisher from *The Autobiography of William Butler Yeats* by William Butler Yeats. Copyright 1916, 1936 by The Macmillan Company. Renewed 1944 by Bertha Georgie Yeats.

a billiard cue to get at the back rows. My father was still at Sligo when I came back from my first lesson and asked me what I had been taught. I said I had been taught to sing, and he said, "Sing then" and I sang

> Little drops of water,
> Little grains of sand,
> Make the mighty ocean,
> And the pleasant land

high up in my head. So my father wrote to the old woman that I was never to be taught to sing again, and afterwards other teachers were told the same thing. Presently my eldest sister came on a long visit and she and I went to a little two-storied house in a poor street where an old gentlewoman taught us spelling and grammar. . . .

The head-master (at Hammersmith) was a clergyman, a good-humored, easy-going man, as temperate, one had no doubt in his religious life as in all else, and if he ever lost sleep on our account, it was from a very proper anxiety as to our gentility. I was in disgrace once because I went to school in some brilliant blue homespun serge my mother had bought in Devonshire, and I was told I must never wear it again. He had tried several times, though he must have known it was hopeless, to persuade our parents to put us into Eton clothes, and on certain days we were compelled to wear gloves. After my first year, we were forbidden to play marbles because it was a form of gambling and was played by nasty little boys, and a few months later told not to cross our legs in class. It was a school for the sons of professional men who had failed or were at the outset of their career, and the boys held an indignation meeting when they discovered that a new boy was an apothecary's son (I think at first I was his only friend), and we all pretended that our parents were richer than they were. I told a little boy who had often seen my mother knitting or mending my clothes that she only mended or knitted because she liked it, though I knew it was necessity.

It was like, I suppose, most schools of its type, an obscene, bullying place, where a big boy would hit a small boy in the wind to see him double up, and where certain boys, too young for any emotion of sex, would sing the dirty songs of the street, but I daresay it suited me better than a better school. I have heard the head-master say, "How has so-and-so done in his Greek?" and the class-master reply, "Very badly, but he is doing well in his cricket," and the head-master reply to that, "Oh, leave him alone." I was unfitted for school work, and though I would often work well for weeks together, I had to give the whole evening to one lesson if I was to know it. My thoughts were a great excitement, but when I tried to do anything with them, it was like trying to pack a balloon into a shed in a high wind. I was always near the bottom of my class, and always making excuses that but added to my timidity; but no master was rough with me. I was known to collect moths and butterflies and to get into no worse mischief than hiding now and again an old tail-less white rat in my coat-pocket or my desk. . . .

My father read out poetry, for the first time, when I was eight or nine years old. Between Sligo and Rosses Point, there is a tongue of land covered with coarse grass that runs out into the sea or the mud according to the state of the tide. It is the place where dead horses are buried. Sitting there, my father read me *The Lays of Ancient Rome*. It was the first poetry that had moved me after the stable-boy's *Orange Rhymes*. Later on he read me *Ivanhoe* and *The Lay of the Last Minstrel,* and they are still vivid in the memory. I re-read *Ivanhoe* the other day, but it has all vanished except Gurth, the swineherd, at the outset and Friar Tuck and his venison pasty, the two scenes that laid hold of me in childhood. *The Lay of the Last Minstrel* gave me a wish to turn magician that competed for years with the dream of being killed upon the seashore.

When I first went to school, he tried to keep me from reading boys' papers, because a paper, by its very nature, as he explained to me, had to be made for the average boy or man and so could not but thwart one's growth. He took away my paper and I had not courage to say that I was but reading and delighting in a prose retelling of the *Iliad*. But after a few months, my father said he had been too anxious and became less urgent about my lessons and less violent if I had learnt them badly, and he ceased to notice what I read. From that on I shared the excitement which ran through all my fellows on Wednesday afternoons when the boys' papers were published, and I read endless stories I have forgotten as I have forgotten *Grimm's Fairy Tales* that I read at Sligo, and all of Hans Andersen except the "Ugly Duckling" which my mother had read to me and to my sisters. I remember vaguely that I liked Hans Andersen better than Grimm because he was less homely, but even he never gave me the knights and dragons and beautiful ladies that I longed for. I have remembered nothing that I read, but only those things that I heard or saw. When I was ten or twelve my father took me to see Irving play *Hamlet,* and did not understand why I preferred Irving to Ellen Terry, who was, I can see now, the idol of himself and his friends.

I could not think of her, as I could of Irving's *Hamlet*, as but myself, and I was not old enough to care for feminine charm and beauty. For many years Hamlet was an image of heroic self-possession for the poses of youth and childhood to copy, a combatant of the battle within myself. My father had read me the story of the little boy murdered by the Jews in Chaucer and the tale of Sir Topaz, explaining the hard words, and though both excited me, I had liked Sir Topaz best and been disappointed that it left off in the middle. As I grew older, he would tell me plots of Balzac's novels, using incident or character as an illustration for some profound criticism of life. Now that I have read all the *Comédie Humaine*, certain pages have an unnatural emphasis, straining and overbalancing the outline, and I remember how in some suburban street, he told me of Lucien de Rubempré's duel after the betrayal of his master, and how the wounded Lucien hearing some one say that he was not dead had muttered, "So much the worse."

I was now fifteen; and as he did not want to leave his painting my father told me to go to Harcourt Street and put myself to school. I found a bleak eighteenth-century house, a small playing-field full of mud and pebbles, fenced by an iron railing, and opposite a long hoarding and a squalid, ornamental railway station. Here, as I soon found, nobody gave a thought to decorum. We worked in a din of voices. We began the morning with prayers, but when the class began the head-master, if he was in the humor, would laugh at Church and Clergy. "Let them say what they like," he would say, "but the earth does go round the sun." On the other hand there was no bullying and I had not thought it possible that boys could work so hard. Cricket and football, the collection of moths and butterflies, though not forbidden, were discouraged. They were for idle boys. I did not know, as I used to, the mass of my school-fellows; for we had little life in common outside the class-rooms. I had begun to think of my school work as an interruption of my natural history studies, but even had I never opened a book not in the school course, I could not have learned a quarter of my night's work. I had always done Euclid easily, making the problems out while the other boys were blundering at the blackboard, and it had often carried me from the bottom to the top of my class; but these boys had the same natural gift and instead of being in the fourth or fifth book were in the modern books at the end of the primer; and in place of a dozen lines of Virgil with a dictionary, I was expected to learn with the help of a crib a hundred and fifty lines. The other boys were able to learn the translation off, and to remember what words of Latin and English corresponded with one another, but I, who it may be had tried to find out what happened in the parts we had not read, made ridiculous mistakes; and what could I, who never worked when I was not interested, do with a history lesson that was but a column of seventy dates? I was worst of all at literature, for we read Shakespeare for his grammar exclusively.

One day I had a lucky thought. A great many lessons were run through in the last hour of the day, things we had learnt or should have learnt by heart overnight, and not having known one of them for weeks, I cut off that hour without anybody's leave. I asked the mathematical master to give me a sum to work and nobody said a word. My father often interfered, and always with disaster, to teach me my Latin lesson. "But I have also my geography," I would say. "Geography," he would reply, "should never be taught. It is not a training for the mind. You will pick up all that you need, in your general reading." And if it was a history lesson, he would say just the same, and "Euclid," he would say, "is too easy. It comes naturally to the literary imagination. The old idea, that it is a good training for the mind, was long ago refuted." I would know my Latin lesson so that it was a nine days' wonder, and for weeks after would be told it was scandalous to be so clever and so idle. No one knew that I had learnt it in the terror that alone could check my wandering mind. I must have told on him at some time or other for I remember the head-master saying, "I am going to give you an imposition because I cannot get at your father to give him one." Sometimes we had essays to write; and though I never got a prize, for the essays were judged by handwriting and spelling, I caused a measure of scandal. I would be called up before some master and asked if I really believed such things, and that would make me angry for I had written what I had believed all my life, what my father had told me, or a memory of the conversation of his friends. I was asked to write an essay on "Men may rise on stepping-stones of their dead selves to higher things." My father read the subject to my mother who had no interest in such matters. "That is the way," he said, "boys are made insincere and false to themselves. Ideals make the blood thin, and take the human nature out of people." He walked up and down the room in eloquent indignation, and told me not to write on such a subject at all, but upon Shakespeare's lines, "To thine own self be true, and it must follow as the night the day thou canst not then be false to any man." At another time, he would denounce the idea of duty; "Imagine," he would say, "how the right sort of woman would despise a dutiful husband"; and he would tell us how much my mother would scorn such a thing. Maybe there were people among whom such ideas were natural, but they were the people with whom one does not dine. All he said was, I now believe right, but he should have taken me away from school. He would have taught me nothing but Greek and Latin, and I would now be a properly educated man, and would not have to look in useless longings at books that have been, through the poor mechanism of translation, the builders of my soul, nor face authority with the timidity born of excuse and evasion. Evasion and excuse were in the event as wise as the house-building instinct of the beaver.

My father's influence upon my thoughts was at its height. We went to Dublin by train every morning, breakfasting in his studio. He had taken a large room with a beautiful eighteenth-century mantelpiece in a York Street tenement house, and at breakfast he read passages from the poets, and always from the play or poem at its most passionate moment. He never read me a passage because of its speculative interest, and indeed did not care at all for poetry where there was generalization or abstraction, however impassioned. He would read out the first speeches of the *Prometheus Unbound*, but never the ecstatic lyricism of that famous fourth act; and another day the scene where Coriolanus comes to the house of Aufidius and tells the impudent servants that his home is under the canopy. I have seen *Coriolanus* played a number of times since then, and read it more than once, but that scene is more vivid than the rest, and it is my father's voice that I hear and not Irving's or Benson's. He did not care even for a fine lyric passage unless he felt some actual man behind its elaboration of beauty, and he was always looking for the lineaments of some desirable, familiar life. When the spirits sang their scorn of Manfred, and Manfred answered, "O sweet and melancholy voices," I was told that they could not, even in anger, put off their spiritual sweetness. He thought Keats a greater poet than Shelley, because less abstract, but did not read him, caring little, I think, for any of that most beautiful poetry which has come in modern times from the influence of painting. All must be an idealization of speech, and at some moment of passionate action or somnambulistic reverie. I remember his saying that all contemplative men were in a conspiracy to overrate their state of life, and that all writers were of them, excepting the great poets. Looking backwards, it seems to me that I saw his mind in fragments, which had always hidden connections I only now begin to discover. He disliked the Victorian poetry of ideas, and Wordsworth but for certain passages or whole poems. He said one morning over his breakfast that he had discovered in the shape of the head of a Wordsworthian scholar, an old and greatly respected clergyman whose portrait he was painting, all the animal instincts of a prizefighter. He despised the formal beauty of Raphael, that calm which is not an ordered passion but an hypocrisy, and attacked Raphael's life for its love of pleasure and its self-indulgence. In literature he was always pre-Raphaelite, and carried into literature principles that, while the Academy was still unbroken, had made the first attack upon academic form.

He no longer read me anything for its story, and all our discussion was of style.

Once when staying with my uncle at Rosses Point where he went for certain months of the year, I called upon a cousin towards midnight and asked him to get his yacht out, for I wanted to find what sea birds began to stir before dawn. He was indignant and refused; but his elder sister had overheard me and came to the head of the stairs and forbade him to stir, and that so vexed him that he shouted to the kitchen for his sea boots. He came with me in great gloom for he had people's respect, he declared, and nobody so far said that he was mad as they said I was, and we got a very sleepy boy out of his bed in the village and set up sail. We put a trawl out, as he thought it would restore his character if he caught some fish, but the wind fell and we were becalmed. I rolled myself in the mainsail and went to sleep for I could sleep anywhere in those days. I was awakened towards dawn to see my cousin and the boy turning out their pockets for money and had to rummage in my own pockets. A boat was rowing in from Roughley with fish and they wanted to buy some and pretend they had caught it, but all our pockets were empty. I had wanted the birds' cries for the poem that became fifteen years afterwards "The Shadowy Waters," and it had been full of observation had I been able to write it when I first planned it. I had found again the windy light that moved me when a child. I persuaded myself that I had a passion for the dawn, and this passion, though mainly histrionic like a child's play, an ambitious game, had moments of sincerity. Years afterwards when I had finished *The Wanderings of Oisin,* dissatisfied with its yellow and its dull green, with all that overcharged color inherited from the romantic movement, I deliberately reshaped my style, deliberately sought out an impression as of cold light and tumbling clouds. I cast off traditional metaphors and loosened my rhythm, and recognizing that all the criticism of life known to me was alien and English, became as emotional as possible but with an emotion which I described to myself as cold. It is a

natural conviction for a painter's son to believe that there may
be a landscape that is symbolic of some spiritual condition and
awakens a hunger such as cats feel for valerian.

We had no scholarship, no critical knowledge of the history
of painting, and no settled standards. A student would show his
fellows some French illustrated paper that we might all admire
now some statue by Rodin or Dalou and now some declamatory
Parisian monument, and if I did not happen to have discussed
the matter with my father I would admire with no more discrimination than the rest. That pretentious monument to Gambetta
made a great stir among us. No influence touched us but that of
France, where one or two of the older students had been already
and all hoped to go. Of England I alone knew anything. Our
ablest student had learnt Italian to read Dante, but had never
heard of Tennyson or Browning, and it was I who carried into
the school some knowledge of English poetry, especially of Browning who had begun to move me by his air of wisdom. I do not
believe that I worked well, for I wrote a great deal and that tired
me, and the work I was set to bored me. When alone and un-
influenced, I longed for pattern, for pre-Raphaelitism, for an
art allied to poetry, and returned again and again to our National Gallery to gaze at Turner's "Golden Bough." Yet I was
too timid, had I known how, to break away from my father's
style and the style of those about me. I was always hoping that
my father would return to the style of his youth, and make pictures out of certain designs now lost, that one could still find in
his portfolios. There was one of an old hunchback in vague medieval dress, going through some underground place where there
are beds with people in the beds: a girl half rising from one has
seized his hand and is kissing it. I have forgotten its story, but
the strange old man and the intensity in the girl's figure are vivid
as in my childhood.[1] There is some passage, I believe in the
Bible, about a man who saved a city and went away and was
never heard of again, and here he was in another design, an old
ragged beggar in the market-place laughing at his own statue.
But my father would say: "I must paint what I see in front of
me. Of course I shall really paint something different because my
nature will come in unconsciously." Sometimes I would try to
argue with him, for I had come to think the philosophy of his
fellow-artists and himself a misunderstanding created by Victorian
science, and science I had grown to hate with a monkish hate;

[1] This little picture has been found and hangs in my house. 1926.

but no good came of it, and in a moment I would unsay what I had said and pretend that I did not really believe it. My father was painting many fine portraits, Dublin leaders of the bar, college notabilities, or chance comers whom he would paint for nothing if he liked their heads; but all displeased me. In my heart I thought that only beautiful things should be painted, and that only ancient things and the stuff of dreams were beautiful. And I almost quarreled with my father when he made a large watercolor, one of his finest pictures and now lost, of a consumptive beggar girl. And a picture at the Hibernian Academy of cocottes with yellow faces sitting before a café by some follower of Manet's made me miserable for days, but I was happy when partly through my father's planning some Whistlers were brought over and exhibited, and did not agree when my father said: "Imagine making your old mother an arrangement in grey!" I did not care for mere reality and believed that creation should be deliberate, and yet I could only imitate my father. I could not compose anything but a portrait and even to-day I constantly see people, as a portrait painter, posing them in the mind's eye before such and such a background. Meanwhile I was still very much of a child, sometimes drawing with an elaborate frenzy, simulating what I believed of inspiration, and sometimes walking with an artificial stride in memory of Hamlet and stopping at shop windows to look at my tie gathered into a loose sailor-knot and to regret that it could not be always blown out by the wind like Byron's tie in the picture. I had as many ideas as I have now, only I did not know how to choose from among them those that belonged to my life.

From our first arrival in Dublin, my father had brought me from time to time to see Edward Dowden. He and my father had been college friends and were trying, perhaps, to take up again their old friendship. Sometimes we were asked to breakfast, and afterwards my father would tell me to read out one of my poems. Dowden was wise in his encouragement, never overpraising and never unsympathetic, and he would sometimes lend me books. The orderly, prosperous house where all was in good taste, where poetry was rightly valued, made Dublin tolerable for a while, and for perhaps a couple of years he was an image of romance. My father would not share my enthusiasm and soon, I noticed, grew impatient at these meetings. He would sometimes say that he had wanted Dowden when they were young to give himself to creative art, and would talk of what he considered Dowden's failure in life. I know now that he was finding in his friend what

he himself had been saved from by the conversation of the pre-
Raphaelites. "He will not trust his nature," he would say, or
"He is too much influenced by his inferiors," or he would praise
"Renunciants," one of Dowden's poems, to prove what Dowden
might have written. I was not influenced for I had imagined a
past worthy of that dark, romantic face. I took literally his verses,
touched here and there with Swinburnian rhetoric, and believed
that he had loved, unhappily and illicitly; and when through the
practice of my art I discovered that certain images about the
love of woman were the properties of a school, I but changed my
fancy and thought of him as very wise.

I was constantly troubled about philosophic questions. I would
say to my fellow-students at the Art School, "Poetry and sculpture exist to keep our passions alive"; and somebody would say,
"We would be much better without our passions." Or I would
have a week's anxiety over the problem: do the arts make us
happier, or more sensitive and therefore more unhappy. And
I would say to Hughes or Sheppard, "If I cannot be certain they
make us happier I will never write again." If I spoke of these
things to Dowden he would put the question away with good-
humored irony; he seemed to condescend to everybody and everything and was now my sage. I was about to learn that if a man
is to write lyric poetry he must be shaped by nature and art to
some one out of half a dozen traditional poses, and be lover or
saint, sage or sensualist, or mere mocker of all life; and that none
but that stroke of luckless luck can open before him the accumulated expression of the world. And this thought before it could
be knowledge was an instinct. . . .

Some one at the Young Ireland Society gave me a newspaper
that I might read some article or letter. I began idly reading
verses describing the shore of Ireland as seen by a returning, dying
emigrant. My eyes filled with tears and yet I knew the verses were
badly written—vague, abstract words such as one finds in a newspaper. I looked at the end and saw the name of some political
exile who had died but a few days after his return to Ireland.
They had moved me because they contained the actual thoughts
of a man at a passionate moment of life, and when I met my
father I was full of the discovery. We should write out our own
thoughts in as nearly as possible the language we thought them
in, as though in a letter to an intimate friend. We should not
disguise them in any way; for our lives give them force as the
lives of people in plays give force to their words. Personal utterance, which had almost ceased in English literature, could be as
fine an escape from rhetoric and abstraction as drama itself. But

my father would hear of nothing but drama; personal utterance was only egotism. I knew it was not, but as yet did not know how to explain the difference. I tried from that on to write out of my emotions exactly as they came to me in life, not changing them to make them more beautiful. "If I can be sincere and make my language natural, and without becoming discursive, like a novelist, and so indiscreet and prosaic," I said to myself, "I shall, if good luck or bad luck make my life interesting, be a great poet; for it will be no longer a matter of literature at all." Yet when I re-read those early poems which gave me so much trouble, I find little but romantic convention, unconscious drama. It is so many years before one can believe enough in what one feels even to know what the feeling is.

Notebook Assignment for Class Discussion

1. Richard Ellmann, one of Yeats's biographers, quotes George Russell (AE) on *Reveries over Childhood and Youth:* "His memories of his childhood are the most vacant things man ever wrote, pure externalities, well written in a dead kind of way, but quite dull except for the odd flashes. The boy in the book might have become a grocer as well as a poet. Nobody could be astonished if this had been issued as a novel, part one, to find in part two the hero had for some reason given up thinking of literature and become a merchant." [1] In the light of the selections you have read from *Reveries,* does this criticism seem to you to be in any degree justified? (With what particular points would you agree or disagree? What seem to you to be the "odd flashes" in the sections you have read? What do you suppose Russell means by saying that *Reveries* is "well written in a dead kind of way"? How can that be? What is the special sense in which he uses the phrase "well written"? Do you think *Reveries* dull?)
2. Edmund Wilson, in *Axel's Castle,* says of Yeats's prose that "in its beginnings, when he is most under the influence of the pre-Raphaelites and Pater, (it) is a little self-consciously archaic—it has a Renaissance elaborateness and pomposity; and it is a little too close to the language of poetry—the meaning is often clotted by metaphor." [2] In the light of this remark

---

[1] Richard Ellmann, *Yeats: The Man and the Masks* (New York: Dutton, 1958), p. 21. Copyright 1948, The Macmillan Co.

[2] Edmund Wilson, *Axel's Castle* (New York: Scribner's, 1959), p. 44.

by Wilson and of your reading of *Reveries,* discuss the relevance of the following passage from *English Prose Style,* by Herbert Read: "... there is a problem which arises when epithets, justified in themselves by the nicety of judgment or subtlety of analysis, threaten merely by their frequency and aggression to obscure the clarity of substantives, the speed of narrative, the *flow* of speech." [3] Read feels that Pater's prose is sometimes enervated. Would you say that this is true of *Reveries,* which is, after all, the autobiography of a young man?

3. Does Yeats, in this example of his prose style, seem to be following his own dictum that "we should write out our own thoughts in as nearly as possible the language we thought them in, as though in a letter to a friend"? Does *Reveries* read like "a letter to a friend"? Does the loose and sometimes rambling sentence structure seem to you to be symptomatic of a loose and rambling mind?

4. Wilson says that Yeats's prose is essentially modern, especially by virtue of "a certain modern terseness and of a characteristically modern trick ... of revealing by unexpected juxtapositions relations of which one had not been aware—"He had been almost poor ... and now, his head full of Flaubert, found himself with ten thousand a year." [4] Can you find other examples of this kind of thing in the passages here reprinted from *Reveries?* What is the special effectiveness of such a device? What might be its limitations, if it is not used with caution and taste?

5. Wilson also points out that another favorite device of Yeats's is to effect "startling transitions from the particular to the general and back again." [5] An example from *Reveries:* "It is a natural conviction for a painter's son to believe that there may be a landscape that is symbolic of some spiritual condition and awakens a hunger such as cats feel for valerian." Find some other examples of this device. What is its special effectiveness, and what are its limitations?

Related Exercises

1. Compare the tones generally taken, when speaking of their fathers, by Yeats, and by Stephen Dedalus in Joyce's *A Por-*

---

[3] Herbert Read, *English Prose Style* (Boston: Beacon Press, 1957), p. 20.
[4] Wilson, *op. cit.,* p. 46.
[5] Wilson, *ibid.,* p. 46.

trait of the Artist as a Young Man. Pay especial attention to the last part of Chapter II of *A Portrait.*[1]

2. What is it about the motto on which the young Yeats is asked to write that so outrages his father? How do you account for John Yeats's saying that "Ideals make the blood thin, and take the human nature out of people"? What does this remark have in common with the one he makes earlier to the effect that Euclid is too easy, since "it comes naturally to the literary imagination"?

3. Stephen Dedalus wants "to meet in the real world the unsubstantial image which his soul so constantly beheld. He did not know where to seek it or how, but a premonition which led him on told him that this image would, without any overt act of his, encounter him." [2] What reaction would John Yeats likely have to Stephen's premonition? Would his reaction differ much from that of the young W. B. Yeats, as presented to us in *Reveries?*

4. William F. Lynch, a literary critic, holds that "the literary process is a highly cognitive passage through the finite and definite realities of man and the world." [3] Might Yeats's father, and Yeats himself, be said to entertain somewhat the same notion themselves? Can you answer this question on the basis of any *concrete* evidence in *Reveries?* How far may we trust John Yeats's assertive outbursts? Can we consider *tone* as a kind of concrete evidence, in answering this last question?

5. Is there the development of an attitude toward or away from Lynch's position on the part of either father or son?

6. What is the *essential* question being asked in items 2, 3, and 4? What relevance to it has Yeats's concluding sentence? Is this sentence merely an offhand remark, or might it be seen as implying an intellectual *position* taken finally by Yeats? Or does the tone and substance of the remark seem to contradict the possibility of Yeats's having arrived at a fixed conviction?

7. Is Yeats's father an effective teacher? How does he compare with Simon Dedalus? With Stephen's Aunt Dante? With Uncle Charles or Mr. Casey? Yeats's autobiography and Joyce's novel are only two instances of many in which young men record, more or less according to the mode of fiction, the progress of their education to the world in its relations to themselves.

1 James Joyce, *A Portrait of the Artist as a Young Man* (New York: Compass Books, 1956), pp. 86–101.

2 *Ibid.,* p. 65.

3 William F. Lynch, *Christ and Apollo* (New York: Mentor, 1963), p. *xiii.*

Some other famous novels are: *Sinister Street,* by Compton Mackenzie; *This Side of Paradise,* by F. Scott Fitzgerald; *Of Human Bondage,* by Somerset Maugham; *The Green Years,* by A. J. Cronin; *The Invisible Man,* by Ralph Ellison. In reading these books you will discover they are all in some way concerned with the processes of education, and with the circumstances of revelation. These are, in fact, the basic concerns of most imaginative literature. How would you, then, particularly distinguish between *Reveries,* and, say, *This Side of Paradise* and *The Invisible Man?* On the basis of the distinction between fiction and non-fiction? What is *that,* by the way? On the basis of the distinction between the authors' emphases: tonal, thematic, formally technical? Read some of these novels, and then try to discover and justify means of comparison and contrast between them and *Reveries.*

Part Four

THE WORLD OF WORDS

Or

Language, Literature, and Criticism

PARTY OF ONE *

By Eric F. Goldman

When I was a student at Johns Hopkins University during the 1930's, I had an unusual relationship with one of my professors, an elderly gentleman named Jacob H. Hollander. The professor had decided, on evidence I never quite understood, that I was a relative of his, and that did it. He would welcome me into his office and, pushing aside the clutter on his desk, would sit musing about the past and the present. I loved the sessions. The professor had a shrewd eye for men and affairs and he had been around— as a prominent economist of his day and as something of a trouble-shooter for Republican Presidents of the United States.

One afternoon he told me a particularly interesting story. He said that just once—I remember how he emphasized "just once" —he had been "one of those ghost-writer fellows" and the occasion was when he drafted the speech in which Warren Harding announced that he was going to take America back to "normalcy." The professor had written the word in its customary form, "normality." Harding ran his sloppy eye over it and it became "normalcy." "Poor Warren Harding," Professor Hollander concluded. "What he did with that word showed a lot that was wrong with the man."

It certainly did, and what Presidents have done with words has expressed a great deal about them, bad and good. A long time ago Georges de Buffon told us, *Le style c'est l'homme,* and the dictum is especially true of the particular human beings who have occupied the White House. The office of President of the United States, with its intensification of all personal qualities, its persistent goad to a man to communicate himself, its sweep of publicity for every utterance, has made Presidential prose an intriguing touchstone of Presidential performance.

This is true even though every Chief Executive from George Washington on has resorted to ghost-writers. After all, no President has had all his written statements prepared for him, and obviously a good many of his oral remarks must be his own. Only now and then have Chief Executives taken over word for word a draft for any important speech. More often they have added and subtracted, shifted emphases, and—especially in recent times

* From *Holiday,* Vol. 31, No. 4 (April, 1962), 11–14. Reprinted by special permission from Holiday, copyright 1962 by The Curtis Publishing Co.

—they have ad-libbed. The way they have delivered the speeches, the context in which they have put the letters, press conferences, and so on, have had a good deal to do with the impression the words have left. And then there is the fundamental fact: there are ghosts and there are ghosts, writing wraiths of all degrees of literary sensitivity, intelligence and human understanding. A President says a good deal about himself by the man he chooses to say things for him.

Go in any place on the long roll of American Chief Executives and the White House words call up the memory of the administrations. Take George Washington, an aging general playing father to a squalling infant nation, and the words are firm, paternal, magisterial. Or Thomas Jefferson, a remarkable combination of the gentleman scholar and the hardheaded politician, using a prose that is a striking amalgam of the elegant and the wily. Or piddling, indecisive James Buchanan, mincing along from flaccidity to inanity. Or Abraham Lincoln, that great President and great human being, incapable of writing even a hasty letter that is not touched with wisdom and compassion. Or the nothing Rutherford B. Hayes, talking and writing a nothing prose. Or the rambunctious Teddy Roosevelt, lecturing the corporations or any other deviator from The Good and The True in sentences that shrill like a runaway calliope.

Naturally the White House words have had the most distinctive flavor when expressed by men of extremes in either ability or personality. Of all thirty-four Presidents, surely none has been more an individual and few have been abler than the presbyter-turned-politician, Woodrow Wilson. First in domestic affairs, then on the world scene, he drove ahead in his God-lashed way, rarely failing to intimate that his program had a decided connection with divine revelation. (The cynical old French Prime Minister Georges Clemenceau put it: "God gave us only Ten Commandments. Wilson brings us Fourteen Points.") The Wilson prose, most of which he hammered out himself on a battered typewriter brought from his Princeton days, had a constant summons to redemption. On the occasion of his famous first inaugural in 1913 the crowd hushed, as if in church, when the new President reached his climax, speaking of lifting "our life as a Nation to the light that shines from the hearthfire of every man's conscience. . . . The feelings with which we face this new age of right and opportunity sweep across our heartstrings like some air out of God's own presence, where justice and mercy are reconciled and the judge and the brother are one."

And then there was Professor Hollander's poor Warren Harding, everybody's nominee for the worst President and the emptiest personality who ever maundered through a term in the White House. There is something magnificently appropriate about the Harding prose. It is bad all right. It is downright atrocious, so atrocious that it moved all kinds of men to their varieties of eloquence. H. L. Mencken took out his heftiest cudgel to declare Harding the master of "the worst English that I have ever encountered. It reminds me of a string of wet sponges; it reminds me of tattered washing on the line; it reminds of stale beansoup, of college yells, of dogs barking idiotically through endless nights."

When Harding died in San Francisco, supposedly as the result of a huge dinner of Japanese crabs, the memory of his tortured prose stirred the poet e. e. cummings to the only song to solecism in American literature:

the first president to be loved by his
bitterest enemies" is dead

the only man woman or child who wrote
a simple declarative sentence with seven grammatical
errors "is dead"
beautiful Warren Gamaliel Harding
"is" dead
he's
"dead"
if he wouldn't have eaten them Yapanese Craps

somebody might hardly never not have been
unsorry, perhaps [1]

The dismal Harding words reflect not only his general ineptitude but many of his specific traits. The man had a profound aversion to work (it was so much more pleasant, he explained, to just "bloviate"), and this was never clearer than in his speechmaking. Once, as he was talking along, he looked up in bafflement and told the audience: "Well, I never saw this before. I didn't write this speech and I don't believe what I just read." The things he did believe were all the danker banalities of American life and his phrases say just that, slithering down to us in a heavy goo of platitudinizing: "I must utter my belief in the divine inspiration of the Founding Fathers"; "Agriculture, the foundation of

our existence"; and of course, "Womanhood, the glory of America." Once in a while Harding would try to think out a speech,
or would get someone he considered a thinker to think for him,
and then the result was awesome. He would rise to the speaker's
stand, flap his wings, and soar into total incomprehensibility. . . .

Notebook Assignment for Class Discussion

1. To reconstruct the author's reasoning: This is the way the
    man wrote, and that is also what the man was. Add to his
    example a number of others, and one comes to the conclusion
    that "what Presidents (*sic*) have done with words has expressed
    a great deal about them, bad and good." His reasoning is
    inductive. Take a complete speech by Harding, Wilson, Cool-
    idge, Kennedy, Johnson, or another President of the United
    States, or one by Hitler, Mussolini, Stalin, and so on, and
    try to see the man himself in his speech. Be prepared to discuss
    and defend your analysis before the class.
2. One could object to Goldman's proposition by noting that
    most presidents do not write their own speeches. How, there-
    fore, could one hope to discover the man in the speech? What
    is Goldman's answer?
3. How can you judge a person who isn't a writer? Or someone
    who exists only in a novel or a play? Could you judge Shakes-
    peare as a person by studying him as a playwright? Do you
    think it more likely to find Shakespeare the person in the
    plays or the sonnets? Why?
4. Does a writer always use the same style, or does he adapt his
    style to the occasion and to the readers for whom he writes?
    If he does change his style, how can you or anyone possibly
    analyze him as a person? Think it out carefully so as to arrive
    at "conclusion instead of confusion."
5. What effect does Goldman hope to achieve by use of quota-
    tion marks in paragraph 2? How strong an impression does
    the word *sloppy* make in characterizing President Harding?
    What single word do you think best characterizes President
    Johnson? Kennedy? Eisenhower? Franklin D. Roosevelt?
6. Does "shrill like a runaway calliope" give you a clear idea
    of the sentence style of Teddy Roosevelt? Would "shrill" alone
    do the job? H. L. Mencken described Harding's prose in terms
    of "wet sponges," "tattered washing on a line," "stale bean-
    soup," "dogs barking," and the like. These are spectacular
    comparisons, likely to provide a chuckle for most readers, but

do they actually say anything critical except that Harding's prose isn't very good? Read three or four of Mencken's essays and then try to decide what kind of man *he* was.

ENGLISH IN 2061: A FORECAST *

By Mario Pei

If a modern-day Rip Van Winkle went to sleep and didn't wake up for 100 years, how well would he be able to understand an American of 2061?

It does not take a linguist to know that language changes. Educated laymen know that the language they speak was once Elizabethan English (a little difficult to follow today, especially in the pronunciation of Shakespearean actors), and before that the half-incomprehensible language of Chaucer, and before that the Anglo-Saxon that no one today can read, let alone speak, unless he has had a graduate course in it.

Yet many people fail to realize that language is also going to change in the future. The English of 1,000 years from now (granted that English is still a living tongue by the year 2961 A.D.) will probably be as different from the language of *Saturday Review* as the latter is from the spoken tongue of the Venerable Bede.

The big difference between the past and the future is that we know, or can reconstruct with some degree of accuracy, what has happened in the past, while we have no way of knowing—or so it sometimes seems—what course the future will take.

But is the last proposition altogether true? We know that governments, business organizations, even private individuals make projections into the future, based on present tendencies and trends. These forecasts do not, of course, have the same value as recorded history, since they may be thrown completely out of kilter by the unexpected or accidental. Nevertheless, barring the unexpected, it is quite possible for our government experts to say: "We anticipate that the population of the United States, growing at an average yearly rate of about 2,000,000, will reach the 200 million mark, more or less, by 1970." In like manner, a business firm may say: "Our profits have grown about $1,000,-

* From *Saturday Review*, Vol. 44 (January 14, 1961), 12–14.

000 a year over the past ten years. Barring a major depression, we estimate that by 1965 they will be about $5,000,000 higher than they are today." When you estimate your income tax for a year that is just beginning, as the Treasury Department somewhat unreasonably asks you to do, you go through this process of reasoning: "My income over the past five years has been about $10,000. As of this moment, I cannot anticipate any sizable change. Therefore, I am putting down the same figures for 1961 that appear in my 1960 declaration."

It is quite possible to do the same thing with language, always with the understanding that some outside factor may come along to knock the calculation into a cocked hat. One such factor in the development of the English language, for instance, was the Danish invasions of England that antedated the Norman Conquest. One effect of them is that today we say, "Take the knife and cut the steak" instead of "Nim the metter and sned the oxflesh," which is the logical development of the Anglo-Saxon of King Alfred without Scandinavian interference. Another factor was 1066 itself, by reason of which we say, "The army pays out large sums of money" instead of "The here tells out great tales of gild."

A projection of the English language into the future on the basis of present-day indications is something like the predictions of an IBM machine on election night when only the first 2,000,-000 votes are in. It can be fascinating, though many things may come along to upset our predictions. Nevertheless, despite the hazards, the questions can legitimately be asked: What can we prophesy at this moment about the English of 100 years hence? How will our descendants of 2061 A.D. speak and write?

By looking at the changes that have taken place in the past, and at the way the language is changing now, I think we can make some reasonable predictions.

Let us first of all recall that language consists of sounds (or phonemes, which are sounds that are distinctively significant to the speakers); of grammatical forms (like *love, loves, loved,* or *see, sees, saw, seen,* or *child, children*); of word arrangements, like the characteristic "John loves Mary," which indicates that John, coming before the verb, is the doer of the action, and Mary, coming after the verb, the recipient; and of individual words, laden with their distinctive meanings. Language change may and does occur in any of these four divisions: phonology, morphology, syntax, and vocabulary.

But the changes do not occur at the same rate or to the same extent in all four. In times of trouble and stress, when communities become isolated, or when an alien tongue comes in direct contact with the native language of an area, changes in sound and grammatical structure seem favored; when conditions are stable, sounds and grammar change moderately, but vocabulary grows quickly.

For this reason, the big sound-and-grammar changes in the English tongue took place primarily in the days of the Anglo-Saxons, the Danes, and the Normans, then again through the troublous times that preceded the stabilization of English society down to the days of Queen Elizabeth I. There were numerous vocabulary changes in those days, too, but the most dramatic vocabulary accretions have come since the dawn of the scientific era.

Our projection for the next hundred years, assuming there will be no major cataclysm (such as an atomic war that plunges us back into medieval conditions), therefore involves a very limited amount of sound changes, a very moderate amount of grammatical transformation, and extensive vocabulary changes, mainly along the lines of accretion.

In the sounds of our language, the omens point to a process of stabilization and standardization, with local dialectal variants tending to be replaced by a uniform style of pronunciation. Indeed, it is likely that even the cleavage between British and American English will tend to be effaced. There are many reasons for this. Large, centralized government units, easy communication between speakers of different areas, widespread trade and travel, and widespread education all favor unification and standardization. This was proved in the days of the Roman Empire, when a strong central government, good roads, unrestricted trade among the provinces and a fairly good educational system (at least for that period) led to the use of a standardized Latin throughout the western part of the Empire and a standardized Greek in the eastern regions. Today we have not only the American Union and British Commonwealth, with their highly centralized features; we also have highways, railroads, swift ships, and jet planes, bringing the speakers of the various English-speaking areas into fast and easy contact with one another; we have public schooling for all social classes, with illiteracy practically eliminated; above all, we have the ubiquitous printing presses, radio, TV, and spoken films, bringing a standard King's English and a standard General American to all readers, viewers, and listeners. The local dialects will probably never quite disappear; but they will be driven more and more underground, particularly with the new generations of speakers. Only those mispronunciations that have spread throughout the country, like *marjerine* for *margarine* and *Febuary* for *February,* will come out on top. As for the cleavage between British and American English, the tendency has been toward reunification since the First World War. Spoken British films were almost incomprehensible to American audiences when they first appeared, while American plays presented in England often were accompanied by printed glossaries in the programs (or should we spell it programmes?). Today, a British accent barely causes us to strain our ears, while the British have grown quite accustomed to the Midwestern voice. Actually, we are slowly and insensibly modifying some of our forms of pronunciation to conform with the British, and they are doing the same with regard to ours.

The pronunciation of the year 2061 will probably not differ very widely from the General American of our best radio and TV announcers today. There will be an elimination of marked vulgarisms and localisms, which will be looked upon as old-fashioned (Cicero, writing in the first century B.C., used such expressions as *rustici dicebant,* "the rustics used to say," and *rustico sermone significabat,* "in rustic speech used to mean"; his use of the imperfect past in this connection is a dead giveaway that these local forms of speech had gone out of fashion by his day).

In the matter of grammatical forms and arrangements, our language today is far too standardized to permit of much change. It is possible that a few stray levelings may take place (*oxes* and *deers* for *oxen* and *deer,* for instance; or *I heared him* in the place of *I heard him*). But despite the widespread rantings of the apostles of "usage" (however that much-belabored word may be defined), it is not likely that substandard forms will make much headway. The primary reason for this is that such substandard forms are normally in the nature of localisms. Such rank atrocities as "Them dogs are us'ns," "I seen the both'n of 'em," and "I'll call you up, without I can't" are too localized to survive the impact of schools and TV. The only grammatical changes that have a real chance of becoming part of the standard language are those that have nation-wide currency, such as "It's me," "Who did you see?" and "ain't." Judgment may be suspended for some ignorant uses in sentences like "I should of done it" and "I seen him."

One historical factor that may blast our calculations to smithereens, however, is the possible growth of a pidginized form of English for international use, and its influence upon the native speakers. If this happens, it is possible that we may get such analogical standardizations as *childs, mouses, gooses, foots* (so that all nouns may form their plurals the same way without exception), and *I did see, I did go* for *I saw, I went* (so that the basically simple English verb may be further simplified by having a universally regular past).

The really big changes will come in vocabulary. It will be the multiplicity of new words that will really make the English of 2061 a startlingly different language from that of today.

Here are several factors at work. As man's activities become increasingly complex and multiform, new words have to be coined, combined, borrowed, or otherwise created to take care of such activities. All we have to do is to go over the list of vocabulary accretions since 1900 to realize what is in store for the language in the next hundred years. Think of *futurama, micromatic, jitterbug, genocide, corny, snafu, gremlin, smog, zoot suit*—all words that would have been meaningless to Dickens or Edgar Allan Poe. Add to these the words of specialized fields of activity (*megavolt* and *psychosomatic, electronic and morphophonemic, isotope* and *positron, kodak* and *latex,* and consider also the words that pre-existed the turn of the century, but which are now used in a variety of new acceptances (*atomic fission, integration, featherbed, release,* etc.). It is easy to see that the language of the future will be only partly comprehensible to the speaker of present-day English, even if the basic sounds, forms, sentence structures, and connecting words remain largely unchanged.

The future tongue will sound, from the point of view of present-day speakers, somewhat like double-talk or, better yet, those nonsense sentences that linguists often construct when they want to get away from meaning and concentrate on form—sentences in which the sounds, the grammatical forms, the word order, and the connecting words are all standard English, but in which the vocabulary is imaginary: something like "Foring mests larry no granning sunners in the rones." Yet this vocabulary will of course be easily understood by speakers who have grown up with it.

How many of our present, current, everyday words will be altogether obsolete, or even archaic, by 2061? A good many, no doubt. All we have to do is to look closely at the vocabulary of 100 years ago and notice how many words were in current use that we can still recognize, but would not think of using ourselves, words like *drawing-room* and *trencher, conscript* and *sparking light, eximious* and *mansuetude,* or, to go a little further, *vocular* and *viduous, gossipaceous* and *dandiacal.* If we care to go a few centuries further back, we can find *deruncinate* and *suppeditate, whirlicote* and *begeck, yuke* and *pringle, toom* and *mizzle, jark-*

men and *priggers, assation* and *clancular, dignotion* and *exolu-
tion.*

Since the language of radio and TV, in the English-speaking
countries, is largely a matter of commercial promotion, a special
word may be in order for the future ramifications of the Madison
Avenue tongue.

In the field of sounds, the promotional language tends to avoid,
save for occasional picturesque effect, localisms and special accents.
It is a powerful, perhaps the most powerful, factor in the standardization we anticipate. It is only occasionally that we get a
deliberate distortion of pronunciation, like *halo* for *hello*. This
laudable conservatism does not, by the way, extend to spelling.
Forms like *nite, kool, Duz,* and *chaise lounge* are there to plague
us, and to confuse the foreigner and even the native learner of
English.

In grammar and syntax, the language of promotion tends toward those vulgarisms that are nation-wide ("like a cigarette
should" is a good example), but not toward local or extreme
forms.

In the advertising vocabulary, two distinct and contradictory
trends are noticeable. One is the tendency to stress the short,
pithy, monosyllabic elements of vocabulary, as when an earlier
"If headaches persist or recur frequently" was replaced by "If
headaches hang on too long or keep coming back." But side by
side with this, we have droves of commercialized scientific and
pseudoscientific long words, like *hydramatic* and *irradiated, ho-
mogenized* and *naugahyde, chlorophyl* and *duridium,* even *olds-
mobility* and *beaverette.*

One grammatical peculiarity of the language of commercialism
is the avoidance of the personal pronouns *it* and *they,* replaced
with endless and annoying repetitions of the name of the sponsor
or product. This may eventually lead an as yet unborn chronicler
of the English language to say in the year 2061: "Personal pronouns, still quite alive in British English, are obsolescent in
American. This is particularly true of the third person neuter
pronoun *it,* which only the older generation of American English
speakers occasionally use today. Instead, Americans prefer to repeat the noun over and over again, often with ludicrous effects."

But all in all, despite the multiplying of human activity, the
advances of science and its nomenclature, the ravages of commercialism, it seems to this writer that we are not justified in
expecting too radical a change in the language, particularly in
its sound-and-grammar structure, provided the present trends
continue.

Remember, though, that this picture may be violently changed by the unexpected and unforeseeable. A historical upset, a political upheaval, a military disaster may place the English language in swift motion once more, so that a century or two could bring on the same differences that appear between the Anglo-Saxon of Aelfric and the Middle English of Chaucer.

Notebook Assignment for Class Discussion

1. Note how the author tries to reach the popular, or average, reader by his allusion to Rip Van Winkle, and by the use of such colloquial expressions as "out of kilter," and "knock . . . into a cocked hat." Does his style change as he gets deeper into his subject? Does it ever become too difficult for the average reader? What is an average reader?
2. The process of making "projections into the future, based on present tendencies and trends," is known as extrapolation. Try to explain why extrapolation is a deductive method of reasoning. Why are public polls which attempt to discover current trends important politically and economically? Wherein does the danger lie that they may be wrong?
3. Why does the author add the parenthetical statement in paragraph 3?
4. Explain whether the comparisons used as examples in paragraph 5 are effective as argument. What other use of comparison and example does Professor Pei make?
5. Look up the meaning of phonology, morphology, syntax, and any other words with which you are unfamiliar.
6. What are several ways an alien tongue may come into direct contact with the native language of an area? Find a dozen words that have thus come into the English language in the past twenty-five years.
7. What does Pei mean by an atomic war plunging us "back into medieval conditions"?
8. Does he make ample allowance for his theory possibly going awry? What are the possibilities he mentions?

Creative Exercises

1. Try an opinion poll of your own, selecting some current campus controversy. Query carefully chosen, representative students to answer your questions. The results will constitute

an inductive conclusion which you may then proceed to apply deductively.

2. Do some research into the *modus operandi* of the principal TV rating systems, then conduct your own poll and compare their results with yours. Do not limit the people to be interviewed to campus residents, but go into the shops and homes in the neighborhood.

3. Listen to a recording of Shakespearean dialogue spoken according to the pronunciation of English in Shakespeare's day (Columbia), and to Chaucerian and Anglo-Saxon English (Linguaphone) to substantiate what Pei says in paragraph 2.

4. Analyze the students in your school who come from many parts of the country, or the world. Do stabilization and standardization tend to make them more, or less, alike? In what ways? In what forms do stabilization and standardization appear in academic or social affairs?

5. Jot down several examples of localisms you hear spoken by people who are "off guard," on "candid camera," so to speak. Would you be in favor of including these localisms in a comprehensive dictionary simply because they are in actual usage, whether by a few or many? What is the policy of the editors of *Webster's Third International Dictionary* regarding actual usage?

6. Listen to several TV special events, sports, panel programs, and the like, and decide what level and quality of language the typical master of ceremonies, or average announcer, uses.

7. Write a report of the result of your findings for any one of the projects listed here.

OF STUDIES

By Francis Bacon

Studies serve for delight, for ornament, and for ability. Their chief use for delight is in privateness and retiring; for ornament, is in discourse; and for ability, is in the judgment and disposition of business. For expert men can execute, and perhaps judge of particulars, one by one; but the general counsels, and the plots and marshaling of affairs, come best from those that are learned. To spend too much time in studies is sloth; to use them too much for ornament is affectation; to make judgment wholly by their rules is the humor of a scholar. They perfect nature, and are perfected by experience; for natural abilities are like natural plants, that need pruning by study; and studies themselves do give forth directions too much at large, except they be bounded in by experience. Crafty men condemn studies; simple men admire them; and wise men use them: for they teach not their own use; but that is a wisdom without them and above them, won by observation. Read not to contradict and confute; nor to believe and take for granted; nor to find talk and discourse; but to weigh and consider. Some books are to be tasted, others to be swallowed, and some few to be chewed and digested: that is, some books are to be read only in parts; others to be read, but not curiously; and some few to be read wholly, and with diligence and attention. Some books also may be read by deputy, and extracts made of them by others; but that would be only in the less important arguments, and the meaner sort of books; else distilled books are like common distilled waters, flashy things. Reading maketh a full man; conference a ready man; and writing an exact man. And therefore, if a man write little, he had need have a great memory; if he confer little, he had need have a present wit; and if he read little, he had need have much cunning, to seem to know that he doth not. Histories make men wise; poets witty; the mathematics subtile; natural philosophy deep; moral, grave; logic and rhetoric able to contend. *Abeunt studia in mores.*[1] Nay, there is no stond or impediment in the wit, but may be wrought out by fit studies: like as diseases of the body may have appropriate exercises. Bowling is good for the stone and reins; shooting for the lungs and breast; gentle walking for the stomach; riding for the head; and the like. So if a man's wit be wandering, let him study the mathematics; for in demonstrations, if his wit be called away never so little, he must begin again: if his wit be not apt to distinguish or find differences, let him study the schoolmen; for they are *cymini sectores:*[2] if he be not apt to beat over matters, and to call up one thing to prove and illustrate another, let him study the lawyers' cases: so every defect of the mind may have a special receipt.

[1] Studies become a way of life. From Ovid's *Heroides*, XV, 83.
[2] Hair-splitters.

Notebook Assignment for Class Discussion

1. Bacon uses several ordinary words in ways probably unfamiliar to you. Look them up in *The Oxford English Dictionary* to discover the meaning he intended, according to his context.
2. How would you logically divide this essay into paragraphs based on topic sentences?
3. What use does Bacon make of metaphors, examples, restatements, and the like, for the sake of clarity?
4. The author's balanced style is compressed and elliptical. What does this mean? Find several examples of elliptical expression and write them out in complete form.
5. Bacon says, "Histories make men wise . . ." Are all the subjects in this balanced, elliptical sentence parallel, or categorically equivalent?
6. Which publications today exemplify Bacon's classification of books that are "read by deputy, and extracts made of them by others"? What is his evaluation of such publications?
7. Analyze this essay as an example of rhetorical division. How does Bacon develop each part of his division?

Related Exercises

1. Bacon makes an important initial distinction between the "expert" and the "learned" man. Does the principle which underlies it serve equally as a basis for the other distinctions which he makes in such matters as application to, and evaluation of, studies; the qualities and determinations of books, readings, the various disciplines, and so on?
2. Can you abstract from this article, and state in a single sentence, the most general principle of evaluation which informs it?
3. A proper approach to studies, according to Bacon, can make a man variously ready, exact, witty, subtle, grave, and able in contention, among other things. Do you think him to be too practical, too satisfied with limited educational objectives, to propose such qualities as the proper ends of studies?
4. What do you consider to be the proper ends of studies? In view of your own special needs and capabilities, what should your education accomplish for you? What should be the *mean* accomplishment of education? Ignoring the accidental requirements of individuals, what should be the value *com-*

mon to all men which is afforded by an education? Does Bacon say?

5. "... every defect of the mind may have a special receipt." Is education, in your opinion, primarily a therapeutic process? Does Bacon suggest that it might be? Or is he prescriptive of studies in another sense?

6. Is Bacon modern in tone? How does what he has to say about education, its aims, effects, and procedures, seem particularly modern? How archaic?

7. Discuss the following in the light of Bacon's elegant little morality on the decorum of studies:

   a. Ovid, *Heroides*, XV, 83
   b. Goethe, *Faust*, Part I, "Night"
   c. Emerson, "The American Scholar"
   d. De Tocqueville, *Democracy in America*, Part II, Book 1

GREEK AND HEBREW STORY-TELLERS *

By Mary Ellen Chase

Although the ancient story-tellers of Greece and of her islands and those living at much the same time among the hills of Canaan were, so far as we know, completely unaware of one another, they possessed in common many similar ideas and points of view. Both were seemingly prompted by the same desires and concerned with much the same general material. Both were keenly aware of the traditions of their respective peoples, knew how these traditions were woven into thoughts and memories, and had, as doubtless their first impetus toward writing, the desire to preserve them.

Although their times seem ancient to us in the twentieth century, their world was already old. They must have realized even in their day that what we now call folklore was in its essence the ways and even the necessities of a people. They understood that it was far more than mere tales and legends; that instead it

* Reprinted from *Life and Language in the Old Testament* by Mary Ellen Chase. By permission of W. W. Norton & Company, Inc. Copyright © 1955 by Mary Ellen Chase.

centered around and tried to answer the eternal questions of simple people about the origins of the world, the means of life, the beginnings of races, the source of human pain. They knew, in brief, that such stories are not simply charming in themselves, but that they are basic to a people's existence since they arise not only from national and racial loyalty, but also from a universal curiosity about the mystery of human existence, the sorrows of human life. Such perceptions on the part of these ancient writers are quite evident in many passages both in the Greek epics and in the Old Testament. Achilles says to Priam, the father of Hector, that the life of man by the mysterious decrees of the gods is destined for sorrow, and the writer of the 3rd chapter of *Genesis* echoes his understanding.

The most brilliantly told legend among the Hebrew narratives, that of Jacob and Joseph, contained in Genesis, chapters 27 to 50, inclusive, is perhaps more accurately termed a saga since it deals with family relationships and is, first of all, a human rather than a national document. Nevertheless, it possesses distinctly epical qualities like those of the *Iliad* and the *Odyssey*. It is an heroic story, the characters of which are the descendants of Abraham and Isaac, and, therefore, in the Hebrew mind the founders of its tribes and the preservers of its race. It is animated throughout by racial pride and patriotic fervor, emotions common to the Greek, and, of course, to all epics.

The *Iliad* and the *Odyssey* and the Jacob-Joseph saga contain alike themes common to most ancient literature. Odysseus and Jacob are both men who escape from perils and who are wanderers; both return home after long years away. In both the Hebrew saga and the Greek epics are familiar motifs. There are dreams which reveal the truth like the dreams of the chief baker and the chief butler, interpreted by Joseph in prison, like Pharaoh's dream of the geese and the eagle; and the origin of these dreams is accorded to God or to the gods. There is in both Greek and Hebrew stories the sense of obligation to the stranger; there is the giving of gifts, Jacob's gifts which he plans for Esau, Joseph's gifts to his brother; and the innumerable gifts which fill the pages of the *Iliad* and the *Odyssey*. There is the time-worn old motif of disguise, in Rebekah's disguise of Jacob so that his father may think he is Esau and in the many instances of disguise in the epics, from the various disguises of the gods and goddesses, who appear in any number of forms, to Odysseus' final disguise as a beggar in tattered rags when he returns at last to Ithaca and plans with the help of Athene to rid his house of the wooers of Penelope who have despoiled it. There are bargainings and tricks and cleverness, whether it is Jacob's shrewdness in gaining Laban's flocks for himself, or Odysseus' desperate cunning in the cave of Polyphemus, the Cyclops. There are touching revelations like that of the final revelation of Joseph to his wondering brothers, or of Odysseus when the old nurse Eurycleia in giving him his bath sees the scar from the tusk of the wild boar. And although the story of Jacob and Joseph is one of peace and that of the *Iliad* and in retrospect, of the *Odyssey* one of war, the atmosphere of both Hebrew and Greek narratives takes us back to the beginnings of things, even although it is a different beginning, and to the portrayal of basic, primitive, changeless human emotions and passions: fear, rage, jealousy, lust, revenge, love, and hatred.

II

But once we have noted the similarities in these ancient stories, each of the childhood of a race, we must become keenly alive to their sharp and pronounced differences, both in form and in methods of literary creation. For in these differences lie not only the singularity of the Hebrew story-tellers, their distinction from all others of any race and time, but, indeed, those characteristics which have marked through centuries the distinction between the Greek literary legacy to Western culture and that of the Hebrew. In studying these differences there is a practical and utilitarian value to the reader of the Old Testament, for in understanding them he becomes more clearly aware of how its narratives must be read in order to gain from them their meaning and significance, quite lost to him without that knowledge.

The first and most obvious difference between the literary conceptions and methods of the Greek and the Hebrew writers lies in the length which they respectively accord to their stories. The *Iliad,* somewhat longer than the *Odyssey* in its number of lines, consists of twenty-four books; the *Odyssey* of an equal number. The Jacob-Joseph saga in its entirety, that is, from the blessing of Isaac to the death of Jacob in Egypt and his burial in the Land of Canaan, comprises twenty-four chapters, and of that number two should be omitted as having no bearing on the story itself.[1] Indeed, the complete epic, or saga, of Jacob and Joseph could be put into any one of the longer books of the *Iliad* or the *Odyssey.*

The reason for this immense disparity in size lies, first, in the *brevity* characteristic of the Hebrew story-tellers, and, second, in

1 We must realize, of course, that the Biblical stories in their original form were not divided into chapters as we know them.

the *principle of omission,* a practice always employed by them. These two literary traits mark all early Old Testament narratives. They are as evident in the account of David's court and in the isolated hero stories as they are in the Jacob-Joseph saga. For the employment of the first of these, *brevity,* and its consequent literary and imaginative effects, let us compare Homer's presentation of certain characters in terms of their background and appearance with that of the Hebrew writers.

Homer's great figures always come from some clearly identified place. Helen, the cause of the Trojan War, whose face in Marlowe's words

> *launched a thousand ships*
> *And burnt the topless towers of Ilium,*

comes from Sparta where, before Paris lured her away, she was the wife of King Menelaus. Andromache, the beautiful wife of Hector, comes from Thebes. The home of Odysseus is in sea-girt Ithaca, but we are told carefully that his grandparents lived at Parnassus. When Achilles, once having overcome his wrath at Agamemnon, proceeds to make havoc among the heroes of Troy, either he takes time before his slaughter of them to ask their homes and their lineage or Homer himself discloses their places of birth and their noble parentage.

In contrast we are told practically nothing of those equally great figures who live and move in the ancient Hebrew saga. Their dwelling-places are never described in even the least detail and often not clearly identified. Apparently Isaac lived at Beersheba, or the *Well of the Oath,* when, old and blind, he was tricked into blessing Jacob instead of the rightful Esau; yet the selling of the birthright, which preceded the blessing, seems to have been near some other well where he had pitched his tent. The time and place of the most important happenings are alike undefined. Are Haran and Padan-aram the same place? They would seem to be from the account in Genesis, and yet one was clearly a town and the other a district. And in what places did Jacob stop on that long journey from Beersheba to Haran? Not one except Bethel is identified although the journey must have occupied many days. We are told only that he went on his journey and came into the land of the people of the east.

Both Odysseus and Jacob spent twenty years away from home, Odysseus on his wanderings, Jacob in the service of Laban. The places of Odysseus' wanderings, as he sails from one to another, are always both named and carefully described: Ogygia, the far-off isle of Calypso; the land of the Phaeacians, who need no rudders for their ships; the drowsy land of the Lotus Eaters and that of the Cyclopes, who dwell in hollow caves; the isle of Circe; and the dreadful Charybdis and Scylla. Jacob presumably wandered a great deal during his long term of service with Laban, since he was a shepherd; but if he did, we know little or nothing about it. We are told once only that he removed himself with his speckled and spotted flocks "a three days' journey" from Laban, but to what place we do not know. Nor are the various stages named of the return journey which he took with his household when he determined to flee from Padan-aram to the Land of Canaan. He is at Mt. Gilead; he wrestles with the angel of God at a place which, in commemoration, he himself names Peniel; he continues to Succoth; then suddenly he is at Shechem in the very land of Canaan. From there, after the sorry tragedy of his daughter Dinah, he seemingly moves on to Bethel and beyond; and yet he is apparently also at Shechem, or at least his flocks are there. Again, time is as if it were not, and place is rarely identified.

Homer describes in careful detail the houses in which people lived. King Priam had a beautiful palace, adorned with polished colonnades, in which were fifty chambers of polished stone. The bronze walls of King Alcinous' house in Phaeacia gave forth a gleam like that of the sun or the moon; round them was a frieze of blue; the doors were of gold and the door-posts of silver; and without the courtyard was a great garden with hedges and fruit trees. Penelope's chamber in Odysseus' great house in Ithaca was reached by a tall staircase, and in the "uttermost part" of the house was a treasure room, the oaken threshold of which had been "planed cunningly by the carpenter."

Such description as this is unimaginable in the Old Testament. The patriarchs "pitch their tents" wherever they find food and water; people in the small Canaanitish villages often, like Rahab, live on the town wall. We are told that the carpenters and masons of Hiram, King of Tyre, built David a house of cedar, but we have no idea what it was like any more than we can picture Solomon's house, which, with his other glories, made the Queen of Sheba breathless. Amos condemns the people of the north for their winter houses and their summer houses, and also for their houses of ivory, but they are only mentioned, never described or located. In the very late book of Esther, which shows various foreign influences, we *are* told of a few elegant furnishings in the palace at Shushan, but this is the one exception. The only house in the Old Testament described in detail is the House of God, the Temple built by Solomon in Jerusalem.

Homer pictures all his characters. His heroes, their hair, their eyes, their stature, their clothing and armor—all receive his utmost care. He is especially susceptible to the charms of his women, whether born of gods or of mortals; and although he pictures them in far less detail than his heroes, each possesses a special grace. Who can forget the white-armed Nausicaa, the daughter of King Alcinous, whose form and comeliness are like to the immortals and who in Odysseus' ravished eyes is like a young palm tree springing by the altar of Apollo in Delos? Odysseus' old nurse, Eurycleia, with her stumbling feet and uncertain hands still holds a graciousness which no age can wither. When she discerns the scar which proves that she is, in very truth, bathing her master and lord, she lets his foot drop so suddenly in her agitation that the water is spilled on the ground. And although Sir Gilbert Murray insists that Helen is described with great restraint in the *Iliad*,[2] she is, in comparison with any woman in the Old Testament, very clearly seen. She may claim that she is but a *dog* to have caused the war between the Greeks and the Trojans; but her enchantment is quite evident to herself as to us when she sits in her chamber in her perfumed raiment with her beautiful hair and in her hands the web of purple wool which she is embroidering with the battles she has caused men to fight. We see her also weeping in her white veil much as the elders on the wall of Troy saw her when they said to one another: "Small wonder that the Trojans and mailed Greeks should endure pain through many years for such a woman!"

It is almost impossible to see any Old Testament character in terms of physical features or of dress. David is perhaps an exception since he is accorded two adjectives instead of one: he is ruddy, that is, red-haired, and of a beautiful countenance. Samson has heavy hair, but that feature is stressed, clearly because in his hair lay the secret of his strength. Absalom is said to be beautiful, "without blemish from the sole of his foot even to the crown of his head." His hair, too, like Samson's is extraordinary, nearly nine pounds in weight at its yearly cutting, but it, too, is obviously emphasized only because it is to be the cause of his death. What did Abraham look like, or Isaac, or Jacob? We do not know. Joseph has a coat of many colors and apparently at seventeen a manner which infuriates his half-brothers, but except for these details and the fact that Potiphar's wife in Egypt thought him well-favored, he is likewise impossible to visualize.

The women who play such dramatic parts not only in the Jacob-Joseph saga, but throughout the Old Testament narratives

2 In *The Rise of the Greek Epic*, pp. 253–54.

are almost never made visible by any definite physical features. Bathsheba, who caused such tragedy, is described only as "very beautiful to look upon" at that fatal hour when David from his roof saw her bathing. We can only imagine what Rebekah with her ruthless cunning must have looked like. Jael, the slayer of Sisera, is presented only in fierce action; Hagar only weeping over her little son in the wilderness. Sarah, whom we remember most clearly for her ironic laughter, is "very fair," so fair indeed, that Abraham fears for his own life at the hand of the covetous Pharaoh and therefore determines to tell the king that she is his sister. Leah and Rachel, most important among Hebrew women because they are the mothers of the tribes of Israel, are contrasted in appearance: "Leah was tender-eyed; but Rachel was beautiful and well-favored." The Jewish translation is more true to the original Hebrew than is the King James in its description of the first wife of Jacob. Leah had *weak,* or sore eyes; and this unfortunate blemish is perhaps one reason why she was less attractive to Jacob than was the beautiful Rachel. . . .

To readers like myself, devoted both to the Homeric epics and to the Old Testament narratives, it is difficult to conceive of literary styles and treatments more different in every respect. The former, with their atmosphere of leisure, their lack of suspense, their fluency, elaboration, and ornament, their complete expression of emotion, stand in direct contrast to the latter, almost even in alienation from them. The Hebrew writers know nothing of the sophistication of the Greek. The language which they employed for their stories was sharp and quick, unfinished, inflexible, fragmentary in comparison; the emotions which it suggested were never fully described. And yet, through its very brevity and bareness and through its empty silences, its writers were able to evoke responses and even understandings impossible to the writers of the epics. Since the Homeric poets reveal everything, conceal nothing, they trail few invisible meanings within their thousands of beautiful phrases and intricate, detailed similes.

Notebook Assignment for Class Discussion

1. Look up the meaning of *motif, singularity, disparity,* and all other words not now in your active vocabulary.
2. Restate fully the author's implied definition of the difference between a saga and an epic, then compare yours with the dictionary's.
3. Just as every positive implies a negative, so every comparison

implies a contrast. List the principal points of similarity and difference in the Greek and Hebrew stories, according to Miss Chase.

4. The topic of paragraph 4 is expressed in its first sentence. The author then uses a series of specific, or concrete, examples to explain and illustrate that topical statement and thus to further the comparison. Where else does she employ a similar technique?

5. What is the structural relation of the final paragraph to the whole essay?

Related Exercises

1. Read *Genesis,* Chapters 27–50, as well as a good modern translation of the *Odyssey* (Rieu, Rouse, or Fitzgerald), looking especially for the truth-dreams, gifts, disguises, trickery, and the like, which Miss Chase claims are to be found in both.

2. In your opinion, which two of the twenty-four chapters in the Jacob-Joseph series have no bearing on the main story?

3. The Hebrew story of Susanna and the elders, which follows, suggests some parallels in the gods lusting after women in the *Odyssey,* and in Greek mythology in general. Try to discover a few such parallels.

4. The story of the marital bed trick involving Jacob, Rachel, and Leah (or Lia) has several parallels in later literature, e.g., Shakespeare's *Measure for Measure* (Angelo, Isabella, and Mariana), and *Morte d'Arthur* (Lancelot, Elaine, and Guenivere). Out of your reading background, can you recall others?

5. Try to find a basis for comparison between other episodes, or persons, in the Hebrew saga, the *Odyssey,* and other literature. Can you find in earlier literature innumerable prototypes of popular TV shows? Movies? Legitimate theater? Novels? Short stories?

6. Miss Chase quotes from the King James version of the *Bible* (1611): "Leah was tender-eyed . . ." but the Douay version (1609–10) says, "Lia was blear-eyed . . ." Did *tender* and *blear* mean the same thing in the early seventeenth century? Compare the two versions for other points of difference.

7. Select one of the episodes of the Jacob-Joseph saga or the *Odyssey* and adapt it to modern short story form and background.

8. Or, develop a serious paper based on your findings for items 3, 4, 5, or 6 in this list of exercises.

SUSANNA *

In those days there was a man that dwelt in Babylon, and his name was Joakim: and he took a wife whose name was Susanna, the daughter of Helcias, a very beautiful woman, and one that feared God: for her parents being just, had instructed their daughter according to the law of Moses. Now Joakim was very rich, and had an orchard near his house: and the Jews resorted to him, because he was the most honorable of them all. And there were two of the ancients of the people appointed judges that year: of whom the Lord said: Iniquity came out from Babylon from the ancient judges that seemed to govern the people. These men frequented the house of Joakim, and all that had any matters of judgment came to them.

And when the people departed away at noon, Susanna went in and walked in her husband's orchard. And the old men saw her going in every day, and walking: and they were inflamed with lust towards her: and they perverted their own mind, and turned away their eyes that they might not look unto heaven, nor remember just judgments. And it fell out, as they watched a fit day, she went in on a time, as yesterday and the day before, with two maids only, and was desirous to wash herself in the orchard: for it was hot weather, and there was nobody there, but the two old men that had hid themselves and were beholding her.

So she said to her maids: Bring me oil and washing balls, and shut the doors of the orchard, that I may wash me. Now when the maids were gone forth, the two elders arose and ran to her, and said: Behold the doors of the orchard are shut, and nobody seeth us, and we are in love with thee: wherefore consent to us and lie with us. But if thou wilt not, we will bear witness against thee, that a young man was with thee, and therefore thou didst send away thy maids from thee.

Susanna sighed, and said: I am straitened on every side: for if I do this thing, it is death to me: and if I do it not, I shall not escape your hands. But it is better for me to fall into your hands without doing it, than to sin in the sight of the Lord.

With that Susanna cried out with a loud voice: and the elders also cried out against her. And one of them ran to the door of the orchard and opened it. So when the servants of the house heard the cry in the orchard, they rushed in by the back door to

* From *Daniel* 13:1–9, 15–17, 19–30, 33–62.

see what was the matter. But after the old men had spoken, the servants were greatly ashamed: for never had there been any such word said of Susanna.

And on the next day, when the people were come to Joakim her husband, the two elders also came full of wicked device against Susanna, to put her to death. And they said before the people: Send to Susanna, daughter of Helcias, the wife of Joakim. And presently they sent. And she came with her parents and children and all her kindred. Therefore her friends and all her acquaintance wept.

But the two elders rising up in the midst of the people laid their hands upon her head. And she weeping looked up to heaven: for her heart had confidence in the Lord. And the elders said: As we walked in the orchard alone, this woman came in with two maids: and shut the doors of the orchard, and sent away the maids from her. Then a young man that was there hid came to her, and lay with her. But we, that were in a corner of the orchard, seeing this wickedness, ran up to them, and we saw them lie together. And him indeed we could not take, because he was stronger than us, and opening the doors he leaped out: but having taken this woman, we asked who the young man was, but she would not tell us: of this thing we are witnesses.

The multitude believed them as being the elders and the judges of the people, and they condemned her to death. Then Susanna cried out with a loud voice, and said: O eternal God, who knowest hidden things, who knowest all things before they come to pass, Thou knowest that they have borne false witness against me: and behold I must die, whereas I have done none of these things which these men have maliciously forged against me.

And the Lord heard her voice. And when she was led to be put to death, the Lord raised up the holy spirit of a young boy, whose name was Daniel. And he cried out with a loud voice: I am clear from the blood of this woman.

Then all the people, turning themselves toward him, said: What meaneth this word that thou hast spoken? But he standing in the midst of them, said: Are ye so foolish, ye children of Israel, that without examination or knowledge of the truth, you have condemned a daughter of Israel? Return to judgment, for they have borne false witness against her. So all the people turned again in haste. And Daniel said to them: Separate these two far from one another, and I will examine them.

So when they were put asunder one from the other, he called one of them, and said to him: O thou art grown old in evil days, now are thy sins come out, which thou hast committed before: in judging unjust judgments, oppressing the innocent, and letting the guilty to go free, whereas the Lord saith: The innocent and the just thou shalt not kill. Now then, if thou sawest her, tell me under what tree thou sawest them conversing together. He said: Under a mastic tree. And Daniel said: Well hast thou lied against thine own head. For behold the angel of God, having received the sentence of Him, shall cut thee in two.

And having put him aside, he commanded that the other should come, and he said to him: O thou seed of Chanaan and not of Juda, beauty hath deceived thee, and lust hath perverted thy heart: thus did you do to the daughters of Israel, and they for fear conversed with you: but a daughter of Juda would not abide your wickedness. Now therefore tell me, under what tree didst thou take them conversing together? And he answered: Under a holm tree. And Daniel said to him: Well hast thou also lied against thy own head: for the angel of the Lord waiteth with a sword to cut thee in two, and to destroy you. With that all the assembly cried out with a loud voice, and they blessed God, who saveth them that trust in Him. And they rose up against the two elders (for Daniel had convicted them of false witness by their own mouth) and they did to them as they had maliciously dealt against their neighbor: and they put them to death, and innocent blood was saved in that day.

Notebook Assignment for Class Discussion

1. Look up the following words in the *Oxford English Dictionary* and write down the definition and sentence example given (with author and date) which best explain the meaning of the word as used in this context:

fear	husband
resort	wife
ancients	kindred
pervert	confidence
fit	forge
straitened	converse

2. Note any strange phrases or idioms, such as "consent *to* us," and others, no longer in common usage.
3. Rewrite this story, using modern language.
4. In what reference book can you find an explanation of "washing balls"?

5. Do you agree with Mary Ellen Chase that the Hebrew stories lack descriptive detail of person, time, and place?

6. Read the "Canticle of Canticles" from a rhetorical point of view, then try to write a series of descriptive sentences, using a minimum number of adjectives, if any, but many inversions and comparisons to produce the effect of Biblical style.

ODYSSEUS AND PENELOPE *

By Homer

Chuckling as she went, the old woman bustled upstairs to tell her mistress that her beloved husband was in the house. Her legs could hardly carry her fast enough, and her feet twinkled in their haste. As she reached the head of the bedstead, she cried: "Wake up, Penelope, dear child, and see a sight you've longed for all these many days. Odysseus has come home, and high time too! And he's killed the rogues who turned his whole house inside out, ate up his wealth, and bullied his son."

Penelope was not caught off her guard. "My dear nurse," she said, "the gods have made you daft. It's as easy for them to rob the wisest of their wits as to make stupid people wise. And now they've addled *your* brains, which used to be so sound. How dare you make sport of my distress by waking me when I had closed my eyes for a comfortable nap, only to tell me this nonsense? Never have I slept so soundly since Odysseus sailed away to that accursed place I cannot bring myself to mention. Off with you now downstairs and back into your quarters! If any of the other maids had come and awakened me to listen to such stuff, I'd soon have packed her off to her own place with a box on the ears. You can thank your age for saving you from that."

But this did not silence the old nurse. "I am not making fun of you, dear child," she said. "Odysseus really has come home, just as I told you. He's the stranger whom they all scoffed at in the hall. Telemachus has known for some time that he was back, but had the sense to keep his father's plans a secret till he'd made those upstarts pay for their villainy."

Penelope's heart leapt up. She sprang from the bed and clung

* From *The Odyssey*, by Homer, Book XXIII, translated by E. V. Rieu. First pub. 1946. Last reprinting 1962 (Baltimore: Penguin Books, Inc.), pp. 341–50.

to the old woman, with the tears streaming from her eyes and the eager words from her lips. "Dear nurse," she cried, "I beg you for the truth! If he is really home, as you say, how on earth did he manage singlehanded against that rascally crew who always hang about the house in a pack?"

"I never saw a thing," said Eurycleia. "I knew nothing about it. All I heard was the groans of dying men. We sat petrified in a corner of our quarters, with the doors shut tightly on us, till your son Telemachus shouted to me to come out. His father had sent him to fetch me. And then I found Odysseus standing among the bodies of the dead. They lay round him in heaps all over the hard floor. It would have done you good to see him, spattered with blood and filth like a lion. By now all the corpses have been gathered together at the courtyard gate, while he has had a big fire made and is fumigating the palace. He sent me to call you to him. So come with me now, so that you two may enter into your happiness together after all the sorrows you have had. The hope you cherished so long is fulfilled for you today. Odysseus has come back to his own hearth alive; he has found both you and his son in the home, and he has had his revenge in his own palace on every one of the Suitors who were doing him such wrong."

"Don't laugh too soon, dear nurse; don't boast about them yet," said Penelope in her prudence. "You know how everyone at home would welcome the sight of him, and nobody more than myself and the son we brought into the world. But this tale of yours does not ring true. It must be one of the immortal gods that has killed the young lords, provoked, no doubt, by their galling insolence and wicked ways. For they respected nobody they met—good men and bad were all the same to them. And now their iniquities have brought them to this pass. Meanwhile Odysseus in some distant land has lost his chance of ever getting home, and with it lost his life."

"My child," her old nurse exclaimed, "how can you say such things! Here is your husband at his own fireside, and you declare he never will get home. What little faith you have always had! But let me tell you something else—a fact that proves the truth. You know the scar he had where he was wounded long ago by the white tusk of a boar? I saw that very scar when I was washing him, and would have told you of it, if Odysseus, for his own crafty purposes, hadn't seized me by the throat and prevented me. Come with me now. I'll stake my life upon it. If I've played you false, then kill me in the cruelest way you can."

"Dear nurse," Penelope replied, "you are a very wise old

woman, but even you cannot probe into the minds of the ever-lasting gods. However, let us go to my son, so that I can see my suitors dead, together with the man who killed them."

As she spoke she left her room and made her way downstairs, a prey to indecision. Should she remain aloof as she questioned her husband, or go straight up to him and kiss his head and hands? What she actually did, when she had crossed the stone threshold into the hall, was to take a chair in the firelight by the wall, on the opposite side to Odysseus, who was sitting by one of the great columns with his eyes on the ground, waiting to see whether his good wife would say anything to him when she saw him. For a long while Penelope, overwhelmed by wonder, sat there without a word. But her eyes were busy, at one moment resting full on his face, and at the next falling on the ragged clothes that made him seem a stranger once again. It was Telemachus who broke the silence, but only to rebuke her.

"Mother," he said, "you strange, hard-hearted mother of mine, why do you keep so far from my father? Why aren't you sitting at his side, talking and asking questions all the while? No other woman would have had the perversity to hold out like this against a husband she had just got back after nineteen years of misadventure. But then your heart was always harder than flint."

"My child, the shock has numbed it," she admitted. "I cannot find a word to say to him; I cannot ask him anything at all; I cannot even look him in the face. But if it really is Odysseus home again, we two shall surely recognize each other, and in an even better way; for there are tokens between us which only we two know and no one else has heard of."

Patient Odysseus smiled, then turning briskly to his son he said: "Telemachus, leave your mother to put me to the proof here in our home. She will soon come to a better mind. At the moment, because I'm dirty and in rags, she gives me the cold shoulder and won't admit that I'm Odysseus. But you and I must consider what is best to be done. When a man has killed a fellow-citizen, just one, with hardly any friends to carry on the feud, he is outlawed, he leaves his kith and kin and flies the country. But we have killed the pick of the Ithacan nobility, the mainstay of our state. There is a problem for you."

"One you must grapple with yourself, dear father," Telemachus shrewdly rejoined. "For at getting out of a difficulty you are held to be the best man in the world, with no one else to touch you. We will follow your lead with alacrity, and I may say with no lack of courage either, so far as in us lies."

Odysseus was not at a loss. "As I see it, then," he said, "our best plan will be this. Wash yourselves first, put on your tunics, and tell the maids in the house to get dressed. Then let our excellent minstrel strike up a merry dance-tune for us, loud as his lyre can play, so that if the music is heard outside by anyone passing in the road or by one of our neighbors, they may imagine there is a wedding-feast. That will prevent the news of the Suitors' death from spreading through the town before we can beat a retreat to our farm among the orchards. Once there, we shall see. Providence may play into our hands."

They promptly put his idea into practice. The men washed and donned their tunics, while the women decked themselves out. The admirable bard took up his hollow lyre and had them soon intent on nothing but the melodies of song and the niceties of the dance. They made the great hall echo round them to the feet of dancing men and women richly clad. "Ah," said the passers-by as the sounds reached their ears. "Somebody has married our much-courted queen. The heartless creature! Too fickle to keep patient watch over the great house till her lawful husband should come back!" Which shows how little they knew what had really happened.

Meanwhile the great Odysseus, in his own home again, had himself bathed and rubbed with oil by the housekeeper Eurynome, and was fitted out by her in a beautiful cloak and tunic. Athene also played her part by enhancing his comeliness from head to foot. She made him look taller and sturdier than ever; she caused the bushy locks to hang from his head thick as the petals of the hyacinth in bloom; and just as a craftsman trained by Hephaestus and herself in the secrets of his art takes pains to put a graceful finish to his work by overlaying silver-ware with gold, she finished now by endowing his head and shoulders with an added beauty. He came out from the bath looking like one of the everlasting gods, then went and sat down once more in the chair opposite his wife.

"What a strange creature!" he exclaimed. "Heaven made you as you are, but for sheer obstinacy you put all the rest of your sex in the shade. No other wife could have steeled herself to keep so long out of the arms of a husband she had just got back after nineteen years of misadventure. Well, nurse, make a bed for me to sleep alone in. For my wife's heart is just about as hard as iron."

"You too are strange," said the cautious Penelope. "I am not being haughty or indifferent. I am not even unduly surprised. But I have too clear a picture of you in my mind as you were when you sailed from Ithaca in your long-oared ship. Come,

Eurycleia, make him a comfortable bed outside the bedroom that
he built so well himself. Place the big bed out there, and make
it up with rugs and blankets, and with laundered sheets."

This was her way of putting her husband to the test. But
Odysseus flared up at once and rounded on his loyal wife. "Penelope," he cried, "you exasperate me! Who, if you please, has
moved my bed elsewhere? Short of a miracle, it would be hard
even for a skilled workman to shift it somewhere else, and the
strongest young fellow alive would have a job to budge it. For
a great secret went into the making of that complicated bed; and
it was my work and mine alone. Inside the court there was a
long-leaved olive-tree, which had grown to full height with a stem
as thick as a pillar. Round this I built my room of close-set stone-
work, and when that was finished, I roofed it over thoroughly,
and put in a solid, neatly fitted double door. Next I lopped all
the twigs off the olive, trimmed the stem from the root up,
rounded it smoothly and carefully with my adze and trued it to
the line, to make my bedpost. This I drilled through where necessary, and used as a basis for the bed itself, which I worked away
at till that too was done, when I finished it off with an inlay of
gold, silver, and ivory, and fixed a set of purple straps across
the frame.

"There is our secret, and I have shown you that I know it.
What I don't know, madam, is whether my bedstead stands where
it did, or whether someone has cut the tree-trunk through and
shifted it elsewhere."

Her knees began to tremble as she realized the complete fidelity
of his description. All at once her heart melted. Bursting into
tears she ran up to Odysseus, threw her arms round his neck and
kissed his head. "Odysseus," she cried, "do not be cross with me,
you who were always the most reasonable of men. All our unhap-
piness is due to the gods, who couldn't bear to see us share the
joys of youth and reach the threshold of old age together. But
don't be angry with me now, or hurt because the moment when
I saw you first I did not kiss you as I kiss you now. For I had
always had the cold fear in my heart that somebody might come
here and bewitch me with his talk. There are plenty of rogues
who would seize such a chance; and though Argive Helen would
never have slept in her foreign lover's arms had she known that
her countrymen would go to war to fetch her back to Argos, even
she, the daughter of Zeus, was tempted by the goddess and fell,
though the idea of such madness had never entered her head till
that moment, which was so fateful for the world and proved the
starting-point of all our sorrows too. But now all's well. You

have faithfully described our token, the secret of our bed, which no one ever saw but you and I and one maid, Actoris, who was my father's gift when first I came to you, and sat as sentry at our bedroom door. You have convinced your unbelieving wife."

Penelope's surrender melted Odysseus' heart, and he wept as he held his dear wife in his arms, so loyal and so true. Sweet moment too for her, sweet as the sight of land to sailors struggling in the sea, when the Sea-god by dint of wind and wave has wrecked their gallant ship. What happiness for the few swimmers that have fought their way through the white surf to the shore, when, caked with brine but safe and sound, they tread on solid earth! If that is bliss, what bliss it was for her to see her husband once again! She kept her white arms round his neck and never quite let go. Dawn with her roses would have caught them at their tears, had not Athene of the flashing eyes bestirred herself on their behalf. She held the long night lingering in the West, and in the East at Ocean's Stream she kept Dawn waiting by her golden throne, and would not let her yoke the nimble steeds who bring us light, Lampus and Phaeton, the colts that draw the chariot of Day.

But there was one thing which Odysseus had the wisdom soon to tell his wife. "My dear," he said, "we have not yet come to the end of our trials. There lies before me still a great and hazardous adventure, which I must see through to the very end, however far that end may be. That was what Teiresias' soul predicted for me when I went down to the House of Hades to find a way home for my followers and myself. So come to bed now, my dear wife, and let us comfort ourselves while we can with a sweet sleep in each other's arms."

Prudent Penelope answered: "Your bed shall be ready the moment you wish to use it, now that the gods have brought you back to your own country and your lovely home. But since it did occur to you to speak of this new ordeal, please tell me all about it; for I shall certainly find out later, and it could be no worse to hear at once."

"Why drag it out of me?" he asked reproachfully. "Well, you shall hear the whole tale. I'll make no secret of it. Not that you'll find it to your liking! I am not pleased myself. For he told me to take a well-cut oar and wander on from city to city, till I come to a people who know nothing of the sea, and never use salt with their food, so that our crimson-painted ships and the long oars that serve those ships as wings are quite beyond their ken. Of this, he said that I should find conclusive proof, as you shall hear, when I met some other traveler who spoke of the 'winnow-ing-fan' I was carrying on my shoulder. Then, he said, the time would have come for me to plant my oar in the earth and offer the Lord Poseidon the rich sacrifice of a ram, a bull, and a breeding boar. After that I was to go back home and make ceremonial sacrifices to the everlasting gods who live in the far-flung heavens, to all of them, this time, in due precedence. As for my end, he said that Death would come to me in his gentlest form out of the sea, and that when he took me I should be worn out after an easy old age and surrounded by a prosperous folk. He swore that I should find all this come true."

"Well then," Penelope sagely replied, "if Providence plans to make you happier in old age, you can always be confident of escaping from your troubles."

While they were talking, Eurynome and the nurse, by the light of torches, were putting soft bedclothes for them on their bed. When the work was done and the bed lay comfortably spread, the old woman went back into her own quarters for the night, and the housekeeper Eurynome, with a torch in her hands, lit them on their way to bed, taking her leave when she had brought them to their room. And glad indeed they were to lie once more together in the bed that had known them long ago. Meanwhile Telemachus, the cowman, and the swineherd brought their dancing feet to rest, made the women finish too, and lay down for the night in the darkened hall.

But Odysseus and Penelope, after their love had taken its sweet course, turned to the fresh delights of talk, and interchanged their news. He heard his noble wife tell of all she had put up with in his home, watching that gang of wreckers at their work, of all the cattle and fat sheep that they had slaughtered for her sake, of all the vessels they had emptied of their wine. And in his turn, royal Odysseus told her of all the discomfiture he had inflicted on his foes and all the miseries which he himself had undergone. She listened spellbound, and her eyelids never closed in sleep till the whole tale was finished.

He began with his first victory over the Cicones and his visit to the fertile land where the Lotus-eaters live. He spoke of what the Cyclops did, and the price he had made him pay for the gallant men he ruthlessly devoured. He told her of his stay with Aeolus, so friendly when he came and helpful when he left; and how the gale, since Providence would not let him reach his home so soon, had caught him up once more and driven him in misery down the highways of the fish. Next came his call at Telepylus on the Laestrygonian coast, where the savages destroyed his fleet and all his fighting men, the black ship that carried him being the only one to get away. He spoke of Circe and her magic arts; of how he sailed across the seas to the mouldering Halls of Hades to consult the soul of Theban Teiresias, and saw all his former comrades and the mother who had borne him and nursed him as a child. He told her how he had listened to the rich music of the Siren's song; how he had sailed by the Wandering Rocks, by dread Charybdis, and by Scylla, whom no sailors pass unscathed; how his men had killed the cattle of the Sun; how Zeus the Thunderer had struck his good ship with a flaming bolt, and all his loyal band had been killed at one fell swoop, though he escaped their dreadful fate himself. He described his arrival at the Isle of Ogygia and his reception by the Nymph Calypso, who had so much desired to marry him that she kept him in her cavern home, a pampered guest, tempted by promises of immortality and ageless youth, but inwardly rebellious to the end. Finally he came to his disastrous voyage to Scherie, where the kind-hearted Phaeacians had treated him like a god and sent him home by ship with generous gifts of bronze ware and of gold, and woven stuffs. He had just finished this last tale, when sleep came suddenly upon him, relaxing all his limbs as it resolved his cares.

Once more Athene of the flashing eyes took thought on his behalf. Not till she was satisfied that he had had his fill of love and sleep in his wife's arms, did she arouse the lazy Dawn to leave her golden throne by Ocean Stream and to bring daylight to the world. At last Odysseus rose from that soft bed of his and told Penelope his plans. "Dear wife," he said, "the pair of us have had our share of trials, you here in tears because misfortune dogged each step I took to reach you, and I yearning to get back to Ithaca but kept in cheerless exile by Zeus and all the gods there are. Nevertheless we have had what we desired, a night spent in each other's arms. So now I leave the house and my belongings in your care. As for the ravages that gang of profligates have made among my flocks, I shall repair the greater part by raiding on my own, and the people must contribute too, till they have filled up all my folds again. But at the moment I am going to our orchard farm, to see my good father, who has been so miserable on my account. And this, my dear, is what I wish you to do, though you are too wise to need my instructions. Since it will be common knowledge, as soon as the sun is up, that I have killed the Suitors in the palace, go with your ladies-in-waiting to your room upstairs and stay quietly there, see nobody, and ask no questions."

Odysseus donned his splendid body-armour, woke up Telem-

achus, the cowman, and the swineherd, and told them all to
arm themselves with weapons. They carried out his orders and
were soon equipped in bronze. Then they opened the doors and
sallied out with Odysseus at their head. It was broad daylight
already, but Athene hid them in darkness and soon had them
clear of the town.

THE WASTELAND OF
WILLIAM BLAKE *

By Frank O'Malley

I. THE TYGERS OF WRATH

The question is: how can you put a prophet in his place when,
by the very character of prophecy, he is eternally slipping out of
place? William Blake was not an eighteenth century or nineteenth
century mind or a typically modern mind at all. What I mean
to say, right at the start, is that, although well aware of his time
and of time altogether, he was not in tune with the main tendencies of his or our own time. Indeed time was a barrier he was
forever crashing against. Blake's talent roved through the world
into the fastnesses of the past and dramatically confronted the
abysses of the future. His age did not confine him. As a poet he
does not seem finally to have had real spiritual or artistic kinship
with any of the rationalist or romantic writers of England. As
a thinker he came to despise the inadequacy of the limited revolutionary effort of the political rebels of the Romantic Revolution.
Blake's name is not to be seen mounted first with that of Paine
or Godwin, of Rousseau or Voltaire, of Wordsworth or Shelley
or Byron or Keats. With these he has, ultimately, little or nothing in common. At any rate, his voice and mood and impact are
thoroughly different from the more publicly successful voices of
the period of his life, older and younger generations alike. The
seething Blake cannot be boundaried. He reached back to Sweden-
borg and Jacob Boehme, to Milton (whom Blake would have
saved from spectre and reintegrated through love), to Pascal and

* From *The Review of Politics Reader* (Notre Dame, Ind.: University of
Notre Dame Press, 1959), pp. 291–310.

Dante, to Virgil and Plato and Homer, to the Old Testament Prophets, especially to Job (Blake could say: "The Prophets Isaiah and Ezekiel dined with me"). Blake was himself, in his own way, a prophet rising out of the spiritual underworld that twists its fibres deep beneath the surface of modern civilization. He belongs with all those who lived or will live in the depths under the wasteland and who will judge the wasteland, directly or symbolically. Blake belongs with de Maistre and Kierkegaard, with Novalis and Nietzsche, with Dostoievski, Solovyev and Berdyaev, with Rimbaud and Baudelaire, with Bergson, with Bloy and Bernanos, with Newman, Hopkins, and Patmore, with Melville, Henry Adams, and T. S. Eliot, with Rilke and Kafka, with Joyce, Yeats, and D. H. Lawrence. For these men, too, have surged against the progress of the physical world and sought, in heaven and hell, the meaning and destiny of man-on-earth.

While it may be a good work to examine Blake's consciousness of the local problems of his particular society and of his particular place, finally such examination is merely academic—notably if the study neglects to emphasize or to realize the spiritual depth and power of Blake's record, in his prophecies, of the barrenness of a creation unnourished by love. I think that Mark Schorer, in his *William Blake, the Politics of Vision,* has been most sensible in discussing Blake as "a man of the world" and in showing that Blake was not just "a little boy lost in a lonely fen" as well as in clearly separating Blake from what Schorer chooses to call "the dubious company" of the mystics. But I think that he has been quite deficient in appreciating the spiritual propulsion of Blake which carried him far and away beyond his moment-of-history, and which makes him the most profound and the most prodigious of the English romantics. Both Schorer and Helen C. White (in her important older study of Blake's mysticism) properly deny Blake's claim to be a genuine mystic. At the same time they fail to do justice to the wonder of his capacity for mystery and eternity, and are content, in niggardly spirit, to conclude that Blake's prophecy is a titanic exercise in obscurity that surely fails. Blake's mythological opaqueness is obvious, of course, and is to be admitted (although S. Foster Damon's classic study of Blake's philosophy and symbols reveals that Blake is not such a dark jungle as he seems). Alfred Kazin, in an immodestly and disdainfully intelligent prefatory essay to the Viking Portable Library edition of Blake, likewise fails to point up the spiritual profundity of Blake. While recognizing that Blake's theme was always the defense of "the integral human personality," Kazin has little insight into the intense spiritual drama of Blake's prophecies, the last of which especially are dismissed as lightless and trackless and as requiring, like Joyce's achievement, the almost fanatical devotion of a lifetime. But, as Christopher Dawson has more wisely and sympathetically suggested, "Whoever has the patience and the imagination to follow Blake through his strange visionary world will gain a more direct insight into the process of spiritual change that was taking place under the surface of European consciousness than is to be found in any other writer." [1]

Let it be accepted that Blake was no authentic mystic. Yet he was a religious mind, able, in radiant though involved revelation, to deal with the death of culture. Let it be accepted that he was conscious of the currents of his time. Yet he was not excessively conscious of them (I do not feel that Blake's political awareness was very obtrusive). In any event, he was not locked into them. And one who simply reads the body of his poetry by itself will not find that "the major currents of opinions of his time" were of great importance to his more searching work. John Middleton Murry, who, according to Schorer, was temerarious in boldly entering Blake's mind and in trying to grasp it "from his own page alone," has shown, I believe, more real insight into Blake than is accomplished by what Schorer terms his own "more halting approach" to Blake's genius. I am afraid that the halting approach of the academy can do little for the splendor of Blake's spiritual genius. This kind of genius is too foreign to the minor tensions and traps of conventional scholarship, which are not quite equal to allowing or holding the greatness of a true and valiant soul. The horses of instruction have never made it evident that they are wiser than the tygers of wrath. Their narrowing formulas and frameworks cannot hold Blake's fiery depiction of the infernal evil and darkness that plague modern civilization, nor can they perceive the strange, burning vision that ministers to the sorrow and savagery of the world.

II. The Heart Full of Futurity

There is to be seen in Blake a juxtaposition of two elements that Nicholas Berdyaev found in himself: "a passionate love of the world above, of the world of the highest, with pity for the lower world, the world of suffering." Blake's mission comes forth

---

[1] C. Dawson, "William Blake and the Religion of Romanticism," *The Tablet*, 168 (London, Sept. 12, 1936), 336–338. All further Dawson quotations are from this incisive and unpretentious essay, to which I acknowledge a special debt.

from this combination. In his letters (and in his marginalia) the first element is given remarkable emphasis. There, with unfaltering conviction, he describes his task: essentially to liberate man and his world from the nets of rationalism, to achieve freedom from the slavery of matter through "Imagination, which is Spiritual Sensation." Out of a deep pit of melancholy, Blake says, he emerged and his eyes expanded into regions of fire and "like a Sea without shore, continue Expanding." Although he tried to chain his feet to the world of duty and reality, it was a vain endeavor. The passion of his love for the higher world, for the mansions of eternity was too great:

> the faster I bind, the better is the Ballast, for I, so far from being bound down, take the world with me in my flights, & often it seems lighter than a ball of wool rolled by the wind. Bacon and Newton would prescribe ways of making the world heavier to me, & Pitt would prescribe distress for a medicinal potion; but as none on Earth can give me Mental Distress, & I know that all Distress inflicted by Heaven is a Mercy, a Fig for all Corporeal! [2]

Blake dwells upon the interest which he keeps closest to his heart, an interest that is "more than life or all that seems to make life comfortable without." His interest, he declares, is

> the Interest of True Religion & Science [in this context true knowledge and wisdom], & whenever anything appears to affect that Interest (Especially if myself omit any duty to my Station as a Soldier of Christ), It gives me the greatest of torments. I am not ashamed, afraid, or adverse to tell you what Ought to be Told: That I am under the direction of Messengers from Heaven, Daily & Nightly; but the nature of such things is not, as some suppose, without trouble or care. Temptations are on the right hand & left; behind, the sea of time & space roars & follows swiftly; he who keeps not right onward is lost, & if our footsteps slide in clay, how can we do otherwise than fear & tremble?

Blake continues the description of his spiritual state and of the spiritual responsibility of his task:

> But if we fear to do the dictates of our Angels, & tremble at the Tasks set before us; if we refuse to do Spiritual Acts

[2] All quotations from Blake in this essay are from the complete *Poetry and Prose of William Blake*, edited by Geoffrey Keynes (New York: Random House, 1939).

because of Natural Fears or Natural Desires! Who can describe the dismal torments of such a state!—I too well remember the Threats I heard!—"If you, who are organized by
Divine Providence for spiritual communion, Refuse, & bury
your Talent in the Earth, even tho' you should want Natural
Bread, Sorrow & Desperation pursues you thro' life, & after
death shame and confusion of face to eternity. Everyone in
Eternity will leave you, aghast at the Man who was crown'd
with glory & honour by his brethren, & betray'd their cause
to their enemies. You will be call'd the base Judas who betray'd his Friend!"—Such words would make any stout man
tremble, & how then could I be at ease? But I am now no
longer in That State, & now go on again with my Task, Fear-
less, and tho' my path is difficult, I have no fear of stumbling
while I keep it.

Reflecting upon his plan to present to "the dwellers upon
earth" by means of his prophecies the history of his spiritual suffering, Blake admonished the children of man for their mockery
of the prophet:

Would to God that they would consider it,—that they would
consider their Spiritual Life, regardless of that faint Shadow
called Natural Life, and that they would Promote Each
other's Spiritual labours, each according to its Rank, & that
they would know that Receiving a Prophet as a Prophet is
a duty which If omitted is more Severely Avenged than Every
Sin and Wickedness beside. It is the Greatest of Crimes to
Depress True Art and Science. I know that those who are
dead from the Earth, & who mocked and Despised the Meekness of True Art . . . I know that such Mockers are Most
Severely Punished in Eternity . . . The Mocker of Art is the
Mocker of Jesus. Let us go on . . . following his Cross: let us
take it up daily, Persisting in Spiritual Labours & the use of
that Talent which it is Death to Bury, and of that Spirit to
which we are called.

The Mocker of Art is the Mocker of Jesus. The Mocker of Art
is the Mocker of Vision. Blake abhorred Bacon and Reynolds and
Burke, because they mocked inspiration and vision: "Inspiration
& Vision was then, & now is, & I hope will always Remain, my
Element, my Eternal Dwelling place; how can I hear it Con-
temned without returning Scorn for Scorn?" For Blake Art was
the creative means of liberation from the stranglehold of reason
and matter. And the action of Imagination was holy, divine.

Christ the Savior became in Blake's sight the Creative Imagination. To him the best Christianity was the exercise of the Divine Art of Imagination: "A poet, a Painter, a Musician, an Architect: the Man or Woman who is not one of these is not a Christian." Blake knew that there existed "a Class of Men whose whole delight is in Destroying." But to be a Christian, one had to be a Creator: "You must leave Fathers & Mothers & Houses & Lands if they stand in the way of Art." If men, Blake declared, remain just and true to their Imagination, they shall have the world of Eternity where they "shall live forever in Jesus Our Lord." Blake's Imagination, as Dawson has pointed out, is "no subjective human faculty; it is the creative and eternal Logos." It rises not out of the world or of man. Blake insisted that the world of Imagination is not the world of the natural man. Rather

> it is the divine bosom into which we shall go after the death of the Vegetative body. This World of Imagination is Infinite & Eternal, whereas the world of Generation, or Vegetation, is Finite and Temporal. There exists in that Eternal World the Permanent Realities of Every Thing which we see reflected in this Vegetative Glass of Nature. All things are comprehended in their Eternal Forms in the divine body of the Saviour, the True Vine of Eternity.

From such beliefs it is easy to see why for Blake the mocker of art became the mocker of Jesus. It is likewise easy to see why he set such great store by the extraordinary products of his own Creative Imagination, the Prophetic Books, why he could rejoice and tremble in his own creations, why he could say that his heart was full of futurity. Blake was rapturous in his enthusiasm for the world above, was convinced of the glory and honor of his utterance and of the self-induced divine sanction for and the insuperability of his mission:

> I see the face of my Heavenly Father; he lays his Hand upon my Head & gives a blessing to all my works; why should I be troubled? why should my heart & flesh cry out? I will go on in the Strength of the Lord; through Hell will I sing forth his Praises, that the Dragons of the Deep may praise him, and that those who dwell in darkness & in the Sea Coasts may be gather'd into his Kingdom.

III. THE FURNACES OF AFFLICTION

Blake's pity for the world of suffering no less than his special vision is marked throughout his poetry, for at least the Songs of Experience onward. He was conscious, like T. S. Eliot, of the wasteland, into which modern civilization was being transformed, of its denial of light and life, love and hope and faith, of its impoverishment of the body through industry and mechanics, of the soul through science, "the Tree of Death." The images, tones, and rhythms of his language become the forms of his lamentation for a lost world, a world without love, which has neglected or perverted the practice of divine arts. The freshness of his enthusiasm for the creativity of the formal revolutionary causes of liberty darkens into portentous voices of anguish. The poet's simple, uncomplicated lyrical pleasure in the innocence of the world is blasted in the furnaces of human affliction. Man has created his world—and it has fallen back into waste and void. And there is darkness again upon the face of the deep.

Like Léon Bloy, Blake had a keen sense of how money had dragged into misery the lives of the poor. Money, he charged, is "the life's blood of Poor Families." Money is the curse of the Art ("The Tree of Life") of Christianity, for "Christianity is Art and not Money." He asserted that the real Christian charity cannot be dependent on money, "on Caesar or Empire or Natural Religion." Money is "the Great Satan of Reason." Blake's "sensitiveness to the suffering of the poor," according to Dawson, marked off his religion from "the orthodox Christianity of the age." Dawson further comments that, although Blake's "ideal of creative imagination and spiritual intuition resembles that of the German romantics, his devotion to social justice has more in common with the utopian socialism of Fourier and the St. Simonians." And the prayer of Los from the second book of Jerusalem is cited as an indication of Blake's attitude towards "the callous indifference of Church and State: and: the facile optimism of the radicals with their cult of enlightened self-interest."

And Los prayed and said, "O Divine Saviour, arise
"Upon the Mountains of Albion as in ancient time! Behold!
"The cities of Albion seek thy face; London groans in pain
"From Hill to Hill, & the Thames laments along the Valleys:
"The little Villages of Middlesex & Surrey hunger & thirst:
"The twenty-eight Cities of Albion stretch their hands to thee
"Because of the Oppressors of Albion in every City & Village.

"They mock at the Labourer's limbs: they mock at his starv'd
Children:
"They buy his Daughters that they may have power to sell
his Sons:
"They compell the Poor to live upon a crust of bread by soft
mild arts:
"They reduce the Man to want, then give with pomp &
ceremony:
"The praise of Jehovah is chaunted from lips of hunger &
thirst. . . ."

In an earlier poem Blake had expressed his concern over the
unholy poverty of "a rich and fruitful land," poverty that, prevailing against all life-giving light and nurture, had created an
"eternal winter."

> Is this a holy thing to see
> In a rich and fruitful land,
> Babes reduc'd to misery,
> Fed with cold and usurious hand?
>
> Is that trembling cry a song?
> Can it be a song of joy?
> And so many children poor?
> It is a land of poverty!
>
> And their sun does never shine,
> And their fields are bleak & bare,
> And their ways are fill'd with thorns:
> It is eternal winter there.
>
> For where-e'er the sun does shine,
> And where-e'er the rain does fall,
> Babe can never hunger there,
> Nor poverty the mind appall.

All his days Blake seemed to be able to hear the spectres of the
dead crying out from the deeps beneath the hills of England and
to hear the English cities groaning in their iron furnaces. D. H.
Lawrence, it may be noted, considered his own mining countryside of Nottingham and said that the real tragedy of England is
"the tragedy of ugliness";

> Now though perhaps nobody knew it, it was ugliness which
> really betrayed the spirit of man in the nineteenth century.
> The great crime which the moneyed classes and promoters

of industry committed in the palmy Victorian days was the condemning of the workers to ugliness, ugliness, ugliness: meanness and formless and ugly surroundings, ugly ideals, ugly religion, ugly hope, ugly love, ugly clothes, ugly furniture, ugly houses, ugly relationship between workers and employers.

Lawrence's words simply reaffirm the much earlier judgment of Hopkins upon the base and bespotted features of the industrial England he observed. British civilization was dirty, Hopkins reflected, and its cities convinced him "of the misery of town life to the poor and more than to the poor, of the misery of the poor in general, of the degradation even of our race, of the hollowness of this century's civilization." But Blake, long before Hopkins or Lawrence, knew this ugliness and baseness. A man-made rationalist and materialist civilization had confined and spoiled and filled with diseases the freshness and loveliness of human and physical nature. It had put its blight upon the action of the mind, upon work, upon patriotism and sacrifice, upon the Church, upon love and marriage:

> I wander thro' each charter'd street,
> Near where the charter'd Thames does flow,
> And mark in every face I meet
> Marks of weakness, marks of woe.
>
> In every cry of every Man,
> In every Infant's cry of fear,
> In every voice, in every ban,
> The mind-forged manacles I hear.
>
> How the Chimney-sweeper's cry
> Every black'ning Church appalls;
> And the hapless Soldier's sigh
> Runs in blood down Palace walls.
>
> But most thro' midnight streets I hear
> How the youthful Harlot's curse
> Blasts the new born Infant's tear
> And blights with plagues the Marriage hearse.

One is reminded of T. S. Eliot's time-kept London:

> Unreal City,
> Under the brown fog of a winter dawn,
> A crowd flowed over London bridge, so many,
> I had not thought death had undone so many.

But Blake did not need to be localizing the miserable conditions of man in London or in England. In his being there was response to the universal withering of man's personality in the midst of murderous rocks, the shattering and smashing of the unity of man's spiritual, intellectual, imaginative, and emotional energies. In the disruptive life of modern man there was no chance for synthesis, for the closing and healing of wounds. Blake had a deep feeling for the loneliness and lost way of man in the wilds of a progressive civilization, the loneliness of man's endurance of the hard and sterile disintegration of life. In countless passages of the Prophetic Books, he explored the wasteland with an art appropriate to his task, sufficiently successful anyway to dispose of Schorer's arbitrary notion that Blake's art is "one of the great casualties in the history of poetry." Blake expressed such anguish and fear as were aroused over a century later in the soul of T. S. Eliot when he contemplated the triumphant civilization that seemed to him, as to Blake, capable of generating only limitless mediocrity and misery and war. Where money exists, Blake declared, only war can be carried on. In Blake's earlier poems there are images of drouth and death enough, of the lightless, stony dread fallen on the head of the earth, "her locks cover'd with grey despair," of the dream of the child starved in the pathless desert, of the Garden of Love flowerless and filled with briars, graves and tombstones, of the snake vomiting out his poison on the Bread and Wine. But the dolorous clangor of sterility is terrific throughout the Prophetic Books. Blake's land is a land of black storms and dark valleys and dreadful ruins. The poet pictures the couches of the dead in "a land of sorrow and tears where never smile was seen." There is often the fright of smoke and thunder and flaming winds, of plagues crippling the world and cutting off man and beast amidst howling and shuddering and the rattling of hollow bones. The furious terrors fly around everywhere. This is Blake's rats' alley, where the dead men have convulsively lost their bones.

Yet in the figure of Urizen the terrors of the void are concentrated, for Urizen is the real spectre of death, the creator of emptiness. Urizen is the unintegrated reasoning power in man, separated from Imagination and framing laws "to destroy Imagination, the Divine Body." In the Blakean mythology, Urizen is the dark, evil god of restriction, the foe that enslaves vision in its frigid horrors:

> . . . his ten thousands of thunders,
> Rang'd in gloom'd array, stretch out across

The dread world; & the rolling of wheels,
As of swelling seas, sound in his clouds,
In his hills of stor'd snows, in his mountains
Of hail & ice; voices of terror
Are heard, like thunders of autumn
When the cloud blazes over the harvests.

Urizen is "self-closed, all-repelling," occupied in vast, silent but unprolific labors. To break the rivets of iron that repressive Urizen has soldered upon the life of man, Blake created Orc, the force of fire, passion and revolutionary energy that will endure no restraints. The poet likewise offered his proverbs of hell: "The road of excess leads to the palace of wisdom"; "He who desires but acts not breeds pestilence"; "The wrath of the lion is the wisdom of God"; "Exuberance is beauty"; "Sooner murder an infant in its cradle than nurse unacted desires"; "The soul of sweet delight can never be defiled." The chorus of the Song of Liberty is sung: "Let the Priests of the Raven of dawn no longer, in deadly black, with hoarse note curse the sons of joy . . . For everything that lives is holy." All this will appear to be not only anarchic and anti-rationalistic, but also anti-Christian. Blake, however, gradually came to realize that the uncontrolled energies of desire and revolt would breed their own pestilences. So the fierce, bright creativity of the romantic revolutionary spirit darkens into "apocalyptic terror and gloom" out of which emerges at last the tender voice of the Lamb of God.

For the Urizen-Orc myth Blake substituted another: "Albion, the universal Man, and Jerusalem, the divine Vision." Blake's lamentation, of course, is no less loud and the sense of suffering and death persists: the groans of Jerusalem are great and storms beat around Albion. But Jesus, the Good Shepherd, reducing to nothing the other voices and phantom figures of the prophecies, has appeared and the breath of divine amity blows over the world. In the fourth book of Jerusalem, the grievous voice of Jerusalem, lost and wandering among precipices of despair, is heard in the darkness of Philisthea:

"How distant far from Albion! his hills & valleys no more
    Receive the feet of Jerusalem: they have cast me quite
    away,
And Albion is himself shrunk to a narrow rock in the
    midst of the sea!
The plains of Sussex & Surrey, their hills of flocks and
    herds

No more seek to Jerusalem nor to the sound of my Holy-
ones.
The Fifty-two Counties of England are harden'd against
me
As if I was not their Mother; they despise me and cast
me out,
London cover'd the Whole Earth: England encompass'd
the Nations,
And all the Nations of the Earth were seen in the Cities
of Albion."

Jerusalem laments that Albion had formerly given her "the whole
Earth to walk up and down, to pour joy upon every mountain,
to teach songs to the shepherd and plowman." Italy, France,
Spain, Germany, Poland, and the North "found my gates in all
their mountains & my curtains in all their vales; the furniture of
their houses was the furniture of my chamber." Turkey and
Greece sounded their thanksgiving to her and Egypt, Libya, and
Ethiopia enquired for Jerusalem. "And thou, America! I once
beheld thee, but now behold no more thy golden mountains."
Now Jerusalem must grieve that her altars run with blood, that
her fires are corrupt, and her innocence become "a cloudy pestilence," rather than "a continual cloud of salvation." Now she has
been closed from the nations "in the narrow passages of the
valleys of destruction." Now she walks "weeping in pangs of a
Mother's torment for her Children":

"I walk in affliction, I am a worm and no living soul!
A worm going to eternal torment, rais'd up in a night
To an eternal night of pain, lost! lost! lost! forever!"

Then Albion is seen lying cold upon his rock, while "the weeds
of Death inwrap his hands & feet, blown incessant and wash'd
incessant by the for-ever restless sea-waves foaming abroad upon
the white Rock" and "England, a Female Shadow, as deadly damps
of the Mines of Cornwall & Derbyshire, lays upon his bosom
heavy." Overhead, "the famish'd Eagle screams on boney Wings,
and around them howls the Wolf of famine." The black ocean
heaves and thunders "around the wormy Garments of Albion."
There comes, however, a pause, a silence like death:

Time was Finished! The Breath Divine Breathed over
Albion
Beneath the Furnaces & starry Wheels and in the
Immortal Tomb,

> And England, who is Britannia, awoke from Death on
>   Albion's bosom:
> She awoke pale & cold; she fainted seven times on the
>   Body of Albion.
> "O piteous Sleep, O piteous Dream! O God, O God
>   awake! I have slain
> In Dreams of Chastity & Moral Law: I have murdered
>   Albion!"

The voice of England pierced the cold ear of Albion, who stirred upon his rock as "the Breath Divine went forth upon the morning hills." Painfully opening his eyelids, Albion looked upon England: "Ah! Shall the Dead live again?" England then rejoiced and entered the bosom of Albion. The inferno of Blake is at this point done and Blake's paradiso (insofar as he achieves one) begins.

The progression through Blake's wasteland is similar to that in T. S. Eliot's. At the very end of Eliot's central poem, "The Waste Land," the thunder, no longer dry and sterile, speaks with the voice of redemption: after the agony in stony places the winds bear life-bringing rains and the poem ends with "the Peace which passeth understanding." Into Blake's wasteland, Jesus finally comes and stands by Albion as "by the lost Sheep that he hath found, & Albion knew that it was the Lord." Albion asks: "Oh Lord, what can I do? My Selfhood cruel marches against thee, deceitful . . . I know it is my Self, O my Divine Creator & Redeemer." Jesus answers: "Fear not Albion: unless I die thou canst not live; but if I die I shall arise again & thou with me. This is Friendship & Brotherhood: without it Man Is Not." And Albion replies: "Cannot Man exist without Mysterious offering of Self for Another? is this Friendship & Brotherhood?" Finally Jesus says:

> ". . . Wouldest thou love one who never died
> For thee, or ever die for one who had not died for thee?
> And if God dieth not for Man & giveth not himself
> Eternally for Man, Man could not exist; for Man is love
> As God is Love: every kindness to another is a little
>   Death
> In the Divine Image, nor can Man exist but by
>   Brotherhood."

Universal man, as Jerusalem laments, has spurned her, the Divine Vision, and has selfishly been preoccupied with his own reason and matter. So the spirit is killed in him. He can be saved from this deadly slavery, this negation of and incrustation upon his immortal spirit, by the constant annihilation of the selfhood. Man must surrender his absolute confidence in rational demonstration and have faith in the Savior and in the mercy of redemption through the Savior. Albion must make a great effort to discard Bacon, Locke, and Newton, must be willing "to take off his filthy garments" and then "clothe himself with Imagination."

This final resolution of Blake is, as Dawson comments, "less Christian than it may appear at first sight, for Blake not only assimilates the Saviour to the Creative Imagination and the Prophet to the artist, but asserts the substantial identity of God and Man in terms that seem to exclude any belief in the divine transcendence." Nevertheless, Blake's attitude is fundamentally religious, full of wonder, love and awe. As Blake himself put it: "I speak of Spiritual Things, Not of Natural." He detested the Spectre of the extreme and sterile rational power that had come to haunt and stupefy man, the Spectre that taught experiment and doubt rather than belief and eternal life and symmetry, the Satanic Accuser that, lacking love and sympathy, had laid waste the world. Here was no water but only rock.

IV. The Conqueror

The Christianity to which Blake came was life-giving for him and for the decayed and groaning world he had constructed. But it was, naturally, a Christianity of his own composition, baffling, gnostic, theosophical, in the mode of St. Martin and Lavater and of the Lutheran mystique of Jacob Boehme. Even at the end he kept his antagonism (based upon his feeling that faith eliminates obligation) towards the dominion of authority and the moral duty imposed by it. Authority remained repressive and fearsome. It is certain, however, that his pantheistic direction and antinomianism did not compel Blake to ignore the implacable presence of evil, its menace to human life and culture, and the importance of the moral struggle against the power of evil. It is also clear that Christianity was no longer the enemy, no longer embodied, as it had in his earlier thought, the calamitous, curbing force in the world of freedom. Christianity now turned the furnaces of affliction into "Fountains of Living Waters flowing from the Humanity Divine." The real enemy of humanity and universal nature, Blake wrote in the Preface to the third book of Jerusalem, is the deist, the preacher of natural morality and natural religion:

Your Religion, O Deists! Deism, is the Worship of the God
of this World by the means of what you call Natural Reli-
gion and Natural Philosophy, and of Natural Morality or
Self-Righteousness, the Selfish Virtues of the Natural Heart.
This was the Religion of the Pharisees who murder'd Jesus.
Deism is the same & ends in the same.

It is the rationalists and natural religionists who are responsible
for the warring and ruin of history, not "the poor Monks & Religious." These profess "the Religion of Jesus, Forgiveness of Sin"
—and this religion "can never be the cause of a War." Those who
cause war are deists, who "never can be Forgivers of Sin." And
Blake concluded: "The Glory of Christianity is To Conquer by
Forgiveness. All the Destruction, therefore, in Christian Europe
has arisen from Deism, which is Natural Religion."

Whatever Blake's contact, adequately investigated by Schorer,
with the currents of his time, he remained essentially "an isolated
figure." But he is still a great clue-figure in the spiritual and intellectual history of the modern world. He reveals, in his odd,
unclassical, and unorthodox ways, as Dawson notes, "the spiritual
conflict which underlies the social changes of the age and which
resulted from the insurgence of the spiritual forces that had been
repressed by the rationalism and moralism of the Enlightenment."
In Dawson's view, this spiritual revolution had a dual realization:
first, as "a movement of return to the tradition of historic Christianity" manifested in the Catholic Revival on the Continent and
in Newman and the Oxford Movement leading to a renewal of
Catholic life and culture in England; secondly, and in contrast,
as "a movement of innovation and change: resulting in new
religions of humanitarianism, nationalism and liberalism." Yet
these two forms are not so contradictory or disparate as they seem.
The religious liberalism of Lamennais, for instance, unfolded out
of the religious traditionalism of de Maistre and de Bonald. Likewise, a number of the intellectual and social reformers, moving
through their new religions, arrived at traditional Christianity.
And although religion did not succeed in giving form to modern
civilization, it was at least recognized as an indispensable element
in the life of modern man. That is why Dawson thinks that "in
comparison with the 18th century, the 19th century, especially
the first half of it, was a religious age." It seems to me that something of all this, writers like Helen C. White and Alfred Kazin
fail to recognize when they intimate, as Miss White does, that
William Blake is not "a prophet for this modern world" or, as
Kazin does, that Blake has not yet spoken "to our modern human-

ity in tones we have learned to prize as our own and our greatest."
In his rather extreme and perverse work, *Blake and Modern
Thought,* Denis Saurat comprehends at least Blake's relevance
and usefulness as a significant "witness of our own mentality."

Blake is not, however, a witness of the prevalent modern mentality, but rather of all those who have, in one shape or another,
fought valiantly in the underground of history for the power of
the spiritual as opposed to the success of the material which is
enough for the surface-dwellers. At the outset of this essay, I listed
the names of some modern seers with whom Blake has relationship. I would not limit his relevance to the fairly familiar figures
who are often brought into the Blakean universe—Yeats and D. H.
Lawrence, for example. Yeats, like Blake, was fascinated by occult-
ism and spiritualism and created in his poetry his own mythological system. Just as Blake managed to encompass, in one phase
of his work, the spirit of the French Revolution and the liberalist
uprising in the world, so did Yeats draw into his mythology the
heroes and events of the Irish Rebellion. As he grew older,
Yeats, much like Blake, became more and more dubious about
the new tyrants enthroned by a society devoted to commerce, science, and the liberal point-of-view, the new tyrants that spat upon
the pride of the people. But Yeats never seems to have gone down
very deep into the inferno—and, in any event, was quite fluid in
dreaming it out of existence. Likewise, the making of analogues
between Blake and D. H. Lawrence is, at first sight anyway, a
quite easy thing to do. Blake, however, is not so one-sided or
obsessed as Lawrence in urging the mind to come down from its
eminence. And Blake does not stop, like Lawrence, with the dark
passional, physical powers; Blake comes closer, as Saurat asserts
(even though misconceivingly), to a synthesis of the human spirit,
a synthesis of "reason, imagination, passion and instinct." Blake
comes toward, I am convinced, many minds whom one might,
without reflection, separate from him entirely. Blake is an enduring, unconquerable, and universal witness because, despite his
faults and confusions, he understood and assailed the evils which
upset and will always upset the great, serious, most worthy thinkers
and artists of the present and future, those particularly who find
it impossible to take it easy and relax when they are braved by
the demons of indifference or compromise, of mediocrity or
venality in man. And, as S. Foster Damon recognized, the evils
damned by Blake "are even stronger now than when he wrote,
and at last the world, beholding the errors, searches for solutions."

In this search for solutions to our evils there are a good many
contemporary spiritual minds who have a real (even if not too

obvious, perhaps) affinity with Blake. I have selected arbitrarily to develop this point some publications of three rather different intellects: Nicholas Berdyaev, the Russian philosopher who lived in exile in Paris; Franz Kafka, the Czech-German writer; and Georges Bernanos, the French Catholic novelist.

Berdyaev, in *Slavery and Freedom*, reveals, like Blake, his kinship with Jacob Boehme and, in general, the characteristic Blakean terror of any destructive tyranny, together with an urgent love of freedom and creativeness. Blake and Berdyaev seem to maintain the same gnostic idea of freedom as coming only when man has been rescued from the cruel grasp of matter. Both have a terrific anxiety to drag modern man out of the snares that seize him. Berdyaev writes: "I discover in myself something elemental and primitive: a reaction against world data; a refusal to accept any sort of objectivity such as the slavery of man; and the opposition of the freedom of the spirit to the compulsion of the world, to violence, and to compliancy." These could readily be the words of Blake. Blake would have understood, too, the large emphasis which Berdyaev puts upon spirit over nature and love over law. Moreover, Berdyaev's strictures upon the "hidden dictatorship" of money in modern society at least echo those of Blake:

> The life of man depends upon money, the most impersonal, the most unqualitative power in the world, and the most readily convertible into everything else alike. It is not directly, by way of physical violence, that a man is deprived of his freedom of conscience, freedom of thought, and freedom of judgment, but he is placed in a position of dependence materially, he finds himself under the threat of death by starvation, and in this way he is deprived of his freedom. Money confers independence: the absence of it places a man in a position of dependence.

And Blake's sensitiveness to the industrialized torture of modern people is repeated in Berdyaev's judgment: "The development of civilization was accompanied by the oppression and exploitation of vast masses of mankind, of the labouring people; and this oppression was held to be justified by the objective values of civilization."

Blake's apocalyptic pessimism is reduced by Berdyaev to this aphorism: "Optimism about the world order is the servitude of man." But the action of the Redeemer (absorbed into gnosticism from Christianity), of Christ suffering for man and striving with man, in opposition to the "falsity and wrong" of the objectivized

world order, will bring man freedom from servitude. Blake no
less than Berdyaev underlines this idea. When Berdyaev writes
that "the slavery of man to nature ... is slavery to the object
world" and that "creativeness is a fight against the object world,"
one cannot fail to remember Blake's annotations upon Wordsworth:

> I see in Wordsworth the Natural Man rising up against the
> Spiritual Man continually, & then he is No Poet but a
> Heathen Philosopher at Enmity against all true Poetry or
> Inspiration. . . . Natural Objects always did & now do weaken,
> deaden & obliterate Imagination in Me. Wordsworth must
> know that what he Writes Valuable is Not to be found in
> Nature.

I think, too, that the beautiful, vast and surging "chaos" of Blake's
poetry which gradually brings itself out to a kind of cosmical
focus in the figure of Jesus, might carry, as an epigraph, this sentence from Berdyaev: "There is no beauty of cosmos without the
background of chaos." That is, without the background of chaos
"there is no tragedy, no climax of human creativeness, no Don
Quixote, no drama of Shakespeare, no Faust, no novels of Dos-
toyevsky." And surely no Blake.

The paradox of the essential chaos of our stupefying efficient
bureaucratic civilization (with its fixation of mechanical order, its
wondrous files and filing systems, its managerial burrows, its inexhaustible forms and guaranteed procedures) imposed itself upon
Franz Kafka. Blake and Kafka are at once alike in that each experienced real hardships and enjoyed no great measure of public
success during his life-time. Each had what Edwin Muir—in the
introduction to Kafka's collection of stories and reflections titled
The Great Wall of China—terms "a passion for rightness." But it
seems that Kafka, unlike Blake, had "no trace of vanity" about
his works. Blake is more humorless in his effort than Kafka, who
had at least "a humour of desperation." Yet Kafka is tied to
Blake in his fantastic fidelity "to himself and what he thought
the right way of conduct." In his art each is able to evoke (Kafka:
quietly, almost geometrically; Blake: tumultuously, even harshly)
an atmosphere of such dread and doom as to make the writer
appear on "the verge of actual madness." But, whereas Kafka
moves in his art "towards proportion and clarity," Blake moves
decidedly towards greater and greater complexity (yet, I suppose,
reaches the more awesome clarity that lies at the heart of complexity).

Kafka's moral and spiritual problem, according to Muir's description, is, in a considerable way, Blake's also: "that of finding one's true vocation . . . and that of acting in accordance with the will of heavenly powers." Kafka, however, grasps the concept of divine authority (although Kafka's God may seem a too darkling and far-removed Jehovah) and its importance for man. Blake, it would seem, exults in his visions of the higher world but very much on his own terms. He has no faith in a personal God, and any idea of authority is intolerable to him. Kafka indicates, in *The Great Wall of China,* that he understands, as well as Blake, the human desire to smash restraints: "Human nature can endure no restraint"; Kafka writes, "if it binds itself it soon begins to tear madly at its bonds, until it rends everything asunder, the wall, the bonds and its very self." Yet Kafka can say, emphasizing the need for "humility and meekness," what Blake could never be expected to say (although he does pray to his Savior to pour upon him the spirit of meekness): "We and here I speak in the name of many people—did not really know ourselves until we had carefully scrutinized the decrees of the high command. . . ." Blake could talk of the direction of messengers from heaven and of the dictates of his angels, but an objectively existing authority remote from his own Imagination could not excite his devotion or gain his obedience.

In their attitude towards progress and science and towards the burdens modern civilization places upon human freedom, there is notable correspondence between Kafka and Blake. Kafka writes, in "Investigations of a Dog":

> Certainly knowledge is progressing, its advance is irresistible, it actually progresses at an accelerating speed, always faster, but what is there to praise in that? It is as if one were to praise someone because with the years he grows older, and in consequence comes nearer and nearer to death with increasing speed. That is a natural and moreover an ugly process, in which I find nothing to praise. I can only see decline everywhere. . . .

And the instinct that invalidates a man's scientific capacity, Kafka suggests, may be the very one that makes him "—perhaps for the sake of science itself but a different science from that of today, an ultimate science—prize freedom higher than everything else." Kafka reflects that the freedom available today may indeed be a "wretched business." But it is still freedom and a possession. Blake would have sympathized with these thoughts, even though his notion of freedom might not have been precisely reconcilable with that of Kafka. And in "Reflections on Sin, Pain, Hope and the True Way," the aphoristic talent of Kafka strikes out in shapes remarkably suggestive of Blake: "There is only a spiritual world; what we call the physical world is the evil in the spiritual one, and what we call evil is only a necessary moment in our endless development"; "The fact that there is only a spiritual world robs us of hope and gives us certainty"; "The spirit only becomes free when it ceases to be a prop"; "We are sinful not merely because we have eaten of the Tree of Knowledge, but also because we have not yet eaten of the Tree of Life"; and "The whole world is full of them [our rationalizations], indeed the whole visible world is perhaps nothing more than the rationalization of a man who wants to find peace for a moment." These, I think, have at least the accent of Blake.

Admittedly, there are great differences in vision and mode of vision between Blake and Kafka. But the ideas and experiences of Kafka, realized in *The Castle, The Trial, Metamorphosis,* and in such a volume as *The Great Wall of China,* are not alien to the being of Blake and are motivated by some likeness of conscience with respect to the chaos of the condition of man and the terror of his life in what Bernanos calls "the vast agglomeration of cities." Blake and Kafka are joined securely in their sight of "the land of snares & traps & wheels & pitfalls & dire mills."

The resemblances between Blake and the formidable French prophet, Georges Bernanos, are numerous and interesting. Of the lineage of Léon Bloy, Bernanos shares with Blake a horror of the merely restrictive and blindly indifferent institutions of education and government. Bernanos, the tyger of wrath, despises the official leaders and teachers of society, the representatives who monstrously break and crush the people or allow them to be broken and exploited. He also shares with Blake an intense sympathy with these poor, weak and oppressed ones of the earth, a savage hostility towards materialist civilization and a passion for liberty. Bernanos sometimes manages nightmarish moments and images of torrid desolation and pain reminiscent of the immense effects, the "gigantic gnawing," of Blake—as in this passage from *Joy* describing a horrible presence of heat:

> It was not so much like the vast universal conflagration of day as an insidious fire over the dry hillside, the quick undulating flame running from one twig to another, like a tiny scarlet tongue. For at certain hours of the day in unusually hot summers, nature instead of relaxing, stretching out under the caress of the sun, seems on the contrary to shrink silently,

timidly into herself, with the motionless, stupid resignation of an animal when it feels the mortal bite of its enemy's teeth sinking into its flesh. And indeed that stiff rain of heat pouring out of the mournful sky, that shower of white-hot arrows, the infinite suction of the sun, made one think of vicious bites, millions upon millions of bites, a gigantic gnawing.

In his novels and essays, Bernanos embodies and assails the spiritual dryness, the talent for compromise and meaninglessness, of the twentieth century Christians, in terms as trenchant as those used by Blake to assail the mediocrity of the Christendom of his age. Blake once said that "Englishmen are all intermeasurable by one another; certainly a happy state of agreement, in which I for one do not agree. God keep you and me from the divinity of yes and no too—the yea, nay, creeping Jesus—from supposing up and down to be the same thing...." Today one might extract many passages similar in tone and text from Bernanos' *Plea for Liberty*. The impact of the voice of Bernanos, appealing to the men of France and England, is often like that of Blake, who could cry out: "Rouse up, O Young Men of the New Age! set your forehead against the ignorant Hirelings! For we have Hirelings in the Camp, the Court & the University...."

With Blake, love is a great word. With Bernanos, Love is the last word. But the Love of Bernanos is clearly a transcendent and consuming Love, flowing out of the charity and grace of the real Christ, about whose nature, Bernanos, unlike Blake, has no confusion. Bernanos is utterly concerned about the freedom of free men. But, different from Blake, he seeks for the truest freedom of man in the authoritative life and strength of the Church and in the profundity of its protection of the life of the Spirit. (Bernanos' feud with ecclesiasticism does not alter in any way the firmness of his belief in the ministry of the Church.) Man will escape from slavery by giving himself up to Christ through the Church which is His Body. The resolution of man's suffering and man's hope is to be expected from the Church which alone in the world today preserves the freedom of the person against the monsters. For, as Bernanos says, it has always been the mission of the Church to fulfill God's expectations "that She shape men truly free, a breed of free men peculiarly effective because freedom is for them not only a right, but an obligation, a duty, for which they must render God an accounting." Naturally, Blake could not have delivered himself in this wise. Still, in his later phase, Blake, without the clear faith of Bernanos, would have been sure that the Christian man is the free man. In Blake's system, of course, this man would be "ever expanding in the Bosom of God, the Human Imagination."

The fiction of Bernanos builds great drama—gloomy but always vital—of the inner life and death, the holiness and evil of man against the background of despiritualized civilization. There is a deep warmth—a density of reality—in Bernanos' recreation of the tragic struggle of the soul against evil, a density that the vaporous although piercing forms projected by the imagination of Blake do not attain. For the mysteries that are transmitted to Bernanos out of the authentic living Christian tradition were not received by Blake. And Blake's Satan, the Accuser, is most indefinite when set beside the reality of the Satan, the stench and ferocity of actual evil and actual sin, that Bernanos can summon. With unique power does *Joy* create such reality: the young, saintly innocence of Mademoiselle de Chantal is confronted full force and violated by diabolical evil. It is the cruel and magnificent strife of earth, of this field between the devil and God. Yet a few might be willing to apply to the soul of Blake the words Bernanos used to describe the soul of the protagonist in *Joy*. By extension, Blake "comes and goes . . . breathes and lives with the light, beyond us, beyond our presence." And, although we may not realize it, he "drags our black souls out of the shadows, and the old sins begin to stir, to yawn, to stretch and show their yellow claws . . . tomorrow, day after tomorrow—who knows—some night, this very night perhaps, they will be altogether wide awake."

This discussion of three writers, stirring in the universe that Blake had entered well over a century before, should help to reveal why his thought and action are not just "interesting" and "suggestive," but really animate and abiding in the present age. It ought also to suggest why Blake was troubled as he reflected upon his tremendous task of opening the Eternal Worlds, and why his hand, as he wrote, trembled "exceedingly upon the rock of ages." But Blake was sure of the eternity of his task. "I will & shall to Eternity Embrace Christianity and Adore him who is the Express image of God; but I have travel'd thro' Perils & Darkness not unlike a Champion. I have Conquer'd & shall Go on Conquering. Nothing can withstand the fury of my Course among the Stars of God & in the Abysses of the Accuser." Blake's then was the conviction of the conqueror. And with reason. I do not suppose that Blake could ever actually have said, like Rimbaud, that in his work the victory over matter is won, that "the gnashing of teeth, the hissings of fire, the pestilential sighs are abating." Still, as one of those who set out "thro' Perils & Darkness" at the dawn of our era to be a vindicator of human life against that which perverts it, he came close to a conquest. His fire touched and still touches the quick of the spirit. Once discovered, all thinkers and artists whose wisdom really burns through the skin of time will give heart to us, will forever help us to know and to be. They become in truth the champions of the soul. We cannot help attaching ourselves to them and depending upon them. For they break the chains that freeze our bones, that require us to live as though dying or already dead.

Part Five

BRUSH, COMPASS, AND PEN

Or

Fine Arts and Shakespeare

RIGOLETTO *

By Carlo Gatti

Early in January 1851 Verdi returned to Busseto, and by the end of that month informed the chairman of the Fenice in Venice that the new opera they had ordered was finished except for the last duet. This too would have been ready had not Verdi been suffering from a severe sore throat, the inevitable penalty he paid for every new opera he wrote.

Verdi sent for Piave to write the lyric, indicating even the particular words he wanted for this or that special point. When he engaged Piave to write the libretto Verdi had urged him first to obtain the censor's approval, and Piave had assured him he need not worry. After all, was he not the librettist at the Fenice and therefore in a position to know the moods of the Austrian censor? That censor had become even more difficult since the return of the imperial troops to that heroic city, victim of exhaustion, starvation, and disease. In his turn Guglielmo Brenna, secretary of the Fenice and a great friend of Verdi's, had also assured the composer that the censor would not put any obstacles in his path. However, Marzari, President of the Fenice, was not of the same opinion. When, a few months after the contract had been signed, he was told the subject of the opera, he informed Verdi that it was doubtful whether the Royal Imperial Council of Public Order would permit the production. Verdi objected violently. *Le Roi s'Amuse* was the best subject he had ever laid hands on up to this point in his career. "The situations are very strong; all the changes of fortune are the result of King Francis's frivolous and libertine character: the fears of Triboulet, the Court jester, the passion of Bianca, Triboulet's daughter, who yields to the love of the Sovereign when he appears to her in disguise." Those situations provide many dramatic highlights, among others the scene of the quartet (in Verdi's and Piave's adaptation) "which will always be one of the most striking effects our (the Italian) theatre can boast."

Verdi had studied the subject and meditated on it profoundly, and in his opinion "the idea, the musical coloring" were real discoveries. "I may say that as far as I am concerned the principal

* From *Verdi, the Man and His Music*, by Carlo Gatti, trans. by Elisabeth Abbott, pp. 121–5. © 1955 by G. P. Putnam's Sons. Reprinted by permission of G. P. Putnam's Sons.

work was already done," he wrote to Marzari. And this was the truth. Verdi himself revealed his own special method of working: "Study your subject, meditate deeply on it; then have a clear vision before your eyes of the actors, see them in their physical and spiritual surroundings as if they were portraits in a luminous frame, standing out in high relief; learn the words by heart, so that you can recite them, pronounce them clearly and distinctly, stress them; then with all the passion in your heart, give full rein to the wave of music."

Donizetti had already said: "Music is only speech accented by sounds, and therefore every composer must create music that rises out of the words. The man who is so unfortunate as to fail in this will produce only superficial music lacking in any emotion."

Checchi tells us that once "when Verdi was present the subject under discussion happened to be the miraculous composition of *The Barber of Seville,* which according to the biographers was written in only thirteen or sixteen days. Someone asked Verdi: 'What is your opinion, Maestro? Is that legend or is it the truth?' Verdi was in an excellent mood that day; in the select circle of intimate friends around him, were none of those terrible bores who were the only persons he cordially detested his whole life long, and he could express himself freely. It was possible, he said, that the great Rossini did not take more than sixteen days to write the *Barber;* but in his opinion the characters were already alive, they moved, had a distinct physiognomy, and each spoke according to his own temperament; scene followed scene and the work of art gradually took on color, acquired its own, one might almost say, supernatural attributes of life. So that on that famous night when Rossini, taking leave of the friends who always accompanied him on those gay nocturnal rambles, went home and sat down to write the first chorus and Fiorello's little aria, the work was already matured. As he filled the sheets of music, the maestro merely transcribed what was written in indelible characters in his brain, and from that sovereign mind the ideas he had accumulated issued forth in their definitive form to be fixed forever on that paper. Who can say how much material is gathered in those hours when, to all appearances, he is merely strolling from one street to another, or calling on some beautiful singer, or in the long hours spent in a restaurant over succulent dinners and merry suppers?"

Verdi also said: "To write well you must write rapidly, almost in one breath, afterward adapting, reworking, polishing the whole rough draft. Unless you do this you run the risk of producing a long-drawn-out work without style or character and with music fitted together laboriously like mosaics."

A friend of the most eminent painters and sculptors, Verdi enjoyed their company, visited them in their studios, and bought their works. He frequented art galleries, and never returned to Rome or to Florence, even for a brief stay, without going to the Vatican or the Uffizi. His home was a little museum of valuable paintings and statues. Often he would call on one or the other of his artist friends to design a scene for him or a character in his opera.

Marzari was right. The Austrian censor, outraged at the idea of confronting a "vile clown" and a glorious sovereign, ordered the management of the Fenice to return the libretto to Verdi for alterations. Marzari then presented the libretto with the required emendations, but the authorities were still unwilling to allow the opera to be performed. Verdi was annoyed and blamed Piave. He had trusted in Piave's written assurance that all would be well and had composed the greater part of the music, working at top speed to finish on time. It was too late now to choose and set to music another subject, even if he were to "work so hard that he would ruin his health." The most he could do was to suggest *Stiffelio*, with a change of ending (the scene in the church) for Venice.

Carlo Martello, General Director of Public Order, was inclined to accept the new opera provided the libretto was modified as he suggested. He proposed changing the name, rank, and attributes of the protagonist. Verdi refused. As a conscientious artist he could not set that libretto to music. Marzari recognized the soundness of these objections, and again appealed to the authorities, who finally consented to allow the opera to be performed with some slight changes to which Verdi agreed. Marzari sent his own secretary, Brenna, and the librettist Piave to Busseto to come to an agreement with the Maestro, who had not budged from his house while the negotiations were in progress.

At last the way was open for Verdi to present his opera. But now he must find the title for it. *Le Roi s'Amuse* was *lèse majesté*; *La Maledizione*, the title Verdi had thought of giving it, offended the religious-minded; *The Duke de Vendôme*, which Martello was at first inclined to accept, might be taken as scorn of a potentate. Better to let the court fool, Triboulet or Triboletto, bear the brunt. His name too was changed to Rigoletto—and at last they had a title for the opera.

Verdi set to work to put the finishing touches to *Rigoletto*, and completed it in a few days. He then hurried off to Venice,

222 *Brush, Compass, and Pen*

where he lodged as usual at the Albergo d'Europa and began rehearsing. The company was excellent: Mme. Brambilla, Mme. Casaloni (a very intelligent woman with a beautiful contralto voice), Mirate, Varesi, and Pons, three fine singers and dramatic actors. A few enthusiastic rehearsals and, on the evening of March 11, the opera was ready for production. The success was tremendous! For the third time Venice gave Giuseppe Verdi a triumphant ovation. Now at last the composer felt that he had attained spiritual and intellectual maturity.

In *Rigoletto* there is warmth and inspired creation: one sees the Maestro's profound knowledge of the elements with which he worked and the confidence with which he handled them. He had been accused of debasing the glorious edifice of traditional Italian opera, of corrupting *bel canto*. Now Italian, French, and English critics accused him of being influenced by the Germanic school. Not the Germans, however, for they knew what an absurd and empty charge that was. Strange that the French should talk of German influence and not realize that Verdi leaned, instead, toward their own *fare svelto*. In Verdi's opinion, Italian opera was overpoweringly monotonous. "Long experience has confirmed the impression I have always had about dramatic effects, though in my first efforts I did not have the courage to express some of them. For example, ten years ago I would not have dared to set *Rigoletto* to music: today I would turn down subjects like *Nabucco, Fescari,* etc. While they offer extremely interesting situations, they lack variety. They strike only one chord, a lofty one if you will, but always the same."

Verdi developed his drama with a flow and swiftness of movement new to Italian opera. Rapid and concise he had always been; now with incomparable daring he let his music sing and weep and smile, blending tears and laughter, joy and sorrow. In *Rigoletto* the lyrical number is greatly extended, though still "closed": in other words, still following the laws of symmetry, in those periods of melodic discourse traditionally reserved for the "aria" and its derivations. In this opera even more than in earlier operas the lyrical number and even the recitative never attain a strictly musical form, but grow out of the force of the dramatic situations and the dialogue. The musical structure of the drama is rich, powerful: it sings, with an eloquence that is sober, moving, intense. Each singer has a distinct musical characterization of his own. Speaking with Somma about *Rigoletto,* Verdi declared that it "was the best subject he had set to music."

That season the Venetians insisted upon hearing *Rigoletto* twenty-one evenings at the Fenice and even more the following season. Soon the opera was playing all over Italy: but to satisfy the angry and suspicious censors of the various States it had to be given other titles—*Viscardello, Clara di Perth, Lionello*. In Austria it was immediately performed at Graz; in Hungary at Pest; in Bohemia at Prague; in Germany at Lübeck, Stuttgart, Bremen, Hanover—always with the greatest success. England saw it the following year; only France waited six years before opening her musical frontiers to the opera. Victor Hugo fought bitterly to keep it off the boards, even hailing Calzado, the impresario, before the Tribunal of the Seine to show cause why he should produce *Rigoletto* in the Italian Theatre of the French capital. In the end *Rigoletto* was produced with Mme. Frezzolini, Mme. Albone, the tenor Mario, and the baritone Corsi singing the principal roles. The opera was received with enthusiasm and had to be repeated one hundred times the first year, nor did public interest diminish as time went on.

With great effort Hugo's friends finally persuaded him to forget his ill will toward Verdi and attend a performance of *Rigoletto*. At last he recognized the composer's genius and the beauty of the opera, and somewhat ruefully expressed his admiration. At the end of the quartet in the last act, he leaped to his feet: "If I could only make four characters in my plays speak at the same time and have the audience grasp the words and sentiments, I would obtain the very same effect," he exclaimed enthusiastically.

Notebook Assignment for Class Discussion

1. Look up the meaning of libretto, aria, maestro, opera, Fenice, lèse majesté, bel canto, fare svelto, protagonist, recitative, impresario.
2. Teachers of prose composition often advise their students: Write about things you are interested in. Involve yourself deeply in your subject; let it grow; live with it; become part of it. What does Verdi say about a similar approach to music composition? What else does he say about the art of writing, whether prose or music?
3. Donizetti was referring to the opera when he said the music must rise out of the words. What happens to Donizetti's principle when Italian opera is sung in English? Is it only the meaning of the words that counts, not the sounds? What about other music, such as the great symphonies, which are without

words? Does it have meaning for you? If so, is it the same kind of meaning that words express or is it different? Explain.
4. Try to substitute another word for *mosaics,* where Verdi uses the simile, "music fitted together laboriously like mosaics."
5. In one of the numerous studies or biographies of Victor Hugo, try to find the reason for his bitter fight to keep *Rigoletto* off the stage in Paris.
6. Suggest several modern counterparts to Verdi's troubles with Hugo, the censors, the State, titles, and red tape in general.

NOTRE DAME OF CHARTRES *

By Henry Adams

If you want to know what churches were made for, come down here on some great festival of the Virgin, and give yourself up to it; but come alone! That kind of knowledge cannot be taught and can seldom be shared. We are not now seeking religion; indeed, true religion generally comes unsought. We are trying only to feel Gothic art. For us, the world is not a schoolroom or a pulpit, but a stage, and the stage is the highest yet seen on earth. In this church the old Romanesque leaps into the Gothic under our eyes; of a sudden, between the portal and the shrine, the infinite rises into a new expression, always a rare and excellent miracle in thought. The two expressions are nowhere far apart; not further than the Mother from the Son. The new artist drops unwillingly the hand of his father or his grandfather; he looks back, from every corner of his own work, to see whether it goes with the old. He will not part with the western portal or the lancet windows; he holds close to the round columns of the choir; he would have kept the round arch if he could, but the round arch was unable to do the work; it could not rise; so he broke it, lifted the vaulting, threw out flying buttresses, and satisfied the Virgin's wish.

The matter of Gothic vaulting, with its two weak points, the flying buttress and the false, wooden shelter roof, is the bête noire of the Beaux Arts. The duty of defence does not lie on tourists,

---

* From *Mount-Saint-Michel and Chartres,* by Henry Adams (Boston: Houghton Mifflin Co., 1913), Chapter VII, pp. 108–117.

who are at best hardly able to understand what it matters whether a wall is buttressed without or within, and whether a roof is single or double. No one objects to the dome of Saint Peter's. No one finds fault with the Pont Neuf. Yet it is true that the Gothic architect showed contempt for facts. Since he could not support a heavy stone vault on his light columns, he built the lightest possible stone vault and protected it with a wooden shelter-roof which constantly burned. The lightened vaults were still too heavy for the walls and columns, so the architect threw out buttress beyond buttress resting on separate foundations, exposed to extreme inequalities of weather, and liable to multiplied chances of accident. The results were certainly disastrous. The roofs burned; the walls yielded.

Flying buttresses were not a necessity. The Merveille had none; the Angevin school rather affected to do without them; Albi had none; Assisi stands up independent; but they did give support wherever the architect wanted it and nowhere else; they were probably cheap; and they were graceful. Whatever expression they gave to a church, at least it was not that of a fortress. Amiens and Albi are different religions. The expression concerns us; the construction concerns the Beaux Arts. The problem of permanent equilibrium which distresses the builder of arches is a technical matter which does not worry, but only amuses, us who sit in the audience and look with delight at the theatrical stage-decoration of the Gothic vault; the astonishing feat of building up a skeleton of stone ribs and vertebrae, on which every pound of weight is adjusted, divided, and carried down from level to level till it touches ground at a distance as a bird would alight. If any stone in any part, from apex to foundation, weathers or gives way, the whole must yield, and the charge for repairs is probably great, but, on the best building the École des Beaux Arts can build, the charge for repairs is not to be wholly ignored, and at least the Cathedral of Chartres, in spite of terribly hard usage, is as solid today as when it was built, and as plumb, without crack or crevice. Even the towering fragment at Beauvais, poorly built from the first, which has broken down oftener than most Gothic structures, and seems ready to crumble again whenever the wind blows over its windy plains, has managed to survive, after a fashion, six or seven hundred years, which is all that our generation had a right to ask.

The vault of Beauvais is nearly one hundred and sixty feet high (48 metres), and was cheaply built. The vault of Saint Peter's at Rome is nearly one hundred and fifty feet (45 metres). That of Amiens is one hundred and forty-four feet (44 metres). Rheims,

Bourges, and Chartres are nearly the same height; at the entrance, one hundred and twenty-two feet. Paris is one hundred and ten feet. The Abbé Bulteau is responsible for these measurements; but at Chartres, as in several very old churches, the nave slopes down to the entrance, because—as is said—pilgrims came in such swarms that they were obliged to sleep in the church, and the nave had to be sluiced with water to clean it. The true height of Chartres, at the croisée of nave and transept, is as near as possible one hundred and twenty feet (36.55 metres).

The measured height is the least interest of a church. The architect's business is to make a small building look large, and his failures are in large buildings which he makes to look small. One chief beauty of the Gothic is to exaggerate height, and one of its most curious qualities is its success in imposing an illusion of size. Without leaving the heart of Paris any one can study this illusion in the two great churches of Notre Dame and Saint-Sulpice; for Saint-Sulpice is as lofty as Notre Dame in vaulting, and larger in its other dimensions, besides being, in its style, a fine building; yet its Roman arches show, as if they were of the eleventh century, why the long, clean, unbroken, refined lines of the Gothic, curving to points, and leading the eye with a sort of compulsion to the culminating point above, should have made an architectural triumph that carried all Europe off its feet with delight. The world had seen nothing to approach it except, perhaps, in the dome of Sancta Sophia in Constantinople; and the discovery came at a moment when Europe was making its most united and desperate struggle to attain the kingdom of Heaven.

According to Viollet-le-Duc, Chartres was the final triumph of the experiment on a very great scale, for Chartres has never been altered and never needed to be strengthened. The flying buttresses of Chartres answered their purpose, and if it were not a matter of pure construction it would be worth while to read what Viollet-le-Duc says about them (article, 'Arcs-boutants'). The vaulting above is heavy, about fifteen inches thick; the buttressing had also to be heavy, and to lighten it, the architect devised an amusing sort of arcades, applied on his outside buttresses. Throughout the church, everything was solid beyond all later custom, so that architects would have to begin by a study of the crypt which came down from the eleventh century so strongly built that it still carries the church without a crack in its walls; but if we went down into it, we should understand nothing; so we will begin, as we did outside, at the front.

A single glance shows what trouble the architect had with the old façade and towers, and what temptation to pull them all down. One cannot quite say that he has spoiled his own church in trying to save what he could of the old, but if he did not quite spoil it, he saved it only by the exercise of an amount of intelligence that we shall never learn enough to feel our incapacity to understand. True ignorance approaches the infinite more nearly than any amount of knowledge can do, and, in our case, ignorance is fortified by a certain element of nineteenth-century indifference which refuses to be interested in what it cannot understand; a violent reaction from the thirteenth century which cared little to comprehend anything except the incomprehensible. The architect at Chartres was required by the Virgin to provide more space for her worshippers within the church, without destroying the old portal and flèche which she loved. That this order came directly from the Virgin, may be taken for granted. At Chartres, one sees everywhere the Virgin, and nowhere any rival authority; one sees her give orders, and architects obey them; but very rarely a hesitation as though the architect were deciding for himself. In his western front, the architect has obeyed orders so literally that he has not even taken the trouble to apologize for leaving unfinished the details which, if he had been responsible for them, would have been his anxious care. He has gone to the trouble of moving the heavy doorways forward, so that the chapels in the towers, which were meant to open on a porch, now open into the nave, and the nave itself has, in appearance, two more spans than in the old church; but the work shows blind obedience, as though he were doing his best to please the Virgin without trying to please himself. Probably he could in no case have done much to help the side aisles in their abrupt collision with the solid walls of the two towers, but he might at least have brought the vaulting of his two new bays, in the nave, down to the ground, and finished it. The vaulting is awkward in these two bays, and yet he has taken great trouble to effect what seems at first a small matter. Whether the great rose window was an afterthought or not can never be known, but any one can see with a glass, and better on the architectural plan, that the vaulting of the main church was not high enough to admit the great rose, and that the architect has had to slope his two tower-spans upward. So great is the height that you cannot see this difference of level very plainly even with a glass, but on the plans it seems to amount to several feet; perhaps a metre. The architect has managed to deceive our eyes, in order to enlarge the rose; but you can see as plainly as though he were here to tell you, that, like a great general, he has concentrated his whole energy on the rose, because the Virgin has told him that the rose symbolized

herself, and that the light and splendor of her appearance in
the west were to redeem all his awkwardnesses.

Of course this idea of the Virgin's interference sounds to you
a mere bit of fancy, and that is an account which may be settled
between the Virgin and you; but even twentieth-century eyes can
see that the rose redeems everything, dominates everything, and
gives character to the whole church.

In view of the difficulties which faced the artist, the rose is
inspired genius—the kind of genius which Shakespeare showed
when he took some other man's play, and adapted it. Thus far,
it shows its power chiefly by the way it comes forward and takes
possession of the west front, but if you want a foot-rule to measure by, you may mark that the old, twelfth-century lancet-win-
dows below it are not exactly in its axis. At the outset, in the
original plan of 1090, or thereabouts, the old tower—the southern
tower—was given greater width than the northern. Such inequalities were common in the early churches, and so is a great deal
of dispute in modern books whether they were accidental or in-
tentional, while no one denies that they are amusing. In these
towers the difference is not great—perhaps fourteen or fifteen
inches—but it caused the architect to correct it, in order to fit his
front to the axis of the church, by throwing his entrance six or
seven inches to the south, and narrowing to that extent the south
door and south lancet. The effect was bad, even then, and went
far to ruin the south window; but when, after the fire of 1194,
the architect inserted his great rose, filling every inch of possible
space between the lancet and the arch of the vault, he made
another correction which threw his rose six or seven inches out
of axis with the lancets. Not one person in a hundred thousand
would notice it, here in the interior, so completely are we under
the control of the artist and the Virgin; but it is a measure of
the power of the rose.

Looking farther, one sees that the rose-motive, which so dominates the west front, is carried round the church, and comes to
another outburst of splendor in the transepts. This leads back to
fenestration on a great scale, which is a terribly ambitious flight
for tourists; all the more, because here the tourist gets little help
from the architect who, in modern times, has seldom the opportunity to study the subject at all, and accepts as solved the problems of early Gothic fenestration. One becomes pedantic and
pretentious at the very sound of the word, which is an intolerable
piece of pedantry in itself; but Chartres is all windows, and its
windows were as triumphant as its Virgin, and were one of her
miracles. One can no more overlook the windows of Chartres

than the glass which is in them. We have already looked at the windows of Mantes; we have seen what happened to the windows at Paris. Paris had at one leap risen twenty-feet higher than Noyon, and even at Noyon, the architect, about 1150, had been obliged to invent new fenestration. Paris and Mantes, twenty years later, made another effort, which proved a failure. Then the architect of Chartres, in 1195, added ten feet more to his vault, and undertook, once for all, to show how a great cathedral should be lighted. As an architectural problem, it passes far beyond our powers of understanding, even when solved; but we can always turn to see what the inevitable Viollet-le-Duc says about its solution at Chartres:

> Toward the beginning of the thirteenth century, the architect of the Cathedral of Chartres sought out entirely new window combinations to light the nave from above. Below, in the side aisles he kept to the customs of the times; that is, he opened pointed windows which did not wholly fill the spaces between the piers; he wanted, or was willing to leave here below, the effect of a wall. But in the upper part of his building we see that he changed the system; he throws a round arch directly across from one pier to the next; then, in the enormous space which remains within each span, he inserts two large pointed windows surmounted by a great rose. . . . We recognize in this construction of Notre Dame de Chartres a boldness, a force, which contrast with the fumbling of the architects in the Ile de France and Champagne. For the first time one sees at Chartres the builder deal frankly with the clerestory, or upper fenestration, occupying the whole width of the arches, and taking the arch of the vault as the arch of the window. Simplicity of construction, beauty in form, strong workmanship, structure true and solid, judicious choice of material, all the characteristics of good work, unite in this magnificent specimen of architecture at the beginning of the thirteenth century.

Viollet-le-Duc does not call attention to scores of other matters which the architect must have had in his mind, such as the distribution of light, and the relations of one arrangement with another; the nave with the aisles, and both with the transepts, and all with the choir. Following him, we must take the choir separately, and the aisles and chapels of the apse also. One cannot hope to understand all the experiments and refinements of the artist, either in their successes or their failures, but, with diffidence, one may ask one's self whether the beauty of the arrange-

ment, as compared with the original arrangement in Paris, did
not consist in retaining the rose-motive throughout, while throwing the whole upper wall into window. Triumphant as the clere-
story windows are, they owe their charm largely to their roses,
as you see by looking at the same scheme applied on a larger
scale on the transept fronts; and then, by taking stand under
the croisée, and looking at all in succession as a whole.

The rose window was not Gothic but Romanesque, and needed
a great deal of coaxing to feel at home within the pointed arch.
At first, the architects felt the awkwardness so strongly that they
avoided it wherever they could. In the beautiful façade of Laon,
one of the chief beauties is the setting of the rose under a deep
round arch. The western roses of Mantes and Paris are treated
in the same way, although a captious critic might complain that
their treatment is not so effective or so logical. Rheims boldly
imprisoned the roses within the pointed arch; but Amiens, toward 1240, took refuge in the same square exterior setting that
was preferred, in 1200, here at Chartres; and in the interior of
Amiens the round arch of the rose is the last vault of the nave,
seen through a vista of pointed vaults, as it is here. All these are
supposed to be among the chief beauties of the Gothic façade,
although the Gothic architect, if he had been a man of logic,
would have clung to his lines, and put a pointed window in his
front, as in fact he did at Coutances. He felt the value of the rose
in art, and perhaps still more in religion, for the rose was Mary's
emblem. One is fairly sure that the great Chartres rose of the west
front was put there to please her, since it was to be always before
her eyes, the most conspicuous object she would see from the high
altar, and therefore the most carefully considered ornament in
the whole church outside the choir. The mere size proves the importance she gave it. The exterior diameter is nearly forty-four feet
(13.36 metres). The nave of Chartres is, next perhaps to the nave
of Angers, the widest of all Gothic naves; about fifty-three feet
(16.31 metres); and the rose takes every inch it can get of this
enormous span. The value of the rose, among architects of the
time, was great, since it was the only part of the church that
Villard de Honnecourt sketched; and since his time, it has been
drawn and redrawn, described and commented by generations of
architects till it has become as classic as the Parthenon.

Yet this Chartres rose is solid, serious, sedate, to a degree unusual in its own age; it is even more Romanesque than the pure
Romanesque roses. At Beauvais you must stop a moment to look
at a Romanesque rose on the transept of the Church of Saint-
Etienne; Viollet-le-Duc mentions it, with a drawing (article,

'Pignon'), as not earlier than the year 1100, therefore about a century earlier than the rose of Chartres; it is not properly a rose, but a wheel of fortune, with figures climbing up and falling over. Another supposed twelfth-century rose is at Étampes, which goes with that of Laon and Saint-Leu-d'Esserent and Mantes. The rose of Chartres is so much the most serious of them all that Viollet-le-Duc has explained it by its material—the heavy stone of Bercheres; —but the material was not allowed to affect the great transept roses, and the architect made his material yield to his object wherever he thought it worth while. Standing under the central croisée, you can see all three roses by simply turning your head. That on the north, the Rose de France, was built, or planned, between 1200 and 1210, in the reign of Philip Augustus, since the porch outside, which would be a later construction, was begun by 1212. The Rose de France is the same in diameter as the western rose, but lighter, and built of lighter stone. Opposite the Rose de France stands, on the south front, Pierre Mauclerc's Rose de Dreux, of the same date, with the same motive, but even lighter; more like a rose and less like a wheel. All three roses must have been planned at about the same time, perhaps by the same architect, within the same workshop; yet the western rose stands quite apart, as though it had been especially designed to suit the twelfth-century façade and portal which it rules. Whether this was really the artist's idea is a question that needs the artist to answer; but that this is the effect, needs no expert to prove; it stares one in the face. Within and without, one feels that the twelfth-century spirit is respected and preserved with the same religious feeling which obliged the architect to injure his own work by sparing that of his grandfathers.

Conspicuous, then, in the west front are two feelings: respect for the twelfth-century work, and passion for the rose fenestration; both subordinated to the demand for light. If it worries you to have to believe that these three things are in fact one; that the architect is listening, like the stone Abraham, for orders from the Virgin, while he caresses and sacrifices his child; that Mary and not her architects built this façade; if the divine intention seems to you a needless impertinence, you can soon get free from it by going to any of the later churches, where you will not be forced to see any work but that of the architect's compasses. According to Viollet-le-Duc, the inspiration ceased about 1250, or, as the Virgin would have dated it, on the death of Blanche of Castile in 1252. The work of Chartres, where her own hand is plainly shown, belongs in feeling, if not in execution, to the last years of the twelfth-century (1195–1200). The great western rose which gives the motive for the whole decoration and is repeated in the great roses of the transepts, marks the Virgin's will—the taste and knowledge of 'cele qui la rose est des roses,' or, if you prefer the Latin of Adam de Saint-Victor, the hand of her who is 'Super rosam rosida.'

Notebook Assignment for Class Discussion

1. Look up the following words in "Glossary of Architectural Terms," *A History of Architecture,* by Sir Banister Fletcher (17th edition; New York: Charles Scribner's Sons, 1961), p. 1255ff.; or a good unabridged, illustrated dictionary:

Gothic	apex	rose windows
Romanesque	nave	axis
portal	transept	fenestration
lancet windows	arcade	pier
arch	crypt	clerestory
buttress	façade	choir
flying buttress	flèche	apse
vault	bay	croisée

2. Why does Henry Adams suggest you "come alone" to Chartres?
3. How is the author justified in using the verb *leaps* in the sentence, "In this church the Romanesque *leaps* into the Gothic under our eyes . . ." ? Also, would *"before* our eyes," or *"above* our eyes" be more consistent with *leaps* than *"under* our eyes"? Why, or why not?
4. What example of causal relationship appears in paragraph 2?
5. Since Adams claims "flying buttresses were not a necessity," why were they used? What other structural methods might have served?
6. Henry Adams repeatedly refers to the Virgin. Do you gather that he personally believed in the Virgin as the mother of God and the true source of the architect's inspiration, or that he believed only that the architect himself sincerely believed so?
7. Which aspect of the cathedral of Notre Dame de Chartres do you think held the primary appeal to the author: the aesthetic, religious, or historical?

Related Exercises

1. There is probably a Romanesque or Gothic building on your campus, or a Gothic church in your city, or nearby. Locate

and study it. Try to identify its characteristic parts. Observe the shape of its windows, design of its vaults, and so on.
2. Work up a comprehensive bibliography on College Gothic.
3. Read some magazine articles about the work of R. Buckminster Fuller, Edward Stone, Eero Saarinen, and Frank Lloyd Wright to inform yourself about modern architecture. Learn to read in depth.
4. Write a paper about the architectural ideas of any one of the men listed in Exercise 3, or Minoru Yamasaki, Gio Ponti, or any other famous architect whose name you discover in the course of your associative reading.
5. Write a paper about a particular building of your choice, but do not depend entirely on your reading. Go to the building, ask about it, study it. (If you are planning a trip overseas, Chartres is only two hours by train from Paris.)
6. Read intensively in the following bibliography on Chartres, and add whatever books and magazine articles your local library provides. Then write a paper on the history of its construction: dates, people, location, source of materials, fires and other disfigurements, architectural irregularities, quality of workmanship, and so on; or more specifically: principal features, including details of the great rose windows, stained glass, sculpture, and the like.

Sample Bibliography

The Cathedrals of France, by T. Francis Bumpus. London: T. W. Laurie, Ltd., 1927. Also, New York: Frederick A. Stokes Co., no date, pp. 90–109.

Gotische Kathedralen in Frankreich, Text (in German) by Paul Clemen. Photographs by Martin Hürlman. Zurich-Berlin: Atlantis Verlag A. G. 1937, pp. XLII–XLVIII, 23–78.

French Cathedrals, by Elizabeth Robins Pennell. New York: The Century Co., 1909, Chapter IX, pp. 213–43.

Cathedrals of France, by Epiphanius Wilson, M.A. New York: The Churchman Co., 1900, pp. 142–9.

Les Cathédrales de France, par A. de Baudot et A. Perrault-Dabot. Paris: Henri Laurens, etc., 1905–7. Text (in French), pp. 11–19, 25–6. Plates.

The Cathedral of Chartres, by René Merlet. Paris: Henri Laurens, 1926. Text in English with illustrations.

An Illustrated Monograph of Chartres Cathedral, by Étienne
Houvet. Chartres: Étienne Houvet, 1930. Text in English.

7. Write a paper in which you first explain, then argue for or
   against, one of the following statements from Henry Adams's
   observations on the cathedral of *Notre Dame de Chartres.*
   a. True religion generally comes unsought.
   b. True ignorance approaches the infinite more nearly than
      any amount of knowledge can do.
   c. A certain element of nineteenth-century indifference ...
      refuses to be interested in that which it cannot understand.
   d. The thirteenth century ... cared little to comprehend any-
      thing except the incomprehensible.

FRA LIPPO LIPPI

By ROBERT BROWNING

I am poor brother Lippo, by your leave!
You need not clap your torches to my face.
Zooks, what's to blame? you think you see a monk!
What, 'tis past midnight, and you go the rounds,
And here you catch me at an alley's end   5
Where sportive ladies leave their doors ajar?
The Carmine's my cloister: hunt it up,
Do,—harry out, if you must show your zeal,
Whatever rat, there, haps on his wrong hole,
And nip each softling of a wee white mouse,   10
Weke, weke, that's crept to keep him company!
Aha, you know your betters! Then, you'll take
Your hand away that's fiddling on my throat,
And please to know me likewise. Who am I?
Why, one, sir, who is lodging with a friend   15
Three streets off—he's a certain ... how d'ye call?
Master—a ... Cosimo of the Medici,
I' the house that caps the corner. Boh! you were best!
Remember and tell me, the day you're hanged,
How you affected such a gullet's-gripe!   20
But you, sir, it concerns you that your knaves
Pick up a manner nor discredit you:
Zooks, are we pilchards, that they sweep the streets
And count fair prize what comes into their net?
He's Judas to a tittle, that man is!   25

Just such a face! Why, sir, you make amends.
Lord, I'm not angry! Bid your hangdogs go
Drink out this quarter-florin to the health
Of the munificent House that harbours me
(And many more beside, lads! more beside!)   30
And all's come square again. I'd like his face—
His, elbowing on his comrade in the door
With the pike and lantern—for the slave that holds
John Baptist's head a-dangle by the hair
With one hand ("Look you, now," as who should say)   35
And his weapon in the other, yet unwiped!
It's not your chance to have a bit of chalk,
A wood-coal or the like? or you should see!
Yes, I'm the painter, since you style me so.
What, brother Lippo's doings, up and down,   40
You know them and they take you? like enough!
I saw the proper twinkle in your eye—
'Tell you, I liked your looks at very first.
Let's sit and set things straight now, hip to haunch.
Here's spring come, and the nights one makes up bands   45
To roam the town and sing out carnival,
And I've been three weeks shut within my mew,
A painting for the great man, saints and saints
And saints again. I could not paint all night—
Ouf! I leaned out of window for fresh air.   50
There came a hurry of feet and little feet,
A sweep of lute-strings, laughs, and whiffs of song—
Flower o' the broom,
Take away love, and our earth is a tomb!
Flower o' the quince,   55
I let Lisa go, and what good in life since?
Flower o' the thyme—and so on. Round they went.
Scarce had they turned the corner when a titter
Like the skipping of rabbits by moonlight,—three slim shapes,
And a face that looked up. . . . zooks, sir, flesh and blood, 60
That's all I'm made of! Into shreds it went,
Curtain and counterpane and coverlet,
All the bed-furniture—a dozen knots,
There was a ladder! Down I let myself,
Hands and feet, scrambling somehow, and so dropped,   65
And after them. I came up with the fun
Hard by Saint Laurence, hail fellow, well met,—
Flower o' the rose,
If I've been merry, what matter who knows?

And so, as I was stealing back again   70
To get to bed and have a bit of sleep
Ere I rise up tomorrow and go work
On Jerome knocking at his poor old breast
With his great round stone to subdue the flesh,
You snap me of the sudden. Ah, I see!   75
Though your eye twinkles still, you shake your head—
Mine's shaved—a monk, you say—the sting's in that!
If Master Cosimo announced himself,
Mum's the word naturally; but a monk!
Come, what am I a beast for? tell us, now!   80
I was a baby when my mother died
And father died and left me in the street.
I starved there, God knows how, a year or two
On fig-skins, melon-parings, rinds and shucks,
Refuse and rubbish. One fine frosty day,   85
My stomach being empty as your hat,
The wind doubled me up and down I went.
Old Aunt Lapaccia trussed me with one hand,
(Its fellow was a stinger as I knew,)
And so along the wall, over the bridge,   90
By the straight cut to the convent. Six words there,
While I stood munching my first bread that month:
"So, boy, you're minded," quoth the good fat father,
Wiping his own mouth, 'twas refection-time—
"To quit this very miserable world?   95
Will you renounce". . ."the mouthful of bread?" thought I;
By no means! Brief, they made a monk of me;
I did renounce the world, its pride and greed,
Palace, farm, villa, shop, and banking-house,
Trash, such as these poor devils of Medici   100
Have given their hearts to—all at eight years old.
Well, sir, I found in time, you may be sure
'Twas not for nothing—the good bellyful,
The warm serge and the rope that goes all round,
And day-long blessed idleness beside!   105
"Let's see what the urchin's fit for"—that came next.
Not overmuch their way, I must confess.
Such a to-do! They tried me with their books;
Lord, they'd have taught me Latin in pure waste!
Flower o' the clove,   110
All the Latin I construe is "amo," I love!
But, mind you, when a boy starves in the streets
Eight years together, as my fortune was,

Watching folk's faces to know who will fling
The bit of half-stripped grape-bunch he desires,   115
And who will curse or kick him for his pains,—
Which gentleman processional and fine,
Holding a candle to the Sacrament,
Will wink and let him lift a plate and catch
The droppings of the wax to sell again,   120
Or holla for the Eight and have him whipped,—
How say I?—nay, which dog bites, which lets drop
His bone from the heap of offal in the street,—
Why, soul and sense of him grow sharp alike,
He learns the look of things, and none the less   125
For admonition from the hunger pinch.
I had a store of such remarks, be sure,
Which, after I found leisure, turned to use.
I drew men's faces on my copy-books,
Scrawled them within the antiphonary's marge,   130
Joined legs and arms to the long music-notes,
Found eyes and nose and chin for A's and B's,
And made a string of pictures of the world
Betwixt the ins and outs of verb and noun,
On the wall, the bench, the door. The monks looked black.   135
"Nay," quoth the Prior, "turn him out, d'ye say?
In no wise. Lose a crow and catch a lark.
What if at last we get our man of parts,
We Carmelites, like those Camaldolese
And Preaching Friars, to do our church up fine   140
And put the front on it that ought to be!"
And hereupon he bade me daub away.
Thank you! my head being crammed, the walls a blank,
Never was such prompt disemburdening.
First, every sort of monk, the black and white,   145
I drew them, fat and lean: then, folk at church,
From good old gossips waiting to confess
Their cribs of barrel-droppings, candle-ends,—
To the breathless fellow at the altar-foot,
Fresh from his murder, safe and sitting there   150
With the little children round him in a row
Of admiration, half for his beard and half
For that white anger of his victim's son
Shaking a fist at him with one fierce arm,
Signing himself with the other because of Christ   155
(Whose sad face on the cross sees only this
After the passion of a thousand years)

Till some poor girl, her apron o'er her head,
(Which the intense eyes looked through) came at eve
On tiptoe, said a word, dropped in a loaf,   160
Her pair of earrings and a bunch of flowers
(The brute took growling), prayed, and so was gone.
I painted all, then cried " 'Tis ask and have;
Choose, for more's ready!"—laid the ladder flat,
And showed my covered bit of cloister-wall.   165
The monks closed in a circle and praised loud
Till checked, taught what to see and not to see,
Being simple bodies,—"That's the very man!
Look at the boy who stoops to pat the dog!
That woman's like the Prior's niece who comes   170
To care about his asthma: it's the life!"
But there my triumph's straw-fire flared and funked;
Their betters took their turn to see and say:
The Prior and the learned pulled a face
And stopped all that in no time. "How? what's here?   175
Quite from the mark of painting, bless us all!
Faces, arms, legs and bodies like the true
As much as pea and pea! it's devil's-game!
Your business is not to catch men with show,
With homage to the perishable clay,   180
But lift them over it, ignore it all,
Make them forget there's such a thing as flesh.
Your business is to paint the souls of men—
Man's soul, and it's a fire, smoke . . . no, it's not . . .
It's vapour done up like a new-born babe—   185
(In that shape when you die it leaves your mouth)
It's . . . well, what matters talking, it's the soul!
Give us no more of body than shows soul!
Here's Giotto, with his Saint a-praising God,
That sets us praising,—why not stop with him?   190
Why put all thoughts of praise out of our head
With wonder at lines, colors, and what not?
Paint the soul, never mind the legs and arms!
Rub all out, try at it a second time.
Oh, that white smallish female with the breasts,   195
She's just my niece . . . Herodias, I would say—
Who went and danced and got men's heads cut off!
Have it all out!" Now, is this sense, I ask?
A fine way to paint soul, by painting body
So ill, the eye can't stop there, must go further   200
And can't fare worse! Thus, yellow does for white

When what you put for yellow's simply black,
And any sort of meaning looks intense
When all beside itself means and looks naught.
Why can't a painter lift each foot in turn,   205
Left foot and right foot, go a double step,
Make his flesh liker and his soul more like,
Both in their order? Take the prettiest face,
The Prior's niece ... patron-saint—is it so pretty
You can't discover if it means hope, fear,   210
Sorrow or joy? won't beauty go with these?
Suppose I've made her eyes all right and blue,
Can't I take breath and try to add life's flash,
And then add soul and heighten them three-fold?
Or say there's beauty with no soul at all—   215
(I never saw it—put the case the same—)
If you get simple beauty and naught else,
You get about the best thing God invents:
That's somewhat: and you'll find the soul you have missed,
Within yourself, when you return him thanks.   220
"Rub all out!" Well, well, there's my life, in short,
And so the thing has gone on ever since.
I'm grown a man no doubt, I've broken bounds:
You should not take a fellow eight years old
And make him swear to never kiss the girls.   225
I'm my own master, paint now as I please—
Having a friend, you see, in the Corner-house!
Lord, it's fast holding by the rings in front—
Those great rings serve more purposes than just
To plant a flag in, or tie up a horse!   230
And yet the old schooling sticks, the old grave eyes
Are peeping o'er my shoulder as I work,
The heads shake still—"It's art's decline, my son!
You're not of the true painters, great and old;
Brother Angelico's the man, you'll find;   235
Brother Lorenzo stands his single peer:
Fag on at flesh, you'll never make the third!"
Flower o' the pine,
You keep your mistr ... manners, and I'll stick to mine!
I'm not the third, then: bless us, they must know!   240
Don't you think they're the likeliest to know,
They with their Latin? So, I swallow my rage,
Clench my teeth, suck my lips in tight, and paint
To please them—sometimes do and sometimes don't;
For, doing most, there's pretty sure to come   245

A turn, some warm eve finds me at my saints—
A laugh, a cry, the business of the world—
(Flower o' the peach,
Death for us all, and his own life for each!)
And my whole soul revolves, the cup runs over,   250
The world and life's too big to pass for a dream,
And I do these wild things in sheer despite,
And play the fooleries you catch me at,
In pure rage! The old mill-horse, out at grass
After hard years, throws up his stiff heels so,   255
Although the miller does not preach to him
The only good of grass is to make chaff.
What would men have? Do they like grass or no—
May they or mayn't they? all I want's the thing
Settled for ever one way. As it is,   260
You tell too many lies and hurt yourself:
You don't like what you only like too much,
You do like what, if given you at your word,
You find abundantly detestable.
For me, I think I speak as I was taught;   265
I always see the garden and God there
A-making man's wife: and, my lesson learned,
The value and significance of flesh,
I can't unlearn ten minutes afterwards.

You understand me: I'm a beast, I know.   270
But see, now—why, I see as certainly
As that the morning-star's about to shine,
What will hap some day. We've a youngster here
Comes to our convent, studies what I do,
Slouches and stares and lets no atom drop: 275
His name is Guidi—he'll not mind the monks—
They call him Hulking Tom, he lets them talk—
He picks my practice up—he'll paint apace,
I hope so—though I never live so long,
I know what's sure to follow. You be judge!   280
You speak no Latin more than I, belike;
However, you're my man, you've seen the world
—The beauty and the wonder and the power,
The shapes of things, their colours, lights and shades,
Changes, surprises—and God made it all!   285
—For what? Do you feel thankful, ay or no,
For this fair town's face, yonder river's line,
The mountain round it and the sky above,

Much more the figures of man, woman, child,
These are the frame to? What's it all about?   290
To be passed over, despised? or dwelt upon,
Wondered at? oh, this last of course!—you say.
But why not do as well as say,—paint these
Just as they are, careless what comes of it?
God's works—paint any one, and count it crime   295
To let a truth slip. Don't object, "His works
Are here already; Nature is complete:
Suppose you reproduce her—(which you can't)
There's no advantage! you must beat her, then."
For, don't you mark? we're made so that we love   300
First when we see them painted, things we have passed
Perhaps a hundred times nor cared to see;
And so they are better, painted—better to us,
Which is the same thing. Art was given for that;
God uses us to help each other so,   305
Lending our minds out. Have you noticed, now,
Your cullion's hanging face? A bit of chalk,
And trust me but you should, though! How much more,
If I drew higher things with the same truth!
That were to take the Prior's pulpit-place,   310
Interpret God to all of you! Oh, oh,
It makes me mad to see what men shall do
And we in our graves! This world's no blot for us,
Nor blank; it means intensely, and means good:
To find its meaning is my meat and drink.   315
"Ay, but you don't so instigate to prayer!"
Strikes in the Prior: "when your meaning's plain
It does not say to folk—remember matins,
Or, mind you fast next Friday!" Why, for this
What need of art at all? A skull and bones,   320
Two bits of stick nailed crosswise, or, what's best,
A bell to chime the hour with, does as well.
I painted a Saint Laurence six months since
At Prato, splashed the fresco in fine style:
"How looks my painting, now the scaffold's down?"   325
I ask a brother: "Hugely," he returns—
"Already not one phiz of your three slaves
Who turn the Deacon off his toasted side,
But's scratched and prodded to our heart's content,
The pious people have so eased their own   330
With coming to say prayers there in a rage:
We get on fast to see the bricks beneath.

Expect another job this time next year,
For pity and religion grow i' the crowd—
Your painting serves its purpose!" Hang the fools!   335

—That is—you'll not mistake an idle word
Spoke in a huff by a poor monk, God wot,
Tasting the air this spicy night which turns
The unaccustomed head like Chianti wine!
Oh, the church knows! don't misreport me, now!   340
It's natural a poor monk out of bounds
Should have his apt word to excuse himself:
And hearken how I plot to make amends.
I have bethought me: I shall paint a piece
... There's for you! Give me six months, then go, see   345
Something in Sant' Ambrogio's! Bless the nuns!
They want a cast o' my office. I shall paint
God in the midst, Madonna and her babe,
Ringed by a bowery, flowery angel-brood,
Lilies and vestments and white faces, sweet   350
As puff on puff of grated orris-root
When ladies crowd to Church at midsummer.
And then i' the front, of course a saint or two—
Saint John, because he saves the Florentines,
Saint Ambrose, who puts down in black and white   355
The convent's friends and gives them a long day,
And Job, I must have him there past mistake,
The man of Uz (and Us without the z,
Painters who need his patience). Well, all these
Secured at their devotion, up shall come   360
Out of a corner when you least expect,
As one by a dark stair into a great light,
Music and talking, who but Lippo! I!—
Mazed, motionless, and moonstruck—I'm the man!
Back I shrink—what is this I see and hear?   365
I, caught with my monk's-things by mistake,
My old serge gown and rope that goes all round,
I, in this presence, this pure company!
Where's a hole, where's a corner for escape?
Then steps a sweet angelic slip of a thing   370
Forward, puts out a soft palm—"Not so fast!"
—Addresses the celestial presence, "nay—
He made you and devised you, after all,
Though he's none of you! Could Saint John there draw—
His camel-hair make up a painting-brush?   375

We come to brother Lippo for all that,
Iste perfecit opus!" So, all smile—
I shuffle sideways with my blushing face
Under the cover of a hundred wings
Thrown like a spread of kirtles when you're gay   380
And play hot cockles, all the doors being shut,
Till, wholly unexpected, in there pops
The hothead husband! Thus I scuttle off
To some safe bench behind, not letting go
The palm of her, the little lily thing   385
That spoke the good word for me in the nick,
Like the Prior's niece . . . Saint Lucy, I would say.
And so all's saved for me, and for the church
A pretty picture gained. Go, six months hence!
Your hand, sir, and good-bye: no lights, no lights!   390
The street's hushed, and I know my own way back,
Don't fear me! There's the gray beginning. Zooks!

Notebook Assignment for Class Discussion

1. Determine the difference between a monologue and a soliloquy.
2. Is Browning's blank verse in this poem strict in rhythmic form, or is it colloquial and idiomatic?
3. Odd words like *zooks, weke, ouf,* and so on, are some of the working parts of the comic grotesque, of which Robert Browning was a master. Find other examples of the comic, or humorous, grotesque in this poem.
4. Select several unusual figures of speech, such as "are we pilchards that they sweep the streets. . . ?"
5. Explain how the rhythm, diction, and imagery of the poem help to reveal the character of Fra Lippo Lippi, the speaker. Is he essentially a serious man, or a playboy? Does his explanation of his worldliness persuade you to his side?
6. What do you think the poet's attitude is toward the Fra? In what ways is this attitude, tone, or point of view made clear?
7. Is it as easy to characterize the watchman to whom the Fra is speaking as it is to characterize the speaker? How does Browning reveal the character of the watchman without ever having him speak?
8. Browning focuses this poem on an exploration of two atti-

tudes toward art. What is the theory which Fra Lippo Lippi
upholds? What is the theory which his superiors uphold?
9. Do you think it is possible for an artist to make clear the
soul without at the same time making clear the flesh? What
objections do the Fra's superiors make to his naturalistic
approach to painting?
10. How do the *stornelli*, or flower songs, contribute to the meaning of the poem? To the revelation of the Fra's character?

Related Exercises

1. Read about one of the most important families of the Renaissance, the Medici's of Florence, who produced powerful
and wealthy statesmen, bankers, popes, and patrons of art
and literature.
2. If you are interested in music, read Browning's "Abt Voglcr,"
"A Toccata of Galuppi's," and "Master Hugues of Saxe-
Gotha."
3. If not many originals are available for your study, look up
good reproductions and critical analyses of some of the paintings of Fra Angelico, Fra Lorenzo (Monaco), Fra Lippo
Lippi, Filippino Lippi (his son), Tommaso Guidi (Masaccio),
Andrea del Sarto and Sandro Botticelli, and try to find the
points of similarity in some and differences in others, as suggested by Browning in "Fra Lippo Lippi."
4. Compare a reproduction of the painting, *The Coronation of
the Virgin*, with Fra Lippo Lippi's detailed description of it
beginning about line 345. If you go to Florence you can see
the original painting in the Accademia delle Velle Arti.
5. Read another of Browning's art poems, "Andrea del Sarto,"
and write a comparison of Fra Lippo Lippi and Andrea as
men and as artists.
6. John Milton said in *Apology for Smectymnuus* that a man
who would write well "in laudable things, ought himself to
be a true Poem; that is, a composition and pattern of the
best and honorablest things; not presuming to sing high
praises of heroic men or famous Citics, unless he have in
himself the experience and the practice of all that which is
praiseworthy." How does Fra Lippo Lippi fit into this frame?
Does he compromise his principles in any way? For what
reasons? Do you think less of him for doing so? Why? Write
about it.
7. Write a comparison of Fra Lippo Lippi and a great author

such as Byron, Shelley, or Oscar Wilde ("Art is above morality"), whose personal and professional lives were, in the
opinion of many people, a moral dichotomy.
8. Defend Fra Lippo Lippi's attitudes toward art, or attack
them. Use as your thesis the following proposition: Religious
art should not call attention to itself, but carry the mind
directly to God. Or, substitute the word *music* for *art* in the
proposition.
9. Read Giorgio Vasari's essay on Filippo Lippi in his *Lives
of Painters, Sculptors, and Architects,* and, in a critical essay,
show to what extent Browning has borrowed from Vasari,
and to what extent he has changed Filippo Lippi's character
for dramatic purposes.

FIRESIDE VERSUS THEATRE *

By H. Granville-Barker

Clearly we cannot blame the art of the theatre for bad perform-
ances; for maltreated text, misguided staging, or unbridled egotism in the actor. These are corrigible things. We must try and
envisage the best performance; dogmatize only upon that. Not,
however, an ideal performance; this will never be possible; the
very use of the human medium forbids it. With much to compen-
sate, the theatre must always be in a sense the most imperfect of
the arts.

The ideal, the omnipercipient reader; he, in the course of
nature, is not to be looked for either. Strange as it may seem,
the dramatist himself will often find a performance of his play
bringing excellent things to life that he did not know were there.

But envisage the best possible reader too, and his task. He
must, so to speak, perform the whole play in his imagination; as
he reads, each effect must come home to him: the succession and
contrast of scenes, the harmony and clash of the music of the dialogue, the action implied, the more physical opposition of characters, or the silent figure standing aloof—for that also can be

* From "Shakespeare's Dramatic Art," by Harley Granville-Barker, in *A
Companion to Shakespeare Studies,* ed. by H. Granville-Barker and G. B. Har-
rison (Cambridge: Cambridge University Press). Reprinted by permission of
Cambridge University Press.

eloquent. Not an easy business even with the simplest play; and
when it comes to the opulent art of an *Antony and Cleopatra*
the most expert of us may feel diffident. But, reasonable excellence on both sides being granted, what upon the balance shall
we gain from reading that performance cannot give us, and of
what will this rob us that solitude and the armchair bring?

There must be no apologizing for the intrusion of the actor.
Fear him as at times we well may, this "foolish Greek" and the
gifts he brings, he and they are an integral part of every practical
playwright's scheme. And however greater a man Shakespeare
became, when did he cease to be this? Even *King Lear* was a contemporary success. Perhaps it ought not to have been, but it was.
One may own that the personality of the actor, which in itself
adds so much to the poor play, will equally be, as such, inadequate to the great one; may even obscure or deform it, unless,
having first let it aggrandize him, he will at last exercise the magnanimity of the interpreter and so suppress himself that the essence of the thing interpreted may shine through. This can be
done; it is not an impossible ideal. We, for our part, can learn
to listen through as well as to the actor. That we habitually do
when it is a question of great music, imperfectly because humanly
performed; and of these very few experts who can, still fewer
seem to be content to sit at home and read the cryptic score. But
what we *ask* of an actor is this very humanity, and to this the
quality of imperfection properly belongs. Pursue it to a paradox,
the more perfect a play's performance the worse it might be, since
this would be lacking. He is asked to use his humanity with force
and freedom; and the greater the play the more he can give
and the more it will absorb. Not to echo the author's voice, nor
count himself a mere moving shadow, but to add to the play
his positive and objective self—and that he can do so devotedly
and unselfishly is no paradox at all.

But just here and in this lies the true difficulty with our solitary firesider. What he really dislikes is not the failings of the
actors but their very virtues. A performance of Shakespeare may
be bad, but the best would not please him. He resents any interference whatever between him and the Shakespeare of his own
private and particular idea. He by no means relishes, to begin
with, the assault on his emotions which it is the business of the
actors to deliver. Their triumph will be to make him laugh or
cry, to "take him out of himself," to "carry him away." He does
not care to be one of the crowd, to have to suspend his judgment,
take what is given him and yield himself in return. He prefers
to go his own pace; to be critical; to exercise taste, savoring what

he likes twice or thrice over, questioning or passing by what he
does not; and now and then he may float off upon the wings of
some notion of his own, which a telling line will have suggested to
him, even though "some necessary question of the play be then
to be considered"—Shakespeare's censure of the clown can serve
for the dilettante reader, too! Only thus, are we to be told, can
great dramatic art be appreciated? Its last refined and ethereal
beauties, perhaps! But even these beauties will be less beautiful,
too insubstantial and vague altogether, unless they have been
reached through the means which the art creating them has provided. The art of the drama makes a primary demand upon us:
to leave our armchair throne of judgment and descend into the
mellay of contradictory passions—which the action of the play is
—and submit for a while to be tossed to and fro in it; and far
less of literature or art there will seem to be in the experience
than of the vulgar emotions of life. It is so; drama's first aim is
to subdue us by submitting us emotionally to the give and take,
the rough and tumble, of some illusion of life. In great plays the
illusion is raised to the highest pitch of emotional intensity, and
out of it their spiritual beauty springs. But the way to this in
its fullness and significance, and the only way, is through experience of the emotion so conveyed and commonly shared; there is
no short cut. With that experience absorbed, by all means let the
reader seek his fireside. The mere structure of the play will then
mean how much more to him; and its texture be a far finer,
richer, and substantial thing! Acting embodies the drama. When
the imperfect human embodiment and the immediate emotion
are all, a case can be made against the theatre; artistically, and
sometimes morally, too. But they need not be all, and they never
have been when great dramatists were about. Even the theatre is
very much what we make it, and the more we ask of the actor
the more he will learn to give. Our cultural Puritans no longer
seem to fear the theatre; they deny it instead. And that is worse;
it is even foolish. For a bodiless drama is a contradiction in terms,
and the demand for one pretty poor humanism besides.

SHAKESPEARE IN
MODERN DRESS *

By Gordon Crosse

In the earlier part of the period covered by this book two different methods of presenting Shakespeare's plays held the stage.
They might be distinguished as Shakespeare illustrated and
Shakespeare interpreted. This puts it too broadly. There was
much faithful interpretation by the actors in the old style, and
sufficient illustration by means of stage setting in the new. Nevertheless the phrase will serve to indicate the two styles. And most
of the productions I have hitherto mentioned have approximated
towards one or other of them, while some, such as Benson's have
combined both.

More recently a third method has grown up. Having no desire
to return to the worn-out style of sheer unsophisticated magnificence, and being dissatisfied with the straightforward simplicity
of the new, producers began to look round for something fresh.
This was not at first a mere desire for novelty for its own sake.
There seems to have been an impression that audiences were becoming too familiar with the accepted manner of playing Shakespeare, were taking him too much for granted, and so were missing
his full value and meaning. They wanted shaking up. They had
got into a rut and must be jolted out of it. And this could best
be done by presenting the plays in some unfamiliar way which
would compel the audience to take fresh notice of them.

The first method of doing this which presented itself was to
act them in modern dress. This, it was thought, would help the
spectators to realize that the characters were real people like
themselves, doing real things, instead of the conventional figures
that, it was assumed, they had hitherto supposed them. Now, the
characters in, say, *Hamlet* may be dressed in various ways. Charles
Kean would spend immense pains in finding out what were the
actual costumes of eleventh-century Denmark and in reproducing
them as closely as convention would allow. The recent custom
has been to give them costumes more or less of the Renaissance.

* From *Shakespearean Playgoing 1890–1952*, by Gordon Crosse (London:
A. R. Mowbray & Co., Limited, 1953), pp. 89–94.

Or they may wear Elizabethan dress so that they appear to us as Shakespeare meant them to appear to playgoers of his own time. And here the modern dress producer thinks he scores a point. Yes, he says, Shakespeare intended his audience to see men and women in the familiar dress of their own day, and that is just what I am letting *you* see. There is some truth in this, but, I think, more fallacy; at least if the methods adopted are those of Sir Barry Jackson's *Hamlet* produced at the Kingsway Theatre in 1925. Eminent persons, I know, stated that they had discovered "new points in Hamlet's soul" from watching this production. To my thinking it was so covered with a blaze of modernity that it was difficult to see anything else. Cigarettes, pocket-lighters, wrist-watches, were always being flourished at us. Here four supers were playing bridge, there some one was mixing a whisky and soda, then a car was heard outside, and all these things by their very novelty on the Shakespearean stage distracted our attention even more effectively than Tree's rabbits.[1]

The producer's problem, then, was to make the play fit into this setting. Clearly certain obstinate lines had to be cut. "He wore his beaver up" could not be said of a ghost in modern uniform, and Hamlet's hysterical outburst after the play scene was omitted as not being the kind of behavior one would expect of a prince in a dinner jacket. His description of his father as having—

Hyperion's curls, the front of Jove himself,

and so on, was also left out, presumably for the same reason. But this policy could not be carried very far or there would be nothing left. The upshot was that no profusion of pocket-lighters could conceal the fact that people in modern dress do not talk and act as these people were talking and acting.

The only character to gain anything by the change from the usual methods was Polonius. Mr. Bromley-Davenport was more convincing as a suave and wily politician than a Polonius in robes usually is. Mr. Frank Vosper, too, was successful in turning the barbaric Claudius into a polished modern royalty. It was significant that for his prayer scene he wore a dressing-gown, presumably thinking that he could express the passion of it more effectively if he covered up his dress trousers.

Sir Barry Jackson's *Macbeth* was more successful because the modernities were not thrust down our throats with the same ve-

---

1 Sir Herbert Tree did not trust the intelligence of the audience and left as little as possible to their imagination. In *A Midsummer Night's Dream*, for example, he let loose a whole cage full of rabbits to scamper about the stage.

hemence. Yet one could not help being aware of them, and they
were nearly always at odds with the words and the action; as
for instance when a general in khaki with a chestful of medal-
ribbons ordered trumpets to sound and called them "clamorous
harbingers of blood and death." Some attempts were made to
avoid incongruity by making the lower-class characters talk
Scotch: "brave Macbaith, weel he desairves that name." And Macbeth himself spoke of "this *blasted* heath" as if the adjective were
an expletive.

Occasionally, I admit, the modern setting helped to bring out
a point. It gave a more vivid impression of Macbeth's charmed
life when they blazed away at him with revolvers at close range
than when they merely poke at him with property swords. But
in spite of a few such moments the general effect was that one
was more interested in the modern setting than in the play. It
was one of the drawbacks to the old style of production that the
scenery and stage effects were apt to draw attention away from
the actors. But now that we had got rid of one distraction it
seemed a mistake to interpose another.

Possibly something of this kind occurred to Sir Barry Jackson.
For in his next production, the *Shrew,* no attempt to illustrate
Shakespeare by the modern trappings could be discerned. It was
a sheer burlesque, the joke lying in the incongruity between the
Elizabethan story and diction, and the modern costumes and business, the motor car, the flashlight photograph of the wedding
group, the electric stove produced when Grumio complains of
the cold; the jokes of the old *Comic History of England* when it
represented William the Conqueror landing from a Channel
steamer. And regarded simply as a burlesque it was amusing
enough.

When Oscar Asche produced the *Merry Wives* in this style in
1929 he carried the same procedure further towards its logical
conclusion by modernizing the language as well as the setting.
Mistress Anne became Miss Anne, her parents Mr. and Mrs. Page,
and her dowry of £700 rose to £7,000. Falstaff called for a jorum
of rum in place of a bottle of sack, talked of "Piccadilly at closing
time" instead of "Bucklersbury at simple time" and shouted
"taxi" whenever he left the stage. It accorded well with this kind
of dialogue that Mrs. Page should give her instructions to Mrs.
Quickly by telephone, that the duel should be a bout of fisticuffs,
and that Pistol's rant, which could not easily be modernized,
should be justified by ingeniously representing him as a broken-
down actor.

On its own lines it was capitally acted. Oscar Asche cleverly distinguished Falstaff as a raffish old sportsman from the Falstaff of Shakespeare, and Hay Petrie's Evans was a triumph. A little, shabby, shaggy Welsh parson, with greyish hair and moustache, and speckled straw hat, he really did modernize the character. But in spite of these and other good pieces of acting the performance was no more than a curiosity. It threw no new light on the play, and was useful only in showing that Shakespeare cannot in any literal sense be modernized.

So when a lady sitting by me said, "I should like to see all Shakespeare's plays in modern dress," I hesitated to agree with her. In fact I have seen eight of them. I pass over the *Merchant*, merely observing that the procedure in the trial when set in the surroundings and costumes of a modern court of justice was the greatest incongruity of all. The *Much Ado* of the Bristol Old Vic, an offshoot of the parent Company, had no such absurdities. Don Pedro and his friends were in uniform, as returned from the wars; Don John was apparently intended to be a Fascist; and the Watch was an amusing burlesque of the Home Guard. The main scene was Leonato's garden, on which a wall of the church abutted, and by an ingenious device this was thrown back to disclose the interior of the church for the wedding scene, at the end of which Benedick and Beatrice returned to the garden.

If we arc to have modern dress productions at all this is how it should be done; the modernity unobtrusive, being confined to the costumes. There were, however, two earlier productions in which the modern setting was employed not to illustrate Shakespeare but to show how his plays may illustrate modern political developments. In *Troilus and Cressida*, in 1938, the Trojans were in khaki and the Greeks in German uniform; and the acting was in that concatenation accordingly. A year later *Julius Caesar* was transposed into a conflict between democracy and the modern brand of dictatorship. These were, to my mind, more legitimate uses of modern dress than those which are described above. Even so the chief interest lay in observing the ingenuity with which the producers would bring in such adjuncts as a cocktail party or morning tea. Nor can I overcome my objection to hearing, for example, officers talking of "my sword" and "my armour" when they are wearing khaki and carrying no weapons but revolvers. And that the rival commanders in *Julius Caesar* should exchange their defiances by telephone was even more far-fetched than the device by which Tree attempted to make that scene plausible.[2]

2 "Tree spent much pains and ingenuity to make the mutual defiances of the opposing generals seem plausible by perching them on high rocks with a ravine between them." Crosse, p. 57.

Both plays were well acted. Shakespeare's Pandarus could not be more skilfully transposed into the modern key than by Mr. Max Adrian's affected, elderly roué and society butterfly. Mr. Walter Hudd's smiling old gentleman, nervously anxious to conciliate everybody, may have been very unlike a real dictator, but was the exact modern counterpart of Shakespeare's neurotic Caesar. Best of all, I thought, was Mr. Antony Hawtrey's Casca. One critic described him as a kind of Bertie Wooster, but this was to mistake the actor's intention. He adopted a pose of blasé boredom to conceal his disgust at having to submit to the dictatorship, and this was exactly Casca interpreted in a modern style.

The sum of all this is that modern dress detracts more from the interest and value of a performance of Shakespeare than it adds to them. Granville-Barker has said that it is when a play has no hold on us that we fall to thinking about the scenery, and that is equally true of the dresses. If the actors are doing their work properly we should not notice the costumes or the properties at all, except when they play a prominent part in the action (for example, Malvolio's stockings), because our attention would be fixed on the story and the characters. And in Shakespeare this end is best attained when the actors are either in the traditional costumes to which we are accustomed or in Elizabethan dress which accords with the words and the action.

Notebook Assignment for Class Discussion

1. Paragraph 1 contains an example of two-part rhetorical division. Restate the two parts in fuller definitive form.
2. Paragraph 2 presents certain causes, or conditions, the effects of which are to be found in paragraph 3. List these causes and effects.
3. Explain the line in paragraph 3, "and that is just what I am letting *you* see." What does the modern dress producer believe he is letting the audience see? Considering the line to be ambiguous, what is another possible meaning to be derived from it?
4. Clearly, Mr. Crosse is not in favor of presenting Shakespeare's plays with the characters in modern dress. What does he say about presenting them in a modern setting, with modern trappings? What of modernizing the language, too?
5. What is Crosse's principal reason for his position, or opposition? Do you think it is a sound reason? What is the etymological relationship between *position* and *opposition?*

6. Look up the term *reductio ad absurdum,* then try to find several instances of it in this essay. Do you think it is an honest and effective device with which to win an argument, i.e., by making the point of view of one's opponent appear to be ridiculous?

Related Exercises

1. The word *drama* originally meant to *act* or to *do* something, i.e., in imitation of others. Therefore, it means also to pretend or make-believe, and in this sense children who "play house," or "play school" are dramatizing their own experiences and observations. They use whatever settings are available: a tree stump may become in their imagination a table or desk, to help the ad-libbed dialogue seem to be more realistic. Is this also the reason for providing scenery and "props" for a stage play? Is a movie version of *Romeo and Juliet* filmed in Italy more realistic for the viewer than one filmed on a Hollywood set? Explain.
2. Do you think that even the most realistic stage settings "fool" anyone in the audience? If the playwright and the players are able to make the audience lose themselves in the play by the force of the play itself, what purpose do the settings serve?
3. If a play were presented in an art gallery, would the play and art be in competition with each other?
4. Shakespeare's *A Midsummer Night's Dream* was presented not long ago in a jungle clearing in Tanganyika. If you had been the director, what kind of stage scenery would you have designed, if any? Would you have constructed a stage for the performance?
5. *Hamlet* has been presented on a bare stage against the blank back walls of the theater. What qualities of Shakespeare were the directors attempting to emphasize in this way?
6. How were Shakespeare's plays presented in his own time? Read a chapter or two of the history of the English stage to discover to what extent he used costume and scenery.
7. In a good rhetoric textbook, study the chapter on argumentation, then write a well-reasoned essay in which you defend or deny the proposition that all is fair in love and war, and also in argumentation.
8. Since Shakespeare's plays, written for his own stage, needed to describe setting rather than construct it, would a radio or

a TV production of *Romeo and Juliet* come closer to the true
Shakespearean technique and intention? Write an argumenta
tive paper in favor of one of the mediums in this respect.

A SCENE FROM OTHELLO

By William Shakespeare

(Edited by Norbert Engels)

In one of Shakespeare's most moving tragedies, Othello, professional soldier and general of the Venetian army, has married
Desdemona, a virtuous and charming young lady of high Venetian society. Iago, his third in command, is determined to destroy
Othello's new-found happiness by making him suspicious of his
wife—accusing her of adultery with Cassio, his close friend and second in command, whom he has recently discharged, but for another reason. In this scene (III:3) Iago shrewdly and gradually
arouses Othello's doubts to the critical point where the husband
reluctantly admits at least the possibility of his wife's infidelity.
"And yet ..." he says, and from that moment he knows not a
single instant of peace or certainty. The tension increases as the
conflict becomes more and more terrifying until in the final
scene Othello murders her and *then* discovers that she had been
a true and faithful wife, whereupon at the play's climax he kills
himself.

At the beginning of this scene Desdemona, Cassio, and Emilia
(Iago's wife) enter the castle garden.

DES. Be thou assured, good Cassio, I will do
All my abilities in thy behalf.

EMIL. Good madam, do.   I warrant it grieves my husband
As if the case were his.

DES. O, that's an honest fellow.   Do not doubt, Cassio,
But I will have my lord and you again
As friendly as you were.

CAS. Bounteous madam,
Whatever shall become of Michael Cassio,
He's never anything but your true servant.

DES. I know it; I thank you. You do love my lord; 10
You have known him long; and be you well assured
He shall in strangeness stand no farther off
Than in a politic distance.

CAS. Ay, but, lady,
That policy may either last so long,
Or feed upon such nice and waterish diet,
Or breed itself so, out of circumstance,
That, I being absent and my place supplied,
My General will forget my love and service.

DES. Do not doubt that. Before Emilia here
I give thee warrant of thy place. Assure thee, 20
If I do vow a friendship, I'll perform it
To the last article. My lord shall never rest;
I'll watch him tame and talk him out of patience;
His bed shall seem a school, his board a shrift;
I'll intermingle everything he does
With Cassio's suit. Therefore be merry, Cassio,
For thy solicitor shall rather die
Than give thy cause away.

EMIL. Madam, here comes my lord.

CAS. Madam, I'll take my leave. 30

DES. Why, stay, and hear me speak.

CAS. Madam, not now, I am very ill at ease,
Unfit for mine own purposes.

DES. Well, do your discretion.

13. **politic:** discreet.
15. **nice ... diet:** weak encouragement.
16. **breed:** develop.
17. **supplied:** i.e., by another, a substitute.
19. **doubt:** fear.
20. **warrant:** promise, guarantee.
24. **shrift:** confessional.

(Cassio, seeing Othello and Iago approach,
makes a hasty exit.)

IAGO Ha! I like not that.

OTH.   What dost thou say?

IAGO Nothing, my lord; or if—I know not what.

OTH. Was not that Cassio parted from my wife?

IAGO Cassio, my lord?   No, sure, I cannot think it,
That he would steal away so guilty-like,
Seeing you coming.

OTH.   I do believe 'twas he.   40

DES. How now, my lord!
I have been talking with a suitor here,
A man that languishes in your displeasure.

OTH. Who is it you mean?

DES. Why, your lieutenant, Cassio.   Good my lord,
If I have any grace or power to move you,
His present reconciliation take;
For if he be not one that truly loves you,
That errs in ignorance and not in cunning,
I have no judgment in an honest face.   50
I prithee call him back.

OTH.   Went he hence now?

DES. Ay, sooth; so humbled
That he hath left part of his grief with me
To suffer with him.   Good love, call him back.

OTH. Not now, sweet Desdemona; some other time.

DES. But shall it be shortly?

47. **present:** immediate.
51. **prithee:** pray thee; **call him back:** reinstate him.
52. **sooth:** truly.

OTH.   The sooner, sweet, for you.

DES. Shall it be tonight at supper?

OTH.   No, not tonight.

DES. Tomorrow dinner, then?

OTH.   I shall not dine at home;
I meet the captains at the citadel.

DES. Why then, tomorrow night or Tuesday morn,   **60**
On Tuesday noon or night, on Wednesday morn.
I prithee name the time, but let it not
Exceed three days.   In faith he's penitent;
And yet his trespass, in our common reason—
Save that they say the wars must make examples
Out of their best—is not almost a fault
To incur a private check.   When shall he come?
Tell me, Othello.   I wonder in my soul
What you would ask me that I should deny,
Or stand so mammering on.   What!   Michael Cassio,   **70**
That came a-wooing with you, and so many a time,
When I have spoke of you dispraisingly,
Hath taken your part, —to have so much to do
To bring him in?   Trust me, I could do much—

OTH. Prithee no more.   Let him come when he will;
I will deny thee nothing.

DES.   Why, this is not a boon.
'Tis as I should entreat you wear your gloves,
Or feed on nourishing dishes, or keep you warm,
Or sue to you to do a peculiar profit
To your own person.   Nay, when I have a suit   **80**
Wherein I mean to touch your love indeed,
It shall be full of poise and difficult weight
And fearful to be granted.

64. **in our common reason:** according to common sense.
66. **almost:** quite.
67. **a private check:** (even) a private rebuke.
70. **mammering:** hesitating.
73. **so . . . do:** so much fuss.
82. **poise:** importance.

OTH.   I will deny thee nothing.
Whereon I do beseech thee, grant me this,
To leave me but a little to myself.

DES. Shall I deny you?   No.   Farewell, my lord.

OTH. Farewell, my Desdemona; I'll come to thee straight.

DES. Emilia, come.   Be as your fancies teach you;
Whate'er you be, I am obedient. (*Desdemona and Emilia leave.*)

OTH. Excellent wretch!   Perdition catch my soul   90
But I do love thee!   and when I love thee not,
Chaos is come again.

IAGO My noble lord—

OTH.   What dost thou say, Iago?

IAGO Did Michael Cassio, when you wooed my lady,
Know of your love?

OTH. He did, from first to last.   Why dost thou ask?

IAGO. But for a satisfaction of my thought;
No further harm.

OTH.   Why of thy thought, Iago?

IAGO I did not think he had been acquainted with her.

OTH. O yes, and went between us very oft.   100

IAGO Indeed!

OTH. Indeed?   Ay, indeed.   Discernest thou aught in that?
Is he not honest?

IAGO   Honest, my lord?

OTH.   Honest?   Ay, honest.

87. **straight:** soon.
100. **between:** i.e., as messenger.

IAGO My lord, for aught I know.

OTH.   What dost thou think?

IAGO Think, my lord?

OTH.   Think, my lord?   By heaven, he echoes me
As if there were some monster in his thought
Too hideous to be shown.   Thou dost mean something.
I heard thee say even now, thou lik'st not that,
When Cassio left my wife.   What didst not like?   110
And when I told thee he was of my counsel
In my whole course of wooing, thou criedst "Indeed!"
And didst contract and purse thy brow together
As if thou then hadst shut up in thy brain
Some horrible conceit.   If thou dost love me,
Show me thy thought.

IAGO My lord, you know I love you.

OTH.   I think thou dost;
And, for I know, thou art full of love and honesty,
And weighest thy words before thou givest them breath,
Therefore these stops of thine fright me the more;   120
For such things in a false disloyal knave
Are tricks of custom; but in a man that's just
They're close delations, working from the heart
That passion cannot rule.

IAGO   For Michael Cassio,
I dare be sworn I think that he is honest.

OTH. I think so too.

IAGO   Men should be what they seem;
Or those that be not, would they might seem none!

OTH. Certain, men should be what they seem.

111. **counsel:** confidence.
115. **conceit:** thought.
120. **stops:** hesitations.
122. **custom:** purpose.
123. **delations:** accusations, denunciations.

IAGO Why, then I think Cassio's an honest man.

OTH. Nay, yet there's more in this,   130
I prithee speak to me as to thy thinkings,
As thou dost ruminate, and give thy worst of thoughts
The worst of words.

IAGO   Good my lord, pardon me.
Though I am bound to every act of duty,
I am not bound to that all slaves are free to.
Utter my thoughts? Why, say they are vile and false?
As where's that palace whereinto foul things
Sometimes intrude not? Who has a breast so pure
But some uncleanly apprehensions
Keep leets and law days and in sessions sit   140
With meditations lawful?

OTH. Thou dost conspire against thy friend, Iago,
If thou but think'st him wronged, and mak'st his ear
A stranger to thy thoughts.

IAGO   I do beseech you:
Though I perchance am vicious in my guess,
As I confess it is my nature's plague
To spy into abuses, and oft my jealousy
Shapes faults that are not—that your wisdom yet
From one that so imperfectly conceits
Would take no notice, nor build yourself a trouble   150
Out of his scattering and unsure observance.
It were not for your quiet nor your good,
Nor for my manhood, honesty, or wisdom,
To let you know my thoughts.

OTH.   What dost thou mean?

129. **then:** i.e., only on the questionable premise that men actually are what
they seem to be.
135. **that:** i.e., the right to keep one's thoughts to one's self.
139. **uncleanly apprehensions:** untrue suspicions.
140. **Keep . . . days:** hold court, rule.
145. **vicious:** wrong.
147. **jealousy:** suspicion.
148. **Shapes:** imagines.
149. **conceits:** conceives, judges.
151. **scattering:** irresponsible.

IAGO Good name in man and woman, dear my lord,
Is the immediate jewel of their souls.
Who steals my purse steals trash; 'tis something, nothing;
'Twas mine, 'tis his, and has been slave to thousands;
But he that filches from me my good name
Robs me of that which not enriches him   160
And makes me poor indeed.

OTH. By heaven, I'll know thy thoughts!

IAGO You cannot, if my heart were in your hand,
Nor shall not whilst 'tis in my custody.

OTH. Ha!

IAGO   O beware, my lord, of jealousy!
It is the green-eyed monster which doth mock
The meat it feeds on.   That cuckold lives in bliss
Who, certain of his fate, loves not his wronger;
But O, what damned minutes tells he o'er
Who doted, yet doubts, suspects, yet strongly loves!   170

OTH. O misery!

IAGO Poor and content is rich, and rich enough,
But riches fineless is as poor as winter
To him that ever fears he shall be poor.
Good heaven, the souls of all my tribe defend
From jealousy!

OTH.   Why, why is this?
Think'st thou I'd make a life of jealousy,
To follow still the changes of the moon
With fresh suspicions?   No, to be once in doubt
Is once to be resolved.   Exchange me for a goat   180
When I shall turn the business of my soul
To such exsufflicate and blown surmises
Matching thy inference.   'Tis not to make me jealous
To say my wife is fair, feeds well, loves company,
Is free of speech, sings, plays, and dances well:

156. **immediate:** closest, dearest.
159. **filches:** steals.
169. **damned:** tormented; **tells:** counts.
173. **fineless:** endless.
180. **resolved:** i.e., convinced, one way or the other.
182. **exsufflicate and blown:** unsubstantial, that come and go with the wind.

Where virtue is, these are more virtuous.
Nor from mine own weak merits will I draw
The smallest fear or doubt of her revolt,
For she had eyes, and chose me. No Iago;
I'll see before I doubt; when I doubt, prove;   190
And on the proof, there is no more but this:
Away at once with love or jealousy!

IAGO I am glad of this; for now I shall have reason
To show the love and duty that I bear you
With franker spirit. Therefore, as I am bound,
Receive it from me—I speak not yet of proof:
Look to your wife; observe her well with Cassio;
Wear your eye thus: not jealous, nor secure.
I would not have your free and noble nature,
Out of self-bounty, be abused; look to it.   200
I know our country disposition well:
In Venice they do let heaven see the pranks
They dare not show their husbands; their best conscience
Is not to leave it undone, but keep it unknown.

OTH. Dost thou say so?

IAGO She did deceive her father, marrying you;
And when she seemed to shake and fear your looks,
She loved them most.

OTH.   And so she did.

IAGO   Why, go to then.
She that so young could give out such a seeming
To seel her father's eyes up close as oak,   210
He thought 'twas witchcraft—but I am much to blame.
I humbly do beseech you of your pardon
For too much loving you.

OTH.   I am bound to thee for ever.

IAGO I see this hath a little dashed your spirits.

187. **weak merits:** i.e., his age, race, and so on.
198. **secure:** unsuspicious.
200. **self-bounty:** generosity, charity (of spirit).
209. **seeming:** pretense.

OTH. Not a jot, not a jot.

IAGO   In faith, I fear it has.
I hope you will consider what is spoke
Comes from my love—but I do see you are moved.
I am to pray you not to strain my speech
To grosser issues nor to larger reach
Than to suspicion.   220

OTH. I will not.

IAGO Should you do so, my lord,
My speech should fall into such vile success
As my thoughts aim not at.   Cassio's my worthy friend—
My lord, I see you are moved.

OTH.   No, not much moved.
I do not think but Desdemona's honest.

IAGO Long live she so! and long live you to think so!

OTH. And yet, how nature erring from itself—

IAGO Ay, there's the point: as—to be bold with you—
Not to affect many proposed matches
Of her own clime, complexion, and degree,   230
Whereto we see in all things nature tends—
Foh! one may smell in such, a will most rank,
Foul disproportion, thoughts unnatural—
But pardon me; I do not in position
Distinctly speak of her, though I may fear
Her will, recoiling to her better judgment,
May fall to match you with her country forms
And happily repent.

OTH.   Farewell, farewell.
If more thou dost perceive, let me know more.
Set on thy wife to observe.   Leave me, Iago.   240

224. **thoughts:** intentions.
229. **affect:** accept.
236. **will:** desire; **recoiling:** reverting.
237. **fall:** begin.
238. **happily:** possibly, perhaps.

IAGO (*Leaving*)   My lord, I take my leave.

OTH. Why did I marry?   This honest creature, doubtless
Sees and knows more, much more, than he unfolds.

IAGO (*Returning*)   My lord, I would I might entreat your honor
To scan this thing no further; leave it to time.
Although 'tis fit that Cassio have his place,
For sure he fills it up with great ability,
Yet if you please to hold him off awhile,
You shall by that perceive him and his means.
Note if your lady strain his entertainment   250
With any strong or vehement importunity.
Much will be seen in that.   In the meantime
Let me be thought too busy in my fears—
As worthy cause I have to fear I am—
And hold her free, I do beseech your honor.

OTH. Fear not my government.

IAGO I once more take my leave.   (*Exit*)

OTH. This fellow's of exceeding honesty,
And knows all qualities, with a learned spirit
Of human dealings.   If I do prove her haggard,   260
Though that her jesses were my dear heartstrings,
I'd whistle her off and let her down the wind
To prey at fortune.   Haply for I am black
And have not those soft parts of conversation
That chamberers have, or for I am declined
Into the vale of years—yet that's not much—
She's gone.   I am abused, and my relief
Must be to loathe her.   O curse of marriage,
That we can call these delicate creatures ours,

245. **scan:** study, probe.
249. **means:** technique.
250. **strain his entertainment:** urge his reinstatement.
251. **importunity:** urging, pleading.
256. **government:** judgment, discretion.
260. **haggard:** wild, like an untamable hawk; faithless.
261. **jesses:** leg thongs to hold hunting hawks.
262. **whistle . . . wind:** be free of her.
263. **Haply for:** perhaps because.
265. **chamberers:** charmers, gallants.

And not their appetites!   I had rather be a toad   **270**
And live upon the vapor of a dungeon
Than keep a corner in the thing I love
For others' uses.   Yet 'tis the plague of great ones;
Prerogatived are they less than the base.
'Tis destiny unshunnable, like death;
Even then this forked plague is fated to us
When we do quicken.

(*Desdemona and Emilia enter.*)

Look where she comes!
If she be false, O, then heaven mocks itself!
I'll not believe it.

DES.   How now, my dear Othello?
Your dinner, and the generous islanders   **280**
By you invited, do attend your presence.

OTH. I am to blame.

DES.   Why do you speak so faintly?
Are you not well?

OTH. I have a pain upon my forehead here.

DES. Faith, that's with watching; 'twill away again.
Let me but bind it hard, within this hour
It will be well.

OTH.   Your napkin is too little.

(*He pushes the handkerchief away and it falls
unnoticed to the ground.*)

Let it alone.   Come, I'll go in with you.

274. **prerogatived:** privileged.
276. **forked plague:** cuckoldry.
277. **quicken:** are born.
280. **generous:** friendly.
281. **attend:** await.
285. **watching:** lack of sleep.
286. **it:** his head.
287. **napkin:** handkerchief.

DES. I am very sorry that you are not well.

(*Othello and Desdemona leave.*)

EMIL. I am glad I have found this napkin.   290
This was her first remembrance from the Moor.
My wayward husband hath a hundred times
Wooed me to steal it; but she so loves the token—
For he conjured her she should ever keep it—
That she reserves it evermore about her
To kiss and talk to.   I'll have the work taken out
And give it Iago.
What he will do with it heaven knows, not I;
I nothing but to please his fantasy.   (*Iago enters.*)

IAGO How now!   What do you here alone?   300

EMIL. Do not you chide.   I have a thing for you.

IAGO A thing for me. It is a common thing—

EMIL. Ha!

IAGO To have a foolish wife.

EMIL. O, is that all?   What will you give me now
For that same handkerchief?

IAGO   What handkerchief?

EMIL. What handkerchief!
Why, that the Moor first gave to Desdemona;
That which so often you did bid me steal.

IAGO Hast stolen it from her?   310

EMIL. No, faith, she let it drop by negligence,
And to the advantage, I, being here, took it up.
Look, here it is.

IAGO   A good wench; give it me.

(*He snatches it from her.*)

296. **work taken out:** pattern copied.
299. **fantasy:** whim.

EMIL. What will you do with it, that you have been so earnest
To have me filch it?

IAGO   Why, what's that to you?

EMIL. If it be not for some purpose of import,
Give it me again.   Poor lady, she'll run mad
When she shall lack it.

IAGO   Be not acknown on it.
I have use for it.   Go, leave me. *(Emilia leaves)*   320
I will in Cassio's lodging lose this napkin
And let him find it.   Trifles light as air
Are to the jealous confirmations strong
As proofs of holy writ.   This may do something:
The Moor already changes with my poison.
Dangerous conceits are in their nature poisons
Which at the first are scarce found to distaste,
But with a little act upon the blood
Burn like the mines of sulphur.   *(Othello enters.)*
                    I did say so.
Look where he comes!   Not poppy nor mandragora.   330
Nor all the drowsy syrups of the world
Shall ever medicine thee to that sweet sleep
Which thou owedst yesterday.

OTH.   Ha!   Ha!   false to me?

IAGO Why, how now, General?   No more of that.

OTH. Avaunt!   Be gone!   Thou hast set me on the rack.
I swear 'tis better to be much abused
Than but to know it a little.

IAGO   How now, my lord!

OTH. What sense had I of her stolen hours of lust?
I saw it not, thought it not, it harmed not me;
I slept the next night well, was free and merry;   340

319. **be . . . it:** pretend you know nothing about it.
324. **holy writ:** holy Scripture.
328. **act:** action.
332. **medicine:** drug.
333. **owedst:** owned, enjoyed.

I found not Cassio's kisses on her lips.
He that is robbed, not wanting what is stolen,
Let him not know it and he's not robbed at all.

IAGO I am sorry to hear this.

OTH. I had been happy if the general camp,
Pioners and all, had tasted her sweet body,
So I had nothing known.   O now for ever
Farewell the tranquil mind!   Farewell content!
Farewell the plumed troop, and the big wars
That makes ambition virtue!   O, farewell!   350
Farewell the neighing steed and the shrill trump,
The spirit-stirring drum, the ear-piercing fife,
The royal banner, and all quality,
Pride, pomp, and circumstance of glorious war!
And O you mortal engines, whose rude throats
The immortal Jove's dread clamors counterfeit,
Farewell!   Othello's occupation's gone!

IAGO Is it possible, my lord?

OTH. Villain, be sure thou prove my love a whore;
Be sure of it; give me the ocular proof;   360
Or by the worth of man's eternal soul,
Thou hadst been better have been born a dog
Than answer my waked wrath!

IAGO   Is it come to this?

OTH. Make me to see it; or at the least so prove it
That the probation bear no hinge nor loop
To hang a doubt on; or woe upon thy life!

IAGO My noble lord—

OTH. If thou dost slander her and torture me,
Never pray more, abandon all remorse;
On horror's head horrors accumulate;   370

346. **pioners:** soldiers of low rank.
355. **mortal engines:** cannons.
356. **dread clamors:** thunder; **counterfeit:** imitate.
360. **ocular:** visual.
365. **probation:** evidence, proof.

Do deeds to make heaven weep, all earth amazed;
For nothing canst thou to damnation add
Greater than that.

IAGO   O grace!   O heaven forgive me!
Are you a man?   Have you a soul or sense?
God be with you; take mine office.   O wretched fool,
That livest to make thine honesty a vice.
O monstrous world!   Take note, take note, O world,
To be direct and honest is not safe.
I thank you for this profit, and from hence
I'll love no friend, sith love breeds such offence.   **380**

OTH. Nay, stay.   Thou shouldst be honest.

IAGO I should be wise; for honesty's a fool
And loses that it works for.

OTH.   By the world,
I think my wife be honest, and think she is not;
I think that thou art just, and think thou art not.
I'll have some proof.   Her name, that was as fresh
As Dian's visage, is now begrimed and black
As mine own face.   If there be cords, or knives,
Poison, or fire, or suffocating streams,
I'll not endure it.   Would I were satisfied!   **390**

IAGO I see, sir, you are eaten up with passion.
I do repent me that I put it to you.
You would be satisfied?

OTH.   Would?   Nay, I will.

IAGO And may; but how?   How satisfied, my lord?
Would you, the supervisor, grossly gape on?
Behold her topped?

375. **wretched fool:** i.e., himself, Iago.
379. **profit:** lesson.
380. **sith:** since.
383. **that:** what.
387. **Dian's:** Diana, goddess of chastity.
395. **supervisor:** onlooker.

OTH.   Death and damnation! O!

IAGO It were a tedious difficulty, I think,
To bring them to that prospect.   Damn them then,
If ever mortal eyes do see them bolster
More than their own!   What then?   How then?   400
What shall I say?   Where's satisfaction?
It is impossible you should see this,
Were they as prime as goats, as hot as monkeys,
As salt as wolves in pride, and fools as gross
As ignorance made drunk.   But yet, I say,
If imputation and strong circumstances
Which lead directly to the door of truth
Will give you satisfaction, you may have it.

OTH. Give me a living reason she's disloyal.

IAGO I do not like the office.   410
But sith I am entered in this cause so far,
Pricked to it by foolish honesty and love,
I will go on.   I lay with Cassio lately,
And being troubled with a raging tooth,
I could not sleep.
There are a kind of men so loose of soul
That in their sleeps will mutter their affairs;
One of this kind is Cassio.
In sleep I heard him say, "Sweet Desdemona,
Let us be wary, let us hide our loves!"   420
And then, sir, would he gripe and wring my hand,
Cry "O sweet creature!" and then kiss me hard,
As if he plucked up kisses by the roots
That grew upon my lips; then laid his leg
Over my thigh, and sighed, and kissed, and then
Cried, "Cursed fate that gave thee to the Moor!"

OTH.   O monstrous!   Monstrous!

IAGO Nay, this was but his dream.

399. **bolster:** bed together.
403. **prime:** primitive, bestial.
404. **salt:** lustful; **pride:** heat.
406. **imputation . . . circumstances:** circumstantial evidence.
412. **Pricked:** spurred.
421. **gripe:** grip.

OTH. But this denoted a foregone conclusion.
'Tis a shrewed doubt, though it be but a dream.

IAGO And this may help to thicken other proofs   430
That do demonstrate thinly.

OTH.   I'll tear her all to pieces!

IAGO Nay, but be wise; yet we see nothing done;
She may be honest yet.   Tell me but this—
Have you not sometimes seen a handkerchief
Spotted with strawberries in your wife's hand?

OTH. I gave her such a one; 'twas my first gift.

IAGO I know not that; but such a handkerchief—
I am sure it was your wife's—did I today
See Cassio wipe his beard with.

OTH.   If it be that—

IAGO If it be that, or any that was hers   440
It speaks against her with the other proofs.

OTH. O that the slave had forty thousand lives!
One is too poor, too weak for my revenge.
Now do I see 'tis true.   Look here, Iago:
All my fond love thus do I blow to heaven.
'Tis gone.
Arise, black vengeance, from thy hollow cell!
Yield up, O love, thy crown and hearted throne
To tyrannous hate!   Swell, bosom, with thy fraught,
For 'tis of aspics' tongues!

IAGO   Yet be content.   450

OTH. O, blood, blood, blood!

428. **foregone conclusion:** previous experience, or perhaps, daydream.
431. **demonstrate:** show proof.
445. **fond:** foolish.
448: **hearted:** deeply placed in the heart.
449. **fraught:** emotional burden.
450. **aspics' tongues:** poison.

IAGO Patience, I say.   Your mind perhaps may change.

OTH. Never, Iago.   Like to the Pontic Sea,
Whose icy current and compulsive course
Ne'er feels retiring ebb, but keeps due on
To the Propontic and the Hellespont,
Even so my bloody thoughts, with violent pace,
Shall ne'er look back, ne'er ebb to humble love,
Till that a capable and wide revenge
Swallow them up.   (*He kneels.*)   Now, by yond marble   **460**
  heaven.
In the due reverence of a sacred vow
I here engage my words.

IAGO   Do not rise yet.   (*Iago kneels.*)
Witness, you ever-burning lights above,
You elements that clip us round about,
Witness that here Iago doth give up
The execution of his wit, hands, heart
To wronged Othello's service!   Let him command,
And to obey shall be in me remorse.
What bloody business ever.   (*They rise.*)

OTH.   I greet thy love
Not with vain thanks but with acceptance bounteous,   **470**
And will upon the instant put thee to it.
Within these three days let me hear thee say
That Cassio's not alive.

IAGO My friend is dead; 'tis done at your request.
But let her live.

OTH.   Damn her, lewd minx!   O, damn her!
Come, go with me apart; I will withdraw
To furnish me with some swift means of death
For the fair devil.   Now art thou my lieutenant.

IAGO I am your own for ever.   (*They both leave.*)

458. **ebb:** return.
464. **clip:** enclose, surround.
466. **execution:** employment.
468. **remorse:** regret, i.e., not to do more.
471. **put . . . it:** put you to your promise.

Notebook Assignment for Class Discussion

1. The poetic form of dialogue used in this scene is known as blank verse. What is blank verse? Does it move stiffly here, with a graceful formality, or almost colloquially?
2. Line 24 is elliptical in structure. What does that mean? What effect does it provide? What are the missing words?
3. The following words are all used figuratively: "board," in line 24, "heart," in line 123, "breast," in line 138, and "honor," in line 255. Analyze them as examples of metonymy.
4. Identify the metaphor in lines 155–6, and lines 165–7; also the simile in line 210, and line 275. What else might Shakespeare have compared unavoidable fate to, besides death: suffering, injustice, war, winter? Could pleasant words serve as substitutions in this simile for "death," such as *love, success, joy?* Explain. Locate and identify other examples of figurative language in this scene.
5. Interpret the analogy in lines 172–4, showing its application specifically to Othello and Desdemona.
6. Analyze the onomatopoeic effects of the diction in lines 351–6, and note the origin of the title of a famous processional march in this passage. What is the title? Who is the composer?
7. Some critics might label lines 453–60 bombastic. What do you think? Are they the words of a man as emotionally charged as Othello is at this moment, or are they more the language of the poet himself?
8. Look up the etymology of *General, lieutenant, ancient.*
9. Exactly where does Desdemona continue to argue when she should have remained silent? What effect might her silence here have had on her husband?
10. In what sense can lines 90–92 be described as "the handwriting on the wall"?
11. Think about line 198. Is there a middle ground between "jealous" and "secure" or must a person be either one or the other (in this play "jealous" means "uncertain")?
12. In lines 214, 217, 224 Iago attempts to *activate* the suspicions he has been planting in Othello's mind. Explain. What is Othello's first reaction (line 215) and later (line 224)? Is there much difference between them, and if so, how serious is it?
13. What is a cuckold? What is the origin of the word? Lines 167–70 describe the different reactions of two cuckolds. In

which parts of the scene does Othello personify the first
cuckold, and in which the second?

14. What is Othello thinking in lines 388–9 when he speaks of
"cords," "knives," "poison," and so on?

Related Exercises

1. Read the complete play quickly to fit this critical scene into
its proper dramatic context, then read it again slowly and
analytically with somewhat the same approach suggested in
the questions under "Notebook assignment..." Try to understand the characters through what they say and do; also
to be aware of Shakespeare's use of diction and imagery.

2. Since a poet usually bases his imagery on his own observations and experience, try to understand the man Shakespeare,
himself, as well as his characters. Select images which you
think help to reveal Shakespeare as a person, i.e., a man of
the countryside, the city, the theater, and so on. What images
does he base on music, sports, the sea? Notice how in Act 5,
Scene 2 the imagery becomes elemental (like murder): "false
as water," "rash as fire," "ignorant as dirt." Why? Analyze
these three elemental similes: Is water false, for example?

3. Why does Shakespeare use "close-ups" in the dialogue, such
as "And yet I fear you; for you are fatal then/When your
eyes roll so," and "Alas, why gnaw you so your nether lip?"
(Act 5, Scene 2) Would such lines be unnecessary in a movie
version of the play?

4. Listen to a dialogue recording of *Othello,* such as London
A4414 (mono. 4–lps), and note the difference between classroom and dramatic reading.

5. Go to the library and draw up a bibliography of book chapters and periodical articles which seek to interpret *Othello.*
Read three or four of these interpretations and compare
them in an essay with your own critical evaluation, being
sure to provide proper documentation for all quoted and
paraphrased materials.

6. Try to find real-life stories in local or metropolitan newspapers which parallel the story of Othello, Desdemona, and
Iago; then write an essay which attempts to reveal the universality of such experience. In what universal sense is jealousy the same as uncertainty, love the same as possessiveness?
How are jealousy and pride equated?

7. Select some epigrammatic line from this scene, or the whole

play, such as "Men are not gods" (Act 3, Scene 4), and write an imaginative interpretation of it, using concrete examples drawn from your own observations of people as they really are.

8. Whitaker Chambers wrote in *Witness:* "Crime, violence, infamy are not tragedy. Tragedy occurs when a human soul awakes and seeks, in suffering and pain, to free itself from crime, violence, infamy, even at the cost of life. The struggle is the tragedy—not defeat or death." [1] Write an essay in which you attempt to show exactly where the tragedy of Othello begins and where it ends, where he awakes and tries to free himself.

9. How does this view of tragedy differ from Aristotle's? Where would the beginning and end of the tragedy of Othello be, according to Aristotle?

[1] From *Witness,* by Whitaker Chambers (New York: Random House, 1952), pp. 4–5.

OTHELLO *

By William Hazlitt

It has been said that tragedy purifies the affections by terror and pity. That is, it substitutes imaginary sympathy for mere selfishness. It gives us a high and permanent interest, beyond ourselves, in humanity as such. It raises the great, the remote, and the possible to an equality with the real, the little and the near. It makes man a partaker with his kind. It subdues and softens the stubbornness of his will. It teaches him that there are and have been others like himself, by showing him as in a glass what they have felt, thought, and done. It opens the chambers of the human heart. It leaves nothing indifferent to us that can affect our common nature. It excites our sensibility by exhibiting the passions wound up to the utmost pitch by the power of imagination or the temptation of circumstances; and corrects their fatal excesses in ourselves by pointing to the great extent of sufferings and of crimes to which they have led others. Tragedy creates a balance of the affections. It makes us thoughtful spectators in the lists of life.

* From *Characters of Shakespeare's Plays,* by William Hazlitt (London, 1817).

It is the refiner of the species; a discipline of humanity. The
habitual study of poetry and works of imagination is one chief
part of a well-grounded education. A taste for liberal art is necessary to complete the character of a gentleman. Science alone is
hard and mechanical. It exercises the understanding upon things
out of ourselves, while it leaves the affections unemployed, or en-
grossed with our own immediate, narrow interests.—OTHELLO
furnishes an illustration of these remarks. It excites our sympathy
in an extraordinary degree. The moral it conveys has a closer
application to the concerns of human life than that of almost
any other of Shakespeare's plays. "It comes directly home to the
bosoms and business of men." The pathos in *Lear* is indeed more
dreadful and overpowering: but it is less natural, and less of
every day's occurrence. We have not the same degree of sympathy
with the passions described in *Macbeth*. The interest in *Hamlet*
is more remote and reflex. That of OTHELLO is at once equally
profound and affecting.

The picturesque contrasts of character in this play are almost
as remarkable as the depth of the passion. The Moor Othello,
the gentle Desdemona, the villain Iago, the good-natured Cassio,
the fool Roderigo, present a range and variety of character as
striking and palpable as that produced by the opposition of costume in a picture. Their distinguishing qualities stand out to the
mind's eye, so that even when we are not thinking of their actions
or sentiments, the idea of their persons is still as present to us
as ever. These characters and the images they stamp upon the
mind are the farthest asunder possible, the distance between them
is immense: yet the compass of knowledge and invention which
the poet has shown in embodying these extreme creations of his
genius is only greater than the truth and felicity with which he
has identified each character with itself, or blended their different
qualities together in the same story. What a contrast the character of Othello forms to that of Iago! At the same time, the force
of conception with which these two figures are opposed to each
other is rendered still more intense by the complete consistency
with which the traits of each character are brought out in a state
of the highest finishing. The making one black and the other
white, the one unprincipled, the other unfortunate in the extreme,
would have answered the common purposes of effect, and satisfied
the ambition of an ordinary painter of character. Shakespeare
has labored the finer shades of difference in both with as much
care and skill as if he had had to depend on the execution alone
for the success of his design. On the other hand, Desdemona and
Emilia are not meant to be opposed with anything like strong

contrast to each other. Both are, to outward appearance, characters of common life, not more distinguished than women usually are, by difference of rank and situation. The difference of their thoughts and sentiments is however laid open, their minds are separated from each other by signs as plain and as little to be mistaken as the complexions of their husbands.

The movement of the passion in Othello is exceedingly different from that of Macbeth. In Macbeth there is a violent struggle between opposite feelings, between ambition and the stings of conscience, almost from first to last: in Othello, the doubtful conflict between contrary passions, though dreadful, continues only for a short time, and the chief interest is excited by the alternate ascendancy of different passions, by the entire and unforeseen change from the fondest love and most unbounded confidence to the tortures of jealousy and the madness of hatred. The revenge of Othello, after it has once taken thorough possession of his mind, never quits it, but grows stronger and stronger at every moment of its delay .The nature of the Moor is noble, confiding, tender, and generous; but his blood is of the most inflammable kind; and being once roused by a sense of his wrongs, he is stopped by no considerations of remorse or pity till he has given a loose to all the dictates of his rage and his despair. It is in working his noble nature up to this extremity through rapid but gradual transitions, in raising passion to its height from the smallest beginnings and in spite of all obstacles, in painting the expiring conflict between love and hatred, tenderness and resentment, jealousy and remorse, in unfolding the strength and the weakness of our nature, in uniting sublimity of thought with the anguish of the keenest woe, in putting in motion the various impulses that agitate this our mortal being, and at last blending them in that noble tide of deep and sustained passion, impetuous but majestic, that "flows on to the Propontic, and knows no ebb," that Shakespeare has shown the mastery of his genius and of his power over the human heart. The third act of OTHELLO is his finest display, not of knowledge or passion separately, but of the two combined, of the knowledge of character with the expression of passion, of consummate art in the keeping up of appearances with the profound working of nature, and the convulsive movements of uncontrollable agony, of the power of inflicting torture and of suffering it. Not only is the tumult of passion in Othello's mind heaved up from the very bottom of the soul, but even the slightest undulation of feeling is seen on the surface, as it arises from the impulses of imagination or the malicious suggestions of Iago. The progressive preparation for the catastrophe is wonderfully managed from the Moor's first gallant recital of the story of his love, of "the spells and witchcraft he had used," from his unlooked-for and romantic success, the fond satisfaction with which he dotes on his own happiness, the unreserved tenderness of Desdemona and her innocent importunities in favor of Cassio, irritating the suspicions instilled into her husband's mind by the perfidy of Iago, and rankling there to poison, till he loses all command of himself, and his rage can only be appeased by blood. She is introduced, just before Iago begins to put his scheme in practice, pleading for Cassio with all the thoughtless gaiety of friendship and winning confidence in the love of Othello.

> What! Michael Cassio?
> That came a wooing with you, and so many a time,
> When I have spoke of you dispraisingly,
> Hath ta'en your part, to have so much to do
> To bring him in? . . . Why this is not a boon:
> 'Tis as I should intreat you wear your gloves,
> Or feed on nourishing meats, or keep you warm;
> Or sue to you to do a peculiar profit
> To your person. Nay, when I have a suit,
> Wherein I mean to touch your love indeed,
> It shall be full of poise, and fearful to be granted.

Othello's confidence, at first only staggered by broken hints and insinuations, recovers itself at sight of Desdemona; and he exclaims:

> If she be false, O then Heav'n mocks itself:
> I'll not believe it.

But presently after, on brooding over his suspicions by himself, and yielding to his apprehensions of the worst, his smothered jealousy breaks out into open fury, and he returns to demand satisfaction of Iago like a wild beast stung with the envenomed shaft of the hunters. "Look where he comes," etc. In this state of exasperation and violence, after the first paroxysms of his grief and tenderness have had their vent in that passionate apostrophe, "I felt not Cassio's kisses on her lips," Iago, by false aspersions, and by presenting the most revolting images to his mind, easily turns the storm of passion from himself against Desdemona, and works him up into a trembling agony of doubt and fear, in which he abandons all his love and hopes in a breath.

> Now do I see 'tis true. Look here, Iago,
> All my fond love thus do I blow to Heaven. 'Tis gone.

Arise black vengeance from the hollow hell;
Yield up, O love, thy crown and hearted throne
To tyrannous hate! Swell bosom with thy fraught;
For 'tis of aspicks' tongues.

From this time, his raging thoughts "never look back, ne'er ebb to humble love," till his revenge is sure of its object, the painful regrets and involuntary recollections of past circumstances which cross his mind amidst the dim trances of passion, aggravating the sense of his wrongs, but not shaking his purpose. Once indeed, where Iago shows him Cassio with the handkerchief in his hand, and making sport (as he thinks) of his misfortunes, the intolerable bitterness of his feelings, the extreme sense of shame, makes him fall to praising her accomplishments and relapse into a momentary fit of weakness, "Yet, oh the pity of it, Iago, the pity of it!" This returning fondness however only serves, as it is managed by Iago, to whet his revenge, and set his heart more against her. In his conversations with Desdemona, the persuasion of her guilt and the immediate proofs of her duplicity seem to irritate his resentment and aversion to her; but in the scene immediately preceding her death, the recollection of his love returns upon him in all its tenderness and force; and after her death, he all at once forgets his wrongs in the sudden and irreparable sense of his loss.

My wife   My wife!   What wife?   I have no wife.
Oh insupportable!   Oh heavy hour!

This happens before he is assured of her innocence; but afterwards his remorse is as dreadful as his revenge has been, and yields only to fixed death-like despair. His farewell speech, before he kills himself, in which he conveys his reasons to the senate for the murder of his wife, is equal to the first speech in which he gave them an account of his courtship of her, and "his whole course of love." Such an ending was alone worthy of such a commencement.

If any thing could add to the force of our sympathy with Othello, or compassion for his fate, it would be the frankness and generosity of his nature, which so little deserve it. When Iago first begins to practise upon his unsuspecting friendship, he answers—

—Tis not to make me jealous,
To say my wife is fair, feeds well, loves company,
Is free of speech, sings, plays, and dances well;
Where virtue is, these are most virtuous.

Nor from my own weak merits will I draw
The smallest fear or doubt of her revolt,
For she had eyes and chose me.

This character is beautifully (and with affecting simplicity) confirmed by what Desdemona herself says of him to Emilia after
she has lost the handkerchief, the first pledge of his love to her.

Believe me, I had rather have lost my purse
Full of cruzadoes. And but my noble Moor
Is true of mind, and made of no such baseness,
As jealous creatures are, it were enough
To put him to ill thinking.
EMILIA. Is he not jealous?
DESDEMONA. Who he? I think the sun where he was born
Drew all such humours from him.

In a short speech of Emilia's, there occurs one of those side-
intimations of the fluctuations of passion which we seldom meet
with but in Shakespeare. After Othello has resolved upon the
death of his wife, and bids her dismiss her attendant for the
night, she answers,

I will, my Lord.
EMILIA. How goes it now? *He looks gentler than he did.*

Shakespeare has here put into half a line what some authors
would have spun out into ten set speeches.
The character of Desdemona is inimitable both in itself, and
as it appears in contrast with Othello's groundless jealousy, and
with the foul conspiracy of which she is the innocent victim. Her
beauty and external graces are only indirectly glanced at: we see
"her visage in her mind"; her character everywhere predominates
over her person.

A maiden never bold:
Of spirit so still and quiet, that her motion
Blush'd at itself.

There is one fine compliment paid to her by Cassio, who exclaims
triumphantly when she comes ashore at Cyprus after the storm,

Tempests themselves, high seas, and howling winds,
As having sense of beauty, do omit
Their mortal natures, letting safe go by
The divine Desdemona.

In general, as is the case with most of Shakespeare's females, we lose sight of her personal charms in her attachment and devotedness to her husband. She is "subdued even to the very quality of her lord"; and to Othello's "honours and his valiant parts her soul and fortunes consecrates." The lady protests so much herself, and she is as good as her word. The truth of conception, with which timidity and boldness are united in the same character, is marvelous. The extravagance of her resolutions, the pertinacity of her affections, may be said to arise out of the gentleness of her nature. They imply an unreserved reliance on the purity of her own intentions, an entire surrender of her fears to her love, a knitting of herself (heart and soul) to the fate of another. Bating the commencement of her passion, which is a little fantastical and headstrong (though even that may perhaps be consistently accounted for from her inability to resist a rising inclination) her whole character consists in having no will of her own, no prompter but her obedience. Her romantic turn is only a consequence of the domestic and practical part of her disposition; and instead of following Othello to the wars, she would gladly have "remained at home a moth of peace," if her husband could have stayed with her. Her resignation and angelic sweetness of temper do not desert her at the last. The scenes in which she laments and tries to account for Othello's estrangement from her are exquisitely beautiful. After he has struck her, and called her names, she says,

> —Alas, Iago,
> What shall I do to win my lord again?
> Good friend, go to him; for by this light of heaven,
> I know not how I lost him.   Here I kneel;
> If e'er my will did trespass 'gainst his love,
> Either in discourse, or thought, or actual deed,
> Or that mine eyes, mine ears, or any sense
> Delighted them on any other form;
> Or that I do not yet, and ever did,
> And ever will, though he do shake me off
> To beggarly divorcement, love him dearly,
> Comfort forswear me.   Unkindness may do much,
> And his unkindness may defeat my life,
> But never taint my love.
> IAGO. I pray you be content: 'tis but his humour.
> The business of the state does him offence.
> DESDEMONA. If 'twere no other!—

The scene which follows with Emilia and the song of the Willow, are equally beautiful, and show the author's extreme power
of varying the expression of passion, in all its moods and in all
circumstances.

> EMILIA. Would you had never seen him.
> DESDEMONA. So would not I: my love doth so approve him,
> That even his stubbornness, his checks, his frowns,
> Have grace and favour in them, etc.

Not the unjust suspicions of Othello, not Iago's unprovoked
treachery, place Desdemona in a more amiable or interesting
light than the conversation (half earnest, half jest) between her
and Emilia on the common behavior of women to their husbands.
This dialogue takes place just before the last fatal scene. If
Othello had overheard it, it would have prevented the whole
catastrophe; but then it would have spoiled the play.

The character of Iago is one of the supererogations of Shakespeare's genius. Some persons, more nice than wise, have thought
this whole character unnatural, because his villainy is *without
a sufficient motive*. Shakespeare, who was as good a philosopher
as he was a poet, thought otherwise. He knew that the love of
power, which is another name for the love of mischief, is natural
to man. He would know this as well or better than if it had been
demonstrated to him by a logical diagram, merely from seeing
children paddle in the dirt or kill flies for sport. Iago in fact belongs to a class of character, common to Shakespeare and at
the same time peculiar to him; whose heads are as acute and
active as their hearts are hard and callous. Iago is to be sure an
extreme instance of the kind; that is to say, of diseased intellectual activity, with the most perfect indifference to moral good or
evil, or rather with a decided preference of the latter, because
it falls more readily in with his favorite propensity, gives greater
zest to his thoughts and scope to his actions. He is quite or nearly
as indifferent to his own fate as to that of others; he runs all risks
for a trifling and doubtful advantage; and is himself the dupe
and victim of his ruling passion—an insatiable craving after action of the most difficult and dangerous kind. "Our ancient" is
a philosopher, who fancies that a lie that kills has more point
in it than an alliteration or an antithesis; who thinks a fatal
experiment on the peace of a family a better thing than watching the palpitations of the heart of a flea in a microscope; who
plots the ruin of his friends as an exercise for his ingenuity, and
stabs men in the dark to prevent *ennui*. His gaiety, such as it is,
arises from the success of his treachery; his ease from the torture

he has inflicted on others. He is an amateur of tragedy in real life; and instead of employing his invention in imaginary characters, or long-forgotten incidents, he takes the bolder and more desperate course of getting up his plot at home, casts the principal parts among his nearest friends and connections, and rehearses it in downright earnest, with steady nerves and unabated resolution. We will just give an illustration or two.

One of his most characteristic speeches is that immediately after the marriage of Othello.

> RODERIGO. What a full fortune does the thick lips owe,
> If he can carry her thus!
> IAGO. Call up her father:
> Rouse him (*Othello*), make after him, poison his delight,
> Proclaim him in the streets, incense her kinsmen,
> And tho' he in a fertile climate dwell,
> Plague him with flies: tho' that his joy be joy,
> Yet throw such changes of vexation on it,
> As it may lose some colour.

In the next passage, his imagination runs riot in the mischief he is plotting, and breaks out into the wildness and impetuosity of real enthusiasm.

> RODERIGO. Here is her father's house: I'll call aloud.
> IAGO. Do, with like timourous accent and dire yell
> As when, by night and negligence, the fire
> Is spied in populous cities.

One of his most favorite topics, on which he is rich indeed, and in descanting on which his spleen serves him for a Muse, is the disproportionate match between Desdemona and the Moor. This is a clue to the character of the lady which he is by no means ready to part with. It is brought forward in the first scene, and he recurs to it, when in answer to his insinuations against Desdemona, Roderigo says,

> I cannot believe that in her—she's full of most blest
>   condition.
> IAGO. Bless'd fig's end.   The wine she drinks is made
>   of grapes.   If she had been blest, she would never
>   have married the Moor.

And again with still more spirit and fatal effect afterwards, when he turns this very suggestion arising in Othello's own breast to her prejudice.

OTHELLO. And yet how nature erring from itself—
IAGO. Ay, there's the point;—as to be bold with you,
Not to affect many proposed matches
Of her own clime, complexion, and degree, etc.

This is probing to the quick. Iago here turns the character of poor Desdemona, as it were, inside out. It is certain that nothing but the genius of Shakespeare could have preserved the entire interest and delicacy of the part, and have even drawn an additional elegance and dignity from the peculiar circumstances in which she is placed. The habitual licentiousness of Iago's conversation is not to be traced to the pleasure he takes in gross or lascivious images, but to his desire of finding out the worst side of everything, and of proving himself an over-match for appearances. He has none of "the milk of human kindness" in his composition. His imagination rejects everything that has not a strong infusion of the most unpalatable ingredients; his mind digests only poisons. Virtue or goodness or whatever has the least "relish of salvation in it," is, to his depraved appetite, sickly and insipid: and he even resents the good opinion entertained of his own integrity, as if it were an affront cast on the masculine sense and spirit of his character. Thus at the meeting between Othello and Desdemona, he exclaims—"Oh, you are well tuned now: but I'll set down the pegs that make this music, *as honest as I am*"—his character of *bonhommie* not sitting at all easy upon him. In the scenes, where he tries to work Othello to his purpose, he is proportionably guarded, insidious, dark, and deliberate. We believe nothing ever came up to the profound dissimulation and dextrous artifice of the well-known dialogue in the third act, where he first enters upon the execution of his design.

IAGO. My noble lord—
OTHELLO. What dost thou say, Iago?
IAGO. Did Michael Cassio,
When you woo'd my lady, know of your love?
OTHELLO. He did from first to last.
Why dost thou ask?
IAGO. But for a satisfaction of my thought,
No further harm.
OTHELLO. Why of thy thought, Iago?
IAGO. I did not think he had been acquainted with her.
OTHELLO. O yes, and went between us very oft—
IAGO. Indeed!
OTHELLO. Indeed? Ay, indeed. Discern'st thou aught of
that? Is he not honest?

IAGO. Honest, my lord?
OTHELLO. Honest?   Ay, honest.
IAGO. My lord, for aught I know.
OTHELLO. What do'st thou think?
IAGO. Think, my lord!
OTHELLO. Think, my lord!   Alas, thou echo'st me;
As if there was some monster in thy thought
Too hideous to be shewn.—

The stops and breaks, the deep workings of treachery under the mask of love and honesty, the anxious watchfulness, the cool earnestness, and if we may so say, the *passion* of hypocrisy, marked in every line, receive their last finishing in that inconceivable burst of pretended indignation at Othello's doubts of his sincerity.

O grace!   O Heaven forgive me!
Are you a man?   Have you a soul or sense?
God be wi' you; take mine office.   O wretched fool,
That lov'st to make thine honesty a vice!
Oh monstrous world!   Take note, take note, O world!
To be direct and honest, is not safe.
I thank you for this profit, and from hence
I'll love no friend, since love breeds such offence.

If Iago is detestable enough when he has business on his hands and all his engines at work, he is still worse when he has nothing to do, and we only see into the hollowness of his heart. His indifference when Othello falls into a swoon, is perfectly diabolical.

IAGO. How is it, General?   Have you not hurt your head?
OTHELLO. Do'st thou mock me?
IAGO. I mock you not, by Heaven, etc.

The part indeed would hardly be tolerated, even as a foil to the virtue and generosity of the other characters in the play, but for its indefatigable industry and inexhaustible resources, which divert the attention of the spectator (as well as his own) from the end he has in view to the means by which it must be accomplished.—Edmund the Bastard in *Lear* is something of the same character, placed in less prominent circumstances. Zanga is a vulgar caricature of it.

Part Six

NO MAN IS AN ISLAND

Or

Cross Sections of Culture and Society

MAN THE TOOL-MAKER *

By Kenneth P. Oakley

Man is a social animal, distinguished by "culture": by the ability to make tools and communicate ideas. Employment of tools appears to be his chief biological characteristic, for considered functionally they are detachable extensions of the forelimb. Other mammals have evolved specialized bodily equipment suited to some particular mode of life. Horses, for example, have teeth and hoofs suited to a plant-eating animal living on grassy plains; beavers are dependent for their way of life on incisor teeth capable of stripping and felling trees; the carnivorous sabre-tooth cats evolved claws like grappling irons and canine teeth like daggers, perfectly adapted for killing prey. In process of evolution man avoided any such specialization, and retained the pliant five-fingered hands which were so useful to his small tree-dwelling ancestors. When the immediate forerunners of man acquired the ability to walk upright habitually, their hands became free to make and manipulate tools—activities which were in the first place dependent on adequate powers of mental and bodily coordination, but which in turn perhaps increased those powers.

The evolution of new bodily equipment in response to a change of environment required millions of years, but relying on extra-bodily equipment of his own making, which could be quickly discarded or changed as circumstances dictated, man became the most adaptable of all creatures. Making fire, constructing dwellings and wearing clothes followed from the use of tools, and these cultural activities have enabled man not only to meet changes of environment, but to extend his range into every climatic zone.

While it is evident that man may be distinguished as the tool-making primate, it is questionable whether this definition gets to the heart of the difference between man and the higher apes. Structurally they are not very different; in fact they are classed by zoologists as members of the same group, the Hominoidea. Moreover, fossil primates transitional between apes and man are known. Sir Wilfrid Le Gros Clark, who has made a special study of these transitional types (the Australopithecines of South Africa)

---

* From *Man the Tool-Maker*, by Kenneth P. Oakley (Phoenix Book P20; Chicago: University of Chicago Press, 1959), pp. 1–4. Reprinted by permission of the trustees of the British Museum (Natural History).

has said: "Probably the differentiation of man from ape will ultimately have to rest on a functional rather than on an anatomical
basis, the criterion of humanity being the ability to speak and
to make tools." This amounts to saying that the real difference
between what we choose to call an ape and what we call man
is one of mental capacity. It is worth considering the psychology
of apes with this point of view in mind.

Observations of Professor W. Kohler, Madame Kohts and
others on the habits of chimpanzees have shown that these apes
are not only adept at learning by trial-and-error, but sometimes
display remarkable insight. For example, Sultan, one of the male
chimpanzees observed by Kohler, fitted together two bamboo
tubes as a means of securing a bunch of bananas dangling beyond
reach outside his cage; and on another occasion he attained the
same end by fitting into one bamboo tube a piece of wood which
he pointed for the purpose with the aid of his teeth. Apes are
thus evidently capable of improvising tools. But it is important
to note that the improvisations effected by Sultan were carried
out with a *visible* reward as incentive. Kohler could obtain no
clear indication that apes are ever capable of conceiving the usefulness of shaping an object for use in an imaginary future eventuality. He expressed this opinon:

"The time in which the chimpanzee lives (mentally) is limited
in past and future. Besides in the lack of speech, it is in the
extremely narrow limits in this direction that the chief difference
is to be found between anthropoids and the most primitive human
beings. The lack of an invaluable technical aid (speech) and a
great limitation of those very important components of thought,
so-called 'images,' would thus constitute the causes that prevent
the chimpanzee from attaining even the smallest beginnings of
cultural development."

One may sum up by saying that apes of the present day are
capable of perceiving the solution of a visible problem, and occasionally of improvising a tool to meet a given situation; but to
conceive the idea of shaping a stone or stick for use in an imagined future eventuality is beyond the mental capacity of any
known apes. Possession of a great capacity for this conceptual
thinking, in contrast to the mainly perceptual thinking of apes
and other primates, is generally regarded by comparative psychologists as distinctive of man. Systematic making of tools implies
a marked capacity for conceptual thought.

THE INDIAN IN
HIS ENVIRONMENT *

By William A. Ritchie

Because of the great range of physical varieties, languages, social and cultural systems found among the Indian tribes of North and South America, it is almost impossible to make specific statements applicable to all. Furthermore, so many changes have taken place within each of these categories (as well as in the physical environment) over the probably more than 20,000 years that man has occupied the New World, that we shall be obliged to limit our observations here to the Indian occupants of the northeastern area during the past few thousand years.

In referring to the Indians' environment, we must clearly distinguish between this term and the mere physical setting, since the environment of any group of people is that part of their physical world with which they have the knowledge and skill to cope; in other words, it is defined for them by their culture. Thus the abundant sources of flint of our natural area are little known or used today, while prehistorically they were of vital significance to the Indians as the chief source of their tool and weapon material.

From the earliest times, the Indians of the Northeast satisfied the primary need for subsistence by a combination of activities based on fishing, hunting and collecting. Much later, simple hoe tillage was added to this pattern. The opening chapter of our drama is difficult to decipher through the obscuring shadow of an estimated minimum of some 7,000 years, but to this first (or Paleo-Indian period) we attribute the distinctive fluted points occasionally found on the surface in our region. So far, in New York State they have not been discovered in association with other stone artifacts, but a single site of this kind is known in three northeastern states—Pennsylvania, Vermont and Massachusetts. Nowhere in the eastern United States, however, are Paleo-Indian implements found with the bones of the animals they

* From *The New York State Conservationist*, Vol. 10, No. 3 (December-January, 1955–56), 23–7. Reprinted by permission of the New York Conservation Department.

were used to kill. In the southern Great Plains, the American Southwest and northern Mexico, the case is very different, for in those areas fluted points have well established connections with an extinct Pleistocene or Ice Age fauna (including the mammoth, mastodon, camel, horse and bison) dating back, in some cases, at least 10,000 years.

In New York, the clearly recorded archeological story begins about 5,500 years ago, on the recently devised radiocarbon scale, with the first influx of what we call Archaic period hunters. These were soon followed by other, and different, groups. For at least 3,500 years these nomadic or seminomadic bands camped along the wooded waterways, on swamp margins, and at advantageous spots along the coast. We believe their temporary settlements of bark or mat-covered houses were small and rude; their political, social and religious organizations simple. In general, such a way of life exists even today among the Algonkian speaking Montagnais, Naskapi and Wabanaki tribes of the Northeast. From the rarely preserved skeletal remains of the Archaic peoples and more abundant implements we infer marked physical as well as cultural differences among the major groups.

An annual cycle of life seems to have prevailed. During the Spring run of fish the bands gathered along stream rifts, a notable locus of this kind formerly existing at Brewerton, on the Oneida River, where some of our most important archeological finds were made. Large marshes, like Montezuma and the district surrounding the foot of Cayuga Lake, were much frequented (as our excavations prove) to exploit the Spring and Fall migrations of waterfowl, as well as the more permanent aquatic life consisting of fish, muskrats, turtles, frogs and even snakes. Winter camps were certainly established in sheltered forest tracts in the vicinity of springs and streams, while the shallow bays of lakes, large rivers, and the sea coast were environmentally well suited to the fishing techniques which employed the barbless bone hook, straight bone gorge, barbed harpoon, and net—the latter inferred from notched stone sinkers and presumed bone net-weaving tools. Traps and weirs certainly existed, leaving few traces, the largest and oldest having been found in digging deep building foundations in Back Bay, Boston.

Perhaps somewhere in the muck may still remain examples of the dugout boats which these Archaic fishermen must have employed. We have found many of their stone axes, adzes and gouges, and other tools so necessary to forest-adapted cultures, but as yet nothing so perishable as the doubtless abundant articles fashioned of wood, bark, fibers and leather.

When the edibility of shellfish became known in later Archaic times, the numerous places along the coast where oysters, clams, scallops and whelk could be gathered were soon discovered and are today marked by accumulations of shells, known as kitchen middens. Inland, the tougher and today neglected *Unio* (fresh water clam) became a source of food, perhaps by transference of the idea of eating shellfish on the coast, since the *Unio* remains occur on even later sites.

Much ingenuity and skill were likewise exercised in hunting—as the stone, bone, antler and occasional native copper weapons testify. Ignoring the important differences which have been defined for specific cultures of the Archaic (for which see the writer's professional monographs and papers), the hunters of this period pursued their game chiefly with the dart or short spear, hurled with the aid of an atlatl or throwing stick, to which was sometimes affixed (to provide momentum) a notched or drilled stone weight, inappropriately termed a bannerstone. The armament of the dart consisted of a chipped flint, or more rarely a bone or antler point, variously fashioned according to patterns current in different times and cultures. Thrusting spears with larger points also served the hunter, but the bow and arrow seem to have been unknown until a much later time. In later Archaic cultures, at least, dogs of large and small breeds were sufficiently esteemed as companions of the hunt to be given careful burial with or near their owners. And we can be sure that traps and snares had wide usage, although they have all disappeared without a trace, save perhaps for what may be considered carved antler trap sticks, bearing rude representations of animal heads. At least one of these suggests a bear, and we may surmise that these effigies served a magical purpose.

From later prehistoric times to the present, we know that certain Indians in the Northeast shared in a reverential attitude toward the bear and conducted ceremonial observances which have been traced to northern Asia. An important food animal of the boreal zone, the bear became the center of a ritual complex involving the manner of its killing, eating, and even the disposition of its bones—all done in order not to offend the spiritual keeper of the bears, who might then withhold the supply of this game.

This example of Indian ritualism, one of many that could be cited, serves to illustrate the tremendous difference between the respective views of the Indian and the white man toward the natural and supernatural worlds. To the white man, with his Mosaic traditions, the earth and all it contained of plants and animals—and also the celestial system in which it moved—were expressly created for human use. Only man was a being with spirit, akin to that of his Creator.

But the Indian, in common with many other preliterate peoples, conceived of no essential distinction between himself and the rest of nature in which he lived. He attributed supernatural qualities of spirit and power to lower animals, as well as to plants, and even to inanimate objects. He responded to a consciousness of unity with nature, with which he identified himself in kind, if not in degree, in a manner culturally comprehensible only to a few so-called mystics in our present society.

If most of the intangible aspects of the Indian's culture—religion, language, social organization, etc.—have escaped us, and only the more durable portions of his material possessions have survived, we are less at loss to account for the kinds and relative quantities of the game taken, since, along with the catching and killing devices in the refuse middens are the discarded bones of mammals, birds, fish and other animals. In the particular localities where food resources were abundant by virtue of natural conditions, repeated temporary human habitation (or more rarely, semipermanent residence) resulted in the accumulation of cultural debris, more or less well preserved by the alkaline medium of the ash content. We learn from such deposits that the primitive dietary tolerated such (to us) unappealing species as the red and gray fox, wolf, mink, marten, lynx, wild cat, mountain lion, eagle, great blue heron, great horned owl, box turtle and various snakes—to mention only a few of the larger forms. Since, however, the bones of these animals were much used in the making of implements and ornaments, we cannot be certain that they were not hunted for this purpose. But when a bone is split or broken, evidently for the extraction of the succulent marrow, we feel safe in listing the species among the food resources.

It is of interest to note that the whitetail deer, black bear and beaver were among the favorite food mammals, with the deer far in the lead. The wild turkey was apparently the most sought after of the larger birds, although duck, goose, and swan remains are also common in some sites. Their bones, too, found wide employment in tool and ornament manufacture.

The well known voracity of the northern pike probably accounts for the frequency of his sharp-toothed jaws among the remains of fishes. On some sites the fin spines of the bullhead tell us that this humble and easily caught species predominated. And the sucker, pike-perch, black bass, brook trout, sturgeon, salmon and several others have also been expertly identified.

The nature of the animal remains sometimes provides an important clue to such interesting matters as the season of occupation of the site and possible local conservation practices, while in addition, the archeologist's data furnished by such remains are of use to students of zoology and ecology.

To the all-protein diet supplied by the hunting and fishing activities referred to, a starch constitutent was added by the consumption of certain wild plants. So few floral vestiges have resisted decomposition that we shall refer only to the acorn, the charred hulls of which occur on some sites along with the stone utensils used in reducing the kernels to meal. These utensils consist of shallow mortars and hand stones or mullers, and of long cylindrical pestles which presumably indicate that the hollowed tree-trunk mortar, so well known in later cultures, was already in use in our area in the earliest Archaic stage.

Since acorns from all of our oaks contain varying amounts of bitter and toxic tannic acid (the black oak group having a higher percentage than the white oaks), the process of leaching must have been known to these early peoples, as was the case among the ancient Indians of California. Roasting or boiling of the hulled nut meats (either before or after pulverizing) and followed by thorough washing in baskets, was doubtless the method employed. Inasmuch as these people had no pottery (the use of baskets is conjectural), boiling was certainly accomplished by the laborious method of heating stones and dropping them into perishable vessels of bark, wood or other materials. Shattered stone "pot boilers" are common on most sites.

Late in the Archaic period, some of the eastern Indians learned the manufacture of steatite or soapstone pots. Even before the dawn of the Christian era, however, these stone vessels began to be supplanted by rude varieties of baked clay pottery. The absorbing story of the subsequent development in our area of pottery, and concurrently of smoking pipes of stone and clay, is too long and complex to relate in this brief generalized account.

When and how our eastern Indians acquired their knowledge and skill as farmers are problems high on the agenda of the archeological investigator. We are confident that in most sections the use of pottery preceded the raising of such storable food products as maize and beans, which is fundamental to a relatively stable pattern of life. It is only when we reach, in our long and involved sequence of Indian occupations in New York, the cultural stages of what is termed the Late Woodland period, that we come upon extensive quantities of carbonized crop foods. The earliest radiocarbon date yet obtained for such a site (which, incidentally, we excavated near St. Johnsville in the Mohawk Valley) is approximately A.D. 300. These sites represent the remains of extensive villages, marked by the post-mold patterns of small round houses, and by deep bark or grass-lined storage pits. The whole assemblage is often surrounded by the evidences of a stout stockade, and is perched on a hilltop for further security. Hunting, fishing and the gathering of wild foods—roots, nuts, berries, etc.—were still relied upon, as is shown both by refuse and the artifact content, which now definitely includes the bow and arrow. This mixed economy survived down into historic times among the Algonkian and Iroquoian speaking tribes of our area, and we are quite certain that its roots go back into the Middle Woodland period cultures, particularly since on current archeological evidence, corn of a very primitive sort was already known in the Southwest around 3,000 B.C.

Certain of the ceremonial attitudes of the earlier hunting cultures have already been referred to. It is of interest to observe that these same reverential attitudes carry over into the agricultural complex and are well recorded for the Iroquoian tribes. Thanksgiving ceremonies and first fruits sacrifices formed an important part of the later Indians' annual cycle. We may say, in sharp contrast to the white man's way, that the Indian trod lightly through his natural environment, merging himself sympathetically into the world of living and even non-living things. This feeling for nature seems almost to have disappeared from our way of life, with its central emphasis on economic values. The deeper emotional levels of response to wildlife, woods and waters still exist, apparently, in some among us, and they are basic to a true feeling for conservation.

The Indians' regard for the land provides us with additional insight into aboriginal philosophy, which was at the farthest remove from European concepts. This is a fact which underlies the numerous difficulties of land transfer during the colonial period: Indian ideology conceived of the land, together with the life-sustaining animals, vegetables and minerals it supported, as supernaturally given for the common use, hence not subject to personal ownership and transfer. Privileges of land use rested with tribe or village, and apparently more than one tribe might synchronously utilize the same large tract in peaceful co-existence, while the removal of a band for a number of years seems to have relinquished even their temporary claim to these holdings. As has recently been argued convincingly, the family hunting territories of the northern Algonkians seem to have been an adaptation to the special conditions imposed by the European fur trade.

These contrasting attitudes of whites and Indians toward the "earth mother" serve once more to emphasize their diverse world views, which we may attempt to express in a final generalization. The goal and purpose of the average Western man centers on the technological domination of his environment; its mastery and control. Seldom is he willing to leave any part of his natural world unmolested. He suffers a cultural compulsion to "improve" everything. He seeks unceasingly to alter the world of nature to conform with his culturally patterned ideals of utility, and he customarily phrases these ideals in economic terms.

The Indian, on the other hand, was content to adjust himself harmoniously into the scheme of nature, to its seasonal cycles and mystically conceived order of life. His sensitive awareness of the ecological relationships existing between plants and animals and their habitats, and the acuity of his perceptions, have often been remarked with wonderment by observers of our race, who attributed them erroneously to qualitative differences in sense perception. Their true source, however, lies rather in evaluative differences of a purely cultural origin.

It is probable that the Indian knew and loved the world of his environment in a way that few white men, reared in the competitive, exploitative and possessive traditions of Western civilization, can ever comprehend.

Notebook Assignment for Class Discussion

1. Look up the following words:

tillage	muck	voracity
artifacts	middens	ecology
paleo	effigy	vestige
Pleistocene	boreal zone	mortar
fauna	ritual	muller
Archaic	Mosaic	pestle
nomad	prehistoric	leaching
locus	preliterate	aboriginal
aquatic	dietary	acuity

2. What is the origin of the word *environment?*
3. What is the exact meaning of the word *culture* as this scientist uses it? What are other meanings of *culture?* In what way do they all mean essentially the same (e.g., the sociological and biological definitions of the word suggest that they have something in common. What is it?)?

4. The first paragraph is one of cause and effect, and the second is one of definition. Explain. What other types of paragraph development can you locate in this essay?

5. What type of scientist is the author: paleontologist, archeologist, anthropologist, sociologist, biologist, or what? What is the specific field of each of these sciences? Name and define at least a dozen other -*ologists*.

6. On what basis does Dr. Ritchie assume that "these Archaic fishermen must have employed [dugout boats]"?

7. List and date (approximately) the various periods into which the author divides the Indian culture of the Northeast. What are the principal characteristics of each period?

Related Exercises

1. Employing a light, popular style, try to explain in three or four hundred words how the radio-carbon test can determine the age of archeological remains.

2. What is the present cultural and economic condition of the Indian in the United States? Be sure to divide and limit your subject as Dr. Ritchie does in the first paragraph of this essay, and read considerably in the library before you attempt to write about it or discuss it orally in class.

3. After reading a good deal about the Indian as he really was during frontier days, write a paper in which you compare him with the modern Western movie and TV versions.

4. The Indians' attitude toward common use of the land and the lack of any sense of personal ownership resemble certain phases of modern Communism. Write a serious paper in which you attempt to show the differences between their "natural" philosophy and modern "political" Communism.

PONY SHOW IN CONNEMARA *

By William Sansom

Often when you are motoring across the broad bog of that distinct part of Ireland called Connemara, one of the final European fingers pointing to the long Atlantic miles Americaward, you see what look like horses standing about. These are not the kind of horses that poke their heads through the windows of your car. They keep themselves to themselves. Nor are they horses at all, but ponies, Connemara ponies, free but not wild, that live out on the lovely land of their birth. They are carefully bred and among ponymen have a rising international reputation.

Against the soggy green of the Irish west, they mark delicate colors: dark yellow, tweedy gray, burnt pink. There are occasional albinos, white with white-lashed pale eyes, like old ladies far gone in the drink. Color is, in any case, one of the Connemara particulars. This mountainous country, with its brilliant estuaries curling miles inland, has little of the brilliant emerald green of the east of Ireland. The green of the west is mistier, and it creeps everywhere, like baize cloth, right up to the tops of the mountains and even flatly down vertical cliff façades; you feel you are living on an old, torn, and humped billiard table, with a cloth that has been left to weather in the sun and the rain. Against such a soft green, whose quality changes with every magical slant and flash of Atlantic-borne light, all isolated colors stand out sharply. Golden-yellow stretches of seaweed line the Prussian-green waters of an estuary miles inland; the crimson bells of the tall wild fuchsia bush dangle everywhere, lining the lanes as though a giant and bloody hand had dripped a bright indication of the path; the mountains may lose their green and in certain lights haze to pale blue or violet, or flower at sunset to a deep blood-red —and all these colors have the inner brightness of plush. Then there is an abundance of black about: the boats are black; the women's shawls are black; and the mounds of black peat and the black rocks and the black cattle all spatter the country with charcoal emphasis. Even the ubiquitous drink, the porter, is black. If ever a martini drifted so far west, the olive would surely be a black one.

* From *The Atlantic Monthly,* Vol. 206, No. 2 (August, 1960), 86–90.

But back to the ponies and a black day in this writer's life, the day of the Connemara Pony Show. This is an annual event that takes place in the westerly small capital of Clifden, an up-and-down slip of a town with a half dozen streets and about a million bars. The purpose of the show is to bring together the best of the pony breed for prizes and for sale, together with other less important local produce, from sheep to sheep's-wool sweaters, from chickens to baked breads, from woven reed whips to the pointed toes of a Gaelic step-dance competition. But the ponies are the mainstay; it is the ponies, each with four hoofs and flying feet, that take up all the room on the muddy, sloping field where the great affair takes place.

Let me state now that I am neither a pony nor horse lover and know little about them, so the following few lines shall be free of words like "withers" and "gaskins," "hands" and "hackney" (from the French *haquenee, an ambling horse*, if this should maybe raise your spirits). The only kinds of things I do know about the horse are such as the length of its fearsome yellow teeth and the force behind the hoof and the mad roll—like that of a jazz drummer deep in the groove—of the eye.

So, on a morning of rain and shine, we bought our tickets and slid muddily into the show. Rain and shine are the normal weather: one minute the sun streams in magic rays from momentous Atlantic cloudscapes; the next, down come the momentous inescapable clouds themselves. The apocalyptic elemental feeling of such godlike weather must, I think, have a large hand in the Gaelic belief in fairies. But there were no fairies at the bottom of our pony field—only mud, viscous gallons of it, down into which the pointed end of my shooting stick vanished at an alarming speed, leaving me seated two feet off the ground, like a cooperative but uncertain uncle in a kiddy car.

From this mildly unelevated position I was perhaps the better equipped to view the goings on and the goers. Previously, being blind to the complex virtues of the ponies themselves, I had been in a position to drink in more of the general atmosphere than others, with their eyes screwed on a fetlock here, a muzzle there; the blessed position of the man who writes of Salzburg without Mozart, or Rome without ruins; and now, here on my low stick, nature had blessed me with another new angle.

I could note the coarse and curiously shaped faces of the copers, the tremendous Irish life in them, cheeks as red as their own fuchsia hedges and eyes under black lashes shining with a Siamese sapphiric blue; and how a wildly handsome young man, strong and fresh and muscular, might open his mouth to show a sudden old row of brown and broken teeth; and his blue-eyed dreamy visionary princess of a colleen raise the red gnarled hand of an old woman to the milk skin of her face, for she has worked hard in a poor country, once sucked dry by my English compatriots and now, somehow, despite the vigilancies of other governments, caught in the habit of apathy. Not that these people today are too poorly off, but they are not by nature builders with an eye to the future; they live, rather, for the day and let tomorrow, and the old turf shed at the back of the house, go to rot. Yet is this really apathy? Is it perhaps not a dream way, near-Arabic, of valuing the moment for its worth? In dripping wet weather, you will be greeted by a local with "Lovely day now!" And this may not be so mad as it sounds; it may, instead, be a way of expressing simply a delight in life, in there being a day at all, whatever its superficial dressing. And on asking the way somewhere and the time it takes, you will be given the answer you *want*, a short way and a short time, in the Eastern manner of giving pleasure at all costs—the cost of mere material truth and shoe leather included. Thus, the most occidental of European peoples are the true orientals, if I might employ a kind of Irishism.

When an industrialist I know proved to an educated Irishman that, by doing this and that and enforcing this or that slightly unpleasant sacrifice, his country could be made as rich as Holland, the reply, wise with many a pint of porter, was both agreement and disavowal, with a final "Och, what do we want with wealth, anyhow?" A key phrase.

So there we were among the ponies. And I didn't stay on my shooting stick for long. To those not only content with living for the day but also surviving it, it was vital to keep on the move and away from the passing hoofs. Mares and their foals strode and staggered hither and thither all the time, arguing, whinnying, kicking, prancing. For the unvalorous discreet, the field was soon turned into a kind of mud lake for an inelegant skater's waltz, as one skidded one's way around a back leg here, a long yellow tooth there, a mountainous muscular haunch to the left, or to the right a forehoof stamping like a bull's.

Not long, indeed, before the awful extent of a horrid truth was forced upon me. Here on this hill of a field, three or four acres bounded by a stream and a few houses and fences, there were enclosed what amounted to about a hundred naked mothers and their children, most of them as yet not properly introduced.

A hundred suspicious females corralled together in one small area! And their young with them! With their protective instincts raised to abnormal levels, and each battle-happy mother and

neurotically thoroughbred infant equipped with four hefty hoofs
and a score of lip-curling teeth!

By now the whinnying, a frightful sound in solo, had become,
in unison, appalling. There was no band, and no wonder; no one
could have heard it. Here and there, above the heaving sea of
rumps and halters, rose a momentary equestrian statue, forefeet
tapping the air and anything else about. As this fell back, so a
hindquarter would flash up, fling out its shoes with a horrid
whack onto a neighboring mother's glossy beige coat, and decline.
The children were no better than the grownups. It says much
for the phlegm of the excitable Irish that nobody seemed to be
the least troubled by any of it. With elevated Hibernian calm,
as if they themselves were not there at all, they led their snorting
matrons to and from the judges, only pausing to exchange the
time of day with a passing friend in a cluck of Gaelic or a brogue
of English that sounded about the same.

Perhaps they were dreaming of big money. For it is true that, in
three years, and largely owing to American buying, prices of the
Connemara breed have risen from nearly nothing to a fairly
sharp something. Or had they half their minds on seaweed? For
fifty miles off, in Galway, a seaweed symposium was being held.
International colloid experts were discussing how best to process
the great seaweed crop of these coasts, and new money is in the
offing here, too. Strange new prosperities loom over the forgotten
land. Perhaps it is wealth they want, after all. But wealth the way
they want it, if you see what I mean.

A sudden shower gleamed like a spider's-web curtain down over
all: over tweedy gentry, fustian farmers, village youth in its blue
Sunday suit; over matrons who still bake their own bread; over
their daughters half in love with home, half with dreams of emigration; over ponies, chickens, judges, sheep. And no one turned
a hair. No scuttling. It was Irish rain, as much to be expected as
not, and was in a few minutes over. Everyone was wetter; no one
had noticed. Except, it seemed, one old ram.

This old ram, a heavy, haughty beast, chose the moment to
smash its pen. As the sun came out, so did the ram, a true batter-
ing ram, head down and flying into the iron-shod feet of the
horse life heaving above it. Never so many upset mothers, never
so startled a pack of children! The whinnying rose, the whole
pony race began to undulate dangerously. Now, whole groups
of equestrian statues reared high, as, like a cannon ball of wool
and horn, the ram bashed its way through a startled forest of
legs beneath and was, in turn, battered and flicked about like a
woolly football, in the course of a new-found liberty. For a few

seconds it looked as if the whole field might go mad and stampede. The ram would loose its grip on the mud and slither a few yards like a fleece-bound Eskimo on a banana skin, then gather its pin legs together and turn, and batter off head down at another fence of horn-shod footballers. You could mark its course from above by the undulation of brownish-colored flanks, as if a tidal wave ran erratically through a heaving brown sea. It looked like the end to me, but not to the phlegmatic excitable Irish. In a matter of a few minutes, cool hands had been laid on the ram, its horns held hard, a rope thrown around. And back, battered, the batterer was led to the safety of his old wood gaol.

After this, mouse-heart in mouth, I left. Anything, I fancied, could happen, including, perhaps, six weeks in hospital.

Out I walked into the gray stone town, deserted but for the bright, near-Mediterranean color washes—pink, blue, green—which occasional houses here wear. Past a humble chemist called a Medical Hall, past shops full of Aran sweaters of white bleached wool, past the groceries that are also bars. Deep below in a ravine lay the dark-green waters of the estuary; high above rolled Atlantic clouds arriving from the Americas.

Peace, peace—and blessed silence.

The danger past, courage returned, and with it a mite of objectivity. Possibly no one was kicked or bitten the whole day through, down there among the ponies and the brave Irish. Possibly my fears were only those of a decadent Saxon townsman. Possibly about it all, I should keep my pony trap shut.

Notebook Assignment for Class Discussion

1. Divide the essay into its introductory, developmental, and concluding passages. How is each related rhetorically to the others?
2. What kind of coherence does this essay display?
3. What are some of the devices and techniques for unity which the author employs?
4. Is the purpose of the essay clear to you? What is the central idea which underlies the whole essay?
5. This essay contains elements of argumentation, exposition, narration, and description. Which seems to predominate? Discuss the interrelationship of all these elements. What seems to you to be the final rhetorical effect of such diversification of technique, purpose, and point of view in a single essay? Is it successful, or not?

6. How would you characterize the diction of this essay?
7. Count the number of verbs, nouns, and adjectives in the first two pages. Which part of speech is used most often? Of what significance is your discovery—can it help you in your effort at answering item 5, or is it merely a useless statistic?
8. Go through this essay cutting out *all* adjectives which seem to you to be not absolutely essential. Has the work been improved or damaged by your editing? How has the tone been altered? Is there any way to gain the effect of adjectives without actually using them? What are the advantages of having nouns and verbs predominate?

Related Exercises

1. What does the writer mean when he says that "the most occidental of European peoples are the true orientals"? Why does he call this statement "a kind of Irishism"?
2. Is the character of the ponies like that of the people? Is the ram more like the sea or the land? Explain.
3. What was your concept of Ireland and Irishmen before you read this sketch? From what had your concept derived? Has this essay changed any preconceived notions you may have had about Ireland? If this is so, in what elements does its power lie to so change your point of view?
4. In "Mowing," one of his early poems, Robert Frost remarks, "Anything more than the truth would have seemed too weak"; and in the same poem he further asserts that "The fact is the sweetest dream that labor knows." In what sense might these statements be taken as making a critical point against this essay?
5. Write an essay in which you describe some incident at a state or county fair which you have attended. Choose an incident which reveals the character of the place, its products, and its people.
6. Write an essay in which you take for your subject some annual gala with which you are acquainted, or a folk festival, such as the Belgian *kermiss* in Northeastern Wisconsin, or the Pennsylvania Dutch Week in Kutztown—anything culturally related to a particular part of the country (but not, for example, a rodeo in New Jersey). Do not attempt to write about a subject with which you are not personally familiar.

NORTHERN PLACES *

By Marya Mannes

Of the long film footage reeled in a returned traveler's head (and mercifully unscreened), three Scandinavian scenes are most brightly retained: in Copenhagen, the distinguished cartoonist of *Politiken,* Denmark's liberal paper, bicycling to work in a natty gray suit, gray bowler, and butterfly tie; on a flight to Norway's Arctic, the awesome, overwhelmingly wild grandeur of fjord and glacier under a coexistent moon and sun; in Stockholm, the high glass slabs rearing to right and left of the historic filigree of stone. And, of course, the girls; reels and reels. Flaxen and flawless, with a dazzling freshness of skin and lip; in Sweden on leisurely promenade; in Norway, fresh and ingenuous under their red tasseled graduation caps. There were differences, some of them significant and having a bearing on the special natures of the three countries so long and closely linked by race and geography. But in editing my interior film for external viewing, I think I would start with the Scandinavian similarities.

These are handsome people. They look clean, as their cities are, as their countryside is; and you feel that sea or mountain air has blown through them for so many centuries that their lungs too are washed. The Scandinavian love of nature has made them natural. To see men without the greenish pallor or larded white of our own city workers, to see girls with unfussed hair and uncaked skin, the blood near the surface of unlipsticked mouths, is to rediscover a lost beauty.

The retinal film would show no slums, for there are none in Scandinavia. Call it socialism, call it homogeneity, call it the lesser problems of small and educated populations. Whatever the reason, squalor is nowhere present. You get the feeling of pervasive human enlightenment in which each person has respect and care and a degree of the small daily pleasures of living. But if the camera should intrude on any gathering of intelligent Swedes, Danes, or Norwegians, you would hear this kind of talk:

"Yes, this is largely true, but the trouble is that we agree too much among ourselves. There is no real difference of aim between

* From *The Reporter,* Vol. 29, No. 3 (August 15, 1963), 55–58. Copyright © 1963 by The Reporter Magazine Company. Reprinted by permission of Harold Ober Associates Incorporated.

our political parties; only of administrative ways and means. We lack the stimulation of opposition, of partisanship, of intense feeling."

You would hear this, too, in Denmark and Norway: "Yes, most of us have accepted the principles, if not all the practices, of the welfare state. But we worry about what it does to the creative juices. We are not really producing anything of great interest at the moment." And then, in a second breath, they point at Sweden —climate of Ingmar Bergman and Dag Hammarskjold, of Gunnar and Alva Myrdal, of live theatre, ballet, and journalism.

In spite of Bergman and his religious preoccupations of film, the Scandinavians are not a church-going people: faith is a private matter, and piety is not considered a public asset. As for temporal homage, you feel that their attitude toward royalty depends as much on affection and respect as on constitutional convention. Sensibly and unemotionally they balance the anachronisms of the monarchy with the continuity, aware that the time may come when the weight of the former will be jettisoned at the possible expense of the latter. For the moment, it works.

So, also, it seems, does the balance of labor and leisure. In Norway and Sweden the distance between office and ski slope or office and sailboat is a matter of minutes instead of hours, and in Denmark the sweet green fields share the cities with open sea. In the northern summer days and nights the Scandinavian returns to his source and rediscovers his senses. In the cities he may—and often does—feel the frustrations and enclosures of a small town in a small country. Out of them he forgets them.

He can also forget the headache of increasing traffic. The rush-hour clutters in Copenhagen and Oslo and Stockholm are no less maddening than ours, and are even worsened by scooters, bicycles, and crooked streets that were never meant for the load they now carry. Stockholm, in fact, is tearing the guts out of its old center to construct the highways, underpasses, and cloverleaves that will take the rising tide of cars to the satellite cities, the high glass slabs, the brand-new suburban tower apartments and shopping centers that make an American wonder whether he has, in fact, left home. What we began or adopted some time ago is happening everywhere, and there are plenty of Norwegians and Swedes who cringe before the gradual obliteration of the handsome old and the rapid growth of the impersonal, unimaginative new.

These, then, are some of the similarities between the little upthrusting peninsula of Denmark and the great down-drooping peninsula of Norway and Sweden. The differences are subtler but no less real.

The Danes, for instance, are the "lightest" of the three peoples: sophisticated, humorous, and experts in the art of accommodation. In their crowded space they can ill afford to judge each other, so they let live. This makes them charming, easy, companionable, but sometimes shallow. To involve yourself in the uninvolved is rare, and with Danes you learn to skim the surface like a waterbug.

Yet they are immensely considerate of each other, particularly of their young and their old, a trait they share with their fellow Nordics. In Tivoli Park, among the fountains and flowers, uniformed boys lift small children onto their ponies with infinite care and obvious affection. Elderly couples beam as little boys, grave with pride, drive miniature vintage cars around winding grooves. There is indeed imagination spent on everything that concerns vulnerable people. The great "town of the old" on the outskirts of Copenhagen brings to every room not only the sight and smell of green but freshness and color to every public hall and meeting place. The segregation of the aged is now considered an ill-advised solution, but so tenderly and warmly administered by the city is this particular place that age is permitted dignity as well as care.

What creativity the Danes possess lies chiefly in design, and a visitor is quite properly directed to the shops and exhibitions that show their clean-lined furniture, silver, stainless-steel cutlery, and remarkable lighting fixtures that are now familiar in American cities. As in Sweden, the level of their design is so high that it's hard to find, in home furnishings and textiles at least, an ugly thing.

But if the Danes are not currently creative in other fields, they are highly receptive to those who are. Copenhagen was agog in early June with the presence of the Romanian-born and Rome-resident conductor Sergiu Celibidache, whom music lovers consider the only worthy successor to Toscanini. Judging from a three-hour rehearsal of Verdi's *Requiem* with the Danish court orchestra, they may be right. I would have liked a good documentary cameraman at another performance too. That week the Ballet School of the Danish Royal Opera was holding its final examination, and my lens was trained on the boys from ten to sixteen who were going through their paces before a row of judges —teachers and dancers. The test was long and rigorous—all the way from the basic positions to jetés and multiple pirouettes— and the marvel was not how well the boys were trained but how soon the winners emerged. Even among the little ones, so serious with their beaded upper lips and their heads held high on their baby necks, there was one with a style, a panache. Among the older ones, every movement made by a tall blond youth with strong legs and a classic head had the breadth and authority of greatness. Like Nureyev, he flowed, and you could see the eyes of the judges widen with attention. It was a moment worthy of immortalization, either on film, or by the Picasso of sixty years past who understood the vulnerable perfection of thin boys.

To fly from Copenhagen Airport—a superlative fusion of airy space and functional detail—to Bergen in Norway is to see at once how a country can mold a people. Instead of the flat lush tidy green—the lily pad of the water skimmers—you approach, by Kristiansand and Stavanger, the powerful and irregular coast of an elemental land. It does not take long after landing on this northwest coast to see why Norwegians are as they are, an elemental people. There is a largeness and directness about them that seems to spring directly from the clear cold water and the hard old mountains that plunge straight down in it, a sort of inviolability that only an unviolated land can sustain. It is not merely that most of them seem physically strong: a life on skis or on ships would account for that, an arduous terrain and a ten-month winter: it is that they are so in balance with their environment that the cancers of frustration have not yet set in. This makes them both tough and innocent, or—if you believe some Danes or Swedes—both good and dumb. Certainly, they are not as sophisticated as the Danes or as devious as the Swedes, but as allies and friends they have no peer.

Bergen itself is a charming town, and SAS (whose flights crisscross these parts like a cat's cradle) was smart to inaugurate a direct flight there from New York this summer. In the mountains that ring it and the fjords that penetrate it is a modest herald of the far mightier scene further north. Funiculars carry you to the top of the hills and boats carry you around their sea-lapped bases, and in the harbor itself more intimate things delight. In the cool afternoon brightness of 10 P.M.—that late gold sun—I wandered along the wharves and the marine machinery, smelling the salt and the fish, watching a coastal steamer load, inspecting the shops in the old wooden houses (peaked, with a hole for a flagpole). Next to one with cheap suits for sailors was an antique shop, and leaning against its inside walls were great mahogany steering wheels from sailing ships. Buoys and winches in another, oilskins in a fourth, and after them a row of Hanseatic houses in stone, each with insignia of the League. Small, clean, tidy gulls mewed on the piers, bright blue ventilators lay on the docks in wait for fitting, and along the waterfront cobbles walked the young: girls in pants chewing gum, boys with stiff blond thatches already resisting the labored haircuts imposed on them—even here.

But Bergen, in spite of new hotels and bright new streets, is not really modern at heart. Norwegians still form a thick and respectful ring around a Salvation Army group playing and singing and preaching on the square by the harbor. With packs on their backs and heavy shoes, the athletic young still walk toward their holidays. And their elders troop yearly, with pride and devotion, to the home of their beloved Edvard Grieg to hear his music played on his piano.

For this is the core of the International Festival that draws the tourists as well. Troldhaugen is only a few miles out of Bergen, and there, in idyllic isolation, overlooking water through trees, Grieg composed. His house—so much a musician's, so much nineteenth-century—is, of course, full of him. Not only all the photos and busts of his bushy head and mustache, his dreaming eyes and rather weak chin, or the memorabilia and the honors, or all the signed photographs of the fellow great. It breathes of the ordered, cloistered, and rather pious peace bestowed on certain creative men as their just due. You felt the deference of female servants, the finger at the lips, the regular meals, the plumping of pillows, and the murmured homage of listeners. The Master must not be disturbed.

The train from Bergen to Oslo is a real cliffhanger. For seven hours it clings to the sides of mountains, peers at glaciers, teeters over ravines, crosses the ice and moraine of high passes, and—with the placid exception of mountain meadows tufted in wildflowers—penetrates some of Norway's wild interior splendor. Antiquated as this day train is, its conductors are models for whatever railways are permitted to survive in our country. They not only give information (in three languages) over an intercom; they are polite, helpful, literate, humorous, and patient.

Oslo is a pleasant town but not a compelling one. The harbor is charming—all things to do with ships have flavor—and my recording eye lit with pleasure on the day-long sale of fresh shrimps from a fishing boat on the quay and the pretty college girls in blue overalls who worked as guides on the tourist boats.

But in visual matters they lag behind their Danish and Swedish relatives. The "modern" Town Hall muffs a superb site on the harbor approach with two heavy squared-off towers, and a spacious interior with decorative derivations of folk art that combine excess of color with banality of design. Between this prevailing folk-art pitch and the muscular horrors of Vigeland Park, intel-

ligent Norwegians are forced to admit that Edvard Munch remains their one proof of genius in the fine arts. And the splendid
new museum housing his paintings and drawings does them
justice: the whole is a visual experience of the first order.

So, indeed, are the Viking ships housed in their special museum in Oslo. The long arch of their hulls—the hulls that sailed
so many thousand miles so long ago—is the purest beauty, moving
in its proud defiance. Simple and brave too is the real Kon-Tiki
raft, the modern Heyerdahl legend, but hardly beautiful. Yet this
clumsy flat ark of wood and sisal and leaves is moving, too, for it
goes to the roots of the sea-borne, sea-conquering Scandinavian
soul and reminds one of noble things.

The thought was inescapable that the Norwegian is presented
with too much external beauty to feel the need of producing his
own. He must be somewhat mad, like Munch or Vigeland in their
wholly opposite ways, to want to try it.

Vigeland, for that matter, may have started that obsession with
the sturdy naked form that imposes so many sexless statues on
the Norwegian scene and raises further thought that the Norwegian may be too healthy to be erotic. Athletics and virility are
certainly compatible, but eroticism seems to flower in more languid and complex natures.

It would seem to flower in Sweden, where love, say observers,
is more of an exercise than an emotion. For with prosperity, again,
has come the removal of all those self-restraints which give meaning to the acts of living.

Perhaps because of this total permissiveness in social and sexual
behavior, because of the constant juxtaposition of shiny new and
weathered old, because of the obvious worldliness of its inhabitants, Stockholm has the feeling of a capital that Copenhagen
and Oslo lack. Its long and potent history is stamped on it, strad-
dled as it is at the confluence of the Baltic Sea and Lake Malaren,
between East and West.

These things are stamped most strongly and in sharp juxtaposition on the retinal film: the late-night ultramarine summer sky
with that particular luminosity you see in stage cycloramas.
Against it the velvet silhouettes of Palace or Opera House or the
low black clutter of the old quarters. . . . The marvelously recon-
structed nineteenth-century bar of the Opera House, full of Tif-
fany glass and shining wood; and two floors below, the ancient
wine cellar, open only to those who possess a key. There in the
vaulted but cozy cool you are offered wine and cheese and quiet
for talk. . . . The glass showcases in public squares where the best
of current design in glass or wood is presented to strollers, and

sculptures are changed each week. (How long would these last in our parks?). . . .

But as far as this eye is concerned, nothing occupied it so intensely as the hull of the great seventeenth-century warship Wasa, raised from Stockholm Harbor two years ago, her enormous oaken hull six stories high, now sheltered in a high-humidity shed while divers daily plunge in the nearby water and bring up treasures. The day before, grappling blindly in the black muddy bottom a hundred feet down, the divers had pulled up a great ornamental wooden swag that belonged, they believed, on the poop deck. The sculpture was intact, the design impressive. It was the Wasa's sad and ludicrous fate to sink, in full splendor, a few minutes after her launching. With carved lions glaring from her gunports, gold glinting fore and aft, and the populace cheering, she keeled over and disappeared. Still no one knows what happened; neither probably did one Wasa sailor whose skeleton, crushed by a gun carriage, was found not long ago with his boots still on.

The cutting-room floor is still full of pieces of Scandinavian tape: an ultramodern hotel on the outskirts of Stockholm that dispenses with service. You wheel your own luggage to your room, you pull your bed from the wall, you fold up your bed cover, you shine your shoes, and you pour yourself a stiff drink. As alternative compensation there is a huge bowling alley in the basement (automated).

After a night flight of unparalleled grandeur along Norway's frosted rib to Bodo on the Arctic Circle, this conversation among passengers eating reindeer meat by the light of the 3 A.M. sun:

South African man: "Jo'burg's a great town. I tell you, it's the place to live, and people outside don't know what it's all about. Those blacks, they're children. They'd be perfectly happy the way they are, if they weren't stirred up. . . ."

Texan woman: "Let me tell you, don't believe all this stuff you hear from the South either. It's all distorted, and anyway the Communists are back of all this. . . . we got a Commie Supreme Court. . . ."

I left the inn to the despoilers and wandered to where, in the still white night, I could see the Lofoten Islands; so far out on the still silver sea that they spelled escape.

But not far enough.

Notebook Assignment for Class Discussion

1. There are many different meanings of the word *culture*. Which dictionary definition best justifies the inclusion of Mannes' "Northern Places" and Sansom's "Pony Show in Connemara" in the category "Culture and Society"?
2. The author has to represent what she considers to be the essential tone of each of three countries in a relatively limited space. Is it, therefore, possible to criticize this essay for being too narrowly selective of detail, too general in its assertions, or too easy in its assumptions?
3. Has this essay too dogmatic a tone to be persuasive?
4. What is the general organization of this essay?
5. What kind of coherence has it?
6. What are some of the organizational devices which the author employs?
7. What is the central unifying concept she employs? Do you find it to be effectively and consistently maintained?
8. Is the author's division of her essay into sections dealing with similarities between the Scandinavian peoples, and with their differences, an effective pattern of organization?
9. Does the author's rather catholic approach to her subject result in a sense of disunity?
10. How does she manage to organize—in her paragraphs on the Danes—such various references as those to the general nature of this national group, Tivoli Park, an old folks' home, the strengths and weaknesses of Danish creativity, and Picasso's insight into the "vulnerable perfection of thin boys"?
11. Are we more concerned in this essay with what the author is observing, than with Miss Mannes as observer?
12. What is the general theme, or organizing proposition, of this essay?
13. Is this essay as argumentative and persuasive as it is descriptive?
14. What is the relevance of the concluding anecdote and observation to what has emerged as the main idea of the essay?

Related Exercises

1. Read a screenplay by Ingmar Bergman, say *The Magician*,[1] and attempt a comparison on the bases of tone, conception,

[1] Included in *Four Screenplays of Ingmar Bergman*, trans. by Lars Malstrom and David Kushner (New York: Simon & Schuster: 1960).

or vision with some works of the painter and print-maker Edvard Munch.

2. Write an essay in which you attempt an impressionistic description of three cities which you have visited, and employ as a unifying device some such concept as Miss Mannes' "retinal camera."

3. What do you think the author means by suggesting that Norwegians "may be too healthy to be erotic," and that "eroticism seems to flower in more languid and complex natures"? How would you square this assertion with the one immediately following which says that in presumably erotic Sweden, "love . . . is more of an exercise than an emotion"?

4. Why should Swedish social and sexual permissiveness in any way contribute to the feeling the author attributes to Stockholm, that of being a *capital?* For that matter, why should the juxtaposition of new and old, or the worldliness of the inhabitants, make Stockholm seem appropriately a capital? Is there an organizing concept underlying this argument which makes the proposition relevant to the train of her discourse?

THINKERS AND DOERS *

By Leo Gurko

"America is the only country in the world," a columnist once observed, "where a man who uses a word that isn't understood by another man, is made to feel inferior to that other man." [1] To be suspected of learning or, what is worse, to display it publicly, is to invite ridicule. In our national stereotype, college professors were long regarded as fogies, usually old, so wrapped up in dry and musty books that they had lost touch with life. Artists— of every genre—were supposed to be unconventional fellows, to be envied perhaps in one's duller moments, but kept firmly outside the pale of respectable society. Many people regard the intellectual as a snob, and the word itself has acquired an unpleasant

---

* From *Heroes, Highbrows, and the Popular Mind,* by Leo Gurko, copyright 1953 by Leo Gurko, reprinted by permission of the publishers, The Bobbs-Merrill Company, Inc.
[1] Samuel Grafton, former columnist on the *New York Post.*

flavor. Women especially are sensitive to it. Call a woman an intellectual, and she is likely to feel insulted. You have as much as said that she is without feminine charm, must make up in brains what Nature denied her in beauty, and cannot be expected to lead a full life. Here, as so often elsewhere, cultivation of mind is regarded as a poor substitute for living.

The same generalized associations are carried over to culture itself. Culture is a heavy and formidable something locked up in libraries and museums, or it is a collection of unfamiliar facts which ladies' literary clubs are forever pursuing in order to set themselves above "ordinary folks." In some parts of the country art is still looked on as foreign and un-American, tied up in a vaguely licentious way with France, and culture generally is denied any sort of usefulness in dealing with the problems of everyday existence. Or it is regarded as a luxury that the very rich perhaps can afford, but that is hardly relevant to the aims of plain people and is utterly alien to the peculiarly American phenomenon summed up under the headings of "just folks," "the average man," or "the common man." An interview with Gary Cooper, as reported in *The New York Times*,[2] illustrates this. When asked to what he attributed his success, the popular movie star replied, speaking in the same patois as his screen characters:

> Shucks, . . . I guess I've just been lucky. I always try to stick pretty much to the type of stuff in which people are accustomed to seeing me—typical, average-guy roles like Mr. Deeds, Sergeant York and Dr. Wassell—people from the middle of the U.S.A. Once in a while I like a good Western—gives me a chance to shoot off guns.
>
> My taste in art and literature is real ordinary. I don't try to pretend I know anything. I don't place myself above other people. I'm the average guy in taste and intelligence. If there's any reason for what you would call my success, that's it.

In colloquial usage, culture is synonymous with pedantry, divorce from reality, phoniness, foreignness, unmanliness in men and unattractiveness in women. At best it is regarded as a harmless pastime for idle females. This is reflected in Helen Hokinson's amusing cartoons of upholstered clubwomen with their synthetic passion for synthetic culture.

When culture cannot simply be laughed out of sight, it is "popularized." Apparently there is no subject so complex that it cannot be reduced to surface terms, none so serious that its

[2] Ezra Goodman, "Average Guy," *The New York Times*, December 19, 1948.

impact cannot be cushioned. Every aspect of science, from the atom bomb to cancer research, has been treated in the newspapers and magazines, nearly always shallowly, often misleadingly. And with a rare exception, such as *The Snake Pit*, the movies have used psychiatry, an involved and vital field, as the basis for a long sequence of sensationalized films in which accuracy is frequently sacrificed to the needs of "entertainment." Religious issues have been diluted to inspirationalism. Ethics and philosophy have been strained through the pragmatic sieve, and formulated in terms of *Does it work?* and *Can I get away with it?*

The process of thinning out culture appears in other fields. Medical investigation of diseases has been funneled into premature announcements of sure cures or overdrawn accounts of sensational cases, dressed up in just enough medical jargon to make them sound authentic. Modern art—resistant to popularizing—has been the target of calumny because, in its rebelliousness, it has been hard to absorb emotionally, and in its experimentalism, it has proved difficult to understand. The same is true of much contemporary music and poetry. When artists have made their way despite this hostility, and have arrived, it is their private lives and the melodramatic sides of their work which have been played up. Culture can be an exotic accessory to brighten dull routine, but it is seldom accepted as an entity in its own right, an experience to be taken on its own terms. In effect, there is little to choose between an outright antagonism to culture and the process by which it is watered down.

Part of the blame for this state of affairs lies with the intellectual himself. He suffers from certain occupational diseases: a sense of superiority; a frequent inability to take a stand on any question because he sees both sides of it too keenly; a tendency to forget that ideas, when divorced from action, can become stuffy and sterile; a contempt for people less educated or attuned than he; an arrogant and dogmatic belief in the rightness of his conclusions; a certain preciousness of attitude with regard to practical problems. All this contributes to the exaggerated conception of him as an ivory-tower resident, a highbrow, an impractical theorist, a person who though "he never met a pay roll" has a pat solution for everything, a philosopher ranging from the amateur of college bull-sessions to the professional operating in the upper echelons of abstract thought. Nor is it surprising that in America he often feels outside the main stream of life, lacking the assured public prestige of the businessman, doctor, engineer, or lawyer; nor that the average American holds him half in awe, half in contempt, and feels generally alienated.

This feeling of alienation is reinforced by the fact that the intellectual is a man who applies himself to disinterested ends, and pursues his profession more for its own sake than for the livelihood to be derived from it. His ranks include writers, artists, teachers, scientists, clergymen, scholars, and nearly everyone who chooses his mode of life for reasons other than the acquisition of money or worldly power. All this in a society dominated by money standards.

By very definition, the man of ideas thinks first and acts afterward, in sharp contrast to the more common American tendency to act first and think afterward. This tendency was brought to a head by the enormous wealth of the country which, in the late nineteenth century especially, was to be won by those who moved most swiftly and were least burdened by a sense of obligation to others. Prompt action, least frightened with reflection on causes and consequences, enabled a man to win the greatest material rewards. Thinking was a bit in the teeth of action, and hence a handicap in the race for success. Contempt for ideas, theories, abstractions, was strong during the middle and late stages of the frontier, when the relatively easy access to free land and forests, to gold and copper mines, through the expenditure of physical energy alone, made anticulturalism inevitable. This easy access helped create the American type, described by Frederick Jackson Turner in *The Frontier in American History:*

> ... self-examination ... is not characteristic of the historic American. He has been an opportunist rather than a dealer in general ideas. Destiny set him in a current and bore him swiftly along through such a wealth of opportunity that reflection and well-considered planning seemed wasted time. He knew not where he was going, but he was on his way, cheerful, optimistic, busy and buoyant.[3]

We became a nation of busy opportunists, of doers rather than thinkers, devotees of the short-range view rather than the long, who piled up mountains of achievement side by side with mountains of waste. Reflection and the long view, we assumed, had no relevance to the building of the country, and so we consigned them to the sidelines.

The great error, still shared by intellectuals and nonintellectuals alike, is this assumption that a gap must exist between "intellectual" and "physical" affairs. Our whole historical experi-

3 Frederick Jackson Turner, *The Frontier in American History* (New York: Holt, 1920), p. 290.

ence shows that, in actuality, no such gap exists, and that when people have acted on the assumption that it does, only damage and confusion have resulted. The very period of the frontier and the tremendous industrial expansion which saw scorn for reflection and the long view at its most intense, witnessed as a result of that scorn the beginning of a disastrous policy in one of the vital national areas of public interest—the conservation of natural resources. For a long time these were regarded as inexhaustible; hence there was no admitting that one could be reckless or profligate in their exploitation. The warnings and efforts of President Theodore Roosevelt went largely unheeded. Deforestation, the unchecked draining-away of topsoil, the impoverishment of petroleum and oil reserves, the denudation of fisheries, did not begin to assume dangerous proportions until the end of the second World War. Industry paid little attention to the problem, partly because it seemed illusory, partly because such attention would have yielded no short-term profit. Professional economists stressed distribution and production as the keys to Utopia, to the virtual exclusion of conservation. Even the Teapot Dome scandal of the twenties, with its focus on naval oil reserves, did little to arouse public interest in the problem.

The stock-market crash of 1929, however, and the ensuing depression jolted the American out of his buoyancy and optimism and forced him, whether he wished to or not, to take stock of his stalled society and think. Desperation hastened this process, paving the way for the emergency measures of the New Deal. Whatever may be said about these measures, they represented an attempt by organized intelligence to get the country back on its feet. Certainly this was true of the government's new policy with regard to natural resources, though this policy, like so many of the New Deal's experiments, was carried out in short, uneven bursts. The establishment of the CCC (Civilian Conservation Corps) initiated activity of a sporadic kind. Under the spur of the quickening social consciousness of the middle '30's and the aggressiveness of Harold L. Ickes, Secretary of the Interior during the four Roosevelt administrations, further organized work in conservation got under way. But it was not until the middle '40's, when the tremendous pressures upon steel, oil and food during the second World War revealed the narrowing margin of our reserves, that a growing awareness of the issue was crystallized on a national scale. The various predictions of the exhaustion of the great Mesabi iron range in Minnesota, and of the once vast petroleum reserves of Texas and Oklahoma, sharpened the edge of this consciousness. Some private industries began investing money in conservation along lines parallel to the government's, in the perfectly rational hope that a relatively small amount invested now would yield incalculable future returns. But this rationality arrived late on the scene, and then only fitfully and piecemeal.

The lack of intelligent foresight in the field of natural resources had political results as well. Foreign policy is made up of many complex elements, economics among them. Our dwindling oil resources forced us to look for oil reserves abroad, which spurred our interest in the Arabian peninsula, which in turn helped to formulate the Truman Doctrine regarding Greece and Turkey as buffers to protect that peninsula. Thus shortsightedness with regard to the single issue of conservation at home helped set in motion a whole chain of events around the world. A refusal to think clearly and over the long view produced consequences which in this instance were almost literally beyond calculation. Perhaps our oil problem will be solved at the last minute by the ingenuity of some scientist who will find a practicable means of extracting oil from coal, and harness petroleum to our coal reserves (which are said to be virtually inexhaustible). Or some other synthetic process might be developed to save us from the results of shortsightedness. Yet it would be compounding the original error to rely blithely on inventiveness always rising up at the right moment to defeat folly. The law of averages aside, this complacency, with its indifference to thinking and planning, creates the very situations in which we are made the enemies of our own self-interest.

A further instance of irrationality in matters vital to the nation has been the frequent reluctance to accept technological change. Often this has been motivated by a narrow zeal for limited profits today at the expense of much larger ones tomorrow, an increase made inevitable by the immense expansion of business activity through technological inventiveness. The whole history of commerce and industry is marked by hostility to new inventions. Suppliers of horses fought against stagecoaches, stagecoaches against canals, canals against railroads, railroads against automobiles, buses, and airplanes, each resisting its successor tooth and nail. Great corporations have bought up patents and suppressed them for varying lengths of time. Devices which ultimately brought about the vast expansion of industries like printing and textiles had to struggle against indifference or outright opposition to make their way. The great transformations effected by the steamboat, the railroad, the sewing machine, and scores of other inventions were postponed by skepticism and antagonism. When the automobile first appeared, it met with the same laughter, ridicule, and distrust that had greeted the steamboat and locomotive—an emotional process repeated with Henry Ford's later application of mass assembly-line techniques and the revolutionary offer of five dollars a day to his workers.

Industrial and technological progress was slowed also by resistance on the part of bankers as well as businessmen and the general public. For a long time many great banking houses tended to look on research and the rapid industrial changes resulting from it as unsettling to the country; and regarded with suspicion and instinctive distaste proposals to launch new contrivances. Bankers even considered labor-saving agricultural machinery as bad for farmers since it might demoralize them with too much leisure time.

The business community has not been alone in failing to foresee the greater benefits that would result from the development of new ideas. Doctors and the medical profession in times past have campaigned against new processes and discoveries in medicine. The history of the great medical researchers in the nineteenth century—Pasteur, Koch, Semmelweis—tells the same bitter story of organized opposition to the future. Farmers, traditionally the most conservative members of society, greeted the iron plow at its first appearance as an instrument of destruction which would surely poison the ground. They regarded the railroad as a great black puffing monster which would scare the cattle, burn down barns by the flames spouting from the locomotives, and even frighten hens so that they would stop laying eggs. Or else the locomotive was looked on as an agent of the Devil, its grinding wheels, belching smoke and hideous noise seeming to come straight from hell itself. These irrational superstitions blinded many farmers to the real benefits that would accrue to them through the rapid transportation of their products to market and the opening of new consumer areas hitherto out of reach.

Workers, too, have been proverbially opposed to technological change. In its modern phase this opposition began in the 1820's with the Luddites smashing weaving looms in the early textile mills. Since then, workers have wrecked new machines which threatened to displace them, forced employers' associations to curtail the introduction of processes that injured them economically, called for periodic moratoriums on labor-saving inventions, and have in many other cases resisted the advance of technology as vigorously as have agriculture and business. Yet this very advance was the basis in the past half century for the unparalleled rise in the standard of living of the American working population.

These several types of unenlightened self-interest sprang in part from indifference or hostility to thinking and planning in broad

perspective. In *The Course of American Democratic Thought,*
Ralph Henry Gabriel describes this hostility to scientific progress:

> ... the age of science has been marked by economic and inter-
> national disaster ... A growing school of thought blamed the
> machine ... for the fact that civilization was faltering. When
> in bleak depression millions of American men and women
> found themselves adrift with no means of earning bread, the
> idea of the machine as Frankenstein spread among the
> masses. The inchoate thoughts of the sufferers found expres-
> sion in a demand for a scientific holiday... A thrill of fear
> ran through the laboratories of the nation. On February 23,
> 1934, in the blackest month of a depression winter the New
> York *Times* published a significant dispatch. "Science struck
> back at its critics yesterday and with the aid of some of its
> own inventions—the radio, sound cameras and loudspeakers
> —it told the world that science makes jobs and does not end
> them ... Two of its leading representatives, Dr. Karl T.
> Compton ... and Dr. R. A. Millikan ... slaughtered with
> words and refuted with figures those who are pressing for a
> 'research holiday' and those who contend that science is the
> root of economic ills." [4]

Resistance, though delaying the advance of science and technology, did not halt it. But the delays caused friction, proved
expensive, and were in every way damaging to the public interest.
Once again the short-range view triumphed over the long, with
injury not only to the country but to the ultimate welfare of the
particular groups whose immediate interests seemed threatened.

The waste of natural resources and the resistance to technological change are but two instances of the price we have paid for
ignoring the long-range values of the intellectual approach to
life. Without the essential elements of that approach, the reflection and well-considered planning of which Turner spoke, we
can look forward to the prospect of further penalties induced by
heedlessness and waste in whatever fields they may appear.
Changes for the better can be effected only when the realization
becomes general that the virtues and resources of the thinking
mind are not confined to vague theorizings and distant abstractions but operate effectively within the world of everyday matter.
As that realization occurs, much of the antipathy to culture and
men of ideas will disappear.

[4] Ralph Henry Gabriel, *The Course of American Democratic Thought.*
Copyright 1940, The Ronald Press Company.

Notebook Assignment for Class Discussion

1. The author's thesis, or central argument, is stated explicitly in the next-to-last paragraph where he says that when the short-range view triumphs over the long, there is injury "not only to the country but to the ultimate welfare of the particular groups whose immediate interests seemed threatened." In how many other places is this thesis stated, either directly or indirectly? What is the purpose and effect of such a repetition of thesis?

2. This is the first chapter of a book which, in subsequent chapters, deals more specifically with the charges which are here made only generally. But considering this essay *as it stands,* why is it not very effective argument?

3. Why does the author place such a heavy emphasis on the subject of conservation? How effectively does it illustrate his thesis?

4. What are some of the author's secondary theses? How does he relate them to his main argument?

5. In what ways does he give substance to his argument?

6. Has his argument been given effective substance by the end of the essay?

7. What are the major rhetorical strengths of this essay? Are there any rhetorical weaknesses?

8. To what audience would you judge this essay to be addressed? How do you arrive at your conclusion?

9. What is the tone of this essay? What elements go to make it up?

Related Exercises

1. Write an essay in which you give an example, from your own experience, of the triumph of the short-range view over the long. Does your experience seem to bear out the author's argument?

2. What might be an argument in *favor* of taking the short-range view most of the time?

3. Isn't it unreasonable of the author to expect the pioneer, for instance, faced with the immediate and impenetrable forests and the need to clear them and wrest from them a living, to take the long-range view? What arguments would you advance against the proposition that the human faculty of foresight is too severely limited to hold the long view very effectively?

4. Write an essay in which you take a clear look at your own past (or present) attitudes, and describe your stock responses to:
   a. Intellectuals: what do you think of when you hear the word?
   b. Politicians: what is the political personality?
   c. College Professors: what is the academic personality?
   d. Artists: what is their social value? What do they try to do?
   e. Corporation Executives: in their zeal to sell their product, do they try to appeal to the highest, lowest, or average mentality of our society?
5. Since the author certainly does not mean to imply that Ford's invention of the techniques of mass production involved *no* rational process, what do you think is the distinction which he makes between "thinking" and "doing"?
6. Can you cite some examples to substantiate the author's claim that "our whole historical experience shows that, in actuality, no such gap (between "intellectual" and "physical" affairs) exists, and that when people have acted on the assumption that it does, only damage and confusion have resulted"?

RECONSTRUCTION OF SOCIAL RELATIONSHIPS IN TRUTH, JUSTICE, AND LOVE

(Part IV of *Mater et Magistra, an Encyclical of Pope John XXIII) ***

1. INCOMPLETE AND ERRONEOUS PHILOSOPHIES OF LIFE

As in the past, so too in our day, advances in science and technology have greatly multiplied relationships between citizens; it seems necessary, therefore, that the relationships themselves,

* Translated by William J. Gibbons, S.J., and a Committee of Catholic Scholars (New York: Paulist Press, 1961), pp. 67–81.

whether within a single country or between all countries, be brought into more humane balance.

In this connection many systems of thought have been developed and committed to writing: some of these already have been dissipated as mist by the sun; others remain basically unchanged today; still others now elicit less and less response from men. The reason for this is that these popularized fancies neither encompass man, whole and entire, nor do they affect his inner being. Moreover, they fail to take into account the weaknesses of human nature, such as sickness and suffering: weaknesses that no economic or social system, no matter how advanced, can completely eliminate. Besides, men everywhere are moved by a profound and unconquerable sense of religion, which no force can ever destroy nor shrewdness suppress.

In our day, a very false opinion is popularized which holds that the sense of religion implanted in men by nature is to be regarded as something adventitious or imaginary, and hence, is to be rooted completely from the mind as altogether inconsistent with the spirit of our age and the progress of civilization. Yet, this inward proclivity of man to religion confirms the fact that man himself was created by God, and irrevocably tends to Him. Thus we read in Augustine: "Thou hast made us for Thyself, O Lord, and our hearts are restless until they rest in Thee." [1]

Wherefore, whatever the progress in technology and economic life, there can be neither justice nor peace in the world, so long as men fail to realize how great is their dignity; for they have been created by God and are His children. We speak of God, who must be regarded as the first and final cause of all things He has created. Separated from God, man becomes monstrous to himself and others. Consequently, mutual relationships between men absolutely require a right ordering of the human conscience in relation to God, the source of all truth, justice, and love.

It is well known and recognized by everyone that in a number of countries, some of ancient Christian culture, many of our very dear brothers and sons have been savagely persecuted for a number of years. Now this situation, since it reveals the great dignity of the persecuted, and the refined cruelty of their persecutors, leads many to reflect on the matter, though it has not yet healed the wounds of the persecuted.

However, no folly seems more characteristic of our time than the desire to establish a firm and meaningful temporal order, but without God, its necessary foundation. Likewise, some wish to

[1] *Confessions*, I, 1.

proclaim the greatness of man, but with the source dried up from
which such greatness flows and receives nourishment: that is, by
impeding and, if it were possible, stopping the yearning of souls
for God. But the turn of events in our times, whereby the hopes
of many are shattered and not a few have come to grief, unques-
tionably confirm the words of Scripture: "Unless the Lord build
the house, they labor in vain who built it." [2]

2. THE CHURCH'S TRADITIONAL TEACHING REGARDING MAN'S SOCIAL LIFE

What the Catholic Church teaches and declares regarding the
social life and relationships of men is beyond question for all
time valid.

The cardinal point of this teaching is that individual men are
necessarily the foundation, cause, and end of all social institutions. We are referring to human beings, insofar as they are social
by nature, and raised to an order of existence that transcends and
subdues nature.

Beginning with this very basic principle whereby the dignity
of the human person is affirmed and defended, Holy Church—
especially during the last century and with the assistance of
learned priests and laymen, specialists in the field—has arrived at
clear social teachings whereby the mutual relationships of men
are ordered. Taking general norms into account, these principles
are in accord with the nature of things and the changed conditions
of man's social life, or with the special genius of our day. Moreover, these norms can be approved by all.

But today, more than ever, principles of this kind must not
only be known and understood, but also applied to those systems
and methods, which the various situations of time or place either
suggest or require. This is indeed a difficult, though lofty, task.
Toward its fulfillment we exhort not only our brothers and sons
everywhere, but all men of good will.

Study of Social Matters

Above all, we affirm that the social teaching proclaimed by the
Catholic Church cannot be separated from her traditional teaching regarding man's life.

Wherefore, it is our earnest wish that more and more attention
be given to this branch of learning. First of all, we urge that atten-

2 Ps. 126, 1.

tion be given to such studies in Catholic schools on all levels, and especially in seminaries, although we are not unaware that in some of these latter institutions this is already being done admirably. Moreover, we desire that social study of this sort be included among the religious materials used to instruct and inspire the lay apostolate, either in parishes or in associations. Let this diffusion of knowledge be accomplished by every modern means: that is, in journals, whether daily or periodical; in doctrinal books, both for the learned and the general reader; and finally, by means of radio and television.

We judge that our sons among the laity have much to contribute through their work and effort, that this teaching of the Catholic Church regarding the social question be more and more widely diffused. This they can do, not merely by learning it themselves and governing their actions accordingly, but also by taking special care that others also come to know its relevance.

Let them be fully persuaded that in no better way can they show this teaching to be correct and effective, than by demonstrating that present day social difficulties will yield to its application. In this way they will win minds today antagonistic to the teaching because they do not know it. Perhaps it will also happen that such men will find some enlightenment in the teaching.

3. Application of Social Teaching

But social norms of whatever kind are not only to be explained but also applied. This is especially true of the Church's teaching on social matters, which has truth as its guide, justice as its end, and love as its driving force.

We consider it, therefore, of the greatest importance that our sons, in addition to knowing these social norms, be reared according to them.

To be complete, the education of Christians must relate to the duties of every class. It is therefore necessary that Christians thus inspired, conform their behavior in economic and social affairs to the teachings of the Church.

If it is indeed difficult to apply teaching of any sort to concrete situations, it is even more so when one tries to put into practice the teaching of the Catholic Church regarding social affairs. This is especially true for the following reasons: there is deeply rooted in each man an instinctive and immoderate love of his own interests; today there is widely diffused in society a materialistic philosophy of life; it is difficult at times to discern the demands of justice in a given situation.

Consequently, it is not enough for men to be instructed, according to the teachings of the Church, on their obligation to act in a Christian manner in economic and social affairs. They must also be shown ways in which they can properly fulfill their duty in this regard.

We do not regard such instructions as sufficient, unless there be added to the work of instruction that of the formation of man, and unless some action follow upon the teaching, by way of experience.

Just as, proverbially, no one really enjoys liberty unless he uses it, so no one really knows how to act according to Catholic teaching in the economic and social fields, unless he acts according to this teaching in the same area.

A Task for Lay Apostolate

Accordingly, in popular instruction of this kind, it seems proper that considerable attention be paid to groups promoting the lay apostolate, especially those whose aim is to ensure that efforts in our present concern draw their inspiration wholly from Christian law. Seeing that members of such groups can first train themselves by daily practice in these matters, they subsequently will be able the better to instruct young people in fulfilling obligations of this kind.

It is not inappropriate in this connection to remind all, the great no less than the lowly, that the will to preserve moderation and to bear difficulties, by God's grace, can in no wise be separated from the meaning of life handed down to us by Christian wisdom.

But today, unfortunately, very many souls are preoccupied with an inordinate desire for pleasure. Such persons see nothing more important in the whole of life than to seek pleasure, to quench the thirst for pleasure. Beyond doubt, grave ills to both soul and body proceed therefrom. Now in this matter, it must be admitted that one who judges even with the aid of human nature alone, concludes that it is the part of the wise and prudent man to preserve balance and moderation in everything, and to restrain the lower appetites. He who judges matters in the light of divine revelation, assuredly will not overlook the fact that the Gospel of Christ and the Catholic Church, as well as ascetical tradition handed down to us, all demand that Christians steadfastly mortify themselves and bear the inconveniences of life with singular patience. These virtues, in addition to fostering a firm and moderate rule of mind over body, also present an opportunity of satisfying the punishment due to sin, from which, except for Jesus Christ and His Immaculate Mother, no one is exempt.

4. Practical Suggestions

The teachings in regard to social matters for the most part are put into effect in the following three stages: first, the actual situation is examined; then, the situation is evaluated carefully in relation to these teachings; then only is it decided what can and should be done in order that the traditional norms may be adapted to circumstances of time and place. These three steps are at times expressed by the three words: *observe, judge, act*.

Hence, it seems particularly fitting that youth not merely reflect upon this order of procedure, but also, in the present connection, follow it to the extent feasible, lest what they have learned be regarded merely as something to be thought about but not acted upon.

However, when it comes to reducing these teachings to action, it sometimes happens that even sincere Catholic men have differing views. When this occurs they should take care to have and to show mutual esteem and regard, and to explore the extent to which they can work in cooperation among themselves. Thus they can in good time accomplish what necessity requires. Let them also take great care not to weaken their efforts in constant controversies. Nor should they, under pretext of seeking what they think best, meanwhile, fail to do what they can and hence should do.

But in the exercise of economic and social functions, Catholics often come in contact with men who do not share their view of life. On such occasions, those who profess Catholicism must take special care to be consistent and not compromise in matters wherein the integrity of religion or morals would suffer harm. Likewise, in their conduct they should weigh the opinions of others with fitting courtesy and not measure everything in the light of their own interests. They should be prepared to join sincerely in doing whatever is naturally good or conducive to good. If, indeed, it happens that in these matters sacred authorities have prescribed or decreed anything, it is evident that this judgment is to be obeyed promptly by Catholics. For it is the Church's right and duty not only to safeguard principles relating to the integrity of religion and morals, but also to pronounce authoritatively when it is a matter of putting these principles into effect.

Manifold Action and Responsibility

But what we have said about the norms of instruction should indeed be put into practice. This has special relevance for those beloved sons of ours who are in the ranks of the laity inasmuch as their activity ordinarily centers around temporal affairs and making plans for the same.

To carry out this noble task, it is necessary that laymen not only should be qualified, each in his own profession, and direct their energies in accordance with rules suited to the objective aimed at, but also should conform their activity to the teachings and norms of the Church in social matters. Let them put sincere trust in her wisdom; let them accept her admonitions as sons. Let them reflect that, when in the conduct of life they do not carefully observe principles and norms laid down by the Church in social matters, and which we ourselves reaffirm, then they are negligent in their duty and often injure the rights of others. At times, matters can come to a point where confidence in this teaching is diminished, as if it were indeed excellent but really lacks the force which the conduct of life requires.

5. A GRAVE DANGER

As we have already noted, in this present age men have searched widely and deeply into the laws of nature. Then they invented instruments whereby they can control the forces of nature; they have perfected and continue to perfect remarkable works worthy of deep admiration. Nevertheless, while they endeavor to master and transform the external world, they are also in danger, lest they become neglectful and weaken the powers of body and mind. This is what our predecessor of happy memory, Pius XI, noted with sorrow of spirit in his Encyclical Letter *Quadragesimo Anno:* "And so bodily labor, which was decreed by divine providence for the good of man's body and soul even after original sin, has too often been changed into an instrument of perversion: for dead matter leaves the factory ennobled and transformed whereas men are there corrupted and degraded." [3]

And our predecessor of happy memory, Pius XII, rightly asserted that our age is distinguished from others precisely by the fact that science and technology have made incalculable progress, while men themselves have departed correspondingly from a sense

[3] *Acta Apostolicae Sedis*, XXIII (1931), p. 221f.

of dignity. It is a "monstrous masterpiece" of this age "to have transformed man, as it were, into a giant as regards the order of nature, yet in the order of the supernatural and the eternal, to have changed him into a pygmy." [4]

Too often in our day is verified the testimony of the Psalmist concerning worshipers of false gods, namely, human beings in their activity very frequently neglect themselves, but admire their own works as if these were gods: "Their idols are silver and gold; the handiwork of men." [5]

Respect for the Hierarchy of Values

Wherefore, aroused by the pastoral zeal wherewith we embrace all men, we strongly urge our sons that, in fulfilling their duties and in pursuing their goals, they do not allow their consciousness of responsibilities to grow cool, nor neglect the order of the more important goods.

For it is indeed clear that the Church has always taught and continues to teach that advances in science and technology and the prosperity resulting therefrom, are truly to be counted as good things and regarded as signs of the progress of civilization. But the Church likewise teaches that goods of this kind are to be judged properly in accordance with their natures: they are always to be considered as instruments for man's use, the better to achieve his highest end: that he can the more easily improve himself, in both the natural and supernatural orders.

Wherefore, we ardently desire that our sons should at all times heed the words of the divine Master: "For what does it profit a man, if he gain the whole world, but suffer the loss of his own soul? Or what will a man give in exchange for his soul?" [6]

Sanctification of Holy Days

Not unrelated to the above admonitions is the one having to o with rest to be taken on feast days.

In order that the Church may defend the dignity with which an is endowed, because he is created by God and because God as breathed into him a soul to His own image, she has never iled to insist that the third commandment: "Remember to keep oly the Sabbath day," [7] be carefully observed by all. It is the

---

4 Radio Broadcast, Christmas Eve, 1953; cf. *A.A.S.*, XLVI (1954), p. 10.
5 Ps. 113, 4.
6 Matt. 16, 26.
7 Exod. 20, 8.

right of God, and within His power, to order that man put aside a day each week for proper and due worship of the divinity. He should direct his mind to heavenly things, setting aside daily business. He should explore the depths of his conscience in order to know how necessary and inviolable are his relations with God.

In addition, it is right and necessary for man to cease for a time from labor, not merely to relax his body from daily hard work and likewise to refresh himself with decent recreation, but also to foster family unity, for this requires that all its members preserve a community of life and peaceful harmony.

Accordingly, religion, moral teaching, and care of health in turn require that relaxation be had at regular times. The Catholic Church has decreed for many centuries that Christians observe this day of rest on Sunday, and that they be present on the same day at the Eucharistic Sacrifice because it renews the memory of the divine Redemption and at the same time imparts its fruits to the souls of men.

But we note with deep sorrow, and we cannot but reprove the many who, though they perhaps do not deliberately despise this holy law, yet more and more frequently disregard it. Whence it is that our very dear workingmen almost necessarily suffer harm, both as to the salvation of their souls and to the health of their bodies.

And so, taking into account the needs of soul and body, we exhort, as it were, with the words of God Himself, all men, whether public officials or representatives of management and labor, that they observe this command of God Himself and of the Catholic Church, and judge in their souls that they have a responsibility to God and society in this regard.

6. Renewed Dedication

From what we have briefly touched upon above, let none of sons conclude, and especially the laity, that they act prudentl in regard to the transitory affairs of this life, they become remiss in their specific Christian contributions. On the con we reaffirm that they should be daily more zealous in carryi this role.

Indeed, when Christ our Lord made that solemn prayer f unity of His Church, He asked this from the Father on L of His disciples: "I do not pray that Thou take them out of world, but that Thou keep them from evil." [8] Let no one imagine

8 John 17, 15.

that there is any opposition between these two things so that they cannot be properly reconciled: namely, the perfection of one's own soul and the business of this life, as if one had no chance but to abandon the activities of this world in order to strive for Christian perfection, or as if one could not attend to these pursuits without endangering his own dignity as a man and as a Christian.

However, it is in full accord with the designs of God's providence that men develop and perfect themselves by exercise of their daily tasks, for this is the lot of practically everyone in the affairs of this mortal life. Accordingly, the role of the Church in our day is very difficult: to reconcile this modern respect for progress with the norms of humanity and of the Gospel teaching. Yet, the times call the Church to this role; indeed, we may say, earnestly beseech her, not merely to pursue the higher goals, but also to safeguard her accomplishments without harm to herself. To achieve this, as we have already said, the Church especially asks the cooperation of the laity. For this reason, in their dealings with men, they are bound to exert effort in such a way that while fulfilling their duties to others, they do so in union with God through Christ, for the increase of God's glory. Thus the Apostle Paul asserts: "Whether you eat or drink, or do anything else, do all for the glory of God." [9] And elsewhere: "Whatever you do in word or in work, do all in the name of the Lord Jesus Christ, giving thanks to God the Father through Him." [10]

Greater Effectiveness in Temporal Affairs

As often, therefore, as human activity and institutions having to do with the affairs of this life, help toward spiritual perfection and everlasting beatitude, the more they are to be regarded as an efficacious way of obtaining the immediate end to which they are directed by their very nature. Thus, valid for all times is that noteworthy sentence of the divine Master: "Seek first the dom of God and His justice, and all these things shall be give. besides." [11] For he who is, as it were, a *light in the Lord*, [12] a. walks as a *son of light*, [13] he perceives more clearly what the requirements of justice are, in the various sectors of human zeal, even in those that involve greater difficulties because of the exces-

9 I Cor. 10, 31.
10 Col. 3, 17.
11 Matt. 6, 33.
12 Eph. 5, 8.
13 Cf. *ibid.*

sive love which many have for their own interests, or those of their country, or race. It must be added that when one is motivated by Christian charity, he cannot but love others, and regard the needs, sufferings and joys of others as his own. His work, wherever it be, is constant, adaptable, humane, and has concern for the needs of others: For "Charity is patient, is kind; charity does not envy, is not pretentious, is not puffed up, is not ambitious, is not self seeking, is not provoked; thinks no evil, does not rejoice over wickedness, but rejoices with the truth; bears with all things, believes all things, hopes all things, endures all things." [14]

7. Living Members of the Mystical Body of Christ

But we do not wish to bring this letter of ours to a close, Venerable Brothers, without recalling to your minds that most fundamental and true element of Catholic teaching, whereby we learn that we are living members of His Mystical Body, which is the Church: "For as the body is one and has many members, and all the members of the body, many as they are, form one body, so also is it with Christ." [15]

Wherefore, we urgently exhort all our sons in every part of the world, whether clergy or laity, that they fully understand how great is the nobility and dignity they derive from being joined to Christ, as branches to the vine, as He Himself said: "I am the vine, you are the branches," [16] and that they are sharers of His divine life. Whence it is, that if Christians are also joined in mind and heart with the most Holy Redeemer, when they apply themselves to temporal affairs, their work in a way is a continuation of the labor of Jesus Christ Himself, drawing from it strength and redemptive power: "He who abides in Me, and I in him, he bears much fruit." [17] Human labor of this kind is so exalted and ennobled that it leads men engaged in it to spiritual perfection, and can likewise contribute to the diffusion and propagation of the fruits of the Redemption to others. So also it results in the flow of that Gospel leaven, as it were, through the veins of civil society wherein we live and work.

Although it must be admitted that the times in which we live

14 I Cor. 13, 4–7.
15 I Cor., 12, 12.
16 John 15, 5.
17 *Ibid.*

are torn by increasingly serious errors, and are troubled by violent disturbances, yet, it happens that the Church's laborers in this age of ours have access to enormous fields of apostolic endeavor. This inspires us with uncommon hope.

Venerable Brothers and beloved sons, beginning with that marvelous letter of Leo, we have thus far considered with you the varied and serious issues which pertain to the social conditions of our time. From them we have drawn norms and teachings, upon which we especially exhort you not merely to meditate deeply, but also to do what you can to put them into effect. If each one of you does his best courageously, it will necessarily help in no small measure to establish the kingdom of Christ on earth. This is indeed: "A kingdom of truth and of life; a kingdom of holiness and grace; a kingdom of justice, of love and peace." [18] And this we shall some day leave to go to that heavenly beatitude, for which we were made by God, and which we ask for with most ardent prayers.

For it is a question here of the teaching of the Catholic and Apostolic Church, mother and teacher of all nations, whose light illumines, sets on fire, inflames. Her warning voice, filled with heavenly wisdom, reaches out to every age. Her power always provides efficacious and appropriate remedies for the growing needs of men, for the cares and solicitudes of this mortal life. With this voice, the age-old song of the Psalmist is in marvelous accord, to strengthen at all times and to uplift our souls: "I will hear what God proclaims; the Lord—for He proclaims peace to His people, and to His faithful ones, and to those who put in Him their hope. Near indeed is His salvation to those who fear Him, glory dwelling in our land. Kindness and truth shall meet; justice and peace shall kiss. Truth shall spring out of the earth, and justice shall look down from heaven. The Lord Himself will give His benefits; our land shall yield its increase. Justice shall walk before Him, and salvation, along the way of His steps." [19]

This is the plea, Venerable Brothers, we make at the close of this Letter, to which we have for a considerable time directed our concern about the Universal Church. We desire that the divine Redeemer of mankind, "who has become for us God-given wisdom, and justice, and sanctification, and redemption" [20] may reign and triumph gloriously in all things and over all things, for centuries on end. We desire that, in a properly organized

[18] *Preface of Jesus Christ the King.*
[19] Ps. 84, 9ff.
[20] I Cor. 1, 30.

order of social affairs, all nations will at last enjoy prosperity, and happiness, and peace.

Notebook Assignment for Class Discussion

1. How is the argument organized? Prepare a précis of this essay so that its organization may become more apparent to you. Prepare both a general outline and a topic-sentence outline. In what different way is each kind of outline an aid to understanding and analyzing this essay?
2. Try to define the pattern of argument employed here. Is it a pattern which may be generally utilized, or only uniquely employed, as in *this* essay on *this* theme?
3. Describe the tone of the essay, and the means by which it is achieved. How is the tone rhetorically appropriate in relation to the pattern of argumentation used here? How is it rhetorically appropriate in relation to the audience to which it is addressed?
4. Describe the diction employed here. How is it rhetorically appropriate?
5. Does Pope John anticipate objections to his arguments? Is it good rhetorical practice to do so? Might it not weaken your case to raise objections to your own arguments?
6. Is the logical progression of the argument disrupted by the arguments from faith and authority in parts 4 and 5?

Related Exercises

1. How does John XXIII feel about the proper relationship between social theorizing and social action? Is his injunction to "observe, judge, act" a good and useful one?
2. Would you agree that "it must be admitted that one who judges even with the aid of human nature alone, concludes that it is the part of the wise and prudent man to preserve balance and moderation in everything, and to restrain the lower appetites"? How is the word "prudent" used here? What is meant by "the lower appetites"?
3. In your experience, is the Pope's concern that men are likely to prefer theory to action well founded? Does it not seem to you that, as often as not, the pattern is reversed? What validity, judged on the basis of your experience, has the Pope's anxiety?

4. Write an essay in which you outline the social values and principles of action which John XXIII reveals, directly or indirectly, to be his. Do you agree with them, or not?
5. Is the tone of this essay authoritarian? Might it not seem to preclude the possibility of liberty for Catholics, especially in view of what is said in paragraph 4 of part 4?
6. What does the Pope mean by saying that no one really "enjoys liberty unless he uses it"? How does one "use" liberty? Is not liberty like saved money: yours, whether you spend it or not?
7. Does John seem negative or critical in his attitude toward science and technology?
8. What relationship does he see between science and technology, and man's "corresponding departure from a sense of dignity"? Is it immediately causal? Do we blame man, or science? *Can* science be blamed? What *is* science?
9. What is the value of leisure, according to John XXIII? How, in your experience, is leisure usually thought of by people? How many attitudes toward leisure can you imagine? What are the broad categories of thought in regard to the nature and value of leisure?
10. Why does the Pope feel that the implementation of Christian social theory will be very difficult?

CULTURE *

By Matthew Arnold

As there is a curiosity about intellectual matters which is futile, and merely a disease, so there is certainly a curiosity—a desire after the things of the mind simply for their own sakes and for the pleasure of seeing them as they are—which is, in an intelligent being, natural and laudable. Nay, and the very desire to see things as they are implies a balance and regulation of mind which is not often attained without fruitful effort, and which is the very opposite of the blind and diseased impulse of mind which is what we mean to blame when we blame curiosity. Montesquieu says: "The first motive which ought to impel us to study is the desire to augment the excellence of our nature, and to render an intelli-

* From *Culture and Anarchy*, Chapter 1.

gent being yet more intelligent." This is the true ground to assign for the genuine scientific passion, however manifested, and for culture, viewed simply as a fruit of this passion; and it is a worthy ground, even though we let the term *curiosity* stand to describe it.

But there is of culture another view, in which not solely the scientific passion, the sheer desire to see things as they are, natural and proper in an intelligent being, appears as the ground of it. There is a view in which all the love of our neighbor, the impulses towards action, help, and beneficence, the desire for removing human error, clearing human confusion, and diminishing human misery, the noble aspiration to leave the world better and happier than we found it—motives eminently such as are called social—come in as part of the grounds of culture, and the main and preeminent part. Culture is then properly described not as having its origin in curiosity, but as having its origin in the love of perfection; it is *a study of perfection*. It moves by the force, not merely or primarily of the scientific passion for pure knowledge, but also of the moral and social passion for doing good. As, in the first view of it, we took for its worthy motto Montesquieu's words: "To render an intelligent being yet more intelligent!" so, in the second view of it, there is no better motto which it can have than these words of Bishop Wilson: "To make reason and the will of God prevail!"

THE NEGRO IS YOUR BROTHER *

By Martin Luther King, Jr.

In any nonviolent campaign there are four basic steps: collection of the facts to determine whether injustices are alive, negotiation, self-purification, and direct action. We have gone through all of these steps in Birmingham. There can be no gainsaying of the fact that racial injustice engulfs this community. Birmingham is probably the most thoroughly segregated city in the United States. Its ugly record of police brutality is known in every section of this country. Its unjust treatment of Negroes in the courts is

* From *The Atlantic Monthly*, Vol. 212, No. 2 (August, 1963), 79–80. Written in "response to a public statement of concern and caution issued by eight white religious leaders of the South."

a notorious reality. There have been more unsolved bombings of Negro homes and churches in Birmingham than in any other city in this nation. These are the hard, brutal, and unbelievable facts. On the basis of them, Negro leaders sought to negotiate with the city fathers. But the political leaders consistently refused to engage in good-faith negotiation.

Then came the opportunity last September to talk with some of the leaders of the economic community. In these negotiating sessions certain promises were made by the merchants, such as the promise to remove the humiliating racial signs from the stores. On the basis of these promises, Reverend Shuttlesworth and the leaders of the Alabama Christian Movement for Human Rights agreed to call a moratorium on any type of demonstration. As the weeks and months unfolded, we realized that we were the victims of a broken promise. The signs remained. As in so many experiences of the past, we were confronted with blasted hopes, and the dark shadow of a deep disappointment settled upon us. So we had no alternative except that of preparing for direct action, whereby we would present our very bodies as a means of laying our case before the conscience of the local and national community. We were not unmindful of the difficulties involved. So we decided to go through a process of self-purification. We started having workshops on nonviolence and repeatedly asked ourselves the questions, "Are you able to accept blows without retaliating?" and "Are you able to endure the ordeals of jail?" We decided to set our direct-action program around the Easter season, realizing that, with exception of Christmas, this was the largest shopping period of the year. Knowing that a strong economic withdrawal program would be the by-product of direct action, we felt that this was the best time to bring pressure on the merchants for the needed changes. Then it occurred to us that the March election was ahead, and so we speedily decided to postpone action until after election day. When we discovered that Mr. Connor was in the runoff, we decided again to postpone action so that the demonstration could not be used to cloud the issues. At this time we agreed to begin our nonviolent witness the day after the runoff.

This reveals that we did not move irresponsibly into direct action. We, too, wanted to see Mr. Connor defeated, so we went through postponement after postponement to aid in this community need. After this we felt that direct action could be delayed no longer.

You may well ask, "Why direct action, why sitins, marches, and so forth? Isn't negotiation a better path?" You are exactly right in your call for negotiation. Indeed, this is the purpose of direct action. Nonviolent direct action seeks to create such a crisis and establish such creative tension that a community that has consistently refused to negotiate is forced to confront the issue. It seeks so to dramatize the issue that it can no longer be ignored. I just referred to the creation of tension as a part of the work of the nonviolent resister. This may sound rather shocking. But I must confess that I am not afraid of the word "tension." I have earnestly worked and preached against violent tension, but there is a type of constructive nonviolent tension that is necessary for growth. Just as Socrates felt that it was necessary to create a tension in the mind so that individuals could rise from the bondage of myths and half-truths to the unfettered realm of creative analysis and objective appraisal, we must see the need of having nonviolent gadflies to create the kind of tension in society that will help men to rise from the dark depths of prejudice and racism to the majestic heights of understanding and brotherhood. So, the purpose of direct action is to create a situation so crisis-packed that it will inevitably open the door to negotiation. We therefore concur with you in your call for negotiation. Too long has our beloved Southland been bogged down in the tragic attempt to live in monologue rather than dialogue.

One of the basic points in your statement is that our acts are untimely. Some have asked, "Why didn't you give the new administration time to act?" The only answer that I can give to this inquiry is that the new administration must be prodded about as much as the outgoing one before it acts. We will be sadly mistaken if we feel that the election of Mr. Boutwell will bring the millennium to Birmingham. While Mr. Boutwell is much more articulate and gentle than Mr. Conner, they are both segregationists, dedicated to the task of maintaining the status quo. The hope I see in Mr. Boutwell is that he will be reasonable enough to see the futility of massive resistance to desegregation. But he will not see this without pressure from the devotees of civil rights. My friends, I must say to you that we have not made a single gain in civil rights without determined legal and nonviolent pressure. History is the long and tragic story of the fact that privileged groups seldom give up their privileges voluntarily. Individuals may see the moral light and voluntarily give up their unjust posture; but, as Reinhold Niebuhr has reminded us, groups are more immoral than individuals.

We know through painful experience that freedom is never voluntarily given by the oppressor; it must be demanded by the oppressed. Frankly, I have never yet engaged in a direct-action movement that was "well timed" according to the timetable of those who have not suffered unduly from the disease of segregation. For years now I have heard the word "wait." It rings in the ear of every Negro with a piercing familiarity. This "wait" has almost always meant "never." It has been a tranquilizing thalidomide, relieving the emotional stress for a moment, only to give birth to an ill-formed infant of frustration. We must come to see with the distinguished jurist of yesterday that "justice too long delayed is justice denied." We have waited for more than three hundred and forty years for our God-given and constitutional rights. The nations of Asia and Africa are moving with jetlike speed toward the goal of political independence, and we still creep at horse-and-buggy pace toward the gaining of a cup of coffee at a lunch counter. I guess it is easy for those who have never felt the stinging darts of segregation to say "wait." But when you have seen vicious mobs lynch your mothers and fathers at will and drown your sisters and brothers at whim; when you have seen hate-filled policemen curse, kick, brutalize, and even kill your black brothers and sisters with impunity; when you see the vast majority of your twenty million Negro brothers smothering in an airtight cage of poverty in the midst of an affluent society; when you suddenly find your tongue twisted and your speech stammering as you seek to explain to your six-year-old daughter why she cannot go to the public amusement park that has just been advertised on television, and see tears welling up in her little eyes when she is told that Funtown is closed to colored children, and see the depressing clouds of inferiority begin to form in her little mental sky, and see her begin to distort her little personality by unconsciously developing a bitterness toward white people; when you have to concoct an answer for a five-year-old son asking in agonizing pathos, "Daddy, why do white people treat colored people so mean?"; when you take a cross-country drive and find it necessary to sleep night after night in the uncomfortable corners of your automobile because no motel will accept you; when you are humiliated day in and day out by nagging signs reading "white" and "colored"; when your first name becomes "nigger" and your middle name becomes "boy" (however old you are) and your last name becomes "John," and when your wife and mother are never given the respected title "Mrs."; when you are harried by day and haunted by night by the fact that you are a Negro, living constantly at tiptoe stance, never quite knowing what to expect next, and plagued with inner fears and outer resentments; when you are forever fighting a degenerating sense of "nobodyness"—then you will understand why we find

it difficult to wait. There comes a time when the cup of endurance runs over and men are no longer willing to be plunged
into an abyss of injustice where they experience the bleakness of
corroding despair. I hope, sirs, you can understand our legitimate
and unavoidable impatience.

Notebook Assignment for Class Discussion

1. This essay, as the footnote points out, is in response to a letter
   written by some Southern clergymen. Try to determine, on
   the basis of King's essay alone, the main issues raised by the
   clergymen.
2. Would you say that this essay, admittedly responsive in nature, is nevertheless integral, or self-contained? Does it make
   sense when read without reference to the letter it answers?
3. Does the author use figurative language effectively? Cite and
   analyze what seems to you to be the most striking metaphor
   in the essay.
4. Is the author effectively epigrammatic? Cite and analyze one
   or two examples of epigrammatic constructions in this essay
   (e.g., "groups are more immoral than individuals").
5. Note the author's use of oratorical progression to a climax.
   One of the final sentences runs over 600 words in length; what
   rhetorical devices, apart from the obvious one of parallel construction, help to determine its effectiveness?
6. Sentimentalism is the danger of rhetorical procedure such as
   the author employs in this sentence. It is a highly personal
   statement which he is making, and one which is emotionally
   charged. It is obviously delivered with passionate conviction.
   How does the author control tone here without at the same
   time impairing the emotional power of the sentence?

Related Exercises

1. It is clear that the author intends literally such flat statements
   as "Freedom is never voluntarily given by the oppressor."
   Does it seem to you a reasonable, or unreasonable, statement?
2. Can you think of any obvious exceptions to this statement?
   Should it be qualified in any way? Try to decide what *you*
   have always understood "radical" to mean; according to your
   standards is Martin Luther King a "radical"?

3. How can it be said that there are "oppressors" in a democratic society such as ours, where it has been agreed that the majority will formulate the social rules?

4. James Baldwin has said that the only "useful definition of the word 'majority' does not refer to numbers, and it does not refer to power. It refers to influence." [1] Does King say, directly or indirectly, anything like this?

5. What has *majority* meant to you? Is "numbers" always "power"? Is "power" always "influence"?

6. What *should* be the limitations upon the majority? Can a majority sanction an evil rule, according to your view? Can a minority properly seek to overthrow a social decision made by a majority? Is there a final sanction for the social order? Does it inhere in, or is it extrinsic to, the society itself?

7. Which of these three propositions seems to you to be King's?
   a. Segregation is a political question which seeks a moral resolution.
   b. Segregation is a moral question which seeks a political resolution.
   c. One cannot with profit distinguish between political and moral actions, so that segregation is a question simultaneously political and moral, and must be resolved accordingly.

8. Write an essay based upon one of the propositions included under item 7.

9. Does King call into question, through such means as the statement cited in item 1, any values which you have long and doubtlessly maintained? What are the primary *personal* bases of your agreement or disagreement with Martin Luther King's argument? What are the sources of your social convictions relating to the question of racial discrimination?

[1] James Baldwin, *Nobody Knows My Name* (New York: Dell Publishing Co., 1961), p. 109.

TRAVELING MAN *

By Peter Matthiessen

November on the Carolina coast is cold at night, a dark clear cold that kills the late mosquitoes.

Toward dusk one evening, a black man slithered from a drainage ditch. He moved swiftly on his belly, writhing out across a greasy bog and vanishing into the sawgrass by the river. The grass stirred a moment and was still. A rail bird rattled nervously, and a hunting gull, drawn inland, cocked a bright, hard, yellow eye. Startled, it dropped a white spot on the brown waste of the bog and banked downwind.

Deep River is dark with piedmont silt and without depth or bottom. It bends its way to its wide delta like a great dead snake slung out across the tidewater, and in the summertime it smells. Alluvial ooze packed tight and rotting on its banks sucks into itself the river debris. Through the grasses near the rim, Traver could see the stranded tree limbs and the prow of the derelict skiff glimpsed earlier in the day.

It was nearly dark. Raising his eyes to the level of the grass, he listened a last time. Then he slid forward and, on his knees in the shallows, wrenched the buried skiff from its sheath of mud. It came with a thick sucking sound and the rank breath of its grave.

Traver knew without experiment that, upright, the skiff would fill immediately. He turned it turtle and waited one moment more, gaining his wind. It was high water, the first of the ebb. The tide and river would be with him. He shivered, moaning softly, though not yet afraid.

In the water, he kicked away from shore. An eddy curled him back upon the bank. He kicked away a second time, and caught the current. But the slimy hulk would not support his weight, and he coasted along beside it, one hand spread-fingered on the keel.

He moved downstream. Across the marsh, the lights switched back and forth like night-time eyes, dancing in the blackness of

* From *Harper's Magazine*, Vol. 214, No. 1281 (February, 1957), 57–65. Copyright © 1957 by Harper & Bros. Reprinted by permission of Russell & Volkening, Inc.

the pines. The voices came vaguely on the shifting river air, and a new sound stirred him. He inched lower in the water, so that only his hand and half his face broke the low outline of the skiff.

Dey gone and put de hounds on dat man Traver.

He giggled, teeth chattering, and cursed.

The river dragged the capsized skiff across the coastal waterway, which parted the mainland from the inner marshes of the barrier islands. Though wisps of clouds at times obscured the moon, the night was clear. No longer able to see the lights, he was alone in the cold river, which widened now as it neared its mouth. He thrashed his legs for warmth, and cursed to restore his courage. Southeast, an arm of woods from Ocean Island reached across the outer marshes toward the bank. He wanted to go aground there, and fearful of drifting past it to the open sea, began to swim the skiff inshore. He swore foully at the balky hulk, the cold, the river, the night world, and then he sang softly, despite himself afraid, a song known long ago in the shanties of Raccoon Creek.

Faraway and gone am I toward dat Judgment Day,
Faraway and gone am I, ain't no one gwine to stay,
Lay down dis haid, lay down dis load,
Gwine to take dat Heaven Road,
Faraway and gone am I toward dat Judgment Day.

His voice hung plaintive in the thin mist over the river, and startled by it, he had a cold premonition of his death. But an inshore current seized the skiff and swept it in beneath the bank. Nearing the piles of the abandoned landing, he forsook the skiff, and struggled through the shallow water. He had to drag himself ashore. Crouched beneath the wharf, too weak to beat his arms, he listened to hoarse, painful breaths he could not help. The skiff disappeared around the final bend, toward the booming where the seas broke on the bar.

Traver scraped coon oysters from the pilings and opened them with his knife. Since the clothes he wore were the property of the state, this knife was his sole possession. He had had it fifteen hours. The knife was long, with a spring blade, and when he had eaten, he played with it before replacing it in his pocket.

Then he rose, peering over the bank at the trees a hundred yards away. Though sure he was alone on Ocean Island, he disliked outlining himself against the river. He went forward in a low crouch, covert, quiet. He liked to think he was quiet as an animal.

In the shelter of the live oaks, for the first time since early morning, he stood straight. Stretching, he threw his shoulders back, legs spread in unconscious arrogance. Traver was a tall man and very strong, with the big hands and haunches of his race. His skin was the mud black of the coastal Negro, and his left eye was obscured by scars which extended in cordy ridges toward the neat, tight ear. The scars seemed to have stretched the skin, which was taut and smooth, like a rubber mask. The expression of the mask was open, almost smiling, the boyish smile of a man enjoying himself without quite knowing why.

Most of the time, this smile was genuine. Traver liked to laugh and, though good-natured, he also liked to fight. He had been fighting since the day when, brought home to Raccoon Creek by a wayward mother, he was nicknamed Traveler.

> His Daddy was a Travelin Man
> Traveled away and left his Mam.

The name became Traver, and stayed with him. And he had traveled north, south, east, and west, in and out of work and jail. He could stay no longer in a job than out of trouble. He had worked on the railroad and the chain gang and the big menhaden boats out of Hampton Roads, and everywhere he laughed like hell and finally fought. Every once in a while, half-drunk, he would come home. And his mother would tell him, You born with too much life in you, dass all, you like you daddy. And you headin straight fo trouble, big mule as you is.

The last time home he had fought with the man who happened to marry his girl. The man had knifed him near the eye. Unable to catch him, Traver, still bleeding, had burned their cabin down and taken the willing girl away. The sheriff followed in his own good time. I got your old place on the road gang saved for you, the sheriff said. We ain't had a good laugh since you left.

But now, a month later, he had escaped. He appeared with the knife in Raccoon Creek, but the man had moved away. The girl's mother reported him, and he took to the woods, and kept on going out across Deep River Marsh. The tide was flooding when he saw the skiff, and he had had to wait. He had scurried, crouched, scurried again, and once submerged, sliding beneath the surface like an alligator. They had not picked up his trail in the green, broken scum and, voices rasping, they had passed.

I a big bull gator, he sang now, a tough-hide long-tail mean ol gator. Opening his open mouth a little more, he chortled soundlessly, still shivering. It growin cold, and dis gator ain't no place to warm hisself. Well, I mean. Cold.

He moved inland through the trees, away from the dark river. Ocean Island is long and large, spreading some four miles from the delta, southwest toward Cape Romaine. The true land is a narrow spine supporting red cedar, cypress, yaupon, live oak, and the old-field pine, and here and there a scattering of small palmettos. There are low ridges and open groves and clearings, and a core of semi-tropic woods. Its south flank is salt marsh and ocean beach, and to the north, diked years ago above the tide, lies a vast, brackish swamp. The swamp is grassy, like a green-and-golden flooded plain, its distances broken by lone, bony trees and hurricane dikes and sluice gates. Here, in a network of overgrown canals, the nut and widgeon grass grows in abandoned rice fields. Wildfowl winter in a diadem of reedy ponds, and coot and rail and gallinule, and predators.

In the swamp, the predators move ceaselessly.

He went to Snake-house. This was a sagging tool shed near the landing, so-called because in other times a worker had been bitten there, and died. In the dark, a sign, NO TRESPASSING, loomed white and new. The door was gone, but the dank interior gave shelter from the breeze. Traver stripped and wrung his clothes, then rubbed his body fiercely with his hands. He found an oily piece of old tarpaulin, and wrapping himself in it, dozed a little, fitful.

He had come to Ocean Island because here he could survive. As a boy he had labored on the rice fields and the dikes, and he knew the name and character of every pond and ditch and slough. He knew where to snare rabbits, stalk birds, ambush deer, and where the wild swine and cattle were which he might outwit and kill. On the salt shores there were razor clams and oysters, and mullet in the canals, if a fish trap could be rigged. He would not starve. He could even eat raccoon and otter and, if necessary, he could eat them raw.

He could survive here, too, because he would not be caught. The island had been unused for years, even for gunning. If he were tracked to this forsaken place, he could always find shelter in the swamp. Hounds could not help them here, and the white did not know the swamp as he did, how to move quickly in it without risking the deep potholes and soft muck. He could elude a wider search than the state would send into the swamp after a black man. For this was black man's country, slow and silent, absorbing the white man's inroads like a sponge. A white man loomed large on Ocean Island, but a black man was swallowed up in it, and disappeared.

In the night, he was awakened by the grunting of a hog. The

grunt was nervous, and there was a skittish stamping of small,
cloven hooves. He smell me, Traver thought. Taking his knife,
he glided to the doorway. Upwind, the hog came toward him
on the island path. He crouched, prepared to ambush it, then
stiffened.

Ol Hawg scairt. And he ain't scairt of Traver.

Traver stooped for his shirt and pants and slipped outside. The
hog snorted and wheeled, crashing off into the brush. Traver slid
down a sand bank behind Snake-house and lay watching. He
heard a rush of bait fish by the landing, the choked cry of a night
heron behind him. A barred owl stole over his head. This was
the hunting time.

The man had not seen Traver. He had stopped short at the
crashing of the hog. Now he came on, down the soft sand path
towards Snake-house. He was a tall, lean man with a rifle slung
over one arm and a flashlight, unlit, in the other hand. His face
was shadowed in the moonlight by his hat brim, lowered all the
way around.

Traver opened the knife blade and lay still. He could not
retreat now without being seen, and if he was seen, he was lost.
He had no doubt that this man was his enemy, an enemy as
natural as a raccoon to a frog, nor did it occur to him to curse
his luck that an enemy was here at all. He was only relieved
that he had heard in time. The rest no longer mattered. Traver
was hardened to hunting and being hunted, and the endless
adaptation to emergencies. He was intelligent and resourceful,
and he was confident. Through the grasses, he gauged the stranger as he passed.

From the man's belt, behind, hung a hatchet and a piece of
rope. The rifle, carried loosely, was ready to be raised, and the
unlit light was also ready. He was hunting. He crossed a patch
of dry grass without sound, and Traver nodded ruefully in
respect.

Dat a poacher. Might be jackin deer.

The man went on, down toward the landing. Stooping on the
wharf, he peered beneath it. Traver, who had moved, could see
him do this, and felt a tightening in his chest.

He see dem feet prints. He see white places where dem oyster
was. You a plain fool nigger, man.

The hunter returned, moving more quickly. Raising his rifle,
he flicked his light into the Snake-house. Traver could see its
gleam through the rotting tongue-and-groove.

Ain't no deer in dar, Boss, ain't no deer in dar.

He repressed a nervous giggle, sweating naked in the cold, and clutched his knife. Upwind, he could hear the hog again, rooting stupidly near the path. The white man turned, bent to one knee, and fired. Traver jumped. The report ricocheted across the grove as the hog kicked, squealing, and lay still.

Ol white folks, he kin shoot. Only why he shootin now and not before? He lookin to fool somebody, he makin pretend he doan know somebody here.

He know, all right. Ol white folks know.

The man dragged the hog into the trees and dressed it quickly, viciously, with the hatchet and a knife. Then he piled brush on the head and hooves and entrails and, rigging a sling with a length of rope, hoisted the carcass to his shoulder. He went away as silently as he had come, and Traver followed.

We stickin close as two peas, man. I got to know what you up to every minute, lest you come sneakin up behind me.

Traver, though uneasy, was excited, jubilant. It seemed to him that he had won some sort of skirmish, and he could scarcely wait to see what would happen next. But because he guessed where the man was going, he kept a safe distance behind. There was a clearing at Back-of-Ocean, and the old cabin of an abandoned shooting camp, and the only beach on the south side steep enough to bring a boat ashore. The poacher would have to have a boat, and he probably had a helper. Realizing this, Traver slowed, and put on his cold clothes.

He circled the clearing and came in from the far side, on his belly. There was kerosene light in the cabin window, and hanging from its eaves on the outside logs were moonlit amorphous carcasses. He made out deer and pig, and what could only be the quarters of a large wild bull. These cattle gone wild were the wariest creatures on the island, and Traver whistled softly at this sign of the hunter's skill. It gave him another start of uneasiness. Backing off again on hands and knees, he cut himself a rabbit club of the right weight. Waiting for dawn, he whittled it, and bound with vine and a piece of shirt two sharp stones to the heavy end. He was skillful with it, and the feel of it in his hand was reassuring.

It was growing light.

The boat appeared at sunup. Traver heard it a long way off, prowling the channel between islands at the southwest end. Now it drummed along the delta, just inside the bar, and headed straight in for the beach. It was a small, makeshift shrimp boat, with rust streaks and scaling gray-green paint. Before it grounded, the hunter came out and, hoisting two small deer onto his shoulders, went down to the shore.

The two men loaded quickly. Then they stood a moment talking, the one on the pale sand of the beach, the other a black silhouette on the bow against the red fireball of the sun.

For once in his life, Traver told himself, he had to stop fooling and be serious. The boatman, who must have been in town the night before, had probably confirmed whatever the hunter had noticed at the landing. He wondered if they would turn him in. He doubted it. In the prison denims, he could be shot on sight, and no questions asked—not that the hunter would require that excuse. He guessed that the latter had some right to be here, for otherwise, even in this lonely place, he would not occupy the cabin. He was probably a hired gamekeeper, poaching on the side. He would not want Traver here, and he would not want the sheriff nosing around the island, either. He would want to take care of Traver by himself.

The man had come in and out of the cabin. He had the rifle in his hands, checking the action. His movements were calm and purposeful, and he gave Traver a good look at his face. It was a gaunt face, creased and hard, under heavy eyebrows, a shrewd face, curiously empty of emotion. Traver recognized that face, he had seen it all his life, throughout the South.

Ol Redneck kill me, do he get the chance. And he meant to get the chance.

The man went off in the direction of Snake-house, moving swiftly into the trees.

For the moment, considering his situation, Traver stayed right where he was. He watched the shrimp boat disappear along the delta. His mouth was dry, and he licked dew from the grass. Though the early sun had begun to warm him, he felt tired and stiff and very hungry, and this hunger encouraged him to loot the cabin.

Unreal in the morning mist, the trees were still. The Spanish moss hung everywhere, like silence. The man would go to Snake-house, to the landing, to pick up Traver's trail, but it would not lead him far. Traver had stayed clear of the sand path, moving wherever possible on the needle ground beneath the pines. Still, if he meant to loot the cabin, he should hurry. And he was half-risen when a huge blue heron, sailing above the cedars into which the hunter had disappeared, flared off with a squawk and thrash of heavy wings.

Traver sank to his knees again, heart pounding.

That was close to bein you last worldly move. I mean, he layin fo you, man, and he like to cotched you. I mean, he *smart*, doan you forget it, nigger. He know what you doin even fore you does it.

Traver waited again. When his heart stopped pounding, he began to laugh, a long quiet laugh that shook his big body like crying, and caused him to press his mouth to the crook of his arm. And he was surprised when tears came to his eyes, and the laughter became sobbing. He was frightened, he knew, and at the same time, he was unbearably excited.

You just a big black mule, you just a fool and a mule and a alligator all wrap into one.

He went on laughing, knowing his delight was dangerous, and all the more elated because of that. And as he laughed, he hummed to himself, in hunger,

> Hambone is good, o so-o good,
> Bacon is sweet, o so-o sweet,
> And possum meat is very, very fine, fine, fine,
> But give me, O give me,
> O, how I wish you would,
> Dat wa-tuh melon smilin on de vine . . .

In a while, far over toward the swamp, he heard the quack of startled black ducks, rising. When he saw their high circle over the trees, he got up on his haunches.

Could be dat a duck hawk, but most likely dat him. He over dar by Snake-house.

A string of ibis, drifting peacefully down the length of woods like bright white sheets of tissue, reassured him. Traver ran. In the open, he tensed for the rifle crack he could never have heard had it come, and zigzagged for the door. In less than a minute, he was back. He had a loaf of bread and matches, and was grinning wildly with excitement.

But now a fresh fear seized him. The hunter might return at any time, from any angle. If he did not hurry, he would no longer be able to maneuver without the terror of being seen. Traver stopped chewing, the stale bread dry in his mouth. Then he cut into the woods, loping in a low, bounding squat in the direction taken by the white man. At Graveyard-over-the-Bank, where once the cattle had been driven, penned, and slaughtered, he hid again. This place, a narrowing of the island, the man would sooner or later have to pass.

Traver stalked him all that day. Toward noon, the hunter went back to the cabin. Traver could hear him rummage for the bread, and he wondered if, in taking it, he might only have endangered himself further by becoming, in the white man's eyes, more troublesome. The man came out again and sat on the doorsill, eating. His face, still calm, was tighter, meaner, Traver thought. The rifle lay across his knees. Then he rose and went away into the woods, heading southwest toward Cottonmouth Dike, and Traver followed.

The man made frequent forays from the path, but he seemed to know that he would not surprise his quarry, that Traver was in all probability behind him, for though he moved stealthily out of habit, he made no real effort to conceal himself. Clearly, his plan was to lure Traver into a poor position, a narrow neck or sparsely wooded place where he might hope to turn and hunt him down. He set a series of ambushes, and now and then wheeled and doubled back along his trail. He was skillful and very quick, quick enough to frighten Traver, who several times was nearly trapped. Traver hung farther and farther behind, using his knowledge of the island to guess where the hunter would come and go, and never remaining directly behind, but quartering.

He was most afraid of the animals and birds which, hunting and hunted, could betray his whereabouts at any time.

The white man was tireless, and this intensity frightened Traver, too. He seemed prepared to stalk forever, carrying his provisions in his pocket. When he ate, he did it in the open, pointedly, knowing that Traver could never relax enough to hunt, could only watch and starve. By noon of the second day, Traver was desperate. When the man went west again, way over past Pig Root and Eagles Grave, Traver fled eastward to the landing, and gorged on the coon oysters. Sated, he realized his mistake. He had a hundred yards of marsh to cross, back to the trees, and for all he knew, the hunter had doubled back again, and had a bead on him. He had done just what the man was waiting for him to do, he had lost the scent, and now any move he made might be the wrong one. He groaned at the thought of the vanished skiff—if only he'd gotten it ashore, and hidden it in the salt grass farther down. But now he was trapped, not only at the landing but on the island.

A bittern broke camouflage with a strangled squawk, causing Traver to spin around. In panic, he clambered up over the river bank and ran back to the trees. The woods were silent. There came a faint cry of snow geese over the delta, and the sharp rattle of a kingfisher back in the slough. Downwind, wild cattle caught his scent, retreating noisily. Or was that the coming of the hunter? He pressed himself to the black earth, in aimless prayer. The silence grew, cut only by the wash of river wind in the old-field pine. Then a wren called, Peter, Peter, Peter, and a hawk flicked quickly overhead in its direction.

Peter, Peter, Peet—

At dark, he fled into the marsh, and tried to rest in the reeds beneath a dike. Under the moon, much later, a raccoon picked its way along the bank, and he stunned it with his rabbit club. The coon played possum. When he crawled up to it, it whirled and bit him on the ankle. He struck it sharply with the stone end of the club, and it dragged itself into the reeds. He could not see it very well and, in a near frenzy of suppressed fear, he beat the dark shape savagely, long after it was dead. Panting, he sat and stared at the wet, matted mound of fur, the sharp teeth in the open, twisted mouth. He dared not light a fire with his stolen matches, and his gut was much too nervous to accept it raw. He left it where it lay and crept back to the woods and, in an agony of stealth, to Back-of-Ocean. He was overjoyed by the lamp in the cabin window.

He finally tuckered out, Traver told himself. The man done give ol Traver up. Traver too spry for him.

The idea restored his confidence a little, and he chuckled without heart. He was still hungry, and he had no idea what his next move should be. Remembering the white man's face, he did not really believe he had given up the hunt, and this instinct was confirmed, at daybreak. The boat appeared again, and the white man met it, but he did not come out of the cabin. He stepped into the clearing from the yaupon on the other side. Traver had almost approached that way the night before. The light in the window had only been another trap.

Traver fought a wild desire to bolt. But he controlled himself, squeezing great fistfuls of earth beween his fingers. He watched the hunter walk slowly to the beach and, resting his rifle butt on the silver roots of a hurricane tree, speak to the boatman. They were silent for a time, as if deciding something. Then the hunter shrugged, and shoved the boat from shore. It backed off with a grinding of worn gears. He returned to the cabin and came out of it a minute later. He had a cooked bone, and he pulled long strings of dry meat from it with his teeth. Traver stared at the lean yellow-brown of his face, the wrinkled neck, the faded khaki clothes and high, cracked boots against the soft greens of the trees and the red cassina berries. He stared at the bone. The man tossed it out in front of him, then tramped it into the ground and lit a cigarette. Breathing smoke, he leaned against the cabin logs and gazed around the clearing. Traver caught the cigarette scent on the air, and stirred uncomfortably. The man flipped the butt into the air, and together they watched it burn away upon the ground. Then he shouldered the rifle and went back to the woods, and once more Traver followed.

Who huntin who heah? Traver tried to smile. Who huntin who?

The fear was deep in him now, like cold. He started at every snap and crackle and cry of bird, sniffing the air for scents which could tell him nothing. There was only the stench of rotting vegetation, and the rank sweat of his fear. He crept along closer and closer to the ground, terrified lest he lose contact with the hunter. In his heart, he knew there was but one course open to him. He could not leave the island, and he could not be killed. Both prospects were unimaginable. But he could kill.

Man, you in de swamp now. It you or him, dass all.

But he could not make himself accept this. He supposed he could kill a black man if he had to, and a white man could kill him. But a black man did not kill a white man unless the black man was insane.

Man, it doan matter what de color is, it just doan matter now. You in de swamp, and de swamp a different world. Dey ain't nobody left in dis heah world but you and him, and he figger dass too crowded. When ol Lo'd passed out de mens's hearts, dis heah man hid behind de do'. A man like dis heah man, you let him run where he de law, and he kill you if you black or white or blue. He ain't no more civilized den a cat gone wild. He doan hate you and he doan feel sorry, no more'n de cat do. You just a varmint dat got in de way, dass all.

But Traver doubted his own sense. Perhaps this man had nothing to hide, perhaps he was hunting legally, perhaps he would do more than remove Traver from the island, or arrest him—how could he, Traver, know that this man, given the chance, would shoot him down?

And yet he knew, as wild animals know, by instinct. He could smell it. He doubted his instinct because, himself civilized, he hated what it told him, because he wanted to believe that this man also was afraid, that a man would not shoot another down without first calling out to him to surrender.

Man, he ain't called, and he know you heah. He quiet as de grave. And you take it in you haid to call you'self, you fixin to get a bullet fo you answer.

His only chance was to live by animal law. It was this that, in the end, he could not bring himself to do.

Again that morning, he was nearly ambushed. This time a rabbit gave the man away. For the first time, Traver lost his nerve entirely. He ran back east along the island and stole out on the marsh, crawling along the dike bank where he had killed the coon, persuading his pounding heart that food was his reason for coming. But he knew before he got there that the raccoon would be gone. Black vultures and an eagle rose in silence from the bank, and there was a flat track in the reeds where an alligator had come and gone, and there were blue crabs clinging upside down to the grass at the edge of the ditch. In the marsh, the weak and dead have a brief existence.

Traver was shifting his position when a bullet slapped into the mudbank by his head. Its whine he heard afterward, a swelling in his ears as he rolled into the water and clawed at the brittle stalks of cane across the ditch. A wind of teal wings, rising out of Dead Oak Pond, blurred his racket in the brake. He crossed a reedy flat and slid into a small pool twenty yards away. The echo of the shot diminished on the marsh, and silence settled, like a cloud across the sun.

Then fiddler crabs snapped faintly on the flat. Where he had passed, their yellow claws protruded, open, from the holes.

But he knew the man would come, and he tried to control the choked rasp of his breath. And the man came, picking his lean way along the dike, stopping to listen, coming on, as Traver himself had often done, tracking crippled ducks for the plantation gunners. Against the bright, high autumn sky, the hunter's silhouette was huge.

Traver slipped the rabbit club from his belt. The game was ending now, and he knew only the intense fear and hate of an animal straining toward survival.

The man had stopped just short of where Traver had lain. He squinted up and down the ditch. Though his face remained set, his right hand, wandering on the trigger guard and breech, betrayed his awareness that Traver might have a weapon.

He came a little farther, stopped again. He seemed on the point of calling out, but did not, as if afraid of intruding a human voice into this primeval silence. He bent and scratched his leg. Then, for a moment, scanning the far side of the dike, he turned his head.

Traver, straightening, tried to hurl the club, but it would not leave his hand. He ducked down and out of sight again. He told himself that the range had been too great, that the chance of a miss, however small, could not be taken. But he also knew he was desperate enough to have thrown it anyway, in agony, simply to bring an end to this suspense.

There was something else.

The man descended from the dike, on the far side. Almost immediately, he sank up to his knees, for there came a heavy, sucking sound as his boots pulled back. The man seemed to know that here, in the black resilience of the marsh, his quarry had him at a disadvantage, for he climbed back up onto the dike and took out a cigarette. This time Traver thought he must call out, but he did not. Instead, he made his way back toward the woods.

Traver cursed him, close to tears. The hunter had only to watch from the trees at the end of the dike. Until dark, Traver was trapped. The hunter would sit down on a log and eat his food, while Traver lay in the cold pool and starved. The whole world was eating, hunting and eating and hunting again, in an endless cycle, while he starved. From where he lay, he could see a marsh hawk quartering wet weadows, and an eagle's patient silhouette in a dead tree. Swaying grass betrayed a prowling otter, and on a mud flat near him, two jack snipe probed for worms. Soon, in that stretch of ditch that he could see, a young alligator surfaced.

Thank de Lo'd it you what stole my coon. Thank de Lo'd dis pool too shaller for you daddy.

The alligator floated, facing him. Only its snout and eyes disturbed the surface, like tips of a submerged branch.

What you waitin on, Ugly? You waitin on ol Traver, man, you got to get in line.

The insects had found Traver, and he smeared black mud on his face and hands. Northeast, a vulture circled slowly down on something else.

Whole world waitin on poor Traver. Whole world hangin round to eat on Traver.

And though he said this to cheer himself, and even chuckled, the sense of the surrounding marsh weighed down on him, the solitude. Inert, half-buried, Traver mourned a blues.

> Black river bottom, black river bottom
> Nigger sinkin down to dat black river bottom
> Ain't comin home no mo'
>
> Ol Devil layin at dat black river bottom
> Black river bottom, black river bottom,

Waitin fo' de nigger man los' on de river
Dat ain't comin home no mo'. . .

At dark, inch by inch, circuitously, Traver came ashore. He knew now he must track the man and kill him. His nerves would not tolerate another day of fear, and he took courage from the recklessness of desperation.

Again the cabin was lit up, but this time he smelled coffee. The man's shadow moved against the window, and the light died out. The man would be sitting in the dark, rifle pointed at the open door.

The hunt ended early the next morning.

Traver bellied across a clearing and slid down a steep bank which here joined the high ground to the marsh. His feet were planted in the water at the end of Red Gate Ditch, and on his right was a muddy, rooted grove of yaupon known as Hog Crawl. The hunter was some distance to the eastward.

Traver had a length of dry, dead branch. He broke it sharply on his knee. The snap rang through the morning trees, and a hog grunted from somewhere in the Crawl. Then Traver waited, peering through the grass. He had his knife out, and his rabbit club. Lifting one foot from the water of the ditch, he kicked a foothold in the bank. Below him, the scum of algae closed its broken surface, leaving no trace of where his foot had been.

The man was coming. Traver could feel him, somewhere behind the black trunks of the trees. The final sun, which filtered through the woods from the ocean side, formed a strange red haze in the shrouds of Spanish moss. Out of this the man appeared. One moment there was nothing and the next he was there, startling the eye like a copperhead camouflaged in fallen leaves. He moved toward Traver until he reached the middle of the clearing, just out of Traver's range, facing the Hog Crawl. There he stood stiff as a deer and listened.

Traver listened, too, absorbing every detail of the scene through every sense. The cardinal song had never seemed so liquid, the foliage so green, the smell of the earth so strong. Though tense to the breaking point, he felt powerfully alive, exultant. For the trap was his, he was the hunter now, on his own ground.

And the white man shifted, stepping a little closer. The hog snuffled again, back in the yaupon. Traver could just make it out beneath the branches, a brown-and-yellow brindle sow, caked with dry mud. Now it came forward, curious. It would see Traver before it saw the white man, and it would give him away.

Traver swallowed. The sow came toward him, red-eyed. The

white man, immobile, waited for it, also. When the sow saw Traver, it stopped, then backed away a little, then grunted and trotted off.

Traver flicked his gaze back to the man.

He was suspicious. Black eyes wide, head up, he froze. Then slowly the rifle swung around until it was pointed a few feet to Traver's left.

He gwine kill me now. Even do I pray, O Lo'd, he gwine kill me now.

Traver was backing down the bank as the man moved forward. Beneath the turned-down brim, the eyes were fixed on the spot to Traver's left. Traver flipped the butt of broken branch in the same direction. When the white man whirled upon the sound, Traver reared and hurled his club. He did not miss. It struck just as the shot went off.

Traver had rolled aside instinctively, but this same instinct drove him to his feet again and forward. The man lay still beside the rifle. The hand which had been groping for it fell back as Traver sprang. He pressed his knife blade to the white, unsunburned patch of throat beneath the grizzled chin.

Kill him, kill him now.

But he did not. Gasping, he stared down at the face a foot from his. It was bleeding badly from the temple but was otherwise unchanged. Pinning the man's arms with his knees, he pushed the eyelids open with his free hand. The eyes regarded him, unblinking, like the eyes of a wounded hawk.

"Wa'nt quite slick enough fo Traver, was you!" Traver panted. He roared hysterically in his relief, his laughter booming in the quiet grove. "You fall fo de oldes trick dey is, dass how smart you is, white folks!" He roared again into the silence. "Ol Traver toss de branch, ol white boy fooled, ol white boy cotch it in de haid! I mean! De oldes trick dey is!"

Traver glared down at him, hoarse, triumphant. The man lay silent.

Traver ran the knife blade back and forth across the throat, leaving a thin red line. He forced his anger, disturbed at how swiftly his relief replaced it.

"You de one dat's scairt now, ain't you? Try to kill dis nigger what never done you harm! You doan know who you foolin with, white trash, you foolin with a man what's mule and gator all wrap into one! And he gwine kill you, what you think 'bout dat?"

The white man watched him.

"Ain't you nothin to say fore I kills you? You gwine pray? Or is I done killed you already?" Uneasy astride the body of the white man, Traver rose to a squat and pricked him with his knife tip. "Doan you play possum with me, now! You ain't foolin me no mo', I gwine kill you, man, you heah me?"

For the first time, Traver heard his own voice in the silence, and it startled him. He glanced around. The sun was bright red over the live oak trees, but quiet hung across the marsh like mist. Out of the corner of his eye, he watched the white man with suspicion, but the other did not stir.

He dead, Traver thought, alarmed. I done killed him dead.

Avoiding the open eyes, he picked up the rifle and stared at it. Then, superstitious, he laid it like a burial fetish back into the grass. Then he stepped back, knife in hand, and prodded the body with his toe.

"Git up, now!" he cried, startling himself again. "You ain't bad hurt. Cap'n, you just kinda dizzy, dass all. Now us is got to do some talkin, heah me now?"

But the body was still. A trail of saliva dribbled from the narrow mouth, and a fly lit on the grass near the bloody temple. Traver bent and crossed the arms upon the narrow chest.

"You fall fo de oldes trick in de world," Traver mourned, and shook his head. "Dass what you done." Badly frightened, he talked to comfort himself, glancing furtively around the clearing.

He started to back away, then bolted.

The man rolled over and up onto his knees, the rifle snatched toward his shoulder. He sighted without haste and fired. Then he reached for his hat and put it on, and turned the brim down all around.

Then he got up.

Traver was a powerful man and did not fall. He could still hear the echo and the clamor in the marsh, and he could not accept what was happening to him. He had never really believed it possible, and he did not believe it now. He dropped the knife and staggered, frowning, as the man walked toward him. The second bullet knocked him over backwards, down the bank, and when he came to rest, his head lay under water.

His instinct told him to wriggle a little further, to crawl away into the reeds. He could not move. He died.

Notebook Assignment for Class Discussion

1. Read the story all the way through, without stopping, before attempting to answer the study questions. Outline the narrative, or chronological sequence of events. How much of the

total meaning of this story depends upon the narrative
alone?

2. *Narrative* (or *story*) is, as we indicated in item 1, the chronological sequence of events, what E. M. Forster calls the "and
then, and then, and then . . ." element. *Plot* is a term which
refers to the pattern of character motivation. Indicate the
various passages which emphasize narrative, and those which
emphasize plot.

3. Does this story emphasize sensory description, character description, or "action" description?

4. What distinction can be made between *logical* and *dramatic*
punctuation? Which kind is most commonly used in this
story? Find and analyze some examples of each.

5. How is the tone of this story established in the first paragraph? Analyze the author's use of details to set the mood.

6. Cite some of the ways in which the author manages to reveal
the passage of time.

7. Attempt to summarize the story, pointing out the basic conflicts of motivation which underlie the whole.

8. How does the author develop those qualities of character of
the white hunter which make Traver fear him?

9. What are the techniques of character development employed
in the case of Traver?

10. Which particular aspects of Traver's character are emphasized by Matthiessen? Explain your answers to items 8, 9,
and 10 by citing action, circumstance, and detail from the
story as evidence.

11. Do you see any important symbolism in the story?

12. What is the final meaning, or structure of values, arising out
of the conflict and its resolution?

Related Exercises

1. How does Traver interpret the movements and sounds of the
animals in relation to his own predicament?

2. At various points in the story, and at the end, the author
speaks of Traver's motivation from instinct, thus, in a sense,
identifying him with the animals. How, then, do we explain
the fact that the animals almost always serve to betray him?

3. How do we reconcile the next-to-the-last sentence in the story
with the author's comment to the effect that Traver could
not bring himself to live by animal law? How do we recon-

cile it with the author's earlier description of Traver as "civilized"?

4. Is Traver truly civilized? Is it really his refusal to live by animal law which finally dooms him? Is it a weakness to be civilized?

5. If we stop to consider that Traver is an uneducated convict living like an animal, in fear of his life, how is it possible to view him as civilized? What does it mean to be civilized?

6. Why does Traver not possess the relentless force of motivation of the hunter? What is the triumph which the author says that Traver feels at one point in the story? What is the reason for the laughter which turns into tears?

7. What is the author's purpose in setting the action on an island?

8. What is his purpose in making one character a Negro and the other a white man? In what essential characteristics would the story differ were Traver to be an escaped *white* convict?

8. The story makes clear that the relationship of the hunter to the hunted, and vice versa, is sometimes ambiguous. In what significant ways do Traver's attitudes toward the hunter change? In what varying relationships does he see himself and the hunter?

9. What is the true nature of this hunt, or, as Traver says, "Who huntin' who"?

A CHAPTER FROM
THE WORLD OF IDELLA MAY *

By Richard Sullivan

As a child and budding social problem, Idella May was spoiled by doting parents. Movies and magazines dealing with romantic love and movie stars impressed her, as did the kind of radio drama known as soap-opera. (Had she been born later she would have been struck hard by television.) Formed by falsity, and

* From *The World of Idella May*, by Richard Sullivan (New York: Doubleday & Co., 1946), Chapter 12, pp. 360–73.

selfish to the core, she came to see herself as the beautiful heroine and glamorous dream girl of a little world made up especially for her. What she never saw was her true self.

Attractive, she engaged the interest of a succession of young men, all of whom found her somehow wanting. But she managed to marry a sound and eventually long-suffering husband who honestly loved her. They lost a baby. She carried on (technically remaining faithful) with other men. She ran away from her husband, but not so far away that she could not return and be regretfully welcomed. Dimly she knew all along that her husband believed in marriage as a permanent commitment.

Aging a bit, yet still seeing herself as the romantic heroine of all time, Idella May remains in this final chapter of the novel which deals with a representative part of her life, a dreamer, with no sense at all of what being alive really signifies. Dreaming, she lies to herself about life itself—and in what may be a symbolic act, nibbles her fingernail in uneasy self-deceit.

On the morning after her mother's funeral Idella May got up earlier than usual and sat for some time in front of the three mirrors of her new dressing table. She was sober and reflective; she admitted to herself, rather formally, that she felt her age. The death of her mother had impressed her with the transitoriness of life. It had made her serious. She had undergone no real grief, but the sense of loss was still strong. There would be no more of her mother's cooking, for example. (For some reason she thought longingly of Erna's apple kuchen.) And there remained such troublesome problems: Alice expected her to take her father to live here; she expected Alice to take her father to live there. She looked at herself in the three mirrors. Her complexion without make-up was blotchy, and on her throat a few of the freckles which had always been there had now turned a noticeable brown. But what disturbed her was the growing little pad beneath her chin. Her profile was clean and clear, still lively; but that bulge of fat beneath the chin seemed to her a kind of menace spreading up from her body. As her fingers worked in massage she looked sharply ahead at the full-face view, and her cheeks appeared all at once puffy and overhanging, too big, too flabby for her own. She sucked them in: that was better, that was the way they really were. I won't do it, she told herself; I won't have him here; Alice knows my health is bad, she's just trying to put something over. Really a person shouldn't look in a mirror until after she's fixed up, she thought. She ran a comb through her tangled hair. One time, before she was ever married, a long time ago, she had used to brush her hair a hundred times every night to make it glossy. Remembering, she felt a fond nostalgia. She picked up the brush now, she set it down. With all the room Alice had in that house, it wouldn't hurt her to accommodate her own father. It was just that our dear Alice didn't want to be bothered. "I suppose you'll be taking Dad," she had announced to Idella May. It was really announcing; she had it all decided. "Well, I think he'd rather live with you," Idella May said. And then, though they had both talked and talked, it was left right there, as an issue, while their poor mother lay in the coffin and everybody knew it made sense that Alice should be the one who took Dad. An early June breeze blew soft and warm across the bedroom. She thought, I'll be damned if I have him here; it's not him but Alice, I won't give in to her.

She stood and fingered the roll of flesh that went round her waist like a flabby tube; she patted her large hips indignantly. She thought, I got to do something. The mean, vague, formless discontent which filled so many of her days now grew to a sudden climax. She turned to the little fuzzy white dog which lay sleeping on the tossed covers at the foot of her bed. *"Chickie!"* she shouted. The little dog lifted its head and blinked at her. Idella May rushed to the bed, batted the little dog's ears and swept it with both hands to the floor. Yelping, Chickie scurried from the room. Idella May, glowering, muttering, with her head thrust forward and her arms swinging, walked over to the closet. She took out the pink rayon satin house coat with the faded blue flowers. Worn out, she thought, slipping it on; I got to get a new one for the summer.

Downstairs she turned on the radio, loud, so that she could hear it in the kitchen. The table was littered with the remains of Tom's breakfast. After all I've done for him, she reflected, you'd think he could at least clean up after himself. But no; gratitude was too much to expect. All he thought about was that newspaper. And lately, since old Barney had been shoving off so many of the editorials on him, he'd been worse than ever. Work, work, work; even at home he worked nights. How any man could think he was getting anything out of life that way was more than she could see. But he was getting ahead, no doubt about that. With my help, she thought complacently; with the help of the little woman here. Oh, never a word of appreciation for the silent partner, never a sign. But she knew how much he owed to her.

Sighing, she lighted the gas under the coffee and started the toast. She filled a bowl with dry cereal and sliced two bananas over the crisp tan heap. There wasn't enough cream in the

pitcher, so she took some off the top of the milk. But before sitting
down she went over to the sink, got the bottle of reducing pills
off the window sill there, and took her customary dose. So far they
hadn't made any difference; she didn't know, she wasn't too hope-
ful about them; they gave her a kind of stomach-ache sometimes.
There was a new kind of tablet called "Slimma" that Dolores
had told her about; she was going to get some of those.

She had just lighted her after-breakfast cigarette when Chickie
yapped sharply in the front hall. "Qui-*yet!*" shouted Idella May.
It was probably the mailman. When he rattled the mailbox the
damn-fool dog always went crazy. She got up, feeling that she
had eaten too much again, and stalked through the house to the
front door. There were a lot of bills in the box, and two of her
magazines. She came back in again and went into the kitchen.

The doorbell rang. Chickie barked frantically. Idella May
jumped up, peeked expertly through a slit of doorway, and saw
a young man on the porch. She ran to the little downstairs bath-
room. Wildly she brushed her hair before the mirror. She patted
her cheeks with a brown powder puff. She smeared the orange
lipstick on with a swift and careless flourish. She shook toilet
water onto her shoulders beneath the housecoat. All the time the
dog kept barking, and the doorbell rang twice more. She got
there just in time. The young man with the black satchel was
going down the steps. He turned quickly when she called him.
He was very young, with a pink face and small, dull eyes; he wore
a hairy gray tweed suit. Behind him the morning was green in
cool sunlight. The tulips, just ready to break into bloom, stood
tall and pointed in the border row along the damp sidewalk.

"Good morning, my name is Petersen, I represent the Kilroy
Publishing Company," said the young man. "May I take up two
minutes of your valuable time?"

He was so precise in speaking his variation of the old lines
which Idella May had been hearing, again and again, for years and
years, so precise and earnest and smiling, that she felt amused.
"Just two minutes?" she asked, cocking her head and blinking at
him. "Well, that sounds reasonable." She opened the door wide,
then stood there so that he had to crowd past very close to her;
it delighted her to see his embarrassment and the obvious way
he braved it out.

"I have here," he said, setting his satchel on a chair and opening it, "a beautiful six-page map of the United States, showing
all principal cities and towns, rivers, lakes, highways, railroad
lines, and points of historical interest—"

"Wait till I turn the radio down," said Idella May.

"—with full notes on leading industries and attractions of various sections, all printed in expensive four-color process as a guide for tourists, or an easy-instruction course for the young. Do you have any children, madam?"

"No," said Idella May. She loved every hackneyed old word he spoke; she liked his boyish looks; his serious manner positively tickled her. For the next half hour she played with him, asking solemn questions with innocent eyes, pretending to be surprised that the map came free with the purchase of Kilroy's *Universal Compendium*, in eight volumes, plus loose-leaf supplements for the three years following date of purchase. "How can you ever afford to be so generous?" she cried. "'Ah, they're lovely books! Is that real leather?"

"I am frequently asked that question, madam, and I always give the same answer. This is what we call a warranted simulated-leather binding."

At last she wore him out of answers. He didn't seem to know quite what to do, now that he had nothing left to say. Sitting back on the davenport, completely relaxed, gratified, her legs crossed, her hands in her lap, she noted the perspiration on his forehead and knew that she had won. "You're tired!" she cried pitifully. "Why don't you sit down for a minute and rest?"

His look of alarm made her angry. She leaned forward. "Of course I've probably just been wasting your time," she said. "I want the books, God knows, but I could never buy them. You don't know my husband!"

The young man, hastily packing his satchel, looked up at her and then looked quickly away.

"I love books," said Idella May. "I love music, all the finer things, you know. But my husband—you just let him catch you trying to sell me those things you got there! Why, he'd beat us both to a pulp!" She stood up as the salesman stumbled awkwardly toward the door.

He was already on the porch. "Thank you very much!" he cried as he ran down the steps.

Going back to the kitchen for another cup of coffee, she felt the release and glow that come of a happy diversion. This was the way poor Mother used to drink coffee, she thought, in the middle of the morning. She looked at the clock: ten forty-eight. That guy had really stayed. She whistled for Chickie, but the dog didn't come. Peeved, thought Idella May; I have to be nicer to Chickie. Poor Mother, she thought, sipping bitter black coffee, her heart was always in the right place; she talked too much and she stuck her nose in everybody's business, but she was a wonderful person.

She had a heart of gold, thought Idella May; we're all going to miss her.

She got up, intending to phone Alice; there was no use postponing things like this, just because they were difficult. Settle it once and for all, she thought. But as she sat down beside the telephone it rang. Coincidences of this kind always pleased her: imagine, somebody calling her, thinking of her, just at this minute when she was right here, planning to call—"Hillo," she said, crisply like a movie actress.

It was Dolores. "Hey, Idell, I got to go to the dentist at half-past eleven. Now I don't know how you'll feel about going out today, right after the funeral. But"—the voice grew lush—"maybe it would be good for you, honey. Would you want to meet me at the Innovation for lunch and then we'll go to the Orpheum?"

"All right," said Idella May somewhat languidly. "I suppose it would help me. Matter of fact, I was just going to call you, Dolly. I was right here at the phone."

"Well, listen, I'll see you at the Innovation, one of those back booths, about twelve-fifteen or so. I have to run now!"

"Run along!" said Idella May. She decided not to call Alice until later, maybe late this afternoon. Sitting there at the telephone, she thought of that salesman—no, not that one, he was too young; but of another one, imagined to suit, older, more experienced, dark, lean, tall, something like the guy who had come during the winter to sell stockings; he was a pistol, that one. She sat there dreaming of a dark lean salesman who strode in and kissed her as she struggled, a masterful intruder. "No!" she muttered, sitting beside the telephone. "No, no! Oh, you mustn't!" Her face was desperate yet joyous. Nothing she could ever say or do would be enough to stop him. "Don't fight against fate!" he told her. "I knew when I stepped through that door that this had to be!" Weak, unable to resist, she breathed her agreement: "I too, Ralph! I knew!" But when he walked out of the house he would be gone forever. She clutched at him wildly. "Ah, Ralph, don't leave me now that you have found me!" But he broke away, dark and heedless; and alone, forevermore she lived with only her memories. Becoming aware of the telephone at which she had been gazing, she sighed deeply. "Chick-ee!" she called in a sweet voice. "Hyuh, hyuh, hyuh, Chickie!"

The little dog came wriggling to her as she crossed the living room. "'At's a little Chickie!" she crooned. "Hyuh, Chickie," she turned up the radio, and when Ma Carter came on announcing the household hints she knew she hadn't missed Miriam Faces Life, which came on immediately afterward. She sat in the big blue chair and patted her knees until Chickie jumped into her lap. The things I've had happen, she thought fondly; the life I've lived. Cuddling the dog, she waited for Miriam, and considered what she would wear downtown this noon.

She wore the green suit. It was bright as a pool table, and so tight on her that with the gold buttons buttoned she couldn't draw a deep breath, and from waist down almost to knees the cloth of the skirt was simply taut. (Buying it two months before, she had insisted, with absoulte truthfulness, that this was the size she had always worn, and she had been indignant at the sales-girl's skepticism.) She did her face over again, wiping off the orange lipstick; the dark shade, the raspberry, was better with green. When she had finished making up she gazed with approval at the thick, moist wine-colored mouth she had given herself. She picked off a few loose hairs which clung to her sleeves. Not bad, she thought, surveying her bright, pneumatic image in the full-length mirror; I've seen worse. She dabbed perfume on her hand-kerchief and behind her ears.

Outside there were small pink worms crawling on the still damp sidewalk. The wind was fresh and sweet. Oh, I love the spring, she thought. Such a sudden bursting urgency filled her that she longed for eloquent, poetic words to express it; really, I ought to keep a diary, she thought. Deep down in her memory there lurked a connection which she could not quite place: this day and some other day just like it in the past. She didn't know when, and it was curiously tantalizing not to know, but sometime before she had experienced this same irrepressible response. Ac-tually, she felt about sixteen years old. There were a million things she had to do, right now, this minute, and they were all terribly important. As she hurried down the sidewalk to the bus corner she wished she would meet somebody; she wanted to talk; she wanted to let loose the beautiful springtime expectancy within her. Across the street in the Parkers' yard the lilacs tossed deli-cately in the breeze. They too were connected: lavender sprays against the cool bright sky. She felt all at once the strange dream-like certainty that this instant was merely the repetition of an earlier, younger existence: all this had happened before; she had already known this seasonal provocation, this compulsive chal-lenge of spring; these dim stirrings were at once new and ancient. When she was just a child, she remembered fondly, she had thought on bright, balmy, glinting days like this, with the wet spots on the sidewalk shining, that it must have rained worms the night before. Gruesome, she decided now, stepping carefully across a tangled pink cluster of the nasty little things. Why did they come out like this? Because it was warm? But did they know? And where did they ever come from? Ah, Nature was really wonderful. She inhaled deeply. That smell, she thought. Honestly, such absolutely refreshing air. She knew that she had to do something.

The restlessness was still on her when she hurried in at half-past twelve to join Dolores at the Innovation.

"Well, hi, there!" cried Dolores, stretching out one lean arm and undulating it until her bracelets clanked. "I was wondering when you'd get here!" Her long, thin, homely face twitched in a welcoming smile. "Sit down!" she urged as Idella May stood there beside the booth staring darkly into the wall mirror.

"Wait!" Idella May's voice was a hoarse whisper; her breath came heavily, almost painfully; she kept staring at her reflection until she saw the heads in the next booth turning to her.

"What's happened?" screeched Dolores. Her whole body writhed; she began to breathe hard herself; as she leaned forward an elaborate festoonery of beads swung from her throat and rattled on the table top. "Idell! What is it?"

Idella May lurched into the seat. "Tell you in a minute," she muttered, covering her face with her hands. Despite the fact that for several months Dolores had been her closest girl friend, Idella May still felt a kind of tolerant contempt for the other woman: she was so gushy and nervous: she heaped herself over with all that cheap jewelry; she wriggled all the time; and though she was absolutely, admittedly, man-crazy, she never had a date. Honestly, if it wasn't for the devotion that Dolores obviously had for her, Idella May wouldn't have wasted too much time on this friendship. As it was, she at least had the satisfaction of feeling that she was a good influence. Now, looking up at Dolores, she said slowly: "How do I look? Do I look all right?"

"Oh, you look so flushed, Idell! Have you had your blood pressure checked since you started getting stout?"

That was the kind of thing you had to put up with. The disgust Idella May felt was something old and familiar: women never gave the right answers. In a single disapproval she swept together all the women she had ever known intimately—Jane Anderson and Bunny and that dirty little no-good Beverly—God, she thought, even my own mother—and now Dolly. None of them ever said the right things. She would have given a lot for a man at that moment across the table. Still, valiant against unappreciative stupidity, she did her best. "When I talked to you on the phone, Dolly," she said, speaking very distinctly, "did I sound funny or anything? Queer?"

"Uh-uh!" The tendons on Dolores's neck stood out long and

stringy as she swung her head; her mouth was wide open, and she snapped it shut like a frog's mouth. "Honey, did something happen? Tell me!"

"It's a wonder," said Idella May, "that I didn't go into hysterics right over the phone!" She nodded meaningfully; then in a slightly louder voice she said: "After what happened to me this morning, honey, I tell you it's a wonder I'm here right now!"

Dolores's face was faintly mottled; her beautiful big eyes were wild. "Honey," she said in a squeaking little voice, "for God's sake don't act this way! Tell Dolly! Whatever it is, it's better if you talk!"

"I don't want to talk about it," declared Idella May. "Why, I can't even bear to think about it! It was one of those book salesmen. You know how I am about books, Dolly. I read all the time! Well, this fella rings the doorbell, I'm just having breakfast, all I got on is my little house coat, see?"

Gasping, Dolores leaned forward; her beads rang against the glass ash tray.

"So I think it's Mrs. Turnbull from across the street; she comes over in the morning that way sometimes to use the phone, see? I run right out just the way I am to the front door. Oh God, if I'd only looked!" She threw an impassioned glance at the ceiling. "So there's this fella standing there, a big tall guy with one of those little mustaches, you know, and the whitest teeth. Oh, I'll say that for him, he was handsome! He didn't say a word when he saw me, he was just going to say good morning or something and then he saw me that way, I'd just got up practically, and he sort of laughed to himself—you know, he had those eyes that crinkle at the corners—and he stuck his foot in the door. I knew —something sort of told me—what he had on his mind. I was trying to close the door, but he had his foot there and he just walked right in, I couldn't stop him!"

"Well!" said Dolores. She sat back and viewed Idella May with a faint affectionate wonder. "More things like that happen to you!"

"Are you trying to suggest," said Idella May, "that you don't believe—"

"Ah, Idell, you know better than that!"

For a moment Idella May hesitated, gazing with squinted eyes at her friend. "I don't know—" she began; but then the waitress came, bringing water, and Dolores ordered the salad plate and Idella May the seventy-five-cent luncheon with creamed beef, and after the waitress left there was a moment of intense silence.

"Well, what did he do when he got in?" demanded Dolores. "You left off at the best part!"

Idella May looked coldly at a red-haired girl sitting alone at one of the tables. "I can't tell you about the rest," she said. She cleared her throat, took a sip of water, leaving a wine-red crescent of lipstick on the glass.

"Ah, Idell!" Dolores made her voice coaxing and penitent.

Idella May carefully ignored her. Keeping her glance fixed on the tables, she let a small smile, reminiscent and aggrieved, work on her lips.

"Now don't be this way, Idell!" All of Dolores's jewelry made noises at once.

"I'm not being any way!" Opening her purse, Idella May studied her face in the mirror there; she sucked in her cheeks; after a moment she took cigarettes out of her purse. "Smoke?" she asked loftily.

"Tell me what happened!"

Idella May blew smoke out her nostrils; that always made her feel disdainful and superior. "You wouldn't be interested," she said. The irony of the remark secretly pleased her; because if there was one thing you could count on Dolly to be interested in, it was men, all sorts and all kinds. Let her wriggle now. Let her beg. "Besides," she went on wearily, "I'm really too upset to talk. The funeral yesterday and then today—this!" She glanced at Dolores, to see how things were going. "Oh, I want to thank you for sending Mother those flowers," she said. "You'll probably get a card about them from my sister—she's handling all that. But they were very pretty." Her sigh was languidly mournful. "She had the most beautiful flowers you ever saw! Honestly, even the undertaker said he'd never seen anything like it!"

Dolores was leaning forward; her large eyes glowed moist and fervid, like an animal's eyes. "Idell," she whispered, "did he—you know—try anything?"

All right, give her what she's looking for, thought Idella May. She spoke slowly, almost contemptuously: "Well, I wouldn't be practically a nervous wreck like this if he just tried selling me books!"

"Tell Dolly!"

Just then the waitress came with her loaded tray, and while she set dishes before them Dolores twitched and Idella May gloated.

"Now I don't want this to get around," said Idella May distinctly, as soon as the waitress had gone. "After all, I got my reputation in this town! But what happened, when he rushed in on me that way, I ran. I know how men like that are! Why, I've had experiences I wouldn't repeat to a living soul! I was scared to death. But right there before I could even get out of the hall he caught me." Grimacing, she fingered her sides. "My ribs are still sore!" she announced happily. "What he said, he said, 'Don't fight against fate!' he said. 'The minute I saw you,' he said, 'I knew we belonged to one another!' "

"Yikes!" cried Dolores.

"I don't know why it is things like this always happen to me," declared Idella May, setting in on the creamed beef. "Honestly, the minute that guy was in the house I knew he was Trouble, you know what I mean? He wasn't trying to sell any of his Kilroy's *Universal Compendium* to me, no ma'am!"

"*Universal Compendium?*" Dolores's mouth gaped, and her long arms flew out in odd angles over her salad plate. "Why, there was a man at my mother's house yesterday selling some kind of *Compendium!* She showed me one of the leaflets he left!" Her breath came quick. "It might have been the same one!" she cried.

"Could be," said Idella May. "Big tall dark fella. I bet he played football wherever he went to college. Of course a woman the age of your mother wouldn't have to worry," she added. "But me, I was scared stiff! If the phone didn't happen to ring just then—"

"Did that stop him? When I called?" Dolores was plainly disappointed.

"No, no, when you called he was gone. This was just a wrong number, but it sort of surprised him. You know, we were right there beside the phone when it rang. He let me answer. Then Mrs. Turnbull came."

"Right then? While he was there? What'd he do?"

Idella May thoughtfully buttered a roll. "What I was going to do," she said after almost ponderous deliberation, "was make out it was somebody I knew on the phone, and they were coming right over, see? That would have been a good way to handle him." She broke away from this attractive little afterthought with reluctance; for some reason it especially pleased her; she began to see herself as cunning, resourceful; no book salesman could put anything over on her. "But of course when Mrs. Turnbull came I didn't have to work that telephone trick. I tell you, I was never so glad to see anybody in my life as I was to see Gladys Turnbull this morning!"

"The fella just went away then, I suppose?" said Dolores sadly.

"He was gone before I could say a word! He said, real quick, 'Thank you very much for your time, Mrs. Logan. I'll put your name on the list and I'll call back again in the near future.' Then he was out the door."

"We-ell! He'll call back in the near future, eh?"

"That's what I'm afraid of," said Idella May. "That's what really worries me. I haven't seen the last of that one, let me tell you!" She shook her head gloomily. "I don't know whether I want ice cream or pie," she said.

Dolores was strangely silent for the rest of the meal. Envy, thought Idella May. Well, that was the way it should be. But then as they walked down Main Street toward the Orpheum, Dolores said, all of a sudden and while they were talking of something else: "You certainly didn't seem very excited when I phoned you!"

"I was petrified," said Idella May.

"Was Mrs. Turnbull surprised?"

Idella May saw the trap; she was so delighted at her own shrewdness that she didn't resent Dolores's attempt until later. "Oh," she said, "I didn't *tell* her. I was at the phone when she came in, you know, and all there was was a book salesman. She couldn't see that anything was wrong. And the guy was gone so fast she probably didn't even get a good look at him." Now, she thought, go see what you can find out from Gladys Turnbull. Still, she felt uneasiness stir in her; the salesman shouldn't have been seen by anybody—

Dolores's face was angry, jealous, ugly; she craned her head at Idella May and somehow managed a hard little laugh. "I should think she'd be able to tell just from the way you looked, if you were so excited and all!"

"I keep my emotions under control," said Idella May. Then— this was the clincher, and it came to her just in time—she went on casually: "Besides, I wouldn't let on to Mrs. Turnbull for anything in the world. You know her heart is so bad a shock like that might kill her. Why, if anybody was even to suggest to her that a man like that was loose in our neighborhood, she'd probably collapse."

That did it, at least for the duration of the double feature. But when they got out of the movie at half-past four Dolores made one last try.

"Idell, he didn't show you books at all, did he?"

"No, ma'am! We never got around to that!"

Dolores stretched her neck triumphantly. "Then, honey, how in the world did you know he was selling this *Universal Compendium?*"

Idella May's laugh went sweetly, lightly, happily down scale.

"Why, he left one of those leaflets, honey. Like at your mother's."

She carried victory home with her, exulting all the way. She thought, It'll be a long time before our little Dolly talks up to me again. As a matter of fact, she thought, I've had about enough of her anyhow. What I got to get is a nice new girl friend, somebody I can really confide in.

The late afternoon was lovely and mild. The sky in the west moved in rosy wreaths as she watched it. Yet the air had the stillness, the clarity, that sometimes precedes a spring storm. Looking upward, however, Idella May estimated that tomorrow would be fair. She still had her lifelong faith that by thinking a thing hard enough, persistently enough, you could make it so. Tomorrow, she determined, would be just the kind of day today was; there would, in fact, be an interminable succession of just such days, they would last forever and ever.

When she opened the front door Chickie came bouncing and whining at her legs. She cooed, stooping to pet the little dog. Virginia, a squat, bowlegged, high-school girl who came in afternoons and Saturdays, stuck her head out the kitchen door. "Mr. Logan phoned he forgot to tell you there's a banquet tonight he has to go to or something. The North Side Business Men or something. He won't be home till late."

"Okay," said Idella May. She opened the buttons of her suit coat, sighed, stepped out of her slippers, gathered Chickie in her arms, and went in to turn on the radio. There was just time for one of her programs before all those awful late-afternoon thrillers for children came on. But as she settled herself in the big chair the telephone rang. "Down, Chickie," she ordered. Then, waiting for Virginia to answer, she took off her hat. "Hello," said Virginia; then she bawled: "It's for you, Mrs. Logan."

"Listen," whispered Idella May as she padded on stocking feet to the phone. "How many times have I told you to answer, 'The Logan residence'?" Honestly, the girl was stupid; she was dumpy; she was a fool. Much as Idella May despised that little devil Beverly Budd for running off to Pittsburgh with that married barber, there were times when she would have welcomed Bev back; she hadn't had a good girl since.

"Ooh, I forgot again!" cried Virginia, clapping one hand over her mouth.

"Well, damn it, stop forgetting!" How could you be companionable with a girl like that? Idella May picked up the phone; her voice went sweet. "Hillo. . . ."

It was Alice; she was sobbing. "Oh, Idell, you know what Dad's going to do? He's going to sell the furniture and go out and live with Art! He said he wouldn't be bothered living with either one of us!"

"*What?*"

"That's what he said! He was over here this afternoon. I would of phoned you before, Idell, but the kids were coming home from school and all. Oh, I feel just terrible!"

"Well, if that's the way he wants it, let him go!"

"But the way he said it, Idell! You didn't hear him! He said he didn't want anything to do with either of us!"

"Huh!" Idella May felt herself growing icy. "What's he ever done for us?" she demanded. "He's sure got reason to talk, he has! Well, if he wants to go out with Art, all right, let him! I certainly don't want him here if he feels that way about his own flesh and blood!"

There were some queer noises at the other end of the phone. Then Alice cried hastily: "I'll have to phone you back! Little Elizabeth just came in with a bloody nose!"

Idella May waited for an instant; the phone went dead. She banged it down on the stand. Well, she thought, that solves one problem. But she was mad. She stamped across the floor; the exertion burst open the top snap of her skirt. Chickie was waiting for her in the big chair. On the radio a man's voice was passionately declaiming; then, "You cannot do this to me, John!" cried a woman's voice, rich and throaty. Idella May sat down beside Chickie, wormed herself over, got the little dog on her lap. She didn't see why what her father did should affect her so deeply. Let him live his own life. Let him go to the devil. But still she felt deserted. She cuddled the dog close; my best friend, she thought. Faithful Chickie would never let her down. "Chickie," she said fondly. The little dog looked up at her and yawned. Idella May leaned back in the chair. Sitting there, big and unmoving, listening to plaintive voices murmuring on the radio, she stared with a frozen malevolence at the wall ahead; then slowly she raised one hand to her mouth and bit—delicately yet eagerly—at a fingertip.

Part Seven

PLANS AND DISPOSITIONS

Or

Odds and Ends of Politics and History

FOREWORD *

By John F. Kennedy

There is little that is more important for an American citizen to know than the history and traditions of his country. Without such knowledge, he stands uncertain and defenseless before the world, knowing neither where he has come from nor where he is going. With such knowledge, he is no longer alone but draws a strength far greater than his own from the cumulative experience of the past and a cumulative vision of the future.

Knowledge of our history is, first of all, a pleasure for its own sake. The American past is a record of stirring achievement in the face of stubborn difficulty. It is a record filled with figures larger than life, with high drama and hard decision, with valor and with tragedy, with incidents both poignant and picturesque, and with the excitement and hope involved in the conquest of a wilderness and the settlement of a continent. For the true historian—and for the true student of history—history is an end in itself. It fulfills a deep human need for understanding, and the satisfaction it provides requires no further justification.

Yet, though no further justification is required for the study of history, it would not be correct to say that history serves no further use than the satisfaction of the historian. History, after all, is the memory of a nation. Just as memory enables the individual to learn, to choose goals and stick to them, to avoid making the same mistake twice—in short, to grow—so history is the means by which a nation establishes its sense of identity and purpose. The future arises out of the past, and a country's history is a statement of the values and hopes which, having forged what has gone before, will now forecast what is to come.

As a means of knowledge, history becomes a means of judgment. It offers an understanding of both the variety and unity of a nation whose credo is E Pluribus Unum—out of many, one. It reminds us of the diverse abundance of our people, coming from all races and all parts of the world, of our fields and mountain ranges, deserts and great rivers, our green farmlands and the thousand voices of our cities. No revolution in communication or transportation can destroy the fact that this continent is, as Walt Whitman said, "a nation of nations." Yet it also reminds us that,

* From the Foreword to The American Heritage New Illustrated History of the United States, published by the Dell Publishing Company, 1963.

in spite of the diversity of ethnic origin, of geographic locale, of occupation, of social status, of religious creed, of political commitment, Americans are united by an ancient and encompassing faith in progress, justice, and freedom.

Our history thus tests our policy: Our past judges our present. Of all the disciplines, the study of the folly and achievements of man is best calculated to foster the critical sense of what is permanent and meaningful amid the mass of superficial and transient questions which make up the day-to-day clamor. The history of our nation tells us that every action taken *against* the freedoms of conscience and expression, *against* equality before the law and equality of opportunity, *against* the ordinary men and women of the country is an action taken *against* the American tradition. And it tells us that every action taken *for* a larger freedom and a more equal and spacious society is one more step toward the realization of what Herbert Croly once called "the promise of American life."

A knowledge of history is more than a means of judgment: It is also a means of sympathy—a means of relating our own experience with the experience of other peoples and lands struggling for national fulfillment. We may sometimes forget, for example, that the United States began as an underdeveloped nation which seized its independence by carrying out a successful revolution against a colonial empire. We may forget that, in the first years of the new republic, George Washington laid down the principle of no "permanent alliances" and enjoined the United States to a course of neutralism in the face of the great-power conflicts then dividing the civilized world. We may forget that, in the first stages of our economic development, our national growth was stimulated to a considerable degree by "foreign aid"—that is, investment from abroad—and by public investment and direction on the part of our state and local as well as our national government. We may forget that our own process of economic change was often accompanied by the issue of wildcat paper money, by the repudiation of bonds, by disorder, fraud, and violence. If we recall the facts of our own past, we may better understand the problems and predicaments of contemporary "new nations" laboring for national development in circumstances far less favorable than our own—and we will, in consequence, become less liable to the national self-righteousness which is both unworthy of our own traditions and a bane of international relations.

A knowledge of history is, in addition, a means of strength. "In times of change and danger," John Dos Passos wrote just before World War II, "when there is a quicksand of fear under men's reasoning, a sense of continuity with generations gone before can stretch like a life line across the scary present." Dos Passos called his book *The Ground We Stand On*—and the title concisely defines the role of the past in preparing us for the crisis of the present and the challenge of the future. When Americans fight for individual liberty, they have Thomas Jefferson and James Madison beside them; when they strive for social justice, they strive alongside Andrew Jackson and Franklin Roosevelt; when they work for peace and a world community, they work with Woodrow Wilson; when they fight and die in wars to make men free, they fight and die with Abraham Lincoln. Historic continuity with the past, as Justice Oliver Wendell Holmes said, "is not a duty; it is only a necessity."

A knowledge of history is, above all, a means of responsibility— of responsibility to the past and of responsibility to the future . . . of responsibility to those who came before us and struggled and sacrificed to pass on to us our precious inheritance of freedom . . . and of responsibility to those who will come after us and to whom we must pass on that inheritance with what new strength and substance it is within our power to add. "Fellow citizens," Abraham Lincoln said, "we cannot escape history. . . . The fiery trial through which we pass will light us down, in honor or dishonor, to the latest generation." American history is not something dead and over. It is always alive, always growing, always unfinished— and every American today has his own contribution to make to the great fabric of tradition and hope which binds all Americans, dead and living and yet to be born, in a common faith and a common destiny.

Notebook Assignment for Class Discussion

1. President Kennedy's style is marked by rhetorical balance and contrast. Select several examples to illustrate this style, such as, "having forged what has gone before, will now forecast what is to come."

2. The style is also closely knit, each topic being linked to, in fact growing out of, the one before. Fill in the following formula with direct quotations:

> History is A, but it is also more; it is B
> But it is even more than B; it is C
> And yet it is more than C; it is also D
> And finally it is E

3. The style is also epigrammatic. Select several succinct and quotable statements, such as, "History . . . is the memory of a nation."
4. Cardinal Newman says that knowledge is its own reward, Kennedy that history is an end in itself. Exactly what do these two eminent writers mean?
5. What strength does quotation lend to a writer's own assertions? Does it lie in the keen perception of the writer who is quoted, in his gift of phrase, or principally in his name, or reputation? Is Kennedy's quotation from Dos Passos appropriate? Does it fortify his argument? Or is it merely topical and convenient? Is it possibly pedantic?
6. Are all the terms of Dos Passos's metaphor consistent, unified? Is the picture, or image, eloquent, or striking?
7. Explain the association of Jefferson and Madison with the fight for individual liberty; Jackson and Franklin Roosevelt with social justice; Wilson with world peace; and Lincoln with men's freedom.
8. Try to explain how Kennedy himself represented all of the principles and the men whom he selected to exemplify them, including Lincoln (even to the circumstances of his death).

Related Exercises

1. Do most people think of history only in terms of political and military movements? What does the word *history* mean? What other kinds of history are there, and what is their relative importance?
2. Do most of our national holidays celebrate political and military persons and events, or is there a good sense of balanced values evident?
3. Do you think that politicians are the most important and capable people on all levels: local, state, national, and international?
4. Can you see in President Kennedy's words any attempt to justify his own national policies by a reference to history? If so, exactly where?
5. Would you consider this foreword to be partially propagandistic, or not at all? What is the meaning of *propaganda?* Does it have only a bad connotation, or may it be also devoted to the dissemination of truth?
6. What *is* truth? Is truth absolute or relative? Give some examples of what you would consider to be true and false

propaganda. Is commercial advertising a form of propaganda? Is it *good*, and if so, in what sense of the word *good?* Good for whom and for what?

7. When Kennedy refers to "circumstances far less favorable than our own," does he mean our *present* national development or our *original* attempt at the time of the Revolutionary War? If he means the former, is the comparison to the struggle of new nations today toward national identification, freedom, and development a fair one? If he means the latter, is it fair to imply that our colonists fought against less favorable odds, or what? Is his statement an example of ambiguity or do our two questions imply a dilemma?

8. When he refers to the "self-righteousness which is . . . unworthy," and so on, do you think he intends a political slur against his opposition? What is the value of opposition in politics?

9. Is it good for a country to have a multi-party system of politics? Why?

10. Write a paper on the advantages and disadvantages of having a single newspaper in an average community.

OF THE PRESENT ABILITY OF AMERICA WITH SOME MISCELLANEOUS REFLECTIONS *

By Thomas Paine

I have never met with a man, either in England or America, who hath not confessed his opinion that a separation between the countries would take place one time or other: and there is no instance, in which we have shown less judgment, than in endeavoring to describe what we call the ripeness or fitness of the continent for independence.

As all men allow the measure, and vary only in their opinion of the time, let us, in order to remove mistakes, take a general survey of things, and endeavor, if possible, to find out the *very*

* From *Common Sense*, by Thomas Paine, Philadelphia, February 14, 1776.

time. But we need not go far, the inquiry ceases at once, for the *time hath found us*. The general concurrence, the glorious union of all things proves the fact.

It is not in numbers, but in unity, that our great strength lies; yet our present numbers are sufficient to repel the force of all the world. The continent hath, at this time, the largest body of armed and disciplined men of any power under heaven: and is just arrived at that pitch of strength, in which no single colony is able to support itself, and the whole when united can accomplish the matter, and either more or less than this might be fatal in its effects. Our land force is already sufficient, and as to naval affairs, we cannot be insensible that Britain would never suffer an American man-of-war to be built while the continent remained in her hands. Wherefore, we should be no forwarder an hundred years hence in that branch than we are now; but the truth is, we should be less so, because the timber of the country is every day diminishing, and that which will remain at last will be far off or difficult to procure.

Were the continent crowded with inhabitants, her sufferings under the present circumstances would be intolerable. The more seaport towns we had, the more should we have both to defend and to lose. Our present numbers are so happily proportioned to our wants, that no man need be idle. The diminution of trade affords an army, and the necessities of an army create a new trade. Debts we have none: and whatever we may contract on this account will serve as a glorious memento of our virtue.

Can we but leave posterity with a settled form of government, an independent constitution of its own, the purchase at any price will be cheap. But to expend millions for the sake of getting a few vile acts repealed, and routing the present Ministry only, is unworthy the charge, and is using posterity, with the utmost cruelty; because it is leaving them the great work to do, and a debt upon their backs from which they derive no advantage. Such a thought is unworthy a man of honor, and is the true characteristic of a narrow heart and a peddling politician.

The debt we may contract doth not deserve our regard, if the work be but accomplished. No nation ought to be without a debt. A national debt is a national bond; and when it bears no interest, is in no case a grievance.

Britain is oppressed with a debt of upwards of one hundred and forty millions sterling, for which she pays upwards of four millions interest. And as a compensation for her debt, she has a large navy; America is without a debt, and without a navy; yet for the twentieth part of the English national debt, could have a navy as large again. The navy of England is not worth, at this time, more than three millions and a half sterling.

The following calculations are given as a proof that the above estimation of the navy is a just one. (See Entick's "Naval History," Intro. page 56.)

The charge of building a ship of each rate, and furnishing her with masts, yards, sails, and rigging, together with a proportion of eight months' boatswain's and carpenter's sea-stores, as calculated by Mr. Burchett, Secretary to the Navy, is as follows:

For a ship of 100 guns	£35,553
90	29,886
80	23,638
70	17,785
60	14,197
50	10,606
40	7,758
30	5,846
20	3,710

And from hence it is easy to sum up the value, or cost rather, of the whole British navy, which in the year 1757, when it was at its greatest glory, consisted of the following ships and guns:

Ships	Guns	Cost of one	Cost of all
6	100	£35,553	£213,318
12	90	29,886	358,632
12	80	23,638	283,656
43	70	17,785	764,755
35	60	14,197	496,895
40	50	10,606	424,240
45	40	7,758	344,110
58	20	3,710	215,180
85 Sloops, bombs, and fire-ships, one with another		2,000	170,000
		Cost	3,270,786
		Remains for guns	229,214
			£3,500,000

No country on the globe is so happily situated, or so internally capable of raising a fleet as America. Tar, timber, iron, and cordage are her natural produce. We need go abroad for nothing. Whereas the Dutch, who make large profits by hiring out their ships of war to the Spaniards and Portuguese, are obliged to import most of the materials they use. We ought to view the building a fleet as an article of commerce, it being the natural manufacture of this country. It is the best money we can lay out. A navy when finished is worth more than it cost: and is that nice point in national policy, in which commerce and protection are united. Let us build; if we want them not, we can sell; and by that means replace our paper currency with ready gold and silver.

In point of manning a fleet, people in general run into great errors; it is not necessary that one-fourth part should be sailors. The privateer *Terrible*, Captain Death, stood the hottest engagement of any ship, last war, yet had not twenty sailors on board, though her complement of men was upwards of two hundred.

A few able and social sailors will soon instruct a sufficient number of active landsmen in the common work of a ship. Wherefore, we never can be more capable to begin on maritime matters than now, while our timber is standing, our fisheries blocked up, and our sailors and shipwrights out of employ. Men-of-war, of seventy and eighty guns, were built forty years ago in New England, and why not the same now?

Ship building is America's greatest pride, and in which she will, in time, excel the whole world. The great empires of the East are mostly inland, and consequently excluded from the possibility of rivaling her. Africa is in a state of barbarism; and no power in Europe hath either such an extent of coast, or such an internal supply of materials. Where nature hath given the one, she hath withheld the other; to America only hath she been liberal of both. The vast empire of Russia is almost shut out from the sea; wherefore, her boundless forests, her tar, iron, and cordage are only articles of commerce.

In point of safety, ought we to be without a fleet? We are not the little people now which we were sixty years ago; at that time we might have trusted our property in the streets, or fields rather; and slept securely without locks or bolts to our doors or windows. The case is now altered, and our methods of defense ought to improve with our increase of property.

A common pirate, twelve months ago, might have come up the Delaware, and laid the city of Philadelphia under instant contribution for what sum he pleased; and the same might have happened to other places. Nay, any daring fellow, in a brig of fourteen or sixteen guns, might have robbed the whole continent, and carried off half a million of money. These are circumstances which demand our attention, and point out the necessity of naval protection.

Some, perhaps, will say, that after we have made it up with

Britain, she will protect us. Can they be so unwise as to mean, that she will keep a navy in our harbors for that purpose? Common sense will tell us that the power which hath endeavored to subdue us, is of all others the most improper to defend us. Conquest may be effected under the pretense of friendship; and ourselves, after a long and brave resistance, be at last cheated into slavery. And if her ships are not to be admitted into our harbors, I would ask, how is she to protect us? A navy three or four thousand miles off can be of little use, and on sudden emergencies, none at all. Wherefore, if we must hereafter protect ourselves, why not do it for ourslves? Why do it for another?

The English list of ships of war is long and formidable but not a tenth part of them are at any one time fit for service, numbers of them are not in being; yet their names are pompously continued in the list if only a plank be left of the ship; and not a fifth part of such as are fit for service can be spared on any one station at one time. The East and West Indies, Mediterranean, Africa and other parts of the world, over which Britain extends her claim make large demands upon her navy.

From a mixture of prejudice and inattention, we have contracted a false notion respecting the navy of England, and have talked as if we should have the whole of it to encounter at once, and, for that reason, supposed that we must have one as large; which not being instantly practicable, has been made use of by a set of disguised Tories to discourage our beginning thereon.

Nothing can be further from the truth than this; for if America had only a twentieth part of the naval force of Britain, she would be by far an over-match for her; because, as we neither have nor claim any foreign dominion, our whole force would be employed on our own coast, where we should, in the long run, have two to one the advantage of those who had three or four thousand miles to sail over before they could attack us, and the same distance to return in order to refit and recruit.

And although Britain, by her fleet, hath a check over our trade to Europe, we have as large a one over her trade to the West Indies, which by lying in the neighborhood of the continent is entirely at its mercy.

Some method might be fallen on to keep up a naval force in time of peace, if we should not judge it necessary to support a constant navy. If premiums were to be given to merchants to build and employ in their service, ships mounted with twenty, thirty, forty or fifty guns (the premiums to be in proportion to the loss of bulk to the merchants) fifty or sixty of those ships with a few guard-ships on constant duty, would keep up a sufficient navy, and that without burdening ourselves with the evil so loudly complained of in England, of suffering their fleet in time of peace to lie rotting in the docks.

To unite the sinews of commerce and defense is sound policy; for when our strength and our riches play into each other's hand we need fear no external enemy.

In almost every article of defense we abound. Hemp flourishes even to rankness, so that we need not want cordage. Our iron is superior to that of other countries. Our small arms equal to any in the world. Cannon we can cast at pleasure. Saltpetre and gunpowder we are every day producing. Our knowledge is hourly improving. Resolution is our inherent character, and courage hath not yet forsaken us. Wherefore, what is it that we want? Why is it that we hesitate?

From Britain we can expect nothing but ruin. If she is once admitted to the government of America again, this continent will not be worth living in. Jealousies will be always arising, insurrections will be constantly happening; and who will go forth to quell them? Who will venture his life to reduce his own countrymen to a foreign obedience?

The difference between Pennsylvania and Connecticut, respecting some unlocated lands, shows the insignificance of a British government, and fully proves that nothing but continental authority can regulate continental matters.

Another reason why the present time is preferable to all others, is that the fewer our numbers are, the more land there is yet unoccupied, which, instead of being lavished by the King on his worthless dependents, may be hereafter applied, not only to the discharge of the present debt, but to the constant support of government. No nation under heaven hath such an advantage as this.

The infant state of the colonies, as it is called, so far from being against, is an argument in favor of independence. We are sufficiently numerous, and were we more so we might be less united. It is a matter worthy of observation, that the more a country is peopled, the smaller their armies are. In military numbers, the ancients far exceeded the moderns: and the reason is evident, for trade being the consequence of population, men became too much absorbed thereby to attend to anything else. Commerce diminishes the spirit both of patriotism and military defense. And history sufficiently informs us, that the bravest achievements were always accomplished in the non-age of a nation.

With the increase of commerce England hath lost its spirit.

The city of London, notwithstanding its numbers, submits to continued insults with the patience of a coward. The more men have to lose, the less willing they are to venture. The rich are in general slaves to fear, and submit to courtly power with the trembling duplicity of a spaniel.

Youth is the seed-time of good habits, as well in nations as in individuals. It might be difficult, if not impossible, to form the continent into one government half a century hence. The vast variety of interests, occasioned by an increase of trade and population, would create confusion. Colony would be against colony. Each being able, might scorn each other's assistance; and while the proud and foolish gloried in their little distinctions, the wise would lament that the union had not been formed before.

Wherefore, the *present time* is the *true time* for establishing it. The intimacy which is contracted in infancy, and the friendship which is formed in misfortune, are of all others, the most lasting and unalterable. Our present union is marked with both these characters; we are young, and we have been distressed; but our concord hath withstood our troubles, and fixes a memorable era for posterity to glory in.

The present time, likewise, is that peculiar time which never happens to a nation but once, viz., the time of forming itself into a government. Most nations have let slip the opportunity, and by that means have been compelled to receive laws from their conquerors, instead of making laws for themselves. First, they had a king, and then a form of government; whereas the articles or charter of government, should be formed first, and men delegated to execute them afterwards: but from the errors of other nations, let us learn wisdom, and lay hold of the present opportunity—*to begin government at the right end.*

When William the Conqueror subdued England, he gave them law at the point of the sword; and until we consent that the seat of government in America be legally and authoritatively occupied, we shall be in danger of having it filled by some unfortunate ruffian, who may treat us in the same manner, and then, where will be our freedom? where our property?

As to religion, I hold it to be the indispensable duty of all governments to protect all conscientious professors thereof, and I know of no other business which government hath to do therewith. Let a man throw aside that narrowness of soul, that selfishness of principle, which the niggards of all professions are so unwilling to part with, and he will be at once delivered of his fears on that head. Suspicion is the companion of mean souls, and the bane of all good society.

For myself, I fully and conscientiously believe, that it is the will of the Almighty, that there should be a diversity of religious opinions among us: it affords a larger field for our Christian kindness. Were we all of one way of thinking, our religious dispositions would want matter for probation, and on this liberal principle, I look on the various denominations among us, to be like children of the same family, differing only in what is called their Christian names.

[Earlier] I threw out a few thoughts on the propriety of a continental charter (for I only presume to offer hints, not plans) and in this place I take the liberty of rementioning the subject, by observing, that a charter is to be understood as a bond of solemn obligation, which the whole enters into, to support the right of every separate part, whether of religion, personal freedom, or property. A firm bargain and a right reckoning make long friends.

In a former page I likewise mentioned the necessity of a large and equal representation; and there is no political matter which more deserves our attention. A small number of electors, or a small number of representatives, are equally dangerous. But if the number of the representatives be not only small, but unequal, the danger is increased. As an instance of this, I mention the following: When the Associators' petition was before the House of Assembly of Pennsylvania, twenty-eight members only were present; all of the Bucks County members, being eight, voted against it, and had seven of the Chester members done the same, this whole province had then been governed by two counties only; and this danger it is always exposed to. The unwarrantable stretch, likewise, which that house made in their last sitting, to gain an undue authority over the delegates of that province, ought to warn the people at large how they trust power out of their own hands.

A set of instructions for their delegates were put together, which in point of sense and business would have dishonored a schoolboy, and after being approved of by a *few*, a *very few* without doors, were carried into the house, and there passed *in behalf of the whole colony;* whereas, did the whole colony know with what ill will that house had entered on some necessary public measures, they would not hesitate a moment to think them unworthy of such a trust.

Immediate necessity makes many things convenient, which if continued would grow into oppressions. Expedience and right are different things. When the calamities of America required a consultation, there was no method so ready, or at that time so proper, as to appoint persons from the several houses of assembly for that purpose; and the wisdom with which they have proceeded hath preserved this continent from ruin.

But as it is more than probable that we shall never be without a *Congress,* every well-wisher to good order must own, that the mode for choosing members of that body, deserves consideration. And I put it as a question to those who make a study of mankind, whether *representation and election* is not too great a power for one and the same body of men to possess? Whenever we are planning for posterity, we ought to remember that virtue is not hereditary.

It is from our enemies that we often gain excellent maxims, and are frequently surprised into reason by their mistakes. Mr. Cornwall (one of the lords of the treasury) treated the petition of the New York Assembly with contempt, because *that* house, he said, consisted but of twenty-six members, which trifling number, he argued, could not with decency be put for the whole. We thank him for his involuntary honesty.[1]

To conclude: However strange it may appear to some, or however unwilling they may be to think so, matters not, but many strong and striking reasons may be given, to show that nothing can settle our affairs so expeditiously as an open and determined declaration for independence. Some of which are:

First. It is the custom of nations, when any two are at war, for some other powers, not engaged in the quarrel, to step in as mediators, and bring about the preliminaries of a peace: but while America calls herself the subject of Britain, no power, however well disposed she may be, can offer her mediation. Wherefore, in our present state, we may quarrel on forever.

Secondly. It is unreasonable to suppose that France or Spain will give us any kind of assistance, if we mean only to make use of that assistance for the purpose of repairing the breach, and strengthening the connection between Britain and America; because, those powers would be sufferers by the consequences.

Thirdly. While we profess ourselves the subjects of Britain, we must, in the eyes of foreign nations, be considered as rebels. The precedent is somewhat dangerous to *their peace,* for men to be in arms under the name of subjects; we, on the spot, can solve the paradox: but to unite resistance and subjection, requires an idea too refined for common understanding.

Fourthly. Were a manifesto to be published and dispatched to foreign courts, setting forth the miseries we have endured, and the peaceful methods which we have ineffectually used for redress;

---

[1] Those who fully understand of what great consequence a large and equal representation is to a state, should read Burgh's "Political Disquisitions."

declaring at the same time, that not being able, any longer, to live happily or safely under the cruel disposition of the British Court, we had been driven to the necessity of breaking off all connection with her; at the same time, assuring all such courts of our peaceable dispositions toward them, and of our desire of entering into trade with them.

Such a memorial would produce more good effects to this continent than if a ship were freighted with petitions to Britain.

Under our present denomination of British subjects, we can neither be received nor heard abroad: the custom of all courts is against us, and will be so, until, by an independence, we take rank with other nations.

These proceedings may at first appear strange and difficult; but like all other steps which we have already passed over, will in a little time become familiar and agreeable; and, until an independence is declared, the continent will feel itself like a man who continues putting off some unpleasant business from day to day, yet knows it must be done, hates to set about it, wishes it over, and is continually haunted with the thoughts of its necessity.

Notebook Assignment for Class Discussion

1. Does this essay make "common sense" to you? Explain.
2. Locate several such lines as, "No man need be idle," and "Debts have we none," which suggest modern parallels or contrasts, then briefly explain their application, or lack of it.
3. Note Paine's usage of punctuation. Is the practice today to use more or less punctuation? If you have written a sentence whose meaning is equally clear with or without a comma, should you use the comma? Why, or why not? Pick out several examples in this essay which suggest that overpunctuation slows up the line.
4. What would you have written instead of "Ministry, only, is unworthy the charge (*sic*)," and "Not a tenth part of them (*sic*)"? The occasional sense of strangeness you encounter in reading Paine and other early writers may be due to idioms which change over the years. What are idioms, and is it true that they sometimes change? What other examples of odd idiomatic phrases can you find in "Common Sense"? How would they be written today? Is it good practice to write idiomatically? On all occasions? What does (*sic*) mean?

5. Paine's style is not only clear and forceful, but also epigrammatic. Do epigrams contribute to a writer's clarity and forcefulness? Which of the three qualities of Paine's style is the most important to his purpose? Why?

6. Select several of Paine's many striking epigrams, such as, "The more men have to lose, the less willing they are to venture," and "A firm bargain and a right reckoning make long friends."

7. In the paragraph beginning, "Wherefore, the present time . . ." there appears to be a mistake in the logic of his rhetoric. The phrase, "of all others" should read simply "of all." Why?

8. Is there a contradiction, or not, between "No man need be idle," and "our sailors and shipwrights [are] out of employ"? Explain.

9. Where does Paine consider objections to his argument and answer them? Is this good practice in argumentation? Why? What does it accomplish?

10. To which idea in the paragraph beginning, "Some, perhaps, will say . . ." might the Russian proverb apply, "Who would send out the goat to guard the cabbage patch?"

Related Exercises

1. Had open hostilities between England and America already broken out when Paine published "Common Sense"? If so, what particular events stand out as being historically important?

2. The first edition of this pamphlet was published on January 10, 1776. Another of the most influential pamphlets of the American Revolution was Paine's "The American Crisis," which opens with the famous words, "These are the times that try men's souls: The summer soldier and the sunshine patriot will, in this crisis, shrink from the service of his country; but he that stands it NOW, deserves the love and thanks of man and woman." (1776) Read the rest of "The American Crisis," Washington's "Farewell Address," Franklin's editorial on Zenger in the *Pennsylvania Gazette* (November 10–17, 1737), and other early American documents to which your reading may lead you. Try to understand these documents and all other history you read, not only in their original historical context but also in their relationship to a total human experience, including our own times and the future. There is no

need for you to make a formal report or write an essay on everything you read and think, but your assimiliation and integration (or the lack of them) will be apparent eventually in almost everything you do or say.

3. However, you might prepare a brief report on the life of Tom Paine, and the circumstances attending his writing of "Common Sense" and "The American Crisis."

4. Write an argumentative essay on this question: How is it possible in our country today for an atheist who is unwilling to have any one else's religion foisted upon him, to foist instead his lack of it upon all the others, as he seeks to do in schools, courts, and other state-constituted assemblies?

5. Paine says, "Whenever we are planning for posterity we ought to remember that virtue is not hereditary." What have our recent administrations planned for our own posterity and at whose expense? Do you believe that we have inherited at least some of our founding fathers' honesty and foresightedness? All of it, and more? Or none of it?

6. Comment on Paine's sense of values when he discusses national debts in the early part of the essay.

IN CONGRESS, JULY 4, 1776
THE UNANIMOUS DECLARATION
OF THE THIRTEEN
UNITED STATES OF AMERICA

When, in the course of human events, it becomes necessary for one people to dissolve the political bands which have connected them with another, and to assume, among the powers of the earth, the separate and equal station to which the laws of nature and nature's God entitle them, a decent respect to the opinions of mankind requires that they should declare the causes which impel them to the separation.

We hold these truths to be self-evident, that all men are created equal; that they are endowed by their Creator with certain unalienable rights; that among these are life, liberty, and the pursuit of happiness. That to secure these rights, governments are instituted among men, deriving their just powers from the consent of the governed; that, whenever any form of government becomes destructive of these ends, it is the right of the people to alter or abolish it, and to institute a new government, laying its foundation on such principles, and organizing its powers in such form, as to them shall seem most likely to effect their safety and happiness. Prudence, indeed, will dictate that governments long established should not be changed for light and transient causes; and, accordingly, all experience hath shown, that mankind are more disposed to suffer, while evils are sufferable, than to right themselves by abolishing the forms to which they are accustomed. But when a long train of abuses and usurpations, pursuing invariably the same object, evinces a design to reduce them under absolute despotism, it is their right, it is their duty, to throw off such government, and to provide new guards for their future security. Such has been the patient sufferance of these colonies, and such is now the necessity which constrains them to alter their former systems of government. The history of the present King of Great Britain is a history of repeated injuries and usurpation, all having, in direct object, the establishment of an absolute tyranny over these States. To prove this, let facts be submitted to a candid world:

He has refused to assent to laws the most wholesome and necessary for the public good.

He has forbidden his governors to pass laws of immediate and pressing importance, unless suspended in their operation till his assent should be obtained; and, when so suspended, he has utterly neglected to attend to them.

He has refused to pass other laws for the accommodation of large districts of people, unless those people would relinquish the right of representation in the legislature; a right inestimable to them, and formidable to tyrants only.

He has called together legislative bodies at places unusual, uncomfortable, and distant from the depository of their public records, for the sole purpose of fatiguing them into compliance with his measures.

He has dissolved representative houses repeatedly, for opposing, with manly firmness, his invasions on the rights of the people.

He has refused, for a long time after such dissolutions, to cause others to be elected; whereby the legislative powers, incapable of annihilation, have returned to the people at large for their exercise; the State remaining, in the meantime, exposed to all the dangers of invasion from without, and convulsions within.

He has endeavored to prevent the population of these States; for that purpose, obstructing the laws for naturalization of foreigners; refusing to pass others to encourage their migration hither, and raising the conditions of new appropriations of lands.

He has obstructed the administration of justice, by refusing his assent to laws for establishing judiciary powers.

He has made judges dependent on his will alone, for the tenure of their offices, and the amount and payment of their salaries.

He has erected a multitude of new offices, and sent hither swarms of officers to harass our people, and eat out their substance.

He has kept among us, in times of peace, standing armies without the consent of our legislatures.

He has affected to render the military independent of, and superior to, the civil power.

He has combined with others, to subject us to a jurisdiction foreign to our constitution, and unacknowledged by our laws; giving his assent to their acts of pretended legislation:

For quartering large bodies of armed troops among us:

For protecting them by a mock trial from punishment, for any murders which they should commit on the inhabitants of these States:

For cutting off our trade with all parts of the world:

For imposing taxes on us without our consent:

For depriving us, in many cases, of the benefit of trial by jury:

For transporting us beyond seas to be tried for pretended offenses:

For abolishing the free system of English laws in a neighboring province, establishing therein an arbitrary government, and enlarging its boundaries, so as to render it at once an example and fit instrument for introducing the same absolute rule into these colonies:

For taking away our charters, abolishing our most valuable laws and altering fundamentally, the powers of our governments:

For suspending our own legislatures, and declaring themselves invested with power to legislate for us in all cases whatsoever.

He has abdicated government here, by declaring us out of his protection, and waging war against us.

He has plundered our seas, ravaged our coasts, burnt our towns, and destroyed the lives of our people.

He is, at this time, transporting large armies of foreign mercenaries to complete the work of death, desolation, and tyranny, already begun, with circumstances of cruelty and perfidy scarcely paralleled in the most barbarous ages, and totally unworthy the head of a civilized nation.

He has constrained our fellow-citizens, taken captive on the high seas, to bear arms against their country, to become the executioners of their friends and brethren, or to fall themselves by their hands.

He has incited domestic insurrections amongst us, and has endeavored to bring on the inhabitants of our frontiers, the merciless Indian savages, whose known rule of warfare is an undistinguished destruction of all ages, sexes, and conditions.

In every stage of these oppressions we have petitioned for redress in the most humble terms; our repeated petitions have been answered only by repeated injury. A prince whose character is thus marked by every act which may define a tyrant, is unfit to be the ruler of a free people.

Nor have we been wanting in attention to our British brethren. We have warned them, from time to time, of attempts made by their legislature to extend an unwarrantable jurisdiction over us. We have reminded them of the circumstances of our emigration and settlement here. We have appealed to their native justice and magnanimity, and we have conjured them, by the ties of our common kindred, to disavow these usurpations, which would inevitably interrupt our connections and correspondence. They, too, have been deaf to the voice of justice and consanguinity. We must, therefore, acquiesce in the necessity which denounces our separation, and hold them, as we hold the rest of mankind, enemies in war—in peace, friends.

We, therefore, the representatives of the United States of America, in General Congress assembled, appealing to the Supreme Judge of the World for the rectitude of our intentions, do, in the name and by the authority of the good people of these colonies solemnly publish and declare, That these United Colonies are, and of right ought to be, Free and Independent States; that they are absolved from all allegiance to the British crown, and that all political connection between them and the State of Great Britain is, and ought to be, totally dissolved, and that as free and independent States, they have full power to levy war, conclude peace, contract alliances, establish commerce and to do all other acts which independent States may of right do. And for the support of this declaration, with a firm reliance on the protection of Divine Providence, we mutually pledge to each other our lives, our fortunes, and our sacred honor.

Notebook Assignment for Class Discussion

1. This declaration, written by Thomas Jefferson, is a good example of cause-and-effect relationship. Analyze it and explain fully and clearly how this relationship appears throughout.
2. For what reason did our founding fathers feel obliged to declare to the world their intention to become a free and independent nation? Is it the same reason that prompts modern nations to scheme and labor to create a favorable "image" of themselves in the mind of the rest of the world? Explain.
3. Is it true that "all men are created equal"? In every sense of the word, in no sense, or in what sense or senses? George Orwell says in *Animal Farm*, "All animals are equal but some animals are more equal than others."
4. Why are "governments instituted among men"?
5. What is the etymological meaning of *evident?*
6. What is the contextual meaning of *pursuit* in the first sentence of paragraph 2?
7. To better read and understand the Declaration of Independence, look up the meaning of the following words:

evince	depository	jurisdiction
sufferance	tenure	magnanimity
colony	harass	conjure
constrain	charter	consanguinity
usurpation	arbitrary	congress
despotism	perfidy	unalienable
tyranny	redress	transient

8. What is the difference between a declaration and a constitution?
9. Why is the balanced form of accumulating causes beginning "He has ..." interrupted by a balanced series beginning "For ..."?
10. How does the word *therefore* reveal the causal relationship between the first part of the declaration and the last paragraph?

Related Exercises

1. Exactly where is the need foreseen in this declaration to provide legal means of preventing usurpation of power by any

political party or any individual, including the president? Cite a prominent instance of attempted usurpation in this country in the field of politics, industry, or organized labor.
2. Has any United States president been impeached or threatened with impeachment? If so, be prepared to outline the general circumstances leading up to and resulting from this action.
3. In which sentence does the essence of this declaration of democracy lie? Evaluate a limited phase of our present administration in terms of this essential statement, using concrete examples.
4. Is it true that men are more disposed to put up with injustices and evils until they become unbearable rather than to rise up and abolish them? What would have been Hamlet's answer to this question?
5. Write a brief report on the drafting, amending, and signing of the Declaration of Independence.
6. Write a long paper on the topic of colonialism, then and now.

BILL OF RIGHTS

Articles in addition to, and amendment of, the Constitution of the United States of America, proposed by Congress, and ratified by the legislatures of the several States pursuant to the fifth article of the original Constitution.

ARTICLE I

Congress shall make no law respecting an establishment of religion, or prohibiting the free exercise thereof; or abridging the freedom of speech, or of the press; or the right of the people peaceably to assemble, and to petition the government for a redress of grievances.

ARTICLE II

A well regulated militia, being necessary to the security of a free State, the right of the people to keep and bear arms, shall not be infringed.

ARTICLE III

No soldier shall, in time of peace be quartered in any house, without the consent of the owner, nor in time of war, but in a manner to be prescribed by law.

ARTICLE IV

The right of the people to be secure in their persons, houses, papers, and effects, against unreasonable searches and seizures, shall not be violated, and no warrants shall issue, but upon probable cause, supported by oath or affirmation, and particularly describing the place to be searched, and the persons or things to be seized.

ARTICLE V

No person shall be held to answer for a capital, or otherwise infamous crime, unless on a presentment or indictment of a grand jury, except in cases arising in the land or naval forces, or in the militia, when in actual service in time of war or public danger; nor shall any person be subject for the same offense to be twice put in jeopardy of life or limb; nor shall be compelled in any criminal case to be a witness against himself, nor be deprived of life, liberty, or property, without due process of law; nor shall private property be taken for public use without just compensation.

ARTICLE VI

In all criminal prosecutions, the accused shall enjoy the right to a speedy and public trial, by an impartial jury of the State and district wherein the crime shall have been committed, which district shall have been previously ascertained by law, and to be informed of the nature and cause of the accusation; to be confronted with the witnesses against him; to have compulsory process for obtaining witnesses in his favor, and to have the assistance of counsel for his defense.

ARTICLE VII

In suits at common law, where the value in controversy shall exceed twenty dollars, the right of trial by jury shall be preserved, and no fact tried by a jury shall be otherwise re-examined in any court of the United States, than according to the rules of the common law.

ARTICLE VIII

Excessive bail shall not be required, nor excessive fines imposed, nor cruel and unusual punishments inflicted.

ARTICLE IX

The enumeration in the Constitution of certain rights shall not be construed to deny or disparage others retained by the people.

ARTICLE X

The powers not delegated to the United States by the Constitution, nor prohibited by it to the States, are reserved to the States respectively, or to the people.

SECOND INAUGURAL ADDRESS *

By Abraham Lincoln

FELLOW-COUNTRYMEN:

At this second appearing to take the oath of the presidential office, there is less occasion for an extended address than there was at the first. Then a statement, somewhat in detail, of a course to be pursued, seemed fitting and proper. Now, at the expiration of four years, during which public declarations have been constantly called forth on every point and phase of the great contest which still absorbs the attention and engrosses the energies of the nation, little that is new could be presented. The progress of our arms, upon which all else chiefly depends, is as well known to the public as to myself; and it is, I trust, reasonably satisfactory and encouraging to all. With high hope for the future, no prediction in regard to it is ventured.

On the occasion corresponding to this four years ago, all thoughts were anxiously directed to an impending civil war. All dreaded it—all sought to avert it. While the inaugural address was being delivered from this place, devoted altogether to saving the

* March 4, 1865, Washington, D.C.

Union without war, insurgent agents were in the city seeking to destroy it without war—seeking to dissolve the Union, and divide effects, by negotiation. Both parties deprecated war; but one of them would make war rather than let the nation survive; and the other would accept war rather than let it perish. And the war came.

One-eighth of the whole population were colored slaves, not distributed generally over the Union, but localized in the Southern part of it. These slaves constituted a peculiar and powerful interest. All knew that this interest was, somehow, the cause of the war. To strengthen, perpetuate, and extend this interest was the object for which the insurgents would rend the Union, even by war; while the government claimed no right to do more than to restrict the territorial enlargement of it.

Neither party expected for the war the magnitude or the duration which it has already attained. Neither anticipated that the cause of the conflict might cease with, or even before, the conflict itself should cease. Each looked for an easier triumph, and a result less fundamental and astounding. Both read the same Bible, and pray to the same God; and each invokes his aid against the other. It may seem strange that any men should dare to ask a just God's assistance in wringing their bread from the sweat of other men's faces; but let us judge not, that we be not judged. The prayers of both could not be answered—that of neither has been answered fully.

The Almighty has his own purposes. "Woe unto the world because of offences! for it must needs be that offences come; but woe to that man by whom the offence cometh." If we shall suppose that American slavery is one of those offences which, in the providence of God, must needs come, but which, having continued through his appointed time, he now wills to remove, and that he gives to both North and South this terrible war, as the woe due to those by whom the offence came, shall we discern therein any departure from those divine attributes which the believers in a living God always ascribe to him? Fondly do we hope—fervently do we pray—that this mighty scourge of war may speedily pass away. Yet, if God wills that it continue until all the wealth piled by the bondman's two hundred and fifty years of unrequited toil shall be sunk, and until every drop of blood drawn with the lash shall be paid by another drawn with the sword, as was said three thousand years ago, so still it must be said, "The judgments of the Lord are true and righteous altogether."

With malice toward none; with charity for all; with firmness in the right, as God gives us to see the right, let us strive on to finish the work we are in; to bind up the nation's wounds; to care for him who shall have borne the battle, and for his widow, and his orphan—to do all which may achieve and cherish a just and lasting peace among ourselves, and with all nations.

NATIONS PRODUCED BY NATURE *

By Montaigne

All things (says Plato) are produced either by nature, by fortune, or by art. The greatest and fairest by one or other of the two first, the least and imperfect by the last. Those nations seem therefore so barbarous to me because they have received very little fashion from human wit, and are yet near their original naturalness. The laws of nature do yet command them which are but little bastardized by ours, and that with such purity as I am sometimes grieved the knowledge of it came no sooner to light, at what time there were men that better than we could have judged of it. I am sorry Lycurgus and Plato had it not, for it seems to me that what in those nations we see by experience not only exceeds all the pictures wherewith licentious Poetry has proudly embellished the golden age, and all her quaint inventions to feign a happy condition of man, but also the conception and desire of Philosophy. They could not imagine a genuineness so pure and simple as we see it by experience; nor ever believe our society might be maintained with so little art and human combination.

It is a nation, would I answer Plato, that hath no kind of traffic, no knowledge of Letters, no intelligence of numbers, no name of magistrate, nor of political superiority; no use of service, of riches or of poverty; no contracts, no successions, no partitions, no occupation but idle; no respect of kindred, but common; no apparel, but natural; no manuring of lands; no use of wine, corn, or metal. The very words that import lying, falsehood, treason, dissimulations, covetousness, envy, detraction, and pardon, were never heard of amongst them. How dissonant would he find his imaginary commonwealth from this perfection! (from "Of the Cannibals.")

* From *The Essayes of Michael, Lord of Montaigne* (1580), trans. by John Florio (1603), and slightly modernized.

THE PERFECT STATE

By WILLIAM SHAKESPEARE

(This excerpt from *The Tempest* is spoken by Gonzalo, "an honest old counselor." The interruptions by Antonio and Sebastian are omitted.)

> Had I plantation of this isle, my lord,
> And were the king on it, what would I do?
> In the commonwealth I would by contraries
> Execute all things; for no kind of traffic
> Would I admit; no name of magistrate;
> Letters should not be known; riches, poverty,
> And use of service, none; contract, succession,
> Bourn, bound of land, tilth, vineyard, none;
> No use of metal, corn, or wine, or oil;
> No occupation, all men idle, all;
> And women, too, but innocent and pure;
> No sovereignty.
> All things in common nature should produce
> Without sweat of endeavor. Treason, felony,
> Sword, pike, knife, gun, or need of any engine
> Would I not have; but nature should bring forth
> Of its own kind all foison, all abundance,
> To feed my innocent people.
> I would with such perfection govern, sir,
> To excel the golden age. (Act 2, Scene 1, lines 144–169)

traffic: business.
admit: allow.
Bourn, bound: boundary.
tilth: working the soil.
metal: money.
women, too: i.e., idle, like the men.
engine: military machine, weapon.
foison: abundance.
golden age: probably a reference to the Garden of Eden, paradise before the fall of Adam and Eve.

THIS ENGLAND

By WILLIAM SHAKESPEARE

This royal throne of kings, this sceptered isle,
This earth of majesty, this seat of Mars,
This other Eden, demi-paradise,
This fortress built by Nature for herself
Against infection and the hand of war;
This happy breed of men, this little world,
This precious stone set in the silver sea,
Which serves it in the office of a wall
Or as a moat defensive to a house
Against the envy of less happier lands;
This blessed plot, this earth, this realm, this England,
This nurse, this teeming womb of royal kings,
Feared by their breed and famous by their birth,
Renowned for their deeds as far from home,
For Christian service and true chivalry,
As is the sepulchre in stubborn Jewry
Of the world's ransom, blessed Mary's Son;
This land of such dear souls, this dear, dear land,
Dear for her reputation through the world,
Is now leased out—I die pronouncing it—
Like to a tenement or pelting farm.
England, bound in with the triumphant sea,
Whose rocky shore beats back the envious siege
Of watery Neptune, is now bound in with shame,
With inky blots and rotten parchment bonds.
That England that was wont to conquer others
Hath made a shameful conquest of itself.
(*Richard II*, Act 2, Scene 1, lines 40–66.)

CONCERNING LIBERALITY
AND MEANNESS *

By Niccolò Machiavelli

Commencing then with the first of the above-named characteristics, I say that it would be well to be reputed liberal. Nevertheless, liberality exercised in a way that does not bring you the reputation for it, injures you; for if one exercises it honestly and as it should be exercised, it may not become known, and you will not avoid the reproach of its opposite. Therefore, any one wishing to maintain among men the name of liberal is obliged to avoid no attribute of magnificence; so that a prince thus inclined will consume in such acts all his property, and will be compelled in the end, if he wish to maintain the name of liberal, to unduly weigh down his people, and tax them, and do everything he can to get money. This will soon make him odious to his subjects, and becoming poor he will be little valued by any one; thus, with his liberality, having offended many and rewarded few, he is affected by the very first trouble and imperiled by whatever may be the first danger; recognizing this himself, and wishing to draw back from it, he runs at once into the reproach of being miserly.

Therefore, a prince, not being able to exercise this virtue of liberality in such a way that it is recognized, except to his cost, if he is wise he ought not to fear the reputation of being mean, for in time he will come to be more considered than if liberal, seeing that with his economy his revenues are enough, that he can defend himself against all attacks, and is able to engage in enterprises without burdening his people; thus it comes to pass that he exercises liberality towards all from whom he does not take, who are numberless, and meanness towards those to whom he does not give, who are few.

We have not seen great things done in our time except by those who have been considered mean; the rest have failed. Pope Julius the Second was assisted in reaching the papacy by a reputation for liberality, yet he did not strive afterwards to keep it

* From *The Prince*, by Niccolò Machiavelli, trans. by W. K. Marriott (F.R.H.S. Everyman's Library; New York: E. P. Dutton & Co.), Chapter 16.

up, when he made war on the King of France; and he made many wars without imposing any extraordinary tax on his subjects, for he supplied his additional expenses out of his long thriftiness. The present King of Spain would not have undertaken or conquered in so many enterprises if he had been reputed liberal. A prince, therefore, provided that he has not to rob his subjects, that he can defend himself, that he does not become poor and abject, that he is not forced to become rapacious, ought to hold of little account a reputation for being mean, for it is one of those vices which will enable him to govern.

And if any one should say: Caesar obtained empire by liberality, and many others have reached the highest positions by having been liberal, and by being considered so, I answer: Either you are a prince in fact, or in a way to become one. In the first case this liberality is dangerous, in the second it is very necessary to be considered liberal; and Caesar was one of those who wished to become pre-eminent in Rome; but if he had survived after becoming so, and had not moderated his expenses, he would have destroyed his government. And if any one should reply: Many have been princes, and have done great things with armies, who have been considered very liberal, I reply: Either a prince spends that which is his own or his subjects' or else that of others. In the first case he ought to be sparing, in the second he ought not to neglect any opportunity for liberality. And to the prince who goes forth with his army, supporting it by pillage, sack, extortion, handling that which belongs to others, this liberality is necessary, otherwise he would not be followed by soldiers. And of that which is neither yours nor your subjects' you can be a ready giver, as were Cyrus, Caesar, and Alexander; because it does not take away your reputation if you squander that of others, but adds to it; it is only squandering your own that injures you.

And there is nothing wastes so rapidly as liberality, for even whilst you exercise it you lose the power to do so, and so become either poor or despised, or else, in avoiding poverty, rapacious and hated. And a prince should guard himself, above all things, against being despised and hated; and liberality leads you to both. Therefore it is wiser to have a reputation for meanness which brings reproach without hatred, than to be compelled through seeking a reputation for liberality to incur a name for rapacity which begets reproach with hatred.

Notebook Assignment for Class Discussion

1. Reduce the second sentence of this excerpt to a short, simple statement. Does your statement sound cynical? Or pessimistic? Or what? Explain.
2. What is a true dilemma? Analyze paragraph 1 to discover the dilemma of the liberal prince, and restate it in not more than fifteen words.
3. How does liberality, according to Machiavelli, lead to being hated and despised?
4. Of the many definitions of *prince, liberal,* and *mean,* which come closest to Machiavelli's usage and apparent intention?
5. Pope Julius II, the King of Spain, and Caesar are cited here as examples. What are they examples of? What other use is made of examples in this short chapter of *Del Principe (The Prince)?*
6. Evaluate the following sentence in an ethical scale: "it does not take away your reputation if you squander that [property] of others . . . it is only squandering your own that injures you." Is it possible that here and elsewhere Machiavelli is being sardonic? If so, would his own uneven, undistinguished political career have anything to do with it? Explain your point of view.
7. There have been many translations of *The Prince* into English. In his introduction, W. K. Marriott says, "My aim has been to achieve at all costs an exact literal rendering of the original, rather than a fluent paraphrase adapted to the modern notions of style and expression." Compare a few lines of his translation with that of one or two others, such as T. G. Bergin (Crofts Classics), and make note of the differences in choice of words and phraseology. Are they equally clear? Is there any serious difference in meaning? Which one in your opinion "reads best"?

Related Exercises

1. Read the rest of *The Prince,* as well as introductory analyses and such critical commentary as Macaulay's essay, "Machiavelli."
2. Although Machiavelli's political *principles* (is the word derived from or related to *prince?*) are based on the activities of the rulers and statesmen of his own time, do they seem to

apply to some political persons and problems of our day as well? To commercial and professional people, too? Would they have any application in the academic world? If so, be sure to support your answer with concrete, typical examples.

3. The *Encyclopedia Americana* says that Pope Julius II "was a farsighted and patriotic sovereign, and a liberal and judicious patron of art and literature." Explain how early popes were temporal as well as spiritual rulers.

4. Write a brief report on the political life of Florence (*Firenze*) under the Medici's. Write another on its artistic life.

5. Since Machiavelli was a practical rather than a moral political theorist, what would have been his reaction to the statement in the Declaration of Independence concerning the people's right to displace a tyrannical ruler?

6. In the Oxford English Dictionary a *Machiavel* is defined as "an unscrupulous schemer." Reread a few chapters of *The Prince* and list all the passages which substantiate or contradict this definition.

GOLD, THE KING-KILLER

By WILLIAM SHAKESPEARE

In *Timon of Athens* Shakespeare dramatizes the folly of giving lavishly of one's fortune to the point where it is depleted. The foolishly generous Timon, hounded by his own creditors, seeks help from those he has befriended but they find one excuse or another to refuse him. In a state of grief and anger he turns his back on man and the city, and while digging for roots to eat he uncovers a huge treasure of gold. The following lines reveal his complete disenchantment with mankind's venal and corrupt nature:

> Destruction fang mankind! Earth, yield me roots.
> Who seeks for better of thee, sauce his palate
> With thy most operant poison. What is here?
> Gold? Yellow, glittering, precious gold? No, gods,
> I am no idle votarist. Roots, you clear heavens!
> Thus much of this will make black white; foul, fair;
> Wrong, right; base, noble; old, young; coward, valiant.
> Ha you gods! Why this? What, this, you gods? Why, this
> Will lug your priests and servants from your sides;

Pluck stout men's pillows from below their heads.
This yellow slave
Will knit and break religions, bless the accursed,
Make the hoar leprosy adored, place thieves,
And give them title, knee, and approbation,
With senators on the bench. This is it
That makes the wappened widow wed again;
She, whom the spital-house and ulcerous sores
Would cast the gorge at, this embalms and spices
To the April day again. Come, damned earth,
Thou common whore of mankind, that puts odds
Among the rout of nations, I will make thee
Do thy right nature. (*He hears distant marching.*)
                                    Ha, a drum? Thou art quick,
But yet I'll bury thee . . .
O thou sweet king-killer, and dear divorce
'Twixt natural son and sire, thou bright defiler
Of Hymen's purest bed, thou valiant Mars,
Thou ever young, fresh, loved, and delicate wooer,
Whose blush doth thaw the consecrated snow
That lies on Dian's lap! Thou visible god,
That solders close impossibilities,
And makest them kiss; that speakest with every tongue,
To every purpose! O thou touch of hearts,
Think, thy slave man rebels, and by thy virtue
Set them into confounding odds, that beasts
May have the world in empire.
                    (Act 4, Scene 3, lines 23–46; 383–394)

hoar leprosy: elephantiasis, a skin disease.
knee: obeisance.
wappened: worn, but in this case, also rich.
spital house: hospital.
April day: youth.
rout: assembly.
quick: alive.
snow: symbol of chastity.

THE DEATH OF CAESAR *

By Plutarch of Charonea

Cicero was the first who proposed that the senate should confer great honors upon Caesar, but honors within the measure of humanity. Those who followed, contending with each other who should make him the most extraordinary compliments, by the absurdity and extravagance of their decrees rendered him odious and unsupportable even to persons of candor. His enemies were supposed to vie with his flatterers in these sacrifices, that they might have the better pretence, and the more cause, to lift up their hands against him. This is probable enough, because in other respects, after the civil wars were brought to an end, his conduct was irreproachable: for he not only pardoned most of those who had appeared against him in the field, but on some of them he bestowed honors and preferments; on Brutus and Cassius for instance: for they were both praetors. The statues of Pompey had been thrown down by his partisans, but he did not suffer them to lie in that posture; he erected them again. On which occasion Cicero said, "That Caesar, by rearing Pompey's statues, had established his own."

His friends pressed him to have a guard, and many offered to serve in that capacity, but he would not suffer it. For he said, "It was better to die once, than to live always in fear of death." He esteemed the affection of the people the most honorable and the safest guard, and therefore endeavored to gain them by feasts and distributions of corn, as he did the soldiers by placing them in agreeable colonies.

The nobility he gained by promising them consulates and praetorships, or, if they were engaged, by giving them other places of honor and profit. To all he opened the prospects of hope; for he was desirous to reign over a willing people.

Caesar had such talents for great attempts, and so vast an ambition, that the many actions he performed, by no means induced him to sit down and enjoy the glory he had acquired; they rather whetted his appetite for other conquests, produced new designs equally great, together with equal confidence of success, and in-

* From "Julius Caesar" in *Plutarch's Lives,* trans. by John and William Langhorne and others (Ithaca, N.Y.: Andrus, Woodruff, & Gauntlett, 1844), pp. 364–70.

spired him with a passion for fresh renown, as if he had exhausted all the pleasures of the old. This passion was nothing but a contest with himself, (as eager as if it had been with another man,) to make his future achievements outshine the past. In this spirit he had formed a design, and was making preparations for war against the Parthians. After he had subdued them, he intended to traverse Hyrcania, and marching along by the Caspian Sea and Mount Caucasus, to enter Scythia; to carry his conquering arms through the countries adjoining to Germany, and through Germany itself: and then to return by Gaul to Rome; thus finishing the circle of the Roman empire, as well as extending its bounds to the ocean on every side.

During the preparations for this expedition, he attempted to dig through the Isthmus of Corinth, and committed the care of that work to Anienus. He designed also to convey the Tiber by a deep channel direct from Rome to Circaei, and so into the sea near Tarracina, for the convenience as well as security of merchants who traded to Rome. Another public-spirited work that he meditated, was to drain all the marshes by Nomentum and Setia, by which ground enough would be gained from the water to employ many thousands of hands in tillage. He proposed farther to raise banks on the shore nearest Rome, to prevent the sea from breaking in upon the land; to clear the Ostian shore of its secret and dangerous obstructions, and to build harbors fit to receive the many vessels that came in there. These things were designed, but did not take effect.

He completed, however, the regulation of the calendar, and corrected the erroneous computation of time, agreeable to a plan which he had ingeniously contrived, and which proved of the greatest utility.

The principal thing that excited the public hatred, and at last caused his death, was his passion for the title of king. It was the first thing that gave offence to the multitude, and it afforded his inveterate enemies a very plausible plea. Those who wanted to procure him that honor, gave it out among the people, that it appeared from the Sibylline books, "The Romans could never conquer the Parthians, except they went to war under the conduct of a king." And one day, when Caesar returned from Alba to Rome, some of his retainers ventured to salute him by that title. Observing that the people were troubled at this strange compliment, he put on an air of resentment, and said, "He was not called king, but Caesar." Upon this, a deep silence ensued, and he passed on in no good humor.

Another time the senate having decreed him some extravagant

honors, the consuls and praetors, attended by the whole body of patricians, went to inform him of what they had done. When they came, he did not rise to receive them, but kept his seat, as if they had been persons in a private station, and his answer to their address, was, "That there was more need to retrench his honors, than to enlarge them." This haughtiness gave pain not only to the senate, but the people, who thought the contempt of that body reflected dishonor upon the whole commonwealth; for all who could decently withdraw, went off greatly dejected.

Perceiving the false step he had taken, he retired immediately to his own house; and laying his neck bare, told his friends, "He was ready for the first hand that would strike." He then bethought himself of alleging his distemper as an excuse; and asserted, that those who are under its influence, are apt to find their faculties fail upon them, when they speak standing; a trembling giddiness coming upon them, which bereaves them of their senses. This, however, was not really the case; for it is said, he was desirous to rise to the senate; but Cornelius Balbus, one of his friends, or rather flatterers, held him, and had servility enough to say, "Will you not remember that you are Caesar, and suffer them to pay their court to you as their superior."

A few days after, his statues were seen adorned with royal diadems; and Flavius and Marullus, two of the tribunes, went and tore them off. They also found out the persons who saluted Caesar king, and committed them to prison. The people followed with cheerful acclamation and called them *Brutuses,* because Brutus was the man who expelled the kings, and put the government in the hands of the senate and people.

Upon this, many applied to Marcus Brutus, who, by the father's side, was supposed to be a descendant of that ancient Brutus, and whose mother was of the illustrious house of the Servilii. He was also nephew and son-in-law to Cato. No man was more inclined than he to lift his hand against monarchy, but he was withheld by the honors and favors he had received from Caesar, who had not only given him his life after the defeat of Pompey at Pharsalia, and pardoned many of his friends at his request, but continued to honor him with his confidence. That very year he had procured him the most honorable praetorship, and he had named him for the consulship four years after, in preference to Cassius, who was his competitor. On which occasion Caesar is reported to have said, "Cassius assigns the strongest reasons, but I cannot refuse Brutus." Some impeached Brutus, after the conspiracy was formed; but, instead of listening to them, he laid his hand on his body, and said, "Brutus will wait for this skin:" inti-

mating, that, though the virtue of Brutus rendered him worthy
of empire, he would not be guilty of any ingratitude or baseness
to obtain it. Those, however, who were desirous of a change, kept
their eyes upon him only, or principally at least; and as they
durst not speak out plain, they put billets night after night in
the tribunal and seat which he used as praetor, mostly in these
terms, "Thou sleepest Brutus"; or, "Thou art not Brutus."

Cassius, perceiving his friend's ambition a little stimulated by
these papers, began to ply him closer than before, and spur him
on to the great enterprise; for he had a particular enmity against
Caesar. Caesar, too, had some suspicion of him, and he even said
one day to his friends, "What think you of Cassius? I do not like
his pale looks."

We are told, there were strong signs and presages of the death
of Caesar. Many report, that a certain soothsayer forewarned him
of a great danger which threatened him on the ides of March,
and that when the day was come, as he was going to the senate-
house, he called to the soothsayer, and said laughing, "The ides
of March are come:" to which he answered softly, "Yes: but they
are not gone." The evening before, he supped with Marcus Lepidus, and signed, according to custom, a number of letters, as
he sat at table. While he was so employed, there arose a question,
"What kind of death was the best?" And Caesar answering before
them all, cried out, "A sudden one." The same night, as he was
in bed with his wife, the doors and windows of the room flew
open at once. Disturbed both with the noise and the light, he
observed, by moonshine, Calpurnia in a deep sleep, uttering
broken words and inarticulate groans. She dreamed that she was
weeping over him, as she held him, murdered, in her arms. Be
that as it may, next morning she conjured Caesar not to go out
that day, if he could possibly avoid it, but to sojourn the senate,
and, if he paid no regard to her dreams, to have recourse to some
other species of divination, or to sacrifices, for information as to
his fate. This gave him some suspicion and alarm; for he had
never known, before, in Calpurnia, any thing of the weakness or
superstition of her sex, though she was now so much affected.

He therefore offered a number of sacrifices, and as the diviners
found no auspicious tokens in them, he sent Antony to dismiss
the senate. In the mean time, Decius Brutus, surnamed Albinus,
came in. He was a person in whom Caesar placed such confidence,
that he had appointed him his second heir, yet he was engaged
in the conspiracy with the other Brutus and Cassius. This man,
fearing that if Caesar adjourned the senate to another day the
affair might be discovered, laughed at the diviners, and told

Caesar he would be highly to blame, if, by such a slight, he gave the senate an occasion to complain against him. "For they were met," he said, "at his summons, and came prepared with one voice to honor him with the title of king in the provinces, and to grant that he should wear the diadem both by land and sea every where out of Italy. But if any one go and tell them, now they have taken their places, they must go home again, and return when Calpurnia happens to have better dreams, what room will your enemies have to launch out against you? Or who will hear your friends when they attempt to show, that this is not an open servitude on the one hand, and tyranny on the other? If you are absolutely persuaded that this is an unlucky day, it is certainly better to go yourself, and tell them you have strong reasons for putting off business till another time." So saying, he took Caesar by the hand, and led him out.

He was not gone far from the door, when a slave, who belonged to some other person, attempted to get up to speak to him, but finding it impossible, by reason of the crowd that was about him, he made his way into the house, and putting himself into the hands of Calpurnia, desired her to keep him safe till Caesar's return, because he had matters of great importance to communicate.

Artemidorus the Cnidian, who, by teaching the Greek eloquence, became acquainted with some of Brutus's friends, and had got intelligence of most of the transactions, approached Caesar with a paper, explaining what he had to discover. Observing that he gave the papers, as fast as he received them, to his officers he got up as close as possible, and said, "Caesar, read this to yourself, and quickly; for it contains matters of great consequence, and of the last concern to you." He took it, and attempted several times to read it, but was always prevented by one application or other. He therefore kept that paper, and that only, in his own hand, when he entered the house.

In the place where the senate was that day assembled, and which proved the scene of that tragedy, there was a statue of Pompey, and it was an edifice which Pompey had consecrated for an ornament to his theatre. Even Cassius himself, though inclined to the doctrines of Epicurus, turned his eye to the statue of Pompey, and secretly invoked his aid, before the great attempt. Antony, who was a faithful friend to Caesar, and a man of great strength, was held in discourse without by Brutus Albinus, who had contrived a long story to detain him.

When Caesar entered the house, the senate rose to do him honor. Some of Brutus's accomplices came up behind his chair, and others before it, pretending to intercede, along with Metillius Cimbri, for the recall of his brother from exile. They continued their instances till he came to his seat. When he was seated, he gave them a positive denial; and as they continued their importunities with an air of compulsion, he grew angry. Cimber, then, with both hands, pulled his gown off his neck, which was the signal for the attack. Casca gave him the first blow. It was a stroke upon the neck with his sword, but the wound was not dangerous: for in the beginning of so tremendous an enterprise he was probably in some disorder. Caesar therefore turned upon him, and laid hold of his sword. At the same time they both cried out, the one in Latin, "Villain! Casca! what dost thou mean?" and the other in Greek, to his brother, "Brother, help!"

After such a beginning, those who knew nothing of the conspiracy were seized with consternation and horror, insomuch that they durst neither fly, nor assist, nor even utter a word. All the conspirators now drew their swords, and surrounded him in such a manner, that whatever way he turned, he saw nothing but steel gleaming in his face, and met nothing but wounds. Like some savage beast attacked by the hunters, he found every hand lifted against him, for they all agreed to have a share in the sacrifice and taste of his blood. Therefore Brutus himself gave him a stroke in the groin. Some say, he opposed the rest, and continued struggling and crying out, till he perceived the sword of Brutus; then he drew his robe over his face, and yielded to his fate. Either by accident, or pushed thither by the conspirators, he expired on the pedestal of Pompey's statue, and dyed it with his blood: so that Pompey seemed to preside over the work of vengeance, to tread his enemy under his feet, and to enjoy his agonies. Those agonies were great, for he received no less than three and twenty wounds. And many of the conspirators wounded each other, as they were aiming their blows at him.

Caesar thus dispatched, Brutus advanced to speak to the senate, and to assign his reasons for what he had done, but they could not bear to hear him; they fled out of the house, and filled the people with inexpressible horror and dismay. Some shut up their houses; others left their shops and counters. All were in motion: one was running to see the spectacle; another running back. Antony and Lepidus, Caesar's principal friends, withdrew and hid themselves in other people's houses. Mean time Brutus and his confederates, yet warm from the slaughter, marched in a body with their bloody swords in their hands, from the senate-house to the capitol, not like men that fled, but with an air of gaiety and confidence, calling the people to liberty, and stopping to talk with every man of consequence whom they met. There were some who even joined them, and mingled with their train; desirous of appearing to have had a share in the action, and hoping for one in the glory. Of this number were Caius Octavius and Lintulus Spinther, who afterwards paid dear for their vanity; being put to death by Antony and young Caesar. So that they gained not even the honor for which they lost their lives; for nobody believed that they had any part in the enterprise; and they were punished, not for the deed, but for the will.

Next day Brutus, and the rest of the conspirators, came down from the capitol, and addressed the people, who attended to their discourse, without expressing either dislike or approbation of what was done. But by their silence it appeared that they pitied Caesar at the same time that they revered Brutus. The senate passed a general amnesty; and to reconcile all parties, they decreed Caesar divine honors, and confirmed all the acts of his dictatorship; while on Brutus and his friends they bestowed governments, and such honors as were suitable: so that it was generally imagined the commonwealth was firmly established again, and all brought into the best order.

But when, upon the opening of Caesar's will, it was found that he had left every Roman citizen a considerable legacy, and they beheld the body, as it was carried through the forum, all mangled with wounds, the multitude could no longer be kept within bounds. They stopped the procession, and tearing up the benches, with the doors and tables, heaped them into a pile, and burnt the corpse there. Then snatching flaming brands from the pile, some ran to burn the houses of the assassins, while others ranged the city, to find the conspirators themselves, and tear them in pieces; but they had taken such care to secure themselves, that they could not meet with one of them.

Caesar died at the age of fifty-six, and did not survive Pompey above four years. His object was sovereign power and authority, which he pursued through innumerable dangers, and which by prodigious efforts he gained at last. But he reaped no other fruit from it, than an empty and invidious title. It is true, the divine power which conducted him through life, attended him after his death, as his avengers pursued and hunted out the assassins over sea and land, and rested not till there was not a man left, either of those who dipt their hands in his blood, or of those who gave their sanction to the deed.

Notebook Assignment for Class Discussion

1. Rewrite the first two sentences in your own words.
2. What civil wars are referred to in paragraph 1?
3. Are the quotations in paragraphs 1 and 2 direct? How would they be punctuated today?
4. What is the modern equivalent of a praetor?
5. Note the division of Romans into (a) the people; (b) the soldiers; and (c) the nobility. Is the trichotomy, or three-part plan of division, complete? Who were included in the first part, the people?
6. Caesar's is known as the Julian calendar. What later calendar supplanted it ?Who compiled it? When? Why? Can you figure out why Shakespeare and Cervantes, though they died on the same date (April 23, 1616), did not die on the same day?
7. What were the Sibylline books? How could they justify Caesar in sometime claiming the title of king? Who was the last king of Rome?
8. Did Caesar refuse the title of king because of humility? What is the relationship between the titles *Tsar, Czar, Kaiser,* and *Caesar?*
9. Explain the reference to the doctrines of Epicurus.
10. What happened to Brutus and Cassius after the death of Caesar?
11. What is the general plan of Plutarch's *Lives?* Did he write a life of Brutus? Of Cassius? Mark Antony? Cleopatra?
12. Which of Shakespeare's plays were based on stories from Plutarch?

Related Exercises

1. Shakespeare knew Plutarch through Sir Thomas North's translation of *The Lives of the Noble Grecians and Romanes* (1579; also 1595, 1603). With which of the noble Grecians was Julius Caesar compared? In which of the three editions did this comparison first appear?
2. The Langhorne translation is from the original Greek of Plutarch, but North's is from the French translation of James Amyot. Locate several other translations and compare a few passages to note differences of phrase if not of fact. Here, as a beginning, is an example from Sir Thomas North:

But when they had opened *Caesar's* testament, and found a liberall legacie of money, bequeathed unto every citizen of ROME, and that they saw his body (which was brought into the market place) al bemangled with gashes of swords; then there was no order to keepe the multitude and common people quiet, but they plucked up formes, tables, and stooles, and layed them all about the body, and setting them a fire, burnt the corpse.

Locate this passage in Langhorne, then compare it with the end of Act 3, Scene 2 of Shakespeare's play to note the dramatic instead of narrative presentation of the same historical detail. A stage representation would, of course, add still another dimension of difference. Write a paper of critical analysis based on your comparison of North, Langhorne, and others or of North, Langhorne, and others with Shakespeare.

3. Discover how Shakespeare renders the quoted line in paragraph 2 of this excerpt from Langhorne by reading *Julius Caesar*, Act 2, Scene 2. Also read *King Lear*, Act 5, Scene 3 to find another expression of the same idea. What are Shakespeare's exact words?

4. Note the difference between historical fact and historical interpretation in such a line as, "Either by accident, or pushed thither by the conspirators, he expired on the pedestal of Pompey's statue, and dyed it with his blood; so that Pompey seemed to preside over the work of vengeance, to tread his enemy under his feet, and to enjoy his agonies." Does Plutarch engage in a good deal of this kind of commentary? Quote a few passages from modern historians, which show a similar treatment of history.

5. Is there still another kind of subjective treatment of history, in which the writer draws not merely moral analogies, as Plutarch does, but attempts to analyze history according to his own highly specialized views? Write a paper of 1000 words, or more, based on an analysis of a deep-dyed historian of this type making sure that you include enough examples to illustrate your point.

FURY OF D-DAY *

By Omar N. Bradley
General of the Army, USA

Standing on the bridge of the USS Augusta in the predawn darkness of June 6, 1944, with just the ghost of a moon glimmering through the overcast, I listened to the steady drone of our heavy bombers high above the clouds and watched the enemy antiaircraft stab blindly at them in the blackened night.

Suddenly the Augusta opened fire with her 8-inch turrets and, as the ship shuddered with each salvo, I plugged up my ears with cotton. Less than five miles off our bow, Omaha Beach lay blurred in the morning mist.

After months of planning and rehearsing, after long weary days of fighting through Africa and Sicily and up through the boot of Italy, our time had come. It was H-Hour on D-Day off the Normandy coast.

Already our demolition teams had gone in to blast out the underwater obstacles so ingeniously planted by Field Marshal Rommel. Already our Rangers were scaling the shingled cliffs to knock out the coastal guns. Already our airborne divisions had been dropped into the hedge-rows behind the beaches, and our Sherman tanks were rolling off the LCTs and trying to "swim" ashore with the aid of the floating canvas skirts that the resourceful British had invented.

Soon the first wave of infantry would be hitting the beach. For better or for worse, Operation Overlord had run beyond the reach of its admirals and generals and was in the hands of the individual unit commanders. The biggest, most ambitious amphibious invasion in military history was irrevocably under way.

That chilly morning off the coast of Normandy left with me many memories that the intervening years have not dimmed.

I remember first scanning the skies and waiting for the Luftwaffe. Why didn't it come? Goering's Stukas and Messerschmitts would never have a more congested or rewarding target. Our assault fleet stretched in an unending line across the channel. Yet throughout the daylight hours I saw no hostile planes.

* As told to Hugh Mulligan. Reprinted by permission of the Associated Press. Copyright AP, 1964.

I remember my surprise at the strength the enemy showed on the left side of Omaha Beach, where our battle-tested 1st Division ran into the crack German 352nd Division. Our intelligence had led us to believe that their coastal defense lines would be weak, manned for the most part by mediocre troops—Poles and Russians who had defected from the Eastern Front. Instead, we learned on the eve of the invasion that the 352nd had been moved in from St. Lo on what was ostensibly a training exercise.

I remember worrying about the weather, and wondering if the decision to go ahead with the invasion after stormy seas had forced a postponement the previous day was the correct one. The waves were much stronger than we would have liked. The first of those floating tanks on which we had relied so heavily sank in the high waves. Later we learned that of the 32 tanks launched from the landing craft only five managed to get ashore.

And, as in every field engagement, I remember thinking with a heavy heart of the day's objectives in terms of the lives it would cost. For a combat commander, this is the real agony of war. Just before the invasion, I had gone down to the staging area and talked with some of the assault battalions, where the statement had been tossed around that none of them would come back, that they would all be killed on the beaches. I remember telling them that yes, there would be casualties, but that with all the firepower we were arranging we would try to keep them at a minimum.

As it turned out, General Eisenhower's decision to go ahead with the invasion was an inspired, courageous decision that undoubtedly changed the course of the war and the course of history. The high winds and heavy overcast that caused our bombers to overshoot their targets had an even more disastrous effect on the enemy.

They kept his navy patrols in port and grounded his reconnaissance flights so that the approach of our invasion fleet went undetected. The bad weather acted as a protective screen for our beach landings. Not only couldn't the Germans see us, but they couldn't believe that we would attack in such dirty weather.

If we had called off our invasion that day we would have had to wait two weeks for favorable tide conditions and available morning light. This would have meant refueling the fleet and depending on 140,000 men to keep the biggest secret of the war in Europe. Besides, two weeks later the channel was lashed by its biggest summer storm in 20 years. We would have had to wait until July and we would have had difficulty in clearing a port (Cherbourg) by September 15, the last date that supplies could be landed over the beach.

By that time, of course, the Germans had developed the V-1 rocket. I sometimes wonder what would have happened had they been able to launch those buzz bombs on our troop concentrations back in England prior to the invasion.

Even though our two airborne divisions, Matt Ridgway's 82nd and Maxwell Taylor's 101st, had missed their jump targets and were badly scattered, this too contributed to the confusion of the enemy. The paratroopers kept their heads and began working their way toward the beaches, cutting communications as they went. It must have been very disconcerting for the Germans to be getting reports of some troops in so many places. They had no way of knowing then how big the invasion was or where it was really centered.

I remember talking with a sergeant and a private on Utah Beach who had been dropped almost as far up as Cherbourg. They knew they were way off the target, so they began working toward the beach, traveling by night and hiding during the daytime. They said their worst experience was one day when our big Navy guns opened up on a German gun battery. The German gun battery personnel came and jumped in the same ditch in which they were hiding.

The big thing, of course, was that Hitler never really became convinced that this was the main attack until about the time that we finally broke out of the beachhead at St. Lo. He thought that another army was getting ready to come across at Calais, and we had taken a lot of pains to get him to think so. We actually sent radio operators to eastern England to send messages back and forth. You know, people experienced in decoding say they can tell an operator by his touch, so we used the same operators they had heard in Africa. We built wooden rafts in the shape of boats so airplanes flying at high altitudes would think they were photographing an invasion fleet.

We knew from our previous dealings with Rommel in Africa that he always committed his reserve divisions as soon as he got his hands on them. We were afraid that he might wait until he got three or four divisions and make a concentrated attempt to throw us back into the sea, but he never did.

For us, the darkest hour on D-Day came about noon. The 1st Division was still pinned down behind the sea wall and locked in a deadly struggle with the 352nd. Because of paralyzing casualties suffered by our demolition teams, only six paths had been blown through the underwater obstacle field and a tremendous traffic jam had developed offshore. Omaha had fallen badly behind schedule. The beach was littered with stove in craft, drowned out vehicles, and burned out tanks. For a time there we didn't know whether to divert the second wave of more than 25,000 troops to another beach.

This would have exposed us to a greater risk in the event of a counterattack. I always say thank God for the 1st Division. This was their fourth amphibious invasion. They had gone in in North Africa, Sicily, and Sardinia. Any inexperienced division might not have made it that day. It was 1:30 P.M. before we learned that the 1st had hurled back one of Rommel's toughest divisions and was advancing up the brush-covered slopes.

For Ike, the vigil must have been even more agonizing. I kept getting messages from him: "Please send me a situation report." I'd been sending him messages all day, but they weren't getting through. Actually, what had happened was they didn't have the capacity to decode messages fast enough, and the ones I was sending went straight to the bottom of the pile.

Despite the traffic jam that morning, the engineers did a terrific job of cleaning up Omaha Beach to keep those supplies moving in, and to bring the wounded out. My supply officer once told me that 7,000 different items of equipment were landed on the beach in the first four hours. When the Germans captured one of our phase maps that first or second day, showing all our objectives for the next 60 days, they concluded the invasion was a failure because we hadn't gotten that far. But the map was only a most optimistic projection for supply purposes, so that we could plan for bridging materials and bulldozers to build airstrips and not have to wait for our supplies to catch up with us.

A few years ago I went back to Omaha Beach.

People were swimming in the surf where Rommel had planted his iron flanges to tear up our tanks, and plowing the fields where he had planted poles to prevent our glider landings.

I even looked for some of those pillboxes that had proved so tough for us on D-Day, but I couldn't find the one I remembered best. I was told that a Frenchman had used it as a foundation for his house.

I spent three days at Omaha then, visiting the cemetery and just walking around. Even then, it all seemed so long ago. It was hard to believe that so many lives, and so much effort, and such bravery on the part of so many had gone into gaining a five-mile sliver of land.

Part Eight

SCIENCE AND PHILOSOPHY

THE CAVE *

By Plato

And now, I said, let me show in a figure how far nature is enlightened or unenlightened:—Behold! human beings living in an underground den, which has a mouth open towards the light and reaching all along the den; here they have been from their childhood, and have their legs and necks chained so that they cannot move, and can only see before them, being prevented by the chains from turning round their heads. Above and behind them a fire is blazing at a distance, and between the fire and the prisoners there is a raised way; and you will see, if you look, a low wall built along the way, like the screen which marionette players have in front of them, over which they show the puppets.

I see.

And do you see, I said, men passing along the wall carrying all sorts of vessels, and statues and figures of animals made of wood and stone and various materials, which appear over the wall? Some of them are talking, others silent.

You have shown me a strange image, and they are strange prisoners.

Like ourselves, I replied; and they see only their own shadows, or the shadows of one another, which the fire throws on the opposite wall of the cave?

True, he said; how could they see anything but the shadows if they were never allowed to move their heads?

And of the objects which are being carried in like manner they would see only the shadows?

Yes he said.

And if they were able to converse with one another, would they not suppose that they were naming what was actually before them?

Very true.

And suppose further that the prison had an echo which came from the other side, would they not be sure to fancy when one of the passers-by spoke that the voice which they heard came from the passing shadow?

No question, he replied.

To them, I said, the truth would be literally nothing but the shadows of the images.

* From *The Republic*.

That is certain.

And now look again, and see what will naturally follow if the prisoners are released and disabused of their error. At first, when any of them is liberated and compelled suddenly to stand up and turn his neck round and walk and look towards the light, he will suffer sharp pains; the glare will distress him, and he will be unable to see the realities of which in his former state he had seen the shadows; and then conceive some one saying to him, that what he saw before was an illusion, but that now, when he is approaching nearer to being and his eye is turned towards more real existence, he has a clearer vision,—what will be his reply? And you may further imagine that his instructor is pointing to the objects as they pass and requiring him to name them,—will he not be perplexed? Will he not fancy that the shadows which he formerly saw are truer than the objects which are now shown to him?

Far truer.

And if he is compelled to look straight at the light, will he not have a pain in his eyes which will make him turn away to take refuge in the objects of vision which he can see, and which he will conceive to be in reality clearer than the things which are now being shown to him?

True, he said.

And suppose once more, that he is reluctantly dragged up a steep and rugged ascent, and held fast until he is forced into the presence of the sun himself, is he not likely to be pained and irritated? When he approaches the light his eyes will be dazzled, and he will not be able to see anything at all of what are now called realities.

Not all in a moment, he said.

He will require to grow accustomed to the sight of the upper world. And first he will see the shadows best, next the reflections of men and other objects in the water, and then the objects themselves; then he will gaze upon the light of the moon and the stars and the spangled heaven; and he will see the sky and the stars by night better than the sun or the light of the sun by day?

Certainly.

Last of all he will be able to see the sun, and not mere reflections of him in the water, but he will see him in his own proper place, and not in another; and he will contemplate him as he is.

Certainly.

He will then proceed to argue that this is he who gives the season and the years, and is the guardian of all that is in the visible world, and in a certain way the cause of all things which he and his fellows have been accustomed to behold?

Clearly, he said, he would first see the sun and then reason about him.

And when he remembered his old habitation, and the wisdom of the den and his fellow-prisoners, do you not suppose that he would felicitate himself on the change, and pity them?

Certainly, he would.

And if they were in the habit of conferring honors among themselves on those who were quickest to observe the passing shadows and to remark which of them went before, and which followed after, and which were together; and who were therefore best able to draw conclusions as to the future, do you think that he would care for such honors and glories, or envy the possessors of them? Would he not say with Homer,

"Better, to be the poor servant of a poor master, and to endure anything, rather than think as they do and live after their manner?"

Yes, he said, I think that he would rather suffer anything than entertain these false notions and live in this miserable manner.

Imagine once more, I said, such an one coming suddenly out of the sun to be replaced in his old situation; would he not be certain to have his eyes full of darkness?

To be sure, he said.

And if there were a contest, and he had to compete in measuring the shadows with the prisoners who had never moved out of the den, while his sight was still weak, and before his eyes had become steady (and the time which would be needed to acquire this new habit of sight might be very considerable) would he not be ridiculous? Men would say of him that up he went and down he came without his eyes; and that it was better not even to think of ascending; and if any one tried to loose another and lead him up to the light, let them only catch the offender, and they would put him to death.

No question, he said.

This entire allegory, I said, you may now append, dear Glaucon, to the previous argument; the prison-house is the world of sight, the light of the fire is the sun, and you will not misapprehend me if you interpret the journey upwards to be the ascent of the soul into the intellectual world according to my poor belief, which, at your desire, I have expressed—whether rightly or wrongly God knows. But, whether true or false, my opinion is that in the world of knowledge the idea of good appears last of all, and is seen only with an effort; and, when seen, is also inferred to be the universal author of all things beautiful and right, parent of light and of the lord of light in this visible world, and the immediate source of reason and truth in the intellectual; and that this is the power upon which he who would act rationally either in public or private life must have his eye fixed.

I agree, he said, as far as I am able to understand you.

Moreover, I said, you must not wonder that those who attain to this beatific vision are unwilling to descend to human affairs; for their souls are ever hastening into the upper world where they desire to dwell; which desire of theirs is very natural, if our allegory may be trusted.

Yes, very natural.

And is there anything surprising in one who passes from divine contemplations to the evil state of man, misbehaving himself in a ridiculous manner; if, while his eyes are blinking and before he has become accustomed to the surrounding darkness, he is compelled to fight in courts of law, or in other places, about the images or the shadows of images of justice, and is endeavoring to meet the conceptions of those who have never yet seen absolute justice?

Anything but surprising, he replied.

Any one who has common sense will remember that the bewilderments of the eyes are of two kinds, and arise from two causes, either from coming out of the light or from going into the light, which is true of the mind's eye, quite as much as of the bodily eye; and he who remembers this when he sees any one whose vision is perplexed and weak, will not be too ready to laugh; he will first ask whether that soul of man has come out of the brighter life, and is unable to see because unaccustomed to the dark, or having turned from darkness to the day is dazzled by excess of light. And he will count the one happy in his condition and state of being, and he will pity the other; or, if he have a mind to laugh at the soul which comes from below into the light, there will be more reason in this than in the laugh which greets him who returns from above out of the light into the den.

That, he said, is a very just distinction.

But then, if I am right, certain professors of education must be wrong when they say that they can put a knowledge into the soul which was not there before, like sight into blind eyes.

They undoubtedly say this, he replied.

Whereas, our argument shows that the power and capacity of learning exists in the soul already; and that just as the eye was unable to turn from darkness to light without the whole body, so too the instrument of knowledge can only by the movement of the whole soul be turned from the world of becoming into that of being, and learn by degrees to endure the sight of being, and of the brightest and best of being, or in other words, of the good.

CHRONOLOGICAL CYCLES
AND ERAS *

By Colin Simkin

Prehistoric man was concerned primarily with the day by day problems of survival. He was, of course, conscious of the alternating periods of light and darkness, and the waxing and waning of the moon. The changing seasons must have impressed him even if he could not predict them with any degree of accuracy. With the formation of organized groups and the development of the ability to communicate, came the desire to calculate and classify time in longer terms. Recorded history depends upon a system of arranging time in periods which permit the fixing of dates and the maintenance of historical sequence. Such chronology requires not only a scale of time but also a point of reference. With these it was possible to regulate civil affairs and to schedule religious rituals. Three major systems evolved: astronomical, religious, and dynastic.

Astronomical calculations were based upon the regular recurrence of natural phenomena such as the lunar and solar cycles and the movements of the planets; sometimes upon the coincidence of two such intervals. This computation required a degree of ability rather above that of the average person. The possessor of this knowledge became an important personage—a high priest, a prophet, a leader, or even a ruler. His indoctrinated successors were quite likely to inherit his prestige. Thus, although the priests seem to have created the calendar, the reverse also deserves some credibility.

Several of the chronological notations are derived from the birth or activities of the founders of the great religions: the Enlightenment of Buddha, the Day of Brahma, the Hegira of Mo-

* From a calendar published by The Travelers Insurance Company, Hartford, Conn., 1963.

hammed from Mecca to Medina, the Birth of Christ. Somewhat related to this category is the cosmogony based on the genesis of the universe. In Constantinople it was believed that the world began in 5508 B.C. The Alexandrian Era began with the creation as occurring in 5500 B.C. This was later modified to 4490 B.C. and thus coincided with the beginning of the Antiochan Era, the date used by the early Syrian Christians. Archbishop Ussher placed the date some fifteen hundred years later and sanctioned the time of creation as 4004 B.C. The Jewish calendar is reckoned from 3761 B.C. and accordingly this (1965) is the year 5726.

The third group of basic dates are those which commemorate the ascendancy of a ruler or of a decisive battle which had a major effect on the course of history. Such dates are very helpful in reviewing history but do not have the continuity of use as do other systems of chronology. Emperors have but a temporal existence. They pass on and are replaced. Even the succession of dynasties comes to an end. Conquests are temporary. The significance and importance of dates fade in the luster of new achievements and new eras.

There is considerable variation in the span of time encompassed by some of the chronological concepts. These vary from a few years to several billion. Possibly the greatest in scope is the vast four-part cycle of the Hindu Yuga. Krita Yuga, or the golden age, is a period of 1,728,000 years. This is followed by Treta Yuga, the silver age, one-fourth less in length and in spiritual light, 1,296,000 years. Dvapara Yuga, the brazen age, shorter and darker by another fourth, extends 864,000 years. The current Kali Yuga, the iron age, began in 3102 B.C. and will endure for 432,000 years. The total of these four periods is 4,320,000 years, representing the span during which Brahma is awake. He then sleeps for an equal amount of time, symbolic of the night. When he awakes the cycle is begun again. After one hundred years, or 36,500 of these Days of Brahma, the world will disintegrate and return to the void from which it came. This schedule will not be completed for some billions of years.

Several of the ancient civilizations in the Central American area arranged their calendars in a fifty-two-year cycle. The Aztecs, who had developed a culture long before America was discovered, employed two calendars. Their civil calendar had eighteen periods of twenty days each, or 360 days. In an effort to make it coincide with the solar cycle, they added five days at the end of each year. Each of the twenty days had a name. They were also numbered from one to thirteen. A combination of name and number was used to identify the day. Substituting letters of the alphabet

for the twenty names, it will be apparent that the sequence is
1–A, 2–B, 3–C, and so on until 13–M. Then the numerical sequence starts over again but the alphabetical continues to 7–T,
after which the alphabetical series starts anew. The sacred calendar had twenty periods of thirteen days each, or a total of 260
days. With these combinations there was no duplication in date
identification for a period of 18,980 days, or fifty-two years.

The completion of a cycle was viewed with great concern and
apprehension, almost as if it were the end of the world. The
priests performed elaborate rituals and called for great sacrifices.
When the Sun rose on the following day, the people rejoiced
that the proper deities had been propitiated and a new cycle of
fifty-two years had begun. The Mayans and the Toltecs had a
similar calendar system. There is no astronomical or natural
phenomena which would suggest the fifty-two-year cycle so it
must be assumed that, in spite of distance and difficulties of travel,
these various groups exchanged information and ideas.

Other than the daily appearance and disappearance of the sun,
the most obvious celestial timepiece is the moon, from which we
derive the word *month*. Many peoples used moon phases to measure time. Since twelve lunar months of 29½ days total only 354,
a lunar year is some eleven days short of the solar year. This
required some means of adjustment to the solar year. The Chinese
accomplished this by adding an extra month every thirty lunations. In a 19-year cycle, twelve of the years had twelve lunations;
seven of the years had thirteen lunations. The New Year started
on the first new moon after the sun entered the zodiacal sign
Aquarius. According to tradition, the Chinese Era dates from
2697 B.C. They were probably the first to determine that the solar
year had approximately 365¼ days.

The Jewish calendar adjusted the nineteen-year lunar cycle by
making the 3rd, 6th, 8th, 11th, 14th, 17th, and 19th years leap
years, during which they added an extra month. The month
names, Babylonian-Assyrian in origin, are Tishri, Heshvan,
Kislev, Tebet, Shebat, Adar, Veadar (in leap years), Nisan, Iyar,
Sivan, Tammuz, Ab, and Elul.

The Metonic cycle, so called after the Athenian astronomer
Meton, was also a 19-year cycle. Its point of reference was the
date on which the new moon returned to the same day of the
year as it had been at the beginning of the cycle. The Greeks
also had a smaller unit—the Olympiad. The first Olympic games
were held in 776 B.C. A four-year interval was established and has
been observed up to present times.

A Roman monk, Dionysius Exiguus, is credited with having

invented in 540 A.D., the system of reckoning dates as before or after the birth of Christ, which he placed as occurring on December 25 in the 753rd year of Rome. This is a great convenience in referring to dates prior to the birth of Christ, for without this device we should have to say, for example, that Romulus founded Rome 2716 years ago, changing that figure every year. With it, we have the constant date of 753 B.C. Although historians believe that Christ was born three or possibly four years earlier than the time established by Dionysius Exiguus, his is the date commonly used as the beginning of the Christian Era.

Notebook Assignment for Class Discussion

1. Outline the general structure and organization of this essay.
2. What is the main thesis of the essay, and where is it first stated? Is it ever restated? What is the purpose of the restatement of a main idea? How many reasons for doing so can you think of?
3. Write a topic sentence outline of this essay. What is the basis of its coherence?
4. Write a précis of this essay. What are some of the devices for unity which the author employs?
5. What is the tone of this essay? Is it appropriate to the subject matter? Is it appropriate to the audience? Who is the audience? How do you know?
6. Is this essay substantial? It attempts a survey of an immense period of time, and completes it in something over 1000 words. Does it do so successfully? What must it sacrifice in order to deal with this topic in such limited space?
7. Does the paper seem to end conclusively? Has it stimulated your interest in the subject matter? By what means has it done so? Or, why has it failed to do so?

Related Exercises

1. Easter is determined as the first Sunday after the first full moon after the vernal equinox. Check this on a popular calendar that includes phases of the moon. Consult past almanacs to prove that this statement is true for Easter dates of earlier years.
2. What procedure would you follow in the library to discover the origins of the means of determining Easter Sunday? What are some of the general headings under which you might look

in beginning your research? What reference texts might prove most useful in helping you to narrow your search?

3. What is an *almanac?* What are the derivations of the word? Write a research paper which treats of the history of almanacs.

4. Write a research paper in which you outline some of the more recent schemes for developing a new calendar. What seem to be the more reasonable arguments advanced in favor of a new calendar system? What seem to be the major disadvantages of the present system? Write an argumentative paper on either of the last two questions.

SONNET—TO SCIENCE

By EDGAR ALLAN POE

Science! true daughter of Old Time thou art!
    Who alterest all things with thy peering eyes.
Why preyest thou thus upon the poet's heart,
    Vulture, whose wings are dull realities?
How should he love thee? or how deem thee wise,
    Who wouldst not leave him in his wandering
To seek for treasure in the jewelled skies,
    Albeit he soared with an undaunted wing?
Hast thou not dragged Diana from her car?
    And driven the Hamadryad from the wood
To seek a shelter in some happier star?
    Hast thou not torn the Naiad from her flood,
The Elfin from the green grass, and from me
The summer dream beneath the tamarind tree?

Notebook Assignment for Class Discussion

1. Compare Poe's use of language in this poem with Whitman's in "The Learn'd Astronomer."

2. Which poet seems the more mannered? Explain.

3. Which poet seems to employ the more "literary" diction? Explain.

4. What kind of sonnet has Poe written? What is a sonnet? How many kinds of sonnets are there?

5. *Denotation* refers to the dictionary meanings of words, while *connotation* refers to the whole complex of associated meanings which a word calls to mind. The scientist's notion of pre-

cision in language is to have each word mean as narrowly as possible, i.e., a single meaning for a single word. But the poet is concerned that a word should mean in as many ways as possible; he is more likely to speak connotatively than is the scientist. Which poet, Poe or Whitman, seems to you to be more concerned with connotative meanings? Point out the passages which best support your conclusion, and explain their connotations.

Related Exercises

1. Compare the meaning of this poem with Whitman's "The Learn'd Astronomer." In what important ways are they similar? In what important ways do they differ?
2. Does Poe view Science as a benefactor of mankind in general, and poets in particular? Define his view of Science. Do you agree with what he says, or have you reservations about his thesis?
3. Poetry, or the spirit of poetry, was often symbolized by the Romantics as a bird taking wing and full of song. Poe uses the image of a bird in this poem to embody his notion of Science. What is significant about his choosing a vulture?
4. Explain the references to Diana, the Hamadryad, the Naiad, and the Elfin in the last six lines of the poem. What charge is Poe making against Science?
5. Why does the poet choose to dream beneath a tamarind tree, when it would have made as good metrical sense to dream beneath a slippery-elm, a crabapple, or a poplar?

CYLINDER SEALS *

By Mary Chubb

I began to find out about cylinder seals. I had discovered something that I now realized I had been missing on this huge dig; something small and concrete and personal which might lead me back towards the shadowy people themselves who had lived so long ago in this ancient land.

* From *City in the Sand*, by Mary Chubb (New York: Thomas Y. Crowell Co., 1957), p. 97.

The cylinder seal was an ingenious invention of very early Sumerian times. Later, as trade routes opened up to other surrounding countries, it was found far away from Sumer, the device being adopted and used for a while in distant lands. But its origin was in Mesopotamia, being first found in the remains of the Uruk period, the second of the prehistoric cultures. These people were the first to use metal, and to fashion cutting tools, without which, of course, a cylinder seal could not have been shaped or carved.

It was first used to seal personal property. When a jar was to be sealed, for instance, a piece of cloth was tied over the mouth with string wound round below the rim. Then the string was covered all round with a thick layer of clay, and before it hardened the owner took his personal cylinder, which he wore on a wristband or necklace, or stuck on the end of the long pin which fastened his cloak, and rolled it round the clay. It had the advantage over the stamp seal that the impression could be made continuous, as long or short as was necessary. Many of the actual clay impressions have been found, sometimes showing on the under side the clear marks of the string which the clay once covered.

ON SCIENTIFIC TRUTH *

By Albert Einstein

(1) It is difficult even to attach a precise meaning to the term "scientific truth." So different is the meaning of the word "truth" according to whether we are dealing with a fact of experience, a mathematical proposition, or a scientific theory. "Religious truth" conveys nothing clear to me at all.

(2) Scientific research can reduce superstition by encouraging people to think and survey things in terms of cause and effect. Certain it is that a conviction, akin to religious feeling, of the rationality or intelligibility of the world lies behind all scientific work of a higher order.

(3) This firm belief, a belief bound up with deep feeling, in a superior mind that reveals itself in the world of experience, rep-

* From *Ideas and Opinions*, by Albert Einstein (New York: Crown Publishers, 1954), p. 261. Reprinted by permission of the Estate of Albert Einstein.

resents my conception of God. In common parlance this may be described as "pantheistic" (Spinoza).

(4) Denominational traditions I can only consider historically and psychologically; they have no other significance for me.

CONCLUSION OF
THE ORIGIN OF SPECIES *

By Charles Darwin

Nothing at first can appear more difficult to believe than that the more complex organs and instincts have been perfected, not by means superior to human reason, but by the accumulation of innumerable slight variations, each good for the individual possessor. I have felt these difficulties far too heavily during many years to doubt their weight. But the more important objections relate to questions on which we are confessedly ignorant; nor do we know how ignorant we are. Serious as they are, in my judgment they are by no means sufficient to overthrow the theory of descent with subsequent modification.

Now let us turn to the other side of the argument. Under domestication we see much variability, caused often in so obscure a manner that we are tempted to consider the variations as spontaneous. On the other hand, we have evidence that variability when it has once come into play never ceases. Under nature during the constant Struggle for Existence, we see a powerful and ever-acting form of Selection. A grain in the balance may determine which individuals shall live and which shall die. What limit can be put to this power, acting during long ages and rigidly scrutinizing the whole constitution, structure, and habits of each creature? I can see no limit to this power, in slowly and beautifully adapting each form to the most complex relations of life. The theory of natural selection, even if we look no farther than this, seems to be in the highest degree probable.

If we admit that the geological record is extremely imperfect, then the facts which the record does give strongly support the

* Reprinted from Charles Darwin's *The Origin of Species,* abridged and edited by Charlotte and William Irvine (Milestones of Thought) by permission of Frederick Ungar Publishing Co.

theory. The grand fact that all extinct beings can be classed with all recent beings follows from the living and the extinct being the offspring of common parents. Lastly, the wonderful law of the long endurance of allied forms on the same continent is intelligible, for the existing and the extinct will be allied by descent.

Looking to geographical distribution, the existence of closely allied or representative species in any two areas implies that the same parent-forms formerly inhabited both areas; and we almost invariably find that some identical species are still common to both. The inhabitants of each area are related to the inhabitants of the nearest source whence immigrants might have been derived. These facts receive no explanation on the theory of creation.

How is it that organs bearing the plain stamp of inutility should so frequently occur? Nature may be said to have taken pains to reveal her scheme of modification by means of rudimentary organs, of embryological and homologous structures, but we are too blind to understand her meaning.

As my conclusions have been much misrepresented, and it has been stated that I attribute the modification of species exclusively to natural selection, I may remark that in the first edition of this work and subsequently, I placed in a most conspicuous position the following words: "I am convinced that natural selection has been the main but not the exclusive means of modification." This has been of no avail. Great is the power of steady misrepresentation; but the history of science shows that fortunately this power does not long endure.

It can hardly be supposed that a false theory would explain so satisfactorily the several large classes of facts above specified. It has been objected that this is an unsafe method of arguing; but it has often been used by the greatest natural philosophers. The undulatory theory of light has thus been arrived at; and the belief in the revolution of the earth on its own axis was until lately supported by hardly any direct evidence. It is no valid objection that science as yet throws no light on the far higher problem of the essence or origin of life. Who can explain what is the essence of the attraction of gravity? Yet no one now objects to following out the results consequent on this unknown element of attraction.

I see no good reason why the views given in this volume should shock religious feelings. The greatest discovery ever made by man, the law of gravity, was also attacked by Leibnitz, "as subversive of natural, and inferentially of revealed, religion." A celebrated author and divine has written to me that "he has gradually learnt to see that it is just as noble a conception of the Deity to believe that He created a few original forms capable of self-development into other and needful forms, as to believe that He required a fresh act of creation to supply the voids caused by the action of His laws."

Why until recently did nearly all eminent naturalists and geologists believe in the immutability of species? The belief was almost unavoidable as long as the history of the world was thought to be of short duration. It is so easy to hide our ignorance under such expressions as the "plan of creation," "unity of design," etc.—and to think that we have given an explanation when we only re-state a fact. A few naturalists, endowed with much flexibility of mind and who have already begun to doubt the immutability of species, may be influenced by this volume; but 1 look to the future—to young and rising naturalists, who will be able to view both sides of the question with impartiality. Whoever is led to believe that species are mutable will do good service by conscientiously expressing his conviction; for thus only can the load of prejudice be removed.

It may be asked how far I extend the doctrine of the modification of species. I believe that animals are descended from at most only four or five progenitors, and plants from an equal or lesser number. Analogy would lead me one step farther, to the belief that all animals and plants are descended from some one prototype. All living things have much in common in their chemical composition, their cellular structure, their laws of growth, and their liability to injurious influences. With all the germinal vesicle is the same; so that all organisms start from a common origin. If we look even to the two main divisions, the animal and vegetable kingdoms, certain low forms are so far intermediate that naturalists have disputed to which kingdom they should be referred. It does not seem incredible that, from such low and intermediate forms, both animals and plants may have been developed; and, if we admit this, we must likewise admit that all the organic beings may be descended from some one primordial form. But this inference is chiefly grounded on analogy and it is immaterial whether or not it be accepted.

When the views advanced by me in this volume, and by Mr. Wallace, or when analogous views on the origin of species are generally admitted, we can dimly foresee that there will be a considerable revolution in natural history. Systemists will not be incessantly haunted by the shadowy doubt whether this or that form be a true species. This, and I speak after experience, will be no slight relief. We shall be compelled to acknowledge that the only distinction between species and well-marked varieties is, that the latter are believed to be connected at the present day by intermediate gradations, whereas species were formerly thus connected.

The other and more general departments of natural history will rise greatly in interest. When we no longer look at an organic being as a savage looks at a ship, as wholly beyond his comprehension; when we contemplate every complex structure and instinct as the summing up of many contrivances, in the same way as any great mechanical invention is the summing up of the labor, the experience, the reason, and even the blunders of numerous workmen—how far more interesting does the study of natural history become!

A grand and almost untrodden field of inquiry will be opened, on the causes and laws of variation, on correlation, on the effects of use and disuse, on the direct action of external conditions, and so forth. Psychology will be securely based on the foundation already well laid by Mr. Herbert Spencer, that of the necessary acquirement of each mental power and capacity by gradation. Much light will be thrown on the origin of man and his history. To my mind it accords better with what we know of the laws impressed on matter by the Creator, that the production and extinction of the inhabitants of the world should have been due to secondary causes, like those determining the birth and death of the individual. When I view all beings not as special creations, but as the lineal descendants of some few beings which lived long before the first bed of the Cambrian system was deposited, they seem to me to become ennobled. Judging from the past, we may safely infer that not one living species will transmit its unaltered likeness to a distant futurity, and very few will transmit progeny of any kind. But we may feel certain that the succession by generation has never once been broken since long before the Cambrian epoch, and that no cataclysm has desolated the whole world. Hence we may look with some confidence to a secure future of great length. And as natural selection works solely by and for the good of each being, all corporeal and mental endowments will tend to progress towards perfection.

It is interesting to contemplate a tangled bank, clothed with many plants, with birds singing on the bushes, with insects flitting about, and with worms crawling through the damp earth, and to reflect that these elaborately constructed forms, dependent upon each other in so complex a manner, have all been produced by laws acting around us, these laws, taken in the largest sense, being Growth and Reproduction; Inheritance; Variability from the indirect and direct action of the conditions of life, and from use and disuse; a Ratio of Increase so high as to lead to a Struggle for Life, and as a consequence to Natural Selection, entailing Divergences of Character and Extinction of less-improved forms. Thus, from the war of nature, from famine and death, the most exalted object which we are capable of conceiving, namely, the production of higher animals, directly follows. There is grandeur in this view of life, with its several powers, having been originally breathed by the Creator into a few forms or into one; and that, whilst this planet has gone cycling on according to the fixed law of gravity, from so simple a beginning endless forms most beautiful and most wonderful have been, and are being evolved.

Notebook Assignment for Class Discussion

1. What is Darwin's purpose in this concluding chapter to *The Origin of Species?*
2. What is it that Darwin chooses to emphasize in summary?
3. What is the central argument which he proposes?
4. What is the motivation for the *apologia?*
5. Is this chapter *primarily* a summary, an argument, or an apologia?
6. How does this essay, which is the concluding chapter of a book, differ in organization from Allport's essay, which is the opening chapter of a book?
7. Does Darwin's prose seem to you "dated"? Explain the rhetorical techniques and conventions as well as the syntactical patterns which differ markedly from modern practices. Give one or two good examples to substantiate your analysis.

Related Exercises

1. Do some basic research in the library to identify the following men in their relationship, direct or indirect, with Darwin and the theory of biological evolution:

   a. William James
   b. James Rawland Angell
   c. Alexander Bain
   d. Harvey A. Carr
   e. Herbert Spencer

   f. Erasmus Darwin
   g. Alfred R. Wallace
   h. Sir Charles Lyell
   i. Thomas Huxley
   j. Jean Lamarck

2. Write a paper in which you explain the process of your research, and include a complete bibliography.
3. Do some basic research in the library to identify the following terms:

   a. Social Darwinism
   b. Laissez-faire economics
   c. Naturalism
   d. Progressionism
   e. Catastrophism
   f. Uniformitarianism
   g. The Law of Divergence
   h. The Great Chain of Being
   i. homunculus
   j. Neptunist Geology

4. Using the information you have gathered in answering item 3, write a research paper of 1500–2000 words on any one of the topics.
5. Do some basic research in the library on the great religious-scientific controversies which arose upon the publication of *The Origin of Species* in 1859.
6. Some suggested reading:
   Eiseley, Loren, *Darwin's Century* (Doubleday)
   Darwin, Charles, *The Voyage of the Beagle* (Bantam FC11)
   Gillispie, Charles C., *Genesis and Geology* (Harvard)
   Irvine, William, *Apes, Angels, and Victorians* (Meridian M78)
   Dart, Raymond A., *Adventures With the Missing Link* (Viking)
7. Write a paper in which you explain the special value and significance to you of any one of the above books. Include a précis of the exposition, or a résumé of the major thesis, of the book you choose to write about.

STANZAS FROM
IN MEMORIAM A.H.H.

By ALFRED LORD TENNYSON

54

Oh yet we trust that somehow good
Will be the final goal of ill,
To pangs of nature, sins of will,
Defects of doubt, and taints of blood;

That nothing walks with aimless feet;
  That not one life shall be destroy'd,
  Or cast as rubbish to the void,
When God hath made the pile complete;

That not a worm is cloven in vain;
  That not a moth with vain desire
  Is shrivell'd in a fruitless fire,
Or but subserves another's gain.

Behold, we know not anything;
  I can but trust that good shall fall
  At last—far off—at last, to all,
And every winter change to spring.

So runs my dream: but what am I?
  An infant crying in the night:
  An infant crying for the light:
And with no language but a cry.

55

The wish, that of the living whole
  No life may fail beyond the grave,
  Derives it not from what we have
The likest God within the soul?

Are God and Nature then at strife,
  That Nature lends such evil dreams?
  So careful of the type she seems,
So careless of the single life;

That I, considering everywhere
  Her secret meaning in her deeds,
  And finding that of fifty seeds
She often brings but one to bear,

I falter where I firmly trod,
  And falling with my weight of cares
  Upon the great world's altar-stairs
That slope thro' darkness up to God,

I stretch lame hands of faith, and grope,
  And gather dust and chaff, and call
  To what I feel is Lord of all,
And faintly trust the larger hope.

56

'So careful of the type?' But no.
    From scarped cliff and quarried stone
    She cries, 'A thousand types are gone:
I care for nothing, all shall go.

'Thou makest thine appeal to me:
    I bring to life, I bring to death:
    The spirit does but mean the breath:
I know no more.' And he, shall he,

Man, her last work, who seem'd so fair,
    Such splendid purpose in his eyes,
    Who roll'd the psalm to wintry skies,
Who built him fanes of fruitless prayer,

Who trusted God was love indeed
    And love Creation's final law—
    Tho' Nature, red in tooth and claw
With ravine, shriek'd against his creed—

Who loved, who suffer'd countless ills,
    Who battled for the True, the Just,
    Be blown about the desert dust,
Or seal'd within the iron hills?

No more? A monster then, a dream,
    A discord. Dragons of the prime,
    That tare each other in their slime,
Were mellow music match'd with him.

O life as futile, then, as frail!
    O for thy voice to soothe and bless!
    What hope of answer, or redress?
Behind the veil, behind the veil.

Notebook Assignment for Class Discussion

1. The subject matter of this poem is highly serious; the tone is elegiac. Do you think the stanza form which the poet employs is appropriate? Should poets, as well as prose writers, observe the rules of good rhetoric?

2. Write a paper in which you defend the poem as formally appropriate. Or, write a paper in which you attack it as formally inappropriate. Can one argue as well on one side of this question as the other? Is the question, in other words, merely academic?

3. The poem is of a speculative and philosophical nature, and yet it is not coldly abstract, but charged with high feeling. By what rather specific means does the poet manage to avoid the "scientific" tone? Give examples to substantiate your analysis.

4. Does the language of this poem seem to you "literary" or "poetic"? Is the poet, in other words, speaking another language from the one he might speak while standing on the street corner with a friend? Point out examples of what seem to you to be especially "literary" passages, and of what seem especially "vulgar," or common-language, passages. Which type predominates? Is the poem better or worse for it? What are the characteristics of "literary-poetic" language? What are the characteristics of the vulgar tongue which differentiate it from the former?

Related Exercises

1. This poem was written some nine years before the publication of Darwin's thesis, but it anticipates certain emotional responses to *The Origin of Species* which followed upon the appearance of that work. It also cites certain geological evidence which was of importance to Darwin and his predecessors.
   a. Try to define the tone of this excerpt from "In Memoriam." Around what thoughts does the mood seem to center?
   b. Point out the use made by the poet of what might be termed "scientific" evidence. How does he transform it so that it adds to the emotional color of the poem, since he regards it, clearly, neither coldly nor objectively?

2. Tennyson is here concerned with the question of man's significance in the scheme of Nature; does Science seem, as far as Tennyson is concerned, to contribute anything toward an answer?

3. The "she" referred to in the poem is Nature; analyze the various references to Nature, and the images which center on Nature, and then attempt a characterization. Which lines in the poem seem to typify Tennyson's feelings about this primal force?

4. What do you suppose Tennyson means by his reference to "dragons of the prime"? How do you account for his assertion that, compared with man, the great beasts were "mellow music"?
5. How is it, in Tennyson's view, that man seems incompatible with his natural environment? Does he propose an orderly argument to back his proposition? Does it strengthen the poem if he does? Does it weaken the poem if he does not?

DOVER BEACH

By MATTHEW ARNOLD

The sea is calm tonight,
The tide is full, the moon lies fair
Upon the straits;—on the French coast the light
Gleams and is gone; the cliffs of England stand,
Glimmering and vast, out in the tranquil bay.
Come to the window, sweet is the night air!
Only, from the long line of spray
Where the sea meets the moon-blanched land,
Listen! you hear the grating roar
Of pebbles which the waves draw back, and fling,
At their return, up the high strand,
Begin, and cease, and then again begin,
With tremulous cadence slow, and bring
The eternal note of sadness in.

Sophocles long ago
Heard it on the Aegean, and it brought
Into his mind the turbid ebb and flow
Of human misery; we
Find also in the sound a thought,
Hearing it by this distant northern sea.

The Sea of Faith
Was once, too, at the full, and round earth's shore
Lay like the folds of a bright girdle furled.
But now I only hear
Its melancholy, long, withdrawing roar,
Retreating, to the breath
Of the night wind, down the vast edges drear
And naked shingles of the world.

Ah, love, let us be true
To one another! for the world, which seems
To lie before us like a land of dreams,
So various, so beautiful, so new,
Hath really neither joy, nor love, nor light,
Nor certitude, nor peace, nor help for pain;
And we are here as on a darkling plain
Swept with confused alarms of struggle and flight
Where ignorant armies clash by night.

Notebook Assignment for Class Discussion

1. How would you describe the mood of the opening of the poem? Does the mood change at any point in the poem?
2. To whom is "come to the window" addressed?
3. Which lines suggest the rhythm of the ebb and flow of the tide?
4. What are the predominant letter sounds in this poem? Why do the last two lines contain so many harsh sounds?
5. In what manner does the movement of the language change in line 9 of the first stanza? Why should it change at this point? How does the poet effect the change in movement?
6. The poet draws an analogy in the third stanza. Attempt a paraphrase of the comparison he makes.
7. Do you find the last four or five lines of the third stanza to be particularly effective? What is it about them that gives them their peculiar power?
8. Compare this poem with the lines from *In Memoriam,* with respect to:
   a. tone (or mood)
   b. formal structure
   c. diction
   d. imagery
   e. theme (or main idea)
   f. thesis (or main argument, if any)

Related Exercises

1. Why does Arnold refer to Sophocles?
2. Does this poem seem to spring from motivations similar to Tennyson's in parts 54, 55, and 56 of *In Memoriam?* Is it a less *specific* poem than Tennyson's?

3. Granting that the poem has a valid application to certain conditions prevalent in the time of Tennyson and Arnold, has it a similarly valid application today? To what conditions? Do these conditions involve matters of religious faith? Politics? Science? Sociology?

4. In the first stanza of the poem, the structure involves a movement from objective description to a subjective note. The first thirteen lines present the image of the English Channel during ebb-tide, in sensible images of sight and sound, while in the fourteenth line is suddenly introduced a less tangible idea: the waves "... bring the eternal note of sadness in." Is this pattern repeated elsewhere in the poem? What is the overall structure of the poem? How does the first stanza fit into this overall structure?

5. Are words such as "calm," "fair," "vast," "tranquil," "sweet," all of which occur in the first stanza, "objectively" descriptive? Can the sea *literally* "bring the eternal note of sadness in"? How can the poet justify such an assertion as occurs in the last two lines of this first stanza?

6. Do you find the opening lines of the last stanza to be weaker in tone than the lines immediately preceding them? Arnold has been criticized for the self-pity which the last stanza exhibits. Do you agree with this criticism? Do you find a similar note in *In Memoriam?*

7. Do you think "Dover Beach" ends nobly and powerfully, or weakly and sentimentally?

8. Can you explain the final image in the light of the whole poem? What justifies the poet's suddenly abandoning the sea imagery he has so carefully built up, in favor of a war image?

THE TWO CULTURES *

By C. P. Snow

"It's rather odd," said G. H. Hardy, one afternoon in the early Thirties, "but when we hear about 'intellectuals' nowadays, it doesn't include people like me and J. J. Thomson and Rutherford." Hardy was the first mathematician of his generation, J. J.

* From the *New Statesman*, Vol. LII (October 6, 1956), 413–414. Reprinted by permission of C. P. Snow and the *New Statesman*.

Thomson the first physicist of his; as for Rutherford, he was one of the greatest scientists who have ever lived. Some bright young literary person (I forget the exact context) putting them outside the enclosure reserved for intellectuals seemed to Hardy the best joke for some time. It does not seem quite such a good joke now. The separation between the two cultures has been getting deeper under our eyes; there is now precious little communication between them, little but different kinds of incomprehension and dislike.

The traditional culture, which is, of course, mainly literary, is behaving like a state whose power is rapidly declining—standing on its precarious dignity, spending far too much energy on Alexandrian intricacies, occasionally letting fly in fits of aggressive pique quite beyond its means, too much on the defensive to show any generous imagination to the forces which must inevitably reshape it. Whereas the scientific culture is expansive, not restrictive, confident at the roots, the more confident after its bout of Oppenheimerian self-criticism, certain that history is on its side, impatient, intolerant, creative rather than critical, good-natured and brash. Neither culture knows the virtues of the other; often it seems they deliberately do not want to know. The resentment which the traditional culture feels for the scientific is shaded with fear; from the other side, the resentment is not shaded so much as brimming with irritation. When scientists are faced with an expression of the traditional culture, it tends (to borrow Mr. William Cooper's eloquent phrase) to make their feet ache.

It does not need saying that generalizations of this kind are bound to look silly at the edges. There are a good many scientists indistinguishable from literary persons, and vice versa. Even the stereotype generalizations about scientists are misleading without some kind of detail—e.g., the generalization that scientists as a group stand on the political Left. This is only partly true. A very high proportion of engineers is almost as conservative as doctors; of pure scientists, the same would apply to chemists. It is only among physicists and biologists that one finds the Left in strength. If one compared the whole body of scientists with their opposite numbers of the traditional culture (writers, academics, and so on), the total result might be a few per cent more towards the Left wing, but not more than that. Nevertheless, as a first approximation, the scientific culture is real enough, and so is its difference from the traditional. For anyone like myself, by education a scientist, by calling a writer, at one time moving between groups of scientists and writers in the same evening, the difference has seemed dramatic.

The first thing, impossible to miss, is that scientists are on the up and up; they have the strength of a social force behind them. If they are English, they share the experience common to us all—of being in a country sliding economically downhill—but in addition (and to many of them it seems psychologically more important) they belong to something more than a profession, to something more like a directing class of a new society. In a sense oddly divorced from politics, they are the new men. Even the staidest and most politically conservative of scientific veterans, lurking in dignity in their colleges, have some kind of link with the world to come. They do not hate it as their colleagues do; part of their mind is open to it; almost against their will there is a residual glimmer of kinship there. The young English scientists may and do curse their luck; increasingly they fret about the rigidities of their universities, about the ossification of the traditional culture which, to the scientists, makes the universities cold and dead; they violently envy their Russian counterparts who have money and equipment without discernible limit, who have the whole field wide open. But still they stay pretty resilient: they are swept on by the same social force. Harwell and Winscale have just as much spirit as Los Alamos and Chalk River: the neat petty bourgeois houses, the tough and clever young, the crowds of children: they are symbols, frontier towns.

There is a touch of the frontier qualities, in fact, about the whole scientific culture. Its tone is, for example, steadily heterosexual. The difference in social manners between Harwell and Hampstead, or as far as that goes between Los Alamos and Greenwich Village, would make an anthropologist blink. About the whole scientific culture, there is an absence—surprising to outsiders—of the feline and oblique. Sometimes it seems that scientists relish speaking the truth, especially when it is unpleasant. The climate of personal relations is singularly bracing, not to say harsh: it strikes bleakly on those unused to it, who suddenly find that the scientists' way of deciding on action is by a full-dress argument, with no regard for sensibilities and no holds barred. No body of people ever believed more in dialectic as the primary method of attaining sense; and if you want a picture of scientists in their off-moments it could be just one of a knock-about argument. Under the argument there glitter egotisms as rapacious as any of ours: but, unlike ours, the egotisms are driven by a common purpose.

How much of the traditional culture gets through to them? The answer is not simple. A good many scientists, including some of the most gifted, have the tastes of literary persons, read the

same things, and read as much. Broadly, though, the infiltration
is much less. History gets across to a certain extent, in particular social history: the sheer mechanics of living, how men ate,
built, travelled, worked, touches a good many scientific imaginations, so they have fastened on such works as Trevelyan's *Social
History*, and Professor Gordon Childe's books. Philosophy, the
scientific culture views with indifference, especially metaphysics.
As Rutherford said cheerfully to Samuel Alexander: "When you
think of all the years you've been talking about those things,
Alexander, and what does it all add up to? Hot *air*, nothing but
hot air." A bit less exuberantly, that is what contemporary scientists would say. They regard it as a major intellectual virtue,
to know what not to think about. They might touch their hats
to linguistic analysis, as a relatively honorable way of wasting
time; not so to existentialism.

The arts? The only one which is cultivated among scientists is
music. It goes both wide and deep; there may possibly be a
greater density of musical appreciation than in the traditional
culture. In comparison, the graphic arts (except architecture)
score little, and poetry not at all. Some novels work their way
through, but not as a rule the novels which literary persons set
most value on. The two cultures have so few points of contact
that the diffusion of novels shows the same sort of delay, and
exhibits the same oddities, as though they were getting into translation in a foreign country. It is only fairly recently, for instance,
that Graham Greene and Evelyn Waugh have become more than
names. And, just as it is rather startling to find that in Italy Bruce
Marshall is by a long shot the best-known British novelist, so it
jolts one to hear scientists talking with attention of the works
of Nevil Shute. In fact, there is a good reason for that: Mr.
Shute was himself a high-class engineer, and a book like *No Highway* is packed with technical stuff that is not only accurate but
often original. Incidentally, there are benefits to be gained from
listening to intelligent men, utterly removed from the literary
scene and unconcerned as to who's in and who's out. One can
pick up such a comment as a scientist once made, that it looked
to him as though the current preoccupations of the New Criticism, the extreme concentration on a tiny passage, had made us
curiously insensitive to the total flavor of a work, to its cumulative effects, to the epic qualities in literature. But, on the other
side of the coin, one is just as likely to listen to three of the most
massive intellects in Europe happily discussing the merits of *The
Wallet of Kai-Lung*.

When you meet the younger rank-and-file of scientists, it often seems that they do not read at all. The prestige of the traditional culture is high enough for some of them to make a gallant shot at it. Oddly enough, the novelist whose name to them has become a token of esoteric literary excellence, is that difficult highbrow Dickens. They approach him in a grim and dutiful spirit as though tackling *Finnegan's Wake,* and feel a sense of achievement if they manage to read a book through. But most young technicians do not fly so high. When you ask them what they read—"As a married man," one says, "I prefer the garden." Another says: "I always like just to use my books as tools." (Difficult to resist speculating what kind of tool a book would make. A sort of hammer? A crude digging instrument?)

That, or something like it, is a measure of the incommunicability of the two cultures. On their side the scientists are losing a great deal. Some of that loss is inevitable: it must and would happen in any society at our technical level. But in this country we make it quite unnecessarily worse by our educational patterns. On the other side, how much does the traditional culture lose by the separation?

I am inclined to think, even more. Not only practically—we are familiar with those arguments by now—but also intellectually and morally. The intellectual loss is a little difficult to appraise. Most scientists would claim that you cannot comprehend the world unless you know the structure of science, in particular of physical science. In a sense, and a perfectly genuine sense, that is true. Not to have read *War and Peace* and *La Cousine Bette* and *La Chartreuse de Parme* is not to be educated; but so is not to have a glimmer of the Second Law of Thermodynamics. Yet that case ought not to be pressed too far. It is more justifiable to say that those without any scientific understanding miss a whole body of experience: they are rather like the tone deaf, from whom all musical experience is cut off and who have to get on without it. The intellectual invasions of science are, however, penetrating deeper. Psychoanalysis once looked like a deep invasion, but that was a false alarm; cybernetics may turn out to be the real thing, driving down into the problems of will and cause and motive. If so, those who do not understand the method will not understand the depths of their own cultures.

But the greatest enrichment the scientific culture could give us is—though it does not originate like that—a moral one. Among scientists, deep-natured men know, as starkly as any men have known, that the individual human condition is tragic; for all its triumphs and joys, the essence of it is loneliness and the end death. But what they will not admit is that, because the individual condition is tragic, therefore the social condition must be tragic, too. Because a man must die, that is no excuse for his dying before his time and after a servile life. The impulse behind the scientists drives them to limit the area of tragedy, to take nothing as tragic that can conceivably lie within men's will. They have nothing but contempt for those representatives of the traditional culture who use a deep insight into man's fate to obscure the social truth—or to do something pettier than obscure the truth, just to hang on to a few perks. Dostoievski sucking up to the Chancellor Pobodonostsev, who thought the only thing wrong with slavery was that there was not enough of it; the political decadence of the *avant garde* of 1914, with Ezra Pound finishing up broadcasting for the Fascists; Claudel agreeing sanctimoniously with the Marshal about the virtue in others' suffering; Faulkner giving sentimental reasons for treating Negroes as a different species. They are all symptoms of the deepest temptation of the clerks—which is to say: "Because man's condition is tragic, everyone ought to stay in their place, with mine as it happens somewhere near the top." From that particular temptation, made up of defeat, self-indulgence, and moral vanity, the scientific culture is almost immune. It is that kind of moral health of the scientists which, in the last few years, the rest of us have needed most; and of which, because the two cultures scarcely touch, we have been most deprived.

Notebook Assignment for Class Discussion

1. Is this a "formal" or an "informal" essay?
2. What are the characteristics of its organization, diction, and style which enable you to define it as "formal" or "informal"?
3. What is the central theme of the essay?
4. What is the central thesis, or proposition to be argued?
5. Are theme and thesis kept in the foreground throughout the essay? How are they emphasized and clarified?
6. Can this essay be very strictly divided into introduction, body (development of thesis), and conclusion?
7. Does it seem logically sturdy?
8. Do you think the author uses illustration and example effectively?
9. Is the essay coherent?
10. Is the essay unified?

Related Exercises

1. S. P. R. Charter, in a review of Aldous Huxley's *Literature and Science*,[1] speaks of "the bland scientism of [Snow's] 'The Two Cultures.' " What do you think he means by the phrase? To what particular characteristics of the essay does the phrase refer? Is Charter's criticism justified, or unjustified, in your opinion?

2. Charter goes on to say, in the same review, "When [poetry and the novel] deny the impact, even the existence, of science and technology, the men of letters aid the men of science in the creation of the partial vacuum within which meaningless turbulence is generated." Does this remark emphasize or contradict, or is it in some other way relevant to, one of the central ideas of "The Two Cultures"?

3. Do some basic research in the library in which you try to discover, and generalize about, the nature of the critical reception given "The Two Cultures" upon its publication in 1956.

4. Write a paper in which you discuss the attack made by F. R. Leavis upon Mr. Snow in 1962. With only this rather undetailed assignment, to what reference works would you go to begin a successful investigation? Write another paper in which you outline the processes of your research.

5. Who is S. P. R. Charter? Is he entitled, by reason of special competency, to criticize C. P. Snow? Why is Mr. Charter a source of some authority in this matter?

6. A common complaint today is that there is only *one* culture, and, far from being humanistic, it is purely scientific. What is C. P. Snow's response to this assertion? What is your feeling about the matter?

[1] From *The New York Times Review of Books*, October 20, 1963, p. 55.

TOUCH AND SIGHT:
THE EARTH AND THE HEAVENS *

By Bertrand Russell

Everybody knows that Einstein did something astonishing, but very few people know exactly what it was that he did. It is generally recognized that he revolutionized our conception of the physical world, but the new conceptions are wrapped up in mathematical technicalities. It is true that there are innumerable popular accounts of the theory of relativity, but they generally cease to be intelligible just at the point where they begin to say something important. The authors are hardly to blame for this. Many of the new ideas can be expressed in non-mathematical language, but they are none the less difficult on that account. What is demanded is a change in our imaginative picture of the world—a picture which has been handed down from remote, perhaps pre-human, ancestors, and has been learned by each one of us in early childhood. A change in our imagination is always difficult, especially when we are no longer young. The same sort of change was demanded by Copernicus, when he taught that the earth is not stationary and the heavens do not revolve about it once a day. To us now there is no difficulty in this idea, because we learned it before our mental habits had become fixed. Einstein's ideas, similarly, will seem easier to generations which grow up with them; but for us a certain effort of imaginative reconstruction is unavoidable.

In exploring the surface of the earth, we make use of all our senses, more particularly of the senses of touch and sight. In measuring lengths, parts of the human body are employed in pre-scientific ages: a "foot," a "cubit," a "span" are defined in this way. For longer distances, we think of the time it takes to walk from one place to another. We gradually learn to judge distance roughly by the eye, but we rely upon touch for accuracy. Moreover it is touch that gives us our sense of "reality." Some things cannot be touched: rainbows, reflections in looking-glasses, and so on. These things puzzle children, whose metaphysical spec-

* From *The ABC of Relativity*, by Bertrand Russell (London: George Allen & Unwin, Ltd., 1958), pp. 9–15.

ulations are arrested by the information that what is in the looking-glass is not "real." Macbeth's dagger was unreal because it was not "sensible to feeling as to sight." Not only our geometry and physics, but our whole conception of what exists outside us, is based upon the sense of touch. We carry this even into our metaphors: a good speech is "solid," a bad speech is "gas," because we feel that a gas is not quite "real."

In studying the heavens, we are debarred from all senses except sight. We cannot touch the sun, or travel to it; we cannot walk around the moon, or apply a foot-rule to the Pleiades. Nevertheless, astronomers have unhesitatingly applied the geometry and physics which they found serviceable on the surface of the earth, and which they had based upon touch and travel. In doing so, they brought down trouble on their heads, which it was left for Einstein to clear up. It turned out that much of what we learned from the sense of touch was unscientific prejudice, which must be rejected if we are to have a true picture of the world.

An illustration may help us to understand how much is impossible to the astronomer as compared with the man who is interested in things on the surface of the earth. Let us suppose that a drug is administered to you which makes you temporarily unconscious, and that when you wake you have lost your memory but not your reasoning powers. Let us suppose further that while you were unconscious you were carried into a balloon, which, when you come to, is sailing with the wind on a dark night—the night of the fifth of November if you are in England, or of the fourth of July if you are in America. You can see fireworks which are being sent off from the ground, from trains, and from aeroplanes travelling in all directions, but you cannot see the ground or the trains or the aeroplanes because of the darkness. What sort of picture of the world will you form? You will think that nothing is permanent: there are only brief flashes of light, which, during their short existence, travel through the void in the most various and bizarre curves. You cannot touch these flashes of light, you can only see them. Obviously your geometry and your physics and your metaphysics will be quite different from those of ordinary mortals. If an ordinary mortal were with you in the balloon, you would find his speech unintelligible. But if Einstein were with you, you would understand him more easily than the ordinary mortal would, because you would be free from a host of preconceptions which prevent most people from understanding him.

The theory of relativity depends, to a considerable extent,

upon getting rid of notions which are useful in ordinary life
but not to our drugged balloonist. Circumstances on the surface
of the earth, for various more or less accidental reasons, suggest
conceptions which turn out to be inaccurate, although they have
come to seem like necessities of thought. The most important of
these circumstances is that most objects on the earth's surface are
fairly persistent and nearly stationary from a terrestrial point of
view. If this were not the case, the idea of going on a journey
would not seem so definite as it does. If you want to travel from
King's Cross to Edinburgh, you know that you will find King's
Cross where it has always been, that the railway line will take
the course that it did when you last made the journey, and that
Waverly Station in Edinburgh will not have walked up to the
Castle. You therefore say and think that you have travelled to
Edinburgh, not that Edinburgh has travelled to you, though the
latter statement would be just as accurate. The success of this
common-sense point of view depends upon a number of things
which are really of the nature of luck. Suppose all the houses in
London were perpetually moving about, like a swarm of bees;
suppose railways moved and changed their shapes like avalanches;
and finally suppose that material objects were perpetually being
formed and dissolved like clouds. There is nothing impossible
in these suppositions. But obviously what we call a journey to
Edinburgh would have no meaning in such a world. You would
begin, no doubt, by asking the taxi-driver: "Where is King's
Cross this morning?" At the station you would have to ask a similar question about Edinburgh, but the booking-office clerk would
reply: "What part of Edinburgh do you mean, sir? Prince's Street
has gone to Glasgow, the Castle has moved up into the High-
lands, and Waverly Station is under the water in the middle of
the Firth of Forth." And, on the journey the stations would not
be staying quiet, but some would be travelling north, some south,
some east or west, perhaps much faster than the train. Under
these conditions you could not say where you were at any moment. Indeed, the whole notion that one is always in some definite "place" is due to the fortunate immobility of most of the
large objects on the earth's surface. The idea of "place" is only
a rough practical approximation: there is nothing logically necessary about it, and it cannot be made precise.

   If we were not much larger than an electron, we should not
have this impression of stability, which is only due to the gross-
ness of our senses. King's Cross, which to us looks solid, would be
too vast to be conceived except by a few eccentric mathematicians. The bits of it that we could see would consist of little tiny

points of matter, never coming into contact with each other, but perpetually whizzing around each other in an inconceivably rapid ballet-dance. The world of our experience would be quite as mad as the one in which the different parts of Edinburgh go for walks in different directions. If—to take the opposite extreme—you were as large as the sun and lived as long, with a corresponding slowness of perception, you would again find a higgledy-piggledy universe without permanence—stars and planets would come and go like morning mists, and nothing would remain in a fixed position relatively to anything else. The notion of comparative stability which forms part of our ordinary outlook is thus due to the fact that we are about the size we are, and live on a planet of which the surface is not very hot. If this were not the case, we should not find pre-relativity physics intellectually satisfying. Indeed we should never have invented such theories. We should have had to arrive at relativity physics at one bound, or remain ignorant of scientific laws. It is fortunate for us that we were not faced with this alternative, since it is almost inconceivable that one man could have done the work of Euclid, Galileo, Newton and Einstein. Yet without such an incredible genius physics could hardly have been discovered in a world where the universal flux was obvious to non-scientific observation.

In astronomy, although the sun, moon, and stars continue to exist year after year, yet in other respects the world we have to deal with is very different from that of everyday life. As already observed, we depend exclusively on sight: the heavenly bodies cannot be touched, heard, smelt, or tasted. Everything in the heavens is moving relatively to everything else. The earth is going round the sun, the sun is moving, very much faster than an express train, towards a point in the constellation Hercules, the "fixed" stars are scurrying hither and thither like a lot of frightened hens. There are no well-marked places in the sky, like King's Cross and Edinburgh. When you travel from place to place on the earth, you say the train moves and not the stations, because the stations preserve their topographical relations to each other and the surrounding country. But in astronomy it is arbitrary which you call the train and which the station: the question is to be decided purely by convenience and as a matter of convention.

In this respect, it is interesting to contrast Einstein and Copernicus. Before Copernicus, people thought that the earth stood still and the heavens revolved about it once a day. Copernicus taught that "really" the earth rotates once a day, and the daily revolution of sun and stars is only "apparent." Galileo and Newton endorsed this view, and many things were thought to prove it—for example, the flattening of the earth at the poles and the fact that bodies are heavier there than at the equator. But in the modern theory the question between Copernicus and his predecessors is merely one of convenience; all motion is relative, and there is no difference between the two statements: "The earth rotates once a day" and "the heavens revolve about the earth once a day." The two mean exactly the same thing, just as it means the same thing if I say that a certain length is six feet or two yards. Astronomy is easier if we take the sun as fixed than if we take the earth, just as accounts are easier in decimal coinage. But to say more for Copernicus is to assume absolute motion, which is a fiction. All motion is relative, and it is a mere convention to take one body as at rest. All such conventions are equally legitimate, though not all are equally convenient.

There is another matter of great importance, in which astronomy differs from terrestrial physics because of its exclusive dependence upon sight. Both popular thought and old-fashioned physics used the notion of "force," which seemed intelligible because it was associated with familiar sensations. When we are walking, we have sensations connected with our muscles which we do not have when we are sitting still. In the days before mechanical traction, although people could travel by sitting in their carriages, they could see the horses exerting themselves and evidently putting out "force" in the same way as human beings do. Everybody knew from experience what it is to push or pull, or to be pushed or pulled. These very familiar facts made "force" seem a natural basis for dynamics. But Newton's law of gravitation introduced a difficulty. The force between two billiard balls appeared intelligible because we know what it feels like to bump into another person; but the force between the earth and the sun, which are ninety-three million miles apart, was mysterious. Newton himself regarded this "action at a distance" as impossible, and believed that there was some hitherto undiscovered mechanism by which the sun's influence was transmitted to the planets. However, no such mechanism was discovered, and gravitation remained a puzzle. The fact is that the whole conception of "force" is a mistake. The sun does not exert any force on the planets; in Einstein's law of gravitation, the planet only pays attention to what it finds in its own neighborhood. The way in which this works will be explained in a later chapter; for the present we are only concerned with the necessity of abandoning the notion of "force," which was due to misleading conceptions derived from the sense of touch.

As physics has advanced, it has appeared more and more that sight is less misleading than touch as a source of fundamental notions about matter. The apparent simplicity in the collision of billiard balls is quite illusory. As a matter of fact the two billiard balls never touch at all; what really happens is inconceivably complicated, but it is more analogous to what happens when a comet penetrates the solar system and goes away again than to what common sense supposes to happen.

Most of what we have said hitherto was already recognized by physicists before Einstein invented the theory of relativity. "Force" was known to be merely a mathematical fiction, and it was generally held that motion is a merely relative phenomenon—that is to say, when two bodies are changing their relative position, we cannot say that one is moving while the other is at rest, since the occurrence is merely a change in their relation to each other. But a great labor was required in order to bring the actual procedure of physics into harmony with these new convictions. Newton believed in force and in absolute space and time; he embodied these beliefs in his technical methods, and his methods remained those of later physicists. Einstein invented a new technique, free from Newton's assumptions. But in order to do so he had to change fundamentally the old ideas of space and time, which had been unchallenged from time immemorial. This is what makes both the difficulty and the interest of his theory.

Notebook Assignment for Class Discussion

1. Leo Gurko says in "Thinkers and Doers" (Part Six): "When culture cannot simply be laughed out of sight, it is 'popularized.' Apparently there is no subject so complex that it cannot be reduced to surface terms." Russell's essay is clearly for a lay audience; a complex scientific theory has been rendered for the people, i.e., "popularly." Would you say that Russell has reduced his topic to surface terms? Do you think Gurko would approve, or disapprove, of this essay?
2. How many instances of example, comparison, and contrast can you find in this essay? How do they serve to strengthen the main thesis?
3. Russell employs the image of the drugged balloonist in a process of slow, methodical revelation; for a time it appears that he is bogged down in his own imagery. Point out the passage in which the light suddenly and dramatically dawns upon you. For what reasons is it particularly effective?

4. Would you say that, by the end of this essay, the author has succeeded in readjusting some of those basic attitudes toward physical reality which he says are so ingrained in us as to be nearly impossible to change?
5. How effectively does he use "shock" statements, such as the assertion that the earth's turning about the sun and the sun's turning about the earth are really the same? For what purpose do you think he employs such assertions?
6. Characterize the author's diction. Is it what you might expect from an eminent philosopher? Does its simplicity suggest that the author does not take his subject matter seriously? Does its simplicity suggest that the subject matter is simple?

Related Exercises

1. Gordon Allport, in "The Case For and Against Psychology," speaks of the penetration of psychology into adjacent disciplines, and suggests that it may be the comprehensive way of viewing man in reaction to all the possibilities of his existence. To what extent is Allport's thesis borne out by this essay? What very basic psychological assumptions does Russell make without which his thesis would not be demonstrable? Might this essay have been as well titled "The Psychology of Touch and Sight"?
2. Is this a "scientific" essay or a "philosophical" essay? What is your conception of what a "scientific" or "philosophical" essay should be? Reexamine items 1 and 6 of the Notebook Assignment, and answer this question in the light of the conclusions to which you have already come.
3. In what respect is the chapter by Darwin similar to this chapter by Russell ("Touch and Sight" is the introductory chapter to *The ABC of Relativity*)?
4. Does Darwin make demands upon your credulity equal to those made by Russell? To which author do you respond more enthusiastically? Analyze the bases for your responses.
5. There is no abstract word which is not derived from concrete reality. Russell gives some examples of words which have lost their original physical connotations and acquired others, e.g., "foot," "cubit," "span." But these are still words which point to something tangible. What do you suppose the original basis in the tangible was for such words as: *revolutionize, numerous, similar, gradually, speculate, arrest, metaphor, good, admin-*

ister? Where in the library would you look, in trying to answer this question?

6. This essay is notable for its clarity. Write an essay in which you analyze the rhetorical techniques employed by the author for the purpose of rendering a difficult subject intelligible.

THE CASE FOR AND AGAINST PSYCHOLOGY *

By Gordon W. Allport

No one who attempts to depict the spirit of the age in which we live can possibly overlook the importance of psychological science in the culture of today. It is gradually assuming a commanding influence upon the thought forms of Western man.

Whether we approve the trend or not we see the evidence on all sides. The common man now talks in the language of Freud and reads an ever mounting output of books and periodicals in popular psychology. If he can afford to do so he may have his private psychiatrist; if not, he may be a client of some mental hygiene clinic, of some guidance center, or of a social agency where a psychiatric point of view prevails. In the modern guises of "human relations" or "group dynamics" psychology is penetrating into industry, community organization, and making its appearance even in the field of international relations. Educational practices show its effect, with teachers and administrators conversing in the idiom of Dewey, Thorndike, Rogers, or psychoanalysis. Mass media and even the arts of biography, fiction, drama and literary criticism borrow themes and techniques from psychology. Adjacent disciplines—especially anthropology, sociology, and political science—often seek their causal laws in the underlying "basic" science of human nature. Even philosophy, the parent of all disciplines, and theology, the "queen science," are to some extent rewriting their principles to accord with the psychological pattern of the time.

* From *Becoming: Basic Considerations for a Psychology of Personality*, by Gordon W. Allport (New Haven: Yale University Press, 1955), pp. 1–7. Reprinted by permission.

In our schools and colleges the demand for training in psychology has reached unprecedented proportions. In the year 1951–52 a total of 2,328 earned doctoral degrees were conferred in the humanities and social sciences in America. Of the 16 fields concerned, psychology was by far the most popular with 450 doctoral degrees, or over 23 per cent of the total number. History, the second most popular field, fell considerably behind with 317 degrees, or 17 per cent of the total. Then came English with 12 per cent, and economics with 10 per cent. Philosophy had a mere 4 per cent of the total.[1] Thus among disciplines dealing with the nature of man psychology, for good or ill, is the fashion.

The Case for and against Psychology

Many critics look askance at the trend. To some of them psychology seems like an illiterate upstart, given to repeating what literature and philosophy have always said, only saying it less artfully and less profoundly. Lord Dunsany once remarked that psychologists, like road-menders, go down only two inches; whereas poets, like miners, go down a mile. Humanists, even while they show its influence, often deplore what they call the arrogance, the superficiality, and the imperialistic character of modern "behavioral science." Specifically they decry the mechanistic assumptions and brittle experimental methods that are the basis of much modern psychology. After examining the present-day science of man one critic, Joseph Wood Krutch, complains that "we have been deluded by the fact that the methods employed for the study of man have been for the most part those originally devised for the study of machines or the study of rats, and are capable, therefore, of detecting and measuring only those characteristics which the three do have in common." [2] Krutch argues for the insights of Hamlet and against the insights of Pavlov.

Neighboring social sciences likewise show alarm. In particular, historians frequently seem to feel threatened by an upstart rival that claims greater precision in interpreting lives and events. At the same time not a few historians employ the rubrics and methods of psychology. Sociologists and anthropologists, unless they capitulate altogether, as some do, frequently take up cudgels against the reduction of their science to psychologism. Some years ago the American Political Science Association appointed a special committee to assess the value of psychology for the science of

[1] Federal Security Agency, Office of Education, Circular No. 360, "Earned Degrees Conferred by Higher Educational Institutions, 1951–52."
[2] J. W. Krutch, *The Measure of Man* (New York: Bobbs-Merrill, 1954), p. 32.

politics. Its verdict, though not entirely unfriendly, was guarded. Political science, it concluded, should view the contributions of the new psychology *con amore ma non troppo*.[3] To these and other critics psychological partisans have a ready reply. It is the scientific temper, they argue, that has brought mankind by successive stages from the Stone Age of husbandry to the modern age of electronics and nuclear fission. Why should not the same temper of mind, applied to man's own nature, lead us out of the Stone Age of human relationships in which we are still enmeshed? The more enthusiastic partisans may add: We already know enough about human nature to improve it vastly in a single generation, and enough to reduce tensions among individuals, within groups, and between nations, if only our knowledge were applied by those who are in a position to use it.

It is true, as most partisans willingly admit, that psychology is not a normative discipline. Up to now only literature, art, philosophy, and religion have given us glimpses of what a mature human society should be. Yet, they argue, these models must be lacking in some particulars, else mankind would not have become so badly mired in anxiety and frustration. Perhaps the models and creeds stand in need of modern restatement or at least of dynamic implementation before they can be made effective in an age of atomic energy and totalitarian peril. Psychology is our chief hope for clarifying man's aims and for discovering the means for achieving them.

The debate could be prolonged, extending freely the case for, and the case against, the psychological revolution that is—whether we approve it or not—now taking place. But it would serve no good purpose so long as the issue is thus coarsely drawn. It is misleading to condemn psychology as a whole, or to exalt it; for psychology is not a unitary thing. Unlike mathematics, physics, or biology, it is not a cumulative science but rather an assortment of facts, presuppositions, and theories, whose relevance to human welfare depends upon the particular theories, presuppositions, and facts we select for inspection. The critic, unless he wishes to be merely cantankerous, should tell us what sort of psychology he is condemning; and the partisan, what sort he is approving.

Except for a common loyalty to their profession, psychologists often seem to agree on little else. Perhaps in a broad sense, all may be said to be committed to the use of the scientific method—though there is dispute as to the legitimate outer boundaries of

3 C. E. Merriam, "The Significance of Psychology for the Study of Politics," *American Political Science Review*, 18 (1924), 469.

this method. Regarding the proper subject matter for study there
is less agreement. Some definitions of psychology put the stress
on *experience,* some on *behavior,* others on *psychophysical relations,* some on *conscious mental processes,* some on the *unconscious,* others on *human nature,* a few on *"the totality of man's
psychic existence."*

Since in this essay our interest centers in the growth and development of personality, we shall consider chiefly those psychological doctrines that advance our understanding of the human person, though we shall also have occasion to criticize doctrines that
retard understanding. Not every brand—indeed no single brand
—of modern psychology is wholly adequate to the problem of
man's individuality and growth. Yet it is to psychology, and to
psychology alone, that the assignment falls—the assignment of
accounting for the organization and growth of the individual person with all his outreachings, downward, upward, inward, outward. If present-day psychology is not fully equal to the task then
we should improve the science until it is.

Other sciences have different concerns. For example, sociology
by contrast views the person as a part of his family, his group, his
nation; the anthropologist views him as part of a culture. The
theologian focuses attention on his spiritual aspects and relates
them to a presumed divine scheme. In a similar way political
science, economics, and other so-called "behavior sciences" ablate
an aspect of personal conduct from the integral nexus of personality, and relate this aspect to some outer frame of reference.
They provide us with a picture of the political man in relation
to a political system, or of the economic man in relation to the
economic system, but not of the whole man in relation to his own
individual system. The biologist, physiologist and biochemist
retreat still further, deliberately avoiding the phenomena both
of total organization and of consciousness, and thus reduce the
person to something less than a complete system for study. To the
psychologist alone falls the problem of the complete psychophysical organization. In principle he cannot be satisfied with segments
of persons related to outer coordinates. He must consider the
system as a whole, and show how part systems are related to one
another.

But his ways of viewing the system as a whole are distressingly
diverse. Is it governed from without, or governed from within?
Is it merely reactive or is it active, mechanically determined or in
some degree spontaneous? (It is on this issue, above all others, that
we find psychologists dividing.) Some current theories of personality are Aristotelian in their acceptance of entelechy; some—a

growing number at the moment—seek an answer, as did Descartes, in the phenomenology of cognition. Many (the Freudians among them) are disciples of Schopenhauer in accepting the primacy of a blindly acting will. Others, the neo-Thomists, see the human person as both a striving and rational being approaching toward, or departing from, an ideal of perfection according to his exercise of freedom.[4] Psychologists gravitate toward one or another philosophical assumption regarding the nature of man, often without being fully aware that they do so.

We cannot here attempt to depict all of the current psychological schools of thought with their diverse philosophical assumptions. It will be helpful for our purposes, however, to have in mind two broadly contrasting approaches to the problem of man's becoming. Virtually all modern psychological theories seem orientated toward one of two polar conceptions, which, at the risk of some historical oversimplifications, I shall call the Lockean and the Leibnitzian traditions, respectively. It is not the total philosophy of Locke or Leibnitz that is here in question. Rather it is their views on one aspect of man's mind—its essentially passive nature (Locke) or its active nature (Leibnitz)—that I wish to contrast. The same polarity, as I say, is found in current theories of growth and change in human personality.

Notebook Assignment for Class Discussion

1. What rhetorical purpose do the first two sentences serve?
2. How effectively does the author employ statistical evidence?
3. What is his purpose in this essay?
4. In what ways does he clearly indicate his purpose?
5. Is this essay *primarily* expository, or argumentative?
6. Dr. Allport is a psychologist; would you say that his argumentation is fairly objective? Or is it clearly biased?
7. Many of the assertions in the second paragraph are of a sweeping and general nature. Would it be necessary or appropriate for the author to undertake their substantiation?
8. What rhetorical evidence would you cite as proof that this is an essay introductory to a larger work?
9. Characterize the diction and tone of this essay.
10. For what audience is this essay intended?

4 Cf. Magda B. Arnold and J. A. Gasson, S. J., *The Human Person: An Approach to an Integral Theory of Personality* (New York: Ronald Press, 1954).

11. This essay is one of a number of lectures delivered by Dr. Allport at Yale University. The tone is certainly not oratorical; is there any internal *rhetorical* evidence that this work was originally written to be read aloud to an audience?

Related Exercises

1. What is the distinction between a psychologist and a psychiatrist?
2. What is the root term from which both *psychology* and *psychiatry* are derived?
3. What does the author mean by saying that psychology is not a normative discipline?
4. In what sense are literature, art, philosophy, and religion "normative disciplines"?
5. In what sense are they "disciplines"?
6. What does the author mean by saying that psychology is not a unitary thing? Is this the same as saying that it is not normative?
7. Identify the following persons alluded to by Dr. Allport in this essay:
   a. E. L. Thorndike
   b. C. R. Rogers
   c. John Dewey
   d. Gottfried Wilhelm Leibnitz
   e. Arthur Schopenhauer
   f. René Descartes
   g. Aristotle
   h. Sigmund Freud
8. Identify the following terms used by Allport:
   a. "group dynamics"
   b. psychoanalysis
   c. behavior sciences
   d. neo-Thomism
   e. phenomenology
   f. entelechy

OF THE ORIGIN OF OUR IDEAS *

By David Hume

All the perceptions of the human mind resolve themselves into two distinct kinds, which I shall call IMPRESSIONS and IDEAS. The difference betwixt these consists in the degrees of force and liveliness with which they strike upon the mind, and make their way into our thought or consciousness. Those perceptions which enter with most force and violence, we may name *impressions;* and under this name I comprehend all our sensations, passions, and emotions, as they make their first appearance in the soul. By *ideas* I mean the faint images of these in thinking and reasoning; such as, for instance, are all the perceptions excited by the present discourse, excepting only those which arise from the sight and touch, and excepting the immediate pleasure or uneasiness it may occasion. I believe it will not be very necessary to employ many words in explaining this distinction. Everyone of himself will readily perceive the difference between feeling and thinking. The common degrees of these are easily distinguished; though it is not impossible but in particular instances they may very nearly approach to each other. Thus in sleep, in a fever, in madness, or in any very violent emotions of soul, our ideas may approach to our impressions: As on the other hand it sometimes happens, that our impressions are so faint and low that we cannot distinguish them from our ideas. But notwithstanding this near resemblance in a few instances, they are in general so very different, that no one can make a scruple to rank them under distinct heads, and assign to each a peculiar name to mark the difference.

There is another division of our perceptions, which it will be convenient to observe, and which extends itself both to our impressions and ideas. This division is into SIMPLE and COM-PLEX. Simple perceptions or impressions and ideas are such as admit of no distinction nor separation. The complex are the contrary to these, and may be distinguished into parts. Though a particular color, taste, and smell are qualities all united together in this apple, it is easy to perceive they are not the same, but are at least distinguishable from each other.

Having by these divisions given an order and arrangement to

* From *A Treatise of Human Nature.*

our objects, we may now apply ourselves to consider with the
more accuracy their qualities and relations. The first circumstance, that strikes my eye, is the great resemblance between our
impressions and ideas in every other particular, except their degree of force and vivacity. The one seem to be in a manner the
reflection of the other; so that all the perceptions of the mind
are double, and appear both as impressions and ideas. When
I shut my eyes and think of my chamber, the ideas I form arc
exact representations of the impressions I felt; nor is there any
circumstance of the one which is not to be found in the other.
In running over my other perceptions, I find still the same resemblance and representation. Ideas and impressions appear
always to correspond to each other. This circumstance seems to
me remarkable and engages my attention for a moment.

Upon a more accurate survey I find I have been carried away
too far by the first appearance, and that I must make use of the
distinction of perceptions into *simple and complex,* to limit this
general decision, *that all our ideas and impressions are resembling.*
I observe, that many of our complex ideas never had impressions
that corresponded to them, and that many of our complex impressions never are exactly copied in ideas. I can imagine to
myself such a city as the New Jerusalem, whose pavement is gold
and walls are rubies, though I never saw any such. I have seen
Paris; but shall I affirm I can form such an idea of that city, as
will perfectly represent all its streets and houses in their real
and just proportions?

I perceive, therefore, that though there is in general a great
resemblance between our *complex* impressions and ideas, yet the
rule is not universally true that they are exact copies of each other.

We may next consider how the case stands with our *simple*
perceptions. After the most accurate examination, of which I am
capable, I venture to affirm, that the rule here holds without any
exception, and that every simple idea has a simple impression
which resembles it; and every simple impression a correspondent
idea. That idea of red, which we form in the dark, and that impression, which strikes our eyes in sunshine, differ only in degree,
not in nature. That the case is the same with all our simple impressions and ideas, it is impossible to prove by a particular
enumeration of them. Everyone may satisfy himself in this point
by running over as many as he pleases. But if any one should
deny this universal resemblance, I know no way of convincing
him, but by desiring him to show a simple impression, that has
not a correspondent idea, or a simple idea, that has not a correspondent impression. If he does not answer this challenge, as

it is certain he cannot, we may from his silence and our own observation establish our conclusion.

Thus we find, that all simple ideas and impressions resemble each other; and as the complex are formed from them, we may affirm in general, that these two species of perception are exactly correspondent. Having discovered this relation, which requires no further examination, I am curious to find some other of their qualities. Let us consider how they stand with regard to their existence, and which of the impressions and ideas are causes, and which effects.

The *full* examination of this question is the subject of the present treatise; and therefore we shall here content ourself with establishing one general proposition, *That all our simple ideas in their first appearance are derived from simple impressions, which are correspondent to them, and which they exactly represent.*

In seeking for phenomena to prove this proposition, I find only those of two kinds; but in each kind the phenomena are obvious, numerous, and conclusive. I first make myself certain, by a new review, of what I have already asserted, that every simple impression is attended with a correspondent idea, and every simple idea with a correspondent impression. From this constant conjunction of resembling perceptions I immediately conclude, that there is a great connection between our correspondent impressions and ideas, and that the existence of the one has a considerable influence upon that of the other. Such a constant conjunction, in such an infinite number of instances, can never arise from chance; but clearly proves a dependence of the impressions on the ideas, or of the ideas on the impressions. That I may know on which side this dependence lies, I consider the order of their *first appearance;* and find by constant experience, that the simple impressions always take the precedence of their correspondent ideas, but never appear in the contrary order. To give a child an idea of scarlet or orange, of sweet or bitter, I present the objects, or in other words, convey to him these impressions, nor do we perceive any color, or feel any sensation merely upon thinking of them. On the other hand we find, that any impression either of the mind or body is constantly followed by an idea, which resembles it, and is only different in the degrees of force and liveliness. The constant conjunction of our resembling perceptions, is a convincing proof, that the one are the causes of the other; and this priority of the impressions is an equal proof, that our impressions are the causes of our ideas, not our ideas of our impressions.

To confirm this I consider another plain and convincing phenomenon; which is, that wherever by any accident the faculties, which give rise to any impressions are obstructed in their operations, as when one is born blind or deaf; not only the impressions are lost, but also their correspondent ideas; so that there never appear in the mind the least traces of either of them. Nor is this only true where the organs of sensations are entirely destroyed, but likewise, where they have never been put in action to produce a particular impression. We cannot form to ourselves a just idea of the taste of a pineapple, without having actually tasted it.

There is however one contradictory phenomenon, which may prove that it is not absolutely impossible for ideas to go before their correspondent impressions. I believe it will readily be allowed, that the several distinct ideas of colors, which enter by the eyes, or those of sounds, which are conveyed by the hearing, are really different from each other, though at the same time resembling. Now if this be true of different colors, it must be no less so of the different shades of the same color, that each of them produces a distinct idea independent of the rest. For if this should be denied, it is possible, by the continual gradation of shades, to run a color insensibly into what is most remote from it; and if you will not allow any of the means to be different, you cannot without absurdity deny the extremes to be the same. Suppose therefore a person to have enjoyed his sight for thirty years, and to have become perfectly well acquainted with colors of all kinds, excepting one particular shade of blue, for instance, which it never has been his fortune to meet with. Let all the different shades of that color, except that single one, be placed before him, descending gradually from the deepest to the lightest; it is plain, that he will perceive a blank where that shade is wanting, and will be sensible, that there is a greater distance in that place between the continuous colors than in any other. Now I ask whether it is possible for him, from his own imagination, to supply this deficiency, and raise up to himself the idea of that particular shade, though it had never been conveyed to him by his own senses? I believe there are few but will be of opinion that he can; and this may serve as a proof, that the simple ideas are not always derived from the correspondent impressions; though the instance is so particular and singular that it is scarce worth our observing, and does not merit that for it alone we should alter our general maxim.

But besides this exception, it may not be amiss to remark on this head, that the principle of the priority of impressions to ideas must be understood with another limitation, *viz.,* that as our ideas are images of our impressions, so we can form secondary ideas, which are images of the primary; as appears from this very reasoning concerning them. This is not, properly speaking, an exception to the rule so much as an explanation of it. Ideas produce the images of themselves in new ideas; but as the first ideas are supposed to be derived from impressions, it still remains true that all our simple ideas proceed either mediately or immediately from their correspondent impressions.

This then is the first principle I establish in the science of human nature; nor ought we to despise it because of the simplicity of its appearance. For it is remarkable, that the present question concerning the precedency of our impressions or ideas, is the same with what has made so much noise in other terms, when it has been disputed whether there be any *innate ideas,* or whether all ideas be derived from sensation and reflection. We may observe, that in order to prove the ideas of extension and color not to be innate, philosophers do nothing but show that they are conveyed by our senses. To prove the ideas of passion and desire not to be innate, they observe that we have a preceding experience of these emotions in ourselves. Now if we carefully examine these arguments, we shall find that they prove nothing but that ideas are preceded by other more lively perceptions, from which they are derived, and which they represent. I hope this clear stating of the question will remove all disputes concerning it, and will render this principle of more use in our reasonings, than it seems hitherto to have been.

Notebook Assignment for Class Discussion

1. This essay is notable for its clarity, and for its close attention to methodical exposition. In order that the reader does not lose the thread of the argument, Hume emphasizes his main idea by repeating it on a number of occasions at strategic points in the essay. How many times does he restate his central proposition, and in what sense are the points at which it is restated "strategic"?
2. In what pattern does he employ abstract statement and illustration?
3. This essay deals with a number of terms and ideas; does it, therefore, seem disunified? What is the basis of its unity?
4. The language is archaic, the work having been published in 1739. Does it seriously interfere with your understanding of the terms of the argument?

5. Point out, and generalize about, the most obviously archaic constructions and syntactical devices.
6. Characterize Hume's style in terms of diction, syntax, punctuation, sentence cadences, and tone.
7. Is the essay logically convincing?
8. Is it persuasive?
9. What qualities of good argumentation are displayed in this work?

Related Exercises

1. *A Treatise of Human Nature* has for its subtitle, "An Attempt to Introduce an Experimental Method of Reasoning into Moral Subjects." In what sense does Hume's pattern of reasoning seem to you truly "experimental"?
2. State in your own words the distinction Hume makes between impressions and ideas. Is it a *reasonable* distinction?
3. Hume says that impressions always precede ideas, but that they resemble each other, are, in fact, "reflections" of one another, or copies. But as the essay proceeds he seems to be saying that although impressions and ideas "look alike," there is no resemblance; that, because they seldom occur at the same time, there is no comparison; that there is, in fact, no basis for saying that they resemble each other. Is his essay hopelessly self-contradictory?
4. Does it seem to you that Hume manages to establish a relationship between ideas and impressions?
5. Is a distinction or separation of ideas and impressions possible, or does it seem to you, *on the basis of your own experience,* that every simple idea corresponds exactly to every simple impression?
6. Does Hume's allusion to the blind and deaf seem to indicate that his definition of *impressions* has changed to mean that which is perceived by the senses?
7. What is Hume's attitude toward the empirical theory that all knowledge is derived from sense experience?
8. Formulate in your own words the argument referred to by Hume between the empiricists and the philosophers who believe in innate ideas.